Charles Seale-Hayne Library
University of Plymouth
(01752) 588 588
LibraryandITenquiries@plymouth.ac.uk

INSIGHT INTO CHINA
THROUGH
COMPARATIVE LAW ANALYSIS
OF
INVISIBLE FACTORS AND CONTEXTS

COMMON LAW v. CHINESE LAW

Dr. VIVEK JAIN

notionpress
.com

INDIA • SINGAPORE • MALAYSIA

INSIGHT INTO CHINA
Through **Comparative Law** Analysis of Invisible Factors & Contexts –
Common Law v. Chinese Law

Notion Press

Old No. 38, New No. 6
McNichols Road, Chetpet
Chennai - 600 031

First Published by Notion Press 2019
Copyright © Dr. Vivek Jain 2019
All Rights Reserved.

ISBN
Paperback: 978-1-64587-742-4
Hardcase: 978-1-64587-743-1

About the Author

Dr. (Capt.) Vivek Jain has qualified as a Barrister in England & Wales in 2003. His academic qualifications include B.Sc. (N. Sc.) (India) with First Class with Distinction, LL. B. (Hons) and LL. M. (Maritime Law) with merit from University of London, B.V.C. (Very Competent) in London, an M.B.A. from Norway and Ph.D. in International Law from a prestigious University in China. His Ph. D. topic was in the area of Comparative International Commercial Law & Civil Procedural Law, where he completed his Ph.D. thesis. After studying for B.Sc. (Nautical Sc.) in prestigious T.S. Rajendra College of Nautical Science (India), where he obtained First Class with Distinction, he had also sailed on merchant vessels and completed his Master Mariner Certificate of Competency (unlimited) from UK with an award.

He is currently working as a Legal Consultant at a firm in Singapore, where he assists its world-wide clients with arbitration, legal and claim matters. He has previously worked for a few years at a law Chambers and a law firm in London along with a few years as a lawyer at marine insurance provider in London and Shanghai. He has also worked as a Senior Lecturer at University of Plymouth in UK for a few years teaching law to graduate and postgraduate students.

Dr. (Capt.) Vivek Jain

Barrister (England & Wales), Master Mariner (UK)
Ph.D. (Int. Law) (China), LL.B. (Hons) (London), LL.M. with Merit (London), B.V.C. with Very Competent (London)
M.B.A. (Norway), Cert. Edu. (Singapore), B.Sc. (N. Sc.) (India) with First Class with Distinction
Ex-Senior Lecturer of University in UK

Preface

The genesis of this *non-political* and *interdisciplinary* work can be traced back to 1999, when I first started to work in the Far East. I was deeply fascinated by the Chinese culture (both visible and invisible) and its approach towards commerce, legal relations, entrepreneurship, networking and so forth. I also found many aspects of Chinese society to be mysterious in many ways. Was it a mystery or was it my ignorance? I was not sure.

The uncertainty in my mind led me to read many books on Chinese history, philosophy & law while focusing at the same time on my practice of commercial and maritime law for my bread and butter. During the last few years, China has indeed become an economic superpower. I was not surprised with this achievement, as I had seen the potential in the invisible part of its culture way back in 1999.

It is a fact, whether one's view of China is favourable or critical, that no one can ignore China in the 21st century. That being the case, one must properly understand the invisible factors and contexts surrounding China. *The legal system and civil justice process in any jurisdiction are the mirror image of any society,* and the comparative law analysis carried out in this book has assisted me to find *reasons behind the reasons* and has provided answers to a lot of my queries. I hope this book serves the same purpose for its readers.

These reasons behind the reasons are often ignored by practising lawyers, judges and laymen. I had to go deeper into the *invisible factors and contexts*, a few of which I had mildly touched on during my Ph.D. research on comparative interim remedies but not in great depth. However, I also made up my mind that I would carry on with my research and find answers for my queries, even after I had finished the studies for my doctorate. This book is a result of this pursuit for answers and trying to understand the invisible factors and contexts.

I owe a great debt to many in relation to this personal project. First, I owe a debt to my better half, Mrs. Lifei Yang Jain, who patiently answered many of my questions and patiently discussed my thoughts, and even assisted in editorial pursuits connected with this book. I also owe a debt to numerous professors, barristers, solicitors and lawyers from various jurisdictions such as the UK, Australia, China, Germany, Singapore, the US, India and many other jurisdictions, with whom I have had philosophical discussions over the last few decades. I also owe a considerable debt to my current employer, who provided me with an opportunity to work in China for a few years. My debt is also owed to the University where I pursued my Ph.D., its professors & administrators, as it gave me the opportunity to interact with learned Chinese law scholars.

Lastly, I owe a debt to the scholars whose books and articles I have read to enrich my knowledge; in order to advance the topic, I have included a detailed Bibliography & Reading List at the end of book to assist other scholars. Any researcher that wishes to study the concept of Comparative Law or Jurisprudence for any jurisdiction in great depth should study it from expert textbooks. I also wish to thank my publisher and the editorial team that has assisted me. With my own experience as a student, I have ensured with the help of publishers that the price is reasonably set to cover the cost to assist the potential readers, who are still studying in Colleges & Universities. The purpose is to ensure that readers appreciate the need for comparative analysis in times of uncertainty that is engulfing our world that is everyone's family.

I owe the greatest debt to my late father, who assisted me to develop a thirst for knowing the reasons behind the reasons from childhood; in fact, he was the first one to introduce me to various global philosophies. I also wish to thank my son and daughter, who have been patient with me for the last few years while I used to work on this project late at night.

I must admit that many advised me that as a commercial lawyer, I must not waste time on finding reasons behind reasons and instead focus on resolving more disputes! However, I felt the comparative analysis of *invisible factors and contexts* is essential to understanding the codes, statutes, case precedents and *law in action*. In fact, as the icing on the cake, I feel that analysis has made me a better lawyer and negotiator. I hope it does the same for readers of this book, who might be professionals in any field.

The law is stated as available to me on 31 March 2019.

Dr. (Capt.) Vivek Jain

Table of Contents

Table I – Primary & Secondary Legislation of England & Wales

Table II – International Legislations

Table III – People's Republic of China ("PRC's") Primary Legislation (translated)

Table IV – PRC's Supreme People's Court – Provisions & Circulars, Interpretations, Replies & Opinions

Opinions

Table V – Table of Cases from England & Wales

Table VI – Abbreviations

Table VI-1 – Abbreviations of Journals

Journal	Abbreviation	Journal	Abbreviation
Akron Law Review	Akron L. Rev.	Harvard Journal of Law and Public Policy	Harv. J. L. & Pub. Pol'y
Alabama Law Review	Ala. L. Rev.	Harvard Law Review	Harv. L. Rev.
American Bar Association	A.B.A.	Hong Kong Law Journal	Hong Kong L.J.
American Journal of Comparative Law	Am. J. Comp. L.	Indiana Law Journal	Ind. L. J.
American Law and Economic Review	Am. L. & Econ. Rev.	Informal Logic	Informal Logic
Archiv für rechts - und Sozialphilosophie	ARSP	International & Comparative Law Quarterly	I.C.L.Q.
Australian Bar Review	Australian Bar Rev.	International Business Law	Int'l Bus. L.
Bond Law Review	Bond L. Rev.	International Business Lawyer	Int'l Bus. Law.
Boston College International and Comparative Law Review	B.C. Int'l & Comp. L. Rev.	Israel Law Review	Israel L. Rev.
Cambridge Law Review	C.L.R.	Journal of Chinese University of Political Science	J. of CUPL
Case Western Reserve Journal of International Law	Case W. Res. J. Int'l L.	Journal of Comparative Law	J. Comp. L.
Chengdu Speed Reading	Chengdu Speed Reading	Journal of Institutional and Theoretical Economics	J. of Inst. And Theoretical Econ.
China Journal	China J.	Journal of Law Application	J. L. App.
China Legal Science	China Legal Science	Journal of Law	Falv Shiyong
China Review	China Rev.	Journal of North China University of Technology	Journal of N. China u. Tech
Chinese Journal of Law	Faxue Yanjiu	Journal of North Western University (Philosophy and Social Science Edition)	J. No. West. U. (P. & So. Sc.)
Civil Justice Quarterly	C.J.Q.	Journal of Northwest University of Political Science and Law	J. Of Northwest U of Pol. Sc. L.
Commonwealth Law Bulletin	Comm. Legal Bulletin	Journal of Political Science and Law	J. Political Sc. L.

Journal	Abbreviation	Journal	Abbreviation
Comparative & International Law Journal of South Africa	Comp. & Int'l L.J. S.Afr.	Journal of South West University of Political Science and law	J. South West U. of Pol. Sc. & L.
Cornell International Law Journal	Cornell Int'l L.J.	Law and History Law Review	Law & Hist. Rev.
Cornell Law Review	Cornell L. Rev.	Law and Social Development	Fazhi Yu Shehui Fazhan
Electronic Journal of Comparative Law	Electronic J. Comp. L.	Law Review of Wuhan University	Law Review
Frontiers Laws of China	Frontiers. L. China	Legal System and Social Development	Legal Sys. & Soc. Dev.
Gansu Social Science	Gansu. So. Sc.	Legal System and Society	Legal Sys. & Soc.
Global Jurist Frontiers	GJF	Max Planck Institute for Research on Collective Goods	MPI Collective Goods
Max Planck Institute for Research on Collective Goods	MPI Collective Goods	The Litigator	The Litigator
Michigan Journal of International Law	Mich. J. Int'l L.	T'Oung Pao	T'Oung Pao
Modern Law Science (Southwest University of Political Science)	Modern L. Science	Tribune of Political Science	Zhengfa Luntan
Monash Law Review	Monash L. Rev.	Tsinghua China Law Review	Tsinghua China L. Rev.
Monash University Law Review	Monash. U. L. Rev.	Tulane Journal of International and Comparative Law	Tul. J. Int'l & Com. L.
Northwest Journal of Technology and Intellectual Property	Northwest J Tech. & Intellectual Prop.	Tulane Law Review	Tul. L. Rev.
Oxford Journal of Legal Studies	Oxford J. of Legal Stud.	Tulsa Law Journal	Tulsa L.J.
Oxford University Commonwealth Law Journal	Oxf. U. Comm. L.J.	UC Davis Journal of International Law and Policy	U.C. Davis J. Int'l L. & Pol'y
Pacific Rim Law & Policy Journal	Pacific Rim L. & Pol. J.	UCLA International Institute	UCLA Int'l Inst.
Peking University Law Journal	Peking U. L.J.	UCLA Law Review	UCLA L. Rev.

Journal	Abbreviation	Journal	Abbreviation
Philosophy and Rhetoric	Phi. & Rh.	University of Detroit Mercy Law Review	U. Det. Mercy. L. Rev.
Rand Journal of Economics	Rand J. Economics	University of Pennsylvania Law Review	U.PA. L. Rev.
Ritsumeikan Law Review	R.L.R.	Washington and Lee Law Review	Wash. & Lee L. Rev.
Scandinavian Law Review	Scandinavian L. Rev.	Washington University Global Studies Law Review	Wash. U. L. Rev.
Scandinavian Studies in Law	Scandinavian Studies L.	Washington University Law Review	Wash. U. L. Rev.
Seton Hall Law Review	Seton Hall L. Rev.	Willamette Journal of International Law and Dispute Resolution	Willeamete J. Int'l L. & Disp. Resol.
Social Sciences in China	Zhonguo Shehui Kexue	Yale Law Journal	Yale L.J.
Southern Californian Law Review	S. Cal. L. Rev.	Yuenan: Legal System and Society	Yuenan L. System Society
The Comparative and International Law Journal of Southern Africa	Comp. & Int'l L.J. S. Afr.	Zeitschrift für Zivilprozeß	ZZP
The George Washington Law Review	Geo.Wash. L. Rev.		

Table VI-2 – Other Abbreviations

Abbreviation	Full Form	Abbreviation	Full Form
A-G	Attorney General	Co-op	Co-operative
AC	Appeal Cases	col/cols	Column/columns
Affd	Affirmed	Com. L	Commercial Law Reports
All ER	All England Reports	Comr/Comrs	Commissioner/Commissioners
ALL ER Rep	All England Law Reports Reprint	Contra.	Direct Contrast
Anon	Anonymous	Corp	Corporation
Ann. Rep.	Annual Report	CPL	Civil Procedural Law 1991 of PRC (as amended)
App	Appendix	CPR	Civil Procedural Rules 1998 (as amended), SI 1998/3132
App Cas	Law Reports, Appeal Cases (UK)	DC	District Council
Art. & Arts.	Article & Articles	Dept	Department
BCE	Before Common Era	Dir	Directive
C	Chapter by which the Act is known in a year	DJ	District Judge
CA	Court of Appeal	ECHR	European Court of Human Rights
CC	County Council	ER	English Reports
CCR	County Court Rules	EU	European Union
CE	Common Era	EWCA Civ	Neutral Citation Court of Appeal Civil Division
cf.	Contrast to text	EWHC (Comm)	Neutral Citation, High Court (Commercial Division)
Ch	Law reports of Chancery Division	EWHC (Admlty)	Neutral Citation High Court (Admiralty)
ch/chs	Chapter/chapters	EWHC (Ch)	Neutral Citation High Court (Chancery Division)
ChD	Chancery Division	EWHC (QB)	Neutral Citation High Court (Queen's Bench Division)
cl/cls	clause/clauses	Fam	Law Reports, Family Division
CLR	Commonwealth Law Reports	FamD	Family Division
CJ	Lord Chief Justices, Chief Justice of Queen's Bench	FLR	Family Law Reports
Co.	Company	Fn	Foot Note

Table VI-2 – Other Abbreviations (continued 1)

Abbreviation	Full Form	Abbreviation	Full Form
FSR	Fleet Street Reports	Para. & Paras.	Paragraph & Paragraphs
GB	Great Britain	PD	Practice Direction
HL	House of Lords	pt/pts	part/parts
Inc	Incorporated	QB	Law Reports, Queen's Bench Division of High
J	Justice of High Court	QBD	Queen's Bench Division
Judge	Circuit Judge	R	Rex/Regina [The Queen (or King)]
Liq	Liquidation	Reg. & regs.	Regulation & Regulations
LJ	Lord/Lady Justice of Appeal	RPC	Reports of Patent, Design and Trademark Cases
Lloyd's Rep	Lloyd's Law Reports	RSC	Rules of the Supreme Court
Lord	Lord of Appeal	S	Section
LR Adm & Eccl	Llyods' Report Admiralty & Ecclesiastical	Sch.	Schedule
LR Ch App	Law Reports, Chancery Appeals Cases	Sch.	Supreme Court
Ltd	Limited	SCJ	Justice of Supreme Court of the United Kingdom
MR	Master of The Rolls	sec.	Section
n.a.	Not Available	UKHL	Neutral Citation, House of Lords
n.d.	No date	UKPC	Neutral Citation, Privy Council
n.p.	No Publisher	V-C	Vice Chancellor
Ors	Others	vol/vols	volume/volumes
		WLR	Weekly Law Reports

Table VII – PRC Related Information

Table VII-1 – PRC Publishers

Beijing Law Press	北京法律出版社
China Procuratorate Press	中国检察出版社
Legal Press	法律出版社
Peking University Press	北京大学出版社
People's Court Press	人民法院出版社
People's Public Security University of China Press	中国人民公安大学出版社
Press of China's University of Political Science and Law	中国政法大学出版社
Shanghai Law Translation & Edition Press	上海法学编译出版社
Shanghai People's House	上海人民出版社
Shanxi People's Publisher	山西人民出版社
The Commercial Press	商务印书馆
The Press of Masses	人民出版社
Wunan Book Co. Ltd.	五南文化事业机构
Wunan Book Publisher	五南图书出版社

Table VII – 2 PRC Journals

China Law	中国法律
China Legal Science	中国法学
Chinese Journal of Law / Cass journal of law	法学研究
Frontiers of Law in China	中国法学前沿
Gansu Social Sciences	甘肃社会科学
Jiangsu Economic Weekly	江苏经济报
Journal of Comparative Law	比较法研究
Journal of Hubei University of Police	湖北警官学院学报
Journal of Law Application	法律适用
Journal of Northwest University	西北大学学报
Journal of Political Science and Law	政法学刊
Journal of Southwest University of Political Science and Law	西南政法大学学报
Law and Social Development	法制与社会发展
Law Review	法学评论
Law Science	法学
Law Science Magazine	法学杂志
Legal System and Social Development	法制与社会发展
Legal System and Society	法律制度与社会 (云南)
Journal of North China University of Technology	北方工业大学学报
Market Modernization	商场现代化
Modern Law Science	现代法学
Peking University Law Journal	中外法学
Science of Law (Journal of Northwest University of Political Science and Law)	法律科学(西北政法大学学报)
Social Sciences in China	中国社会科学
Speed Reading	速读 (成都)
Tribune of Political Science and Law	政法论坛
Tsinghua China Law Review	清华中国法学评论

List of Figures

List of Tables

CHAPTER ONE — INTRODUCTION

1.1. Global Undercurrents and China's rise

As international trade has become more globalized over the last few decades, another important parallel development has also taken place in the past eighteen years: The People's Republic of China ("PRC") has emerged as an economic powerhouse. A sizable amount of global trade in goods and services either originates in the PRC or is destined for the PRC. Nowadays, therefore, International Trade includes numerous connections and networks with the PRC, centered around trade in goods and services. These developments have had a profound impact, comparable to the changes that occurred in the late nineteenth century,[1] when the Qing dynasty was coerced into opening up the economy to western powers. This opening up led to demands by the Qing elites to gradually introduce changes in then-existing laws.

---

[1] Refer to Table VIII – Ancient Chinese Dynasties.

1

Table VIII – Ancient Chinese Dynasties

Dynasties	Year	Comments
Xia Dynasty	2300-1800 BCE	
Shang Dynasty	1600-1045 BCE	1800-1200 BCE, according to a few other historians.
Western Zhou	1046-771 BCE	1122-255 BCE, Combined Western and Eastern according to a few historians. It covered the central plains of present PRC.
Zheng Kingdom	806-375 BCE	
Kingdom of Lu	722-481 BCE	Around the present-day Shandong province.
Jin	772-468 BCE	Vassal state of Zhou.
Eastern Zhou	771-221 BCE	Spring and Autumn Period (c. 771–476 BCE) & the Warring States Period (c. 476–221 BCE).
Qin Dynasty	221-205 BCE	Famous for reuniting various provinces in a big land mass, into what is now called China.
Han Dynasty	206 BCE - 220 CE	
Three Kingdoms	220-280 CE	
Jin Dynasty	265-420 CE	
Northern & Southern Dynasties	420-589 CE	
Sui Dynasty	581-618 CE	
Tang Dynasty	681-906 CE	
Song Dynasty	960-1279 CE	
Yuan Dynasty	1206-1367 CE	
Ming Dynasty	1368-1644 CE	
Qing Dynasty	1644-1911 CE	Last Dynasty before Imperial system was abolished.

In a somewhat similar way, the profound economic prosperity that has occurred in the PRC over the last two decades has created a demand for a thorough analysis of current laws to enable future legal reforms to reach specific outcomes to continue this momentum of economic growth in the PRC.

In order to appreciate just how profound these economic changes of the last two decades have been to the PRC, it is necessary to look back at the history of its economy since the early 20th century. At the end of the 1940s, the Chinese economy was nearly bankrupt. Still greater economic suffering came about as a result of the Great Leap Forward (1958-60) and the Cultural Revolution (1966-76).[2] The decades of economic suffering were followed by market reforms in 1978, and from that time until 2008, real GDP growth in the PRC was at an annual rate of almost 10%.[3] This economic growth was nearly double that of India and even higher than that of newly industrialised economies in the Asia-Pacific region, such as South Korea and Singapore. This striking economic growth must be seen in the context of the PRC's land mass, which is much bigger than that of most of these other countries.[4]

The impressive rate of economic growth was supported by an increase in consumption of commodities, as the reserves of these commodities available in the PRC are lower on a per capita basis.[5] The growth in consumption led to the growth, at an unprecedented level never seen before in human history, of numerous PRC-related commodity transactions, contracts, and finalised business deals.

It has also transformed the PRC's agriculture-based society into an industrial society in a very short span of time.[6] The PRC's Human Development Index ("HDI") in some provinces/cities such as Shanghai, Beijing and Tianjin is comparable to that in advanced economies, and currently the PRC's overall HDI itself is in the category of middle-income countries.[7] However, the unprecedented economic development observed in the PRC is not matched by an equivalent political development; this has led to a massive drop in accountability and control of corruption, most notably from 2002-2007.[8]

---

[2]Rongxing Guo, *An Introduction to the Chinese Economy: The Driving Forces Behind Modern Day China* (Singapore: John Wiley & Sons, 2010), 11.
[3]Ibid.
[4]Ibid., 111.
[5]Ibid., 35-37.
[6]Ibid., 61.
[7]Ibid., 63.
[8]Ibid., 104–5.

The economic development discussed above was supported by a high saving rate and a large supply of labour, keeping the rate of return on investment profitable.[9] The PRC's economic growth was supported by the intensifying undercurrents of globalisation, as a result of which the PRC gained massively through access to Foreign Direct Investment ("FDI"), technology, modern management techniques, demand for its manufactured goods, and increased efficiency due to the competition in the globalised market. This rapid economic growth was accompanied by rising income levels at the start of reforms to foster increased competition, due to the official policy of "getting some people rich first." A discussion of rapid economic growth and economic philosophy cannot be complete without mention of PRC's core leader Deng Xiaoping, who said:

> To take the road to socialism is to realize common prosperity step by step. Our plan is as follows: where conditions permit, some areas may develop faster than others; those that develop faster can help promote the progress of those that lag behind, until all become prosperous. If the rich keep getting richer and the poor poorer, polarization will emerge. The socialist system [emphasis added] must and can avoid polarization. One way is for the areas that become prosperous first to support the poor areas by paying more taxes or turning in more profits to the state. Of course, this should not be done too soon. At present, we don't want to dampen the vitality of the developed areas or encourage the practice of having everyone "eat from the same big pot." We should study when to raise this question and how to settle it.[10]

The PRC, as a socialist nation founded in 1949, remained a closed economy for a number of years, as it preferred to limit itself to trading with other socialist states. This was similar to the *Hanjin policy* of the Qing Dynasty (1644-1911) banning particular kinds of maritime voyages.[11] However, due to the economic woes suffered during the Cultural Revolution, the PRC abandoned this closed economic policy and initiated market reforms. As early as 1979 it implemented a law concerning *Joint Ventures with Chinese and Foreign Investment*; also in 1979 it granted a few provinces such as Guangdong the authority to initiate flexible measures to advance commerce, called *xian zhou yibu*.[12] In 1984, a further fourteen coastal cities were

---

[9]Ibid., 113.
[10]Deng Xioping in 1992 as quoted in Guo, *Introduction to the Chinese Economy*, 110.
[11]Guo, *Introduction to the Chinese Economy*, 130-31.
[12]Ibid., 134.

allowed to form Special Economic Zones; later, Economic Development Zones were created to enhance economic development.

The gradual movement of the PRC towards a market economy gained momentum and impetus when it joined the World Trade Organisation ("WTO") on December 11, 2001.[13] From the point of view of legal reforms, the PRC abolished laws that were deemed inconsistent with the then-existing WTO regulations. Market reforms, meanwhile, followed the four-stage process of decentralisation followed by centralisation (*shou*), which was followed by rigidity and again followed by decentralisation (*fang*) as a result of political compromises made at the level of the top leadership of the PRC.[14]

Even though the PRC's economic growth is unprecedented, it has to be seen from a global perspective as its GDP per capita is still considerably less than that of the US and other developed countries, which signifies that there remain challenges that need to be overcome. The analysis or comparison of law must be seen within this context as well. Income disparity exists between rural and urban areas and the gap ratio in per capita income in these two areas has increased in the last few years, rising to nearly 3.5 in 2008.[15] Based on the above quote from Deng, and to reduce the income disparities between provinces, the "western region Development Strategy" (*xibu da kaifa*) was introduced to raise the prosperity level of the PRC's western regions.

In the author's view, the rate of legal development is affected by the level of prosperity and income disparity, and this factor should not be overlooked in any comparison between the legal systems. The understanding of the country through its legal system can be achieved by understanding this context. Income disparity has a direct effect on the less privileged, and also on the ability of new or developing corporations to access the investments with a higher rate of return. Another equally important factor affecting them is a general lack of credit liquidity in the system. All such factors directly affect the legal system as it will have the effect of reducing access to justice and thereby affecting litigants' ability to seek remedies in court against powerful business corporations.

It is no secret that even though there is a body of PRC laws to govern commerce, the experience at ground level can differ widely. It is apparent from the experiences of

---

[13] For many experts, the making of the PRC as a market economy is still a work in progress due to the domination of state enterprises in the PRC's economy. It is also a major bone of contention in the current trade war between the two largest economies of the world, that is, the US and the PRC.

[14] Guo, *Introduction to the Chinese Economy*, 163.

[15] Ibid., 119.

many businessmen that there is wide discretion in terms of enforcement of these central regulations as exhibited by central, provincial and local officials in the PRC.[16] This issue, in the author's own experience, is evident in many provincial courts in the PRC, which are at a considerable distance from Beijing.In the author's view, this type of economic development, which is unprecedented in human history, has also led to enormous changes in society.

To sustain such unprecedented economic growth, the level of economic growth brought about through increased exports, imports, business and commercial transactions must be maintained to avoid catastrophic social unrest. This has necessitated immense changes in the PRC legal system in the last two decades; for example, new laws have been introduced with the intention of improving the PRC legal system at provincial level (*sheng*), autonomous body level (*zizhiqu*), municipalities controlled by the central government in Beijing (*zhixiashi*), and in the special administrative regions of Hong Kong and Macao.

1.2. Role of Legal Systems in Business Disputes

As economic growth accelerates in any country, it boosts commerce and all-round development within its frontiers. This increase in commerce & trade leads to even further investments (domestic & foreign direct investment), contracts, trade, and movements of people; as a result, augmented transactions are carried out by that country's own citizens and organisations. These transactions transpire within domestic trade as well as international trade through export or import of goods and services from other countries.

However, if disputes occur during these transactions, and the parties involved cannot resolve their differences amicably, they will have to turn to the courts in a particular jurisdiction. This jurisdiction could have been selected by the parties in their contracts, or it could be the jurisdiction which is closely related to the dispute. In developed countries with fully developed legal systems, the courts are the source of economic development as they are not only involved in resolving the commercial disputes of stakeholders in its economy, but also assist in restraining legislative and bureaucratic excesses.[17]

---

[16]Ibid., 117.
[17]John Gillespie, "Rethinking the Role of Judicial Independence in Socialist-Transforming East Asia," *I.C.L.Q.* 56, no. 4 (2007): 838.

However, the courts in many East Asian countries, which have been experiencing breakneck economic growth for a while, are not given high status, and as a result are considered as secondary to the legislature. In some cases, the judiciary is not fully independent. The claimants in any civil litigation will endeavour to establish the validity of their claims, and thereafter will try to succeed in their claims, or to reach an outcome as close as possible to what they are demanding from the defendants. The defendant will try to avoid any of the two outcomes that the claimants are hoping for by using the civil justice system.[18]

At the same time, there are stakeholders in the civil courts, and in the businesses that may be affected by the filing of a case by the claimants. These other stakeholders in the courts are the judges and even the states where these courts are located. The aim of the judges is to reach a just resolution to the dispute before them; the states' purpose, however, will be similar in most scenarios, as both the executive and legislative branch of any country will expect the civil courts that are manned by an independent judiciary to resolve commercial disputes in such a way as to enhance trade between the parties.

Any potential commercial or business disputes in commerce and trade are hurdles to enhancing trade and increasing the Gross Domestic Product ("GDP") of any country, it is in the interests of the state that citizens, foreign investors and traders, businessmen and business organisations, all have trust in its civil courts.

The trust of these stakeholders, who carry out commercial activities, is the vital factor to sustain and enhance the economic activities that ultimately benefit citizens through increased GDP per person, which will raise their standard of living, improve their quality of life and even encourage sustainable development. For example, England & Wales, a common law jurisdiction, has been a popular destination for resolving commercial, maritime and corporate disputes for over one hundred fifty years, even where the parties or the subject matter of the disputes have no connection whatsoever with England & Wales.

Wales has a unified justice system with England, and all laws of England in commercial matters and civil procedure are applicable in Wales. England & Wales are also the most popular centers for resolving disputes through arbitration. The author will refer to the courts of England & Wales following common law as *'English Courts'*.

---

[18]J. A. Jolowicz, "Civil Litigation: What's it For?" *Camb. L.J.* 67, no. 3 (2008): 67.

Initially, the popularity of English courts in the Commonwealth was because Great Britain was the major imperial power of the world for over two centuries. However, the major factor for the popularity of English courts in recent years is that its legal system is readily accepted by litigants around the world due to its ability to evolve and impart justice in commercial disputes. Most importantly, in general, English judges feel confident to employ their discretionary power within the common law system. In the author's view, these English judges are also empowered to a certain extent due to their training in a common law system.

On the other hand, the PRC has become an economic superpower only in the twenty-first century. Therefore, commercial stakeholders, both domestic and foreign, have an interest in the legal system and philosophy of PRC not only to resolve disputes, but also to provide necessary assurances that their hard-earned money will be protected without bias, if anything were to go wrong. Furthermore, the expectations of these stakeholders for the PRC courts would be in relation to the remedies available through these PRC courts.

These stakeholders will expect that these remedies are well founded in its civil procedural law and will assist them in time of need. Therefore, a comparison of the two jurisdictions is appropriate in the contemporary context. Because businessmen and commercial interests from the PRC are investing abroad or involved in big-ticket projects, this book will provide a timely and relevant comparison of the two legal systems & philosophies.

An important question that could be asked by the readers is whether the jurisdiction of England & Wales, a common law jurisdiction can really be compared with the jurisdiction of PRC. A few of the reasons to argue against such comparison could be the rapid advent of PRC as an economic superpower and a completely different system from England & Wales. A justification for the comparison of a Western legal system with the jurisdiction of the rising economic superpower such as the PRC has been suggested by Eberle.[19] In particular, Eberle has praised old civilisations such as the PRC for their rules and norms that could assist even scholars trained in advanced common law legal system such as England & Wales:

> Evaluation of older cultures in place before the rise of legal
> systems can yield important information about the basic elements
> and structure of modern societies. Looking at ourselves through

---

[19]Edward J. Eberle, "The Method and Role of Comparative Law," *Wash. U. Global Stud. L. Rev.* 8, no. 3 (2009): 454.

these mirrors could reveal important ideas, norms, rules or principles, forcing a reevaluation that may improve the social order or, alternatively, lead us to confirm the tenets of our own legal system.[20]

As a means to show the comparative difference between the philosophies, let us start by highlighting the difference of philosophy in Civil Procedure Law of both the systems. These differences have a profound effect on the way the disputes are litigated in the respective courts. For example, Civil Procedure Rules 1998 ("*CPR 1998*")[21] of England & Wales, in particular *CPR 1998* r.1.1 (1) states *inter alia* that:

> These Rules are a new procedural code with the *overriding objective* of enabling the court to deal with cases justly and at proportionate cost [emphasis added].

Similarly, Article 2 of *Civil Procedural Law 1991* ("*CPL 1991*") of the People's Republic of China ("PRC") provides *inter alia* very similar objectives as *CPR 1998*:[22]

> ...
>
> apply the law correctly, try civil cases promptly; and the law, [to] *maintain the social and economic order*; and to guarantee the smooth progress of the *socialist* construct [sic] [emphasis added].
>
> ...

The reader can clearly appreciate that the judges in the PRC must consider the public interests in private disputes between the parties as can be seen from the above. PRC judges must take into account issues such as social and economic order, and in that sense function as guarantors of socialist society of PRC. This is surely a huge burden for the PRC judges as compared to the English or any common-law judges in respect of litigation of ordinary civil and commercial disputes. In addition, the author will

---

[20]Ibid., 454–55.
[21]*Civil Procedure Rules 1998*, No. 3132 (L.17)*, as amended by Civil Procedure (Amendment No. 3) Rules 2016,* No. 788 (L.11) that came into force on October, 3, 2016. *CPR 1998. CPR 1998* is regularly amended, and the author has taken into account all the amendments until this date. The old Civil Procedural Rules before *CPR 1998* will be hereinafter called as *pre-CPR*.
[22]*Civil Procedure Law 1991 (as amended in 2012)*, Order 44 of President of PRC on April, 9, 1991.

highlight that such burdens are also not defined precisely in the relevant statutes in the PRC Code.

It may moreover mean that a great deal of leeway is given to the PRC judges, when they are litigating private civil and commercial law disputes. The litigants, who are financially stronger, can usually employ their financial might in the commercial/civil litigation in any jurisdiction, unless the courts are equipped with the proper case management power or have power to order mediation or assist in mediation themselves. For example, in order to assist the judges in the English Courts, discretionary power is provided for them through the development and evolution of law through case precedents in the common law system in England & Wales, or through the drafting of new procedural codes & subsequent interpretations, opinions or replies to ensure the objectives of civil procedure are met.

Another issue that will have a deep impact on how cases are progressed through civil litigation in the courts is whether judges are entitled to find the truth in any case, or their focus is just on resolving the dispute before them, as per the overriding objectives and to achieve procedural fairness. Administrative reasons, legal philosophies, and jurisprudence behind the civil procedural system are some of the factors affecting how the cases are progressed from their first contact with the legal system.

These philosophies will have a profound effect upon the outcome for any case, and it is quite possible that the same case can be lost in one jurisdiction but can be won easily in another. The success or failure will all depend on the jurisprudence and philosophy behind the procedural systems. These factors will affect the judges' discretionary powers in granting the relevant remedies in commercial or civil litigation and so forth.

The approach in England & Wales is to ensure that civil procedural rules encourage settlement as a first resort, thus avoiding these cases progressing all the way to costly civil trials before the courts.[23] The above factors are ordinarily not appreciated by laymen, traders and so forth.

This approach of English courts will avoid the tying up of judicial resources of the courts in deciding mere questions of fact, as opposed to the more important matter of deciding questions of law. The issues of questions of law are, in fact, essential for

---

[23]Lord Woolf, *Access to Justice: Final Report to the Lord Chancellor on the Civil Justice System in England and Wales* (London: HMSO, 1996).

development of laws that could benefit societies with the common law systems. This philosophical approach is one of the factors that led to the development of various remedies as a substitute for litigation in the common-law courts, such as freezing injunctions or interim injunctions during litigation. This approach is essential in times of breakneck technological advances, digital connections, and globalisation, all of which affect commercial transactions and communications.

The jurisprudential theories dominating the legal and administrative thought processes of these jurisdictions will also affect how such remedies, if any, are granted in commercial disputes that reach the courts in any jurisdiction. Factors such as jurisprudence, legal philosophy, legal history, culture, evolution of law, substantive law and civil procedural law, and methods of judicial activities are the **invisible factors and contexts** that are responsible for differences or similarities between the two jurisdictions' practice. **The focus of the book is on understanding these invisible factors and contexts in which the law is developed, created, interpreted, and then applied in the courts.** Each of the invisible factors and contexts for both common law and PRC law will be examined in separate chapters in this book. The author has tried to ensure that each of these invisible factors and contexts can be read as a stand-alone chapter.

The two jurisdictions, that is the common law system of England & Wales and PRC law, have different terminology for similar remedies or court processes. In any comparative analysis, the real challenge lies in comparing the relevant laws from the perspective of these invisible factors and contexts. Otherwise, merely comparing exercise of laws and codes will remain a superficial exercise. Even when comparing the remedies in commercial and/or civil litigation, there is a need to have the invisible factors and contexts in mind. It is appropriate at this juncture to quote Rable at length:

> [T]he student of the problem must encompass the law of the whole world, past and present, and everything that affects the law, such as geography, climate and race, developments and events shaping the course of country's history - war, revolution, colonisation, subjugation - religion and ethics, the ambition and creativity of individuals, the needs of production and consumption, the interests of groups, parties and classes. Ideas of every kind have their effect, for it is not just feudalism, liberalism and socialism which produce different types of law; legal institutions once adopted may have logical consequences; and not least important is the striving for a political or legal ideal. Everything in the social, economic and legal fields interacts. The law of every developed

people is in constant motion, and the whole kaleidoscopic picture is one which no one has ever clearly seen.[24]

The granting of remedies in courts, from the initial stage when the applications are made by the claimant, to the stage when any orders granted are to be enforced, is always dependent, in any jurisdiction, on the administrative setup and framework of a legal system, including its administrative aspects. These factors cannot be overlooked.

1.2.1. Administration of Disputes in Market economy

'Market economy' in any country or an economic zone refers to an economic system where economic decisions as to investments, distribution and price of goods and services are steered only on the basis of transactions and dealings of citizens and business, and there is no planned state intervention. Civil dispute resolution and how parties are assisted by this system are an important part of any market economy, as they are instrumental in reducing transaction costs. It is important that civil litigation is considered as part of the service sector of the economy, especially with the increasing clout of the PRC in global economic spheres.[25]

A legal system with a proper framework to manage the expectations of commercial interests will ensure that many of these cases are resolved satisfactorily; this can even improve the local economy. The vital factor is the perception of fairness, and in a market economy, any negative view cannot be swept under the carpet. A good legal system will assist in disposal of commercial disputes without full civil trials or without determination by the courts, and thus assist in achieving the aim of legislators in any country.

The following quote from a 2013 OECD Report describes succinctly the importance of the civil justice system:

> Judicial systems serve important purposes in up-holding [sic] social values but also in <u>determining economic performance.</u>

---

[24]Hein Kotz, "Comparative Law in Germany Today," *Revue Internationale de Droit Compare* 51, no. 4 (1999): 756, where the author quoted Ernest Rable.

[25]Peter Middleton, *Review of Civil Justice and Legal Aid*, Report to the Lord Chancellor (London: Lord Chancellor's Department, 1997), Ch 1, where he wrote in the article that "Justice- by which I mean the satisfactory resolution of disputes - is part of the service sector of the economy."

> Well-functioning judiciaries guarantee security of property rights and enforcement of contracts. Security of property rights strengthens incentives to save and invest, by protecting returns from these activities. A good enforcement of contracts stimulates agents to enter into economic relationships, by dissuading opportunistic behaviour and reducing transaction costs. This has a positive impact on growth through various channels: it promotes competition, fosters specialisation in more innovative industries, contributes to the development of financial and credit markets and facilitates firm growth [emphasis added].[26]

This is also an appropriate time to introduce Rawls' concept of *formal justice*,[27] which states that there is a need to impart consistent, impartial administration of procedural rules where the decision makers (the judges) do not exercise their own personal discretion that is available to any one of them at the personal level. The sheer size of the PRC means that it will have to overcome the challenge of applying the rules uniformly and consistently, and it is the author's view that it will need to bring in the concept of formal justice within the legal framework.

This brings the author to the principle of rule of law, namely the formal rules and procedures, the formal application of which will control the exercise of human discretion. In such a system, Dicey's concept of the primacy of rules over all institutions is established, with the aim to curb the arbitrary power of officials.[28] This requirement of formal justice is important, in spite of the achievement of having almost all procedural codes and substantive law established in the span of just a few years, as stated by the ex-chairman of the Standing Committee of NPC, Mr. Wu Bangguo, who stated that a socialist legal system with Chinese characteristics was established in China in 2011.

2011 was the year when the PRC established a good system of PRC Codes to cover various aspects of trade and society. In the history of a civilisation and relative to other countries' legal systems, the PRC's codes are new and recently established. This has to be appreciated by the readers of the book from the start, as do the challenges that the implementation of any law brings to the PRC.

---

[26]OECD, *What Makes Civil Justice Effective*, OECD Economic Department Policy Notes, No. 18 June 2013 (2013), 2, 1–12. www.oecd.org/eco/growth/civil%20Justice%20Policy%20note.pdf.
[27]Refer, Chapter 5, § 5.3.1 & Chapter 6, § 6.2 for the concept of Rawls' formal justice in context of discretionary powers of the decision-makers.
[28]Ibid. Dicey is discussed in the same section of Chapter 6, §6.2.

1.3. Background to the Book

When there are commercial and civil disputes and all attempts to resolve those disputes have failed, in that scenario, civil litigation before the courts is the most important medium to resolve the disputes. This will hold true, as long as there are no mandatory arbitration and/or other alternative dispute resolution clauses in the contracts governing that dispute. However, civil litigation is principally an adversarial process, where the final judgments after a civil trial ultimately settle the respective position of the parties to the commercial dispute. In the author's view, this statement is true not only for the common law systems such as England & Wales, but also for jurisdictions like the PRC that follow the civil law system. In order to understand the differences between the two systems, it is important to focus on the contemporary philosophies and then link them subtly to the invisible factors and contexts.

Therefore, the author will discuss the practical example of civil dispute between parties, and how the respective courts in both the jurisdictions approach the issues currently; the purpose of this is to understand the differences in the current philosophy and what has led to this thought process. **By taking civil dispute as a background, the author hopes to help the readers to understand the similarities and differences between the two systems.**

Civil procedures have evolved in both the common law systems and the civil law systems to ensure fairness to both parties; however, these formal civil procedures have costs implications for the parties to commercial disputes. In addition, civil procedures can result in complexities, tactical moves and even obstructions by one of the parties to the commercial dispute, exploiting the civil procedural rules by the parties concerned. England & Wales follow a common law system, whereas the PRC follows a civil law system. The jurisprudence affecting both these civil procedural systems is a bit different, even though it is a fact that most of the objectives of the civil law systems, as far as the parties to disputes are concerned, are similar to the common law systems.

Civil litigation, in general, is all about 'winning the case', and sometimes the parties are baffled by the need for formal civil procedures that are costly and are, in fact, the principal reason for delay as observed by the parties to commercial disputes. In addition, at times the civil and commercial cases are won just on tactical procedural moves rather than arguments on relevant substantive law. Effective civil/commercial lawyers in any jurisdiction will usually utilise the civil procedural rules effectively and aptly; in particular, they will not hesitate to issue many tactical interim applications to the court.

Recently, in England & Wales, as a result of the Woolf Reforms in April 1999, civil procedures went through drastic changes to reduce legal costs and delays by the introduction of case management powers for the courts. As a result of this power, courts can set timetables, by demanding more cooperation between the parties and increasing focus on *overriding objective*. Even though the procedural rules have, in fact, developed over the centuries in England & Wales, the new *CPR 1998* was meant to break with the past. In order to accomplish that, the English courts have resisted the use of old cases to interpret the fresh rules from *CPR 1998*, except where the form and intention of written rules in the new *CPR 1998* are the same as in the old cases pursuant to *City and County Properties Ltd v Kamali*.[29]

The most important change in the *CPR 1998* was the setting out of the overriding objective in Part 1 of *CPR 1998* to ensure fairness between the parties to litigation; cases are dealt with expeditiously; costs are saved; and the courts' resources are safeguarded. In *CPR 1998* r. 1.4 active case management powers were given to the courts. In spite of these remarkable additions and the judges' power over case management, an effective litigator would never lose sight of the fact that the client's objectives are the prime factor, which cannot be put on the back burner. In addition, the lawyers have obligations pursuant to the Solicitors' professional code of conduct to identify clients' clear objectives. In England & Wales, which is a common law system, judges do not have the power to seek evidence in order to establish the truth but must determine the case based on the best case presented by the lawyers acting on behalf of the parties.

In any legal system, these are the stages in any civil litigation:

- Pre-action stage where issues are identified and information is collated, to decide how the case is to be framed; the right court is chosen in which to commence the action; and a strategy is developed for applying for any pre-action interim orders;

- Issuance of a claim form at a tactical time chosen by the lawyer through which a relevant court is notified; followed by

---

[29][2007] 1 WLR 1219.

the service of the claim form and exchange of statements of claim by the parties, defence and any counterclaims;

- Court's powers to allocate the case and manage the case;

- Interim applications such as disclosure of evidence, attachment of assets, interim or behavior injunctions and so forth;

- Trial;

- Judgment and assessment of costs.

In any litigation, there are numerous interim applications. Even though the main purpose for the development of *CPR 1998* was to ensure fairness for all parties, in the last few decades, the commercial burdens and the money involved have ensured that astute lawyers are using these civil procedure rules as a tool to fit the individual case. Accordingly, numerous interim applications are made in the courts. Interim applications can be made any time during the civil process. A large percentage of cases do not reach the stage of out-and-out civil trials as one of the parties to the commercial dispute would have used the route of an interim application to its advantage or there some sort of settlement has been put in place.

Scholars have highlighted that Comparative law is a special branch of jurisprudence,[30] and therefore, this branch of law has been used less often in comparison to the procedural laws between the two jurisdictions. Comparative law though has been employed in research about issues pertaining to private international law, forum shopping and so forth.

In this book, the author has eschewed the assumptions based on views usually advocated by western practitioners and academics. The main reason for adopting this approach is that many western experts' views are largely based on the fact that they have failed to comprehend fully the cultural aspects of law. Western scholars have

---

[30] Peter Gottwald, "Comparative Civil Procedure," *Ritsumeikan L. Rev.* 22 (2005): 23, where Martinek ideas were discussed. *See also*, M. Martinek, "Rechtsverglechung Als Akademische Disziplin in Deutschland," *Ritsumeikan Law Review (International Edition)* 17 (2000): 84.

viewed PRC law as lacking 'formal-rational rules' as understood by them.[31] The two very common misunderstandings and assumptions that are prevalent amongst western scholars are that there is absence of law in East Asia or law is not that developed in East Asia as compared to the western common law system or even civil law system.[32] The book therefore focuses on the legal traditions and invisible factors behind the rules, to eschew such ready-made assumptions.

The only limitation in pursuing this project is whether the two jurisdictions can be compared, as Scott has elaborated in his paper associated with the Comparative law lectures. In the eighteenth to early twentieth centuries, as a big colonial power, England was the center of International trade. Meanwhile in this decade and for the foreseeable future, the PRC as a current economic superpower will remain a major exporter and importer of goods and services.

As discussed earlier, this will involve commercial people/merchants having trust in the PRC courts and a clear understanding of how the PRC civil procedural law can protect their assets, businesses and commercial interests, when they carry out commercial transactions with PRC connections. In parallel, there is another development that is evolving, where cash rich organisations from the PRC are expanding abroad in other countries, and therefore, have to grapple with other jurisdictions' laws, or understand the contexts and invisible factors in these jurisdictions. The PRC's investors in these other countries are facing similar issues as foreign investors are currently facing in the PRC, arising due to a lack of understanding of foreign laws and the cultural framework in which these foreign laws operate. This raises the importance of such Comparative law analysis.

1.4. Comparative Law – Definition, Meaning and Various Approaches

This book involves the comparison of the legal systems in the two quite distinct jurisdictions, focusing on the contexts and invisible factors underpinning issues within these jurisdictions. In order to carry out a systematic scientific study, it is important to first analyse the concept of Comparative law.

---

[31]Teemu Ruskola, "The East Asian Legal Tradition," in *The Cambridge Companion to Comparative Law*, in *The Cambridge Companion to Comparative Law*, ed. M. Bussani and U. Mattei (Cambridge; New York: Cambridge University Press, 2012), 261.
[32]Ruskola, "The East Asian Legal Tradition," 261.

G. Swanson has highlighted, with reference to comparative research, that any scientific thinking devoid of comparison is unthinkable and cannot be classed even as scientific research or thought. [33] In simple terms, Comparative law is the comparison of the different legal systems of the world. Many jurists have avoided any kind of definition of Comparative law or of comparative methodology as they feel that it is a very complex area of study that cannot be condensed into a brief definition or an abridged version of study.[34]

Comparative law, however, is described in an influential book on Comparative law as the comparison of law with the extra dimension of internationalism.[35] For example, for an English common-law lawyer, just to study and research a few elements of PRC law, or to compare superficially the codes or statutes, will not be considered research into Comparative Law. [36] Scott in his article has translated a definition of the comparative method as provided by the famous jurist Venter:

> The comparative method [of legal research] is that unique, systematic, jurisprudential method, which we apply to gain new knowledge about the legal systems in respect of which we apply it, by taking cognisance of the similarities and differences of those legal systems [emphasis added].[37]

Comparative law is quite distinct from Private International Law, but they do interact with each other.[38] Disciplines such as Private International Law, Public International Law, and Transactional Law consist of a body of positive legal rules, but Comparative

---

[33]G. Swanson, "Framework for Comparative Research: Anthropology and the Theory of Action," in *Comparative Methods in Sociology: Essays on Trends and Applications*, ed. Vallier Ivan and Aptter. David E. (Berkeley: University of California Press, 1971), 141-202.

[34]Scott, "The Comparative Method of Legal Research," 1. The article was accessed on 21 April 2016. Scott used the Latin adage '*Omnis definition periculosa est*' to highlight the patent truism that it is not easy for any jurist to discuss the definition of concepts like Comparative law or comparative methodology; however, there is a contrasting adage, '*tot hominess, quot sententiae*', which reveals the simple truth that academics are brave enough to provide a definition of some kind for any concepts including Comparative law.

[35]Konrad Zweigert, Hein Kotz, and Tony Weir, trans., *An Introduction to Comparative Law: Volume I: The Framework*, 2nd Revised ed. (Oxford: Clarendon Press, 1987), 2.

[36] Ibid., 6. Authors were of the view that merely studying another country's law is not Comparative law.

[37]Scott, "The Comparative Method of Legal Research," 1-2, where he translated the quote that was taken from Venter, *F et al Regsnavorsing - Metode en Publikasie Juta* (1990), 206-244.

[38]Zweigert, Kotz, and Weir, *Introduction to Comparative Law*, 6.

law is a 'method of studying law and stock of academic knowledge'.[39] Many issues in Private International Law are resolved by using Comparative law rather than using national tests. Article 38(1)(c) of *Statute of the International Court of Justice* 1945 ("ICJ") laid down the guidelines for 'general principles of law recognized by civilised nations'; a decision as to how many countries need that common general principle of law enshrined in ICJ's articles can be resolved in a way by Comparative law.[40]

Legal historians have also compared the law over a period of time, and their systematic approach could be classed as similar to scholars comparing laws existent at a particular time.[41] Zweigert and Kotz have discussed Genzmer's ideas in the context of legal historians and Comparative law, saying that experts:

> ...no longer believe that legal history unrolls independently, but see law and history as fully interfused and try to illuminate the extra-legal context and hidden stimuli of legal development. Legal history is therefore not simply self-serving, but contributes to a critical evaluation of the policy of law which is, after all, the principal aim of pure comparative law [emphasis added].[42]

In addition, according to Zweigert and Kotz, Comparative law can be classified as '*vertical comparative law*' when practised by legal historians, and '*horizontal comparative law*' when comparing the modern systems of law in different countries.[43]

Legal Ethnologists, on the other hand, study the history of law to understand the evolution of civilisation. There are many theories propounded by Legal Ethnologists, but they do not focus on studying the evolution of law in societies that are not touched by modern civilisation.[44] These studies could have shed light on the evolution of modern societies as well. This area of law too could make an important contribution in studying Comparative law.[45]

---

[39]Mathias Reimann, "Comparative Law and Neighbouring Disciplines," in *The Cambridge Companion to Comparative Law*, ed. Mauro Bussani and Ugo Mattei, Cambridge Companions to Law (Cambridge; New York: Cambridge University Press, 2012), 14.

[40]See also, Zweigert, Kotz, and Weir, *Introduction to Comparative Law*, 8.

[41]It succinctly described the approach of legal historians in Zweigert, Kotz, and Weir, *Introduction to Comparative Law*, 8.

[42]Zweigert, Kotz, and Weir, *Introduction to Comparative Law*, 9, where they quoted Genzmer. *See also*, Genzmer E., "Verhaltnis von Rechtsgeschichte und Rechtvergleichung," *ARSP 41* (1954/55): 334.

[43]Zweigert, Kotz, and Weir, *Introduction to Comparative Law*, 9.

[44]Adam, "Ethonologische Rechtsforschung," in *Lehrbuch der Volkerkunde*, ed. Adam and Trimborn (1958), 192.

[45]Zweigert, Kotz, and Weir, *Introduction to Comparative Law*, 10.

In the author's view, the above studies could even be useful in analysing methodologies in all areas of substantive law such as contract, tort and so forth, and relevant civil procedures that have been developed over the years to resolve civil disputes germane to these various substantive laws. These aspects will form part of the context in this book and will be discussed in the subsequent Chapters.

For example, if the author were to analyse injunctions, the analysis would not be complete without a discussion of the evolution of equitable remedies in laws of equity and their interaction with common law courts a few hundred years previously. Similarly, if one were to analyse the procedural remedy in the PRC, the analysis would have to take into account the lack of civil procedure for many centuries, and the very recent evolution of such remedies in the 1990s.

Modern comparative scholars believe that there are many more disciplines that Comparative law seems to be related to in practice, such as disciplines of transnational law, legal anthropology and economic analysis of law. Transnational law is also related to this branch, as suggested by Jessup's definition of transnational law "all law which regulates actions or events that transcends national frontiers".[46]

1.4.1. Aims & Objectives of Comparative Law with respect to the Book

From the perspective of this book, with the advent of globalisation, businessmen are trading more across the nations. Common people are travelling more and are therefore exposed to laws of other nations. Even businessmen trading across frontiers are forced to resolve their disputes in unfamiliar jurisdictions. Commercial lawyers have to give advice to such businessmen from other nations/jurisdictions, who are only familiar with their own legal system. Comparative law touches all aspects of laws in the modern globalised world, and it is particularly important for commercial lawyers. Both the PRC and England & Wales are influential players in the global economy due to high GDP, advanced technical capabilities, and strong military powers.

Laws across the nations are not uniform, and there is no law than can be aptly called a common law of mankind.[47] This problem is compounded by the fact that most lawyers in almost all jurisdictions are not exposed to Comparative law at an early stage. According to Zweigert and Kotz, "legal studies only become scientific when

---

[46]P. Jessup, *Transnational Law* (New Haven: Yale University Press, 1956), 2.
[47]Lambert ideally wished for law of humanity as "*droit, commun de l'humanite*" in "Conception Generale et Definition de la Science Due Droit Compare, Proces-Verbaux Des Seances et Documents, Congress International de Droit Compare I," *Congress International de Droit Compare I* (1905): 26.

they rise above the actual rules of any national system, as it happens in legal philosophy, legal history, the sociology of law, and comparative law." [48] This succinctly describes the importance of Comparative law. In addition, Zweigert and Kotz have defined the main purpose of Comparative law as being:

> ...practical, namely reform and improvement of the law [emphasis added] at home, rather than theoretical, philosophical, or speculative; but a part was played also by natural curiosity about other peoples' law and by the impartial feeling that perhaps those others had something to offer - a contrast with the haughty concentration of legal scholars on their own newly codified systems. [49]

The above quote is certainly relevant to this book, as we are comparing English common law with PRC law.

It seems to be the case that Comparative law cannot help to find all the answers due to internal debate within the field. However, one issue is crystal clear: Comparative law is one branch of Jurisprudence that can assist the author in the interpretation of existing laws and analysis of invisible factors & contexts in both the PRC and England & Wales.[50] Comparative law can also assist in understanding the laws within one's home jurisdiction and developing proposals for reforms, and even can be a means and guide for unification and harmonisation of law, including the development of model codes.[51]

This book will avoid the trap of exhibiting mere curiosity, or of limiting the research to the purely philosophical level. In the author's view, the objective should be to provide a practical guide that can be used to resolve real issues for commercial lawyers in the globalised world, where the PRC is the economic powerhouse, and London is still one of the leading financial centers around the world.

---

[48]Zweigert, Kotz, and Weir, *Introduction to Comparative Law*, 4.

[49]Ibid., 53.

[50]It is a branch of jurisprudence and as discussed also in Gottwald, "Comparative Civil Procedure," 23. The author of this book chose to introduce the readers to Comparative law in the Chapter 1 itself to appreciate the phenomenon of comparing the two legal systems.

[51]J.A. Jolowicz, "On the Comparison of Procedures," in *Law and Justice in Multistate World: Essays in Honour of Arther T. Von Mehren*, ed. James Nafziger and Symeon Symeonides (New York: Transnational Publishers, 2002), 721.

1.4.2. Methodology of Comparative Law - Warnings to be kept in mind from the beginning

There are inherent risks in pursuing Comparative law methodology, and the author will keep those in mind from the beginning. Palmer has also mentioned that Comparative law needs to prove that it is cost-effective when resolving day to day problems.[52] In the author's view, a realist way of doing a comparative process may involve just focusing on textual comparisons,[53] and/or in words of Palmer, "...simple juxtapositions of material without elaboration or comment, -- all of these could have legitimacy and value in practical forms of legal research."[54]

However, Comparative law for *law in practice and in action* is crucial for its utility to lawyers and stakeholders with an interest in the area, and the realist mode of comparison will not capture the essence of a law without also having knowledge of when the law came into existence, sources of law and above all its social context. To capture this essence, a high cognitive bar is expected from the author.[55] Palmer even suggested, "... it [comparative law process] *always* requires total immersion and deep preparation [emphasis added] in specific foreign languages and cultures before being attempted: the foreign system should always be seen with the inside and in socio-cultural context [emphasis added]."[56]

The *limit of what the book, the author* and the readers can manage needs to be appreciated from the start in light of the PRC's phenomenal economic growth in the last few decades. Each year in the PRC, the changes in terms of urbanisation, prosperity levels, rising levels of migration, etc., are unprecedented and probably unimaginable in other societies and jurisdictions. This also affects the role of commercial law & commercial/ civil litigation in the fast-changing PRC; therefore, even a snapshot of such rapid change is difficult for any local Chinese researcher/lawyer in the PRC, let alone for a foreign researcher such as the author embarking upon a Comparative law study by comparing the PRC legal system with the common law system. It will be important for the readers to understand the need

---

[52]V.V. Palmer, "From Lerotholi to Lando: Some Examples of Comparative Law Methodology," *Global Jurist Frontiers* 4, no. 2 (2004): 3.
[53]See also, Palmer was of the same view in Palmer, "Comparative Law Methodology," 4.
[54]Palmer, "Comparative Law Methodology," 4.
[55]Ibid.
[56]Ibid., 5. The author of this book has spent a considerable number of years in the PRC. He attempted to immerse himself in the Chinese culture and tried to maintain an objective view of the things around him. The author has avoided the trap of either just appeasing the hosts by praising everything or being overly critical of things after seeing them from the prism of west or a different kind of system. This approach helped the author to maintain an objective view for pursuing research for the book.

to analyse the *sub-context* behind the law, and to ensure that factors such as culture, language, socio-cultural context are clearly understood.[57]

However, there is a counter argument from post-modern critics that the criticism of Comparative law is unfair, and that even within a researcher's own jurisdiction, they are unable to comprehend completely the socio-cultural concepts that underpin the legal concepts and subsequent law, which have evolved in that jurisdiction. Accordingly, scholars have argued that even lawyers who only practise law within their own jurisdictions, should also free themselves from the 'limitations and distortions of their legal culture.'[58]

Ainsworth has succinctly described the dangers for researchers, if they were to rely on legal terminology taken from their own jurisdiction and then try to understand the same concept in a similar way in another jurisdiction. According to Ainsworth, "the very concepts and categories with which the scholar organizes this purportedly universal legal framework are freighted with culturally contingent normative baggage."[59] The author has tried his best to avoid such pitfalls in this book, but the readers should accept some errors in this difficult and complicated task.

1.4.3. Comparative Law Methodology - Most Suited for the Book

The methodology is based upon the classification of the legal systems and the six to eight families into which jurisdictions can be divided:[60] according to Church and Edwards, there are six groupings for the purposes of Comparative law - *Romano-Germanic family*, which comprises civil law countries such as France and Germany; *Common law family* such as England & Wales, USA, India, Australia, Singapore, Malaysia; *Socialist legal family* such as China, Russia, many of which are also Civil Law countries; Religious-philosophical laws such as *Islamic* or *Hindu Law*, *African*

---

[57]Janet E. Ainsworth, "Categories and Culture: On the 'Rectification of Names' in Comparative Law," *Cornell L. Rev.* 82, no. 1 (1996): 19–42. http://scholarship.law.cornell.edu/clr/vol82/iss1/3. In addition, the theories of post-modern critiques have highlighted that criticism of Comparative law is unfair as even within England, the law researchers will not be able to know the entire context. In relation to the PRC, the knowledge of any sub-context is in fact impossible due to the size and constant changes within the PRC.

[58]Palmer, "Comparative Law Methodology," 15, where they cited Gordley. *See also*, James Gordley, "Comparative Legal Research: Its Function in the Development of Harmonized Law," *Am. J. Comp. L.* 43, no. 4 (1995): 555–68.

[59]Ainsworth, "Categories and Culture," quoted in Palmer, "Comparative Law Methodology," 17, n53.

[60]Scott, "The Comparative Method of Legal Research," 4. Cf Pier Giuseppe Monateri, "Methods in Comparative Law: An Intellectual Overview," in *Methods of Comparative Law* (Cheltenham, U.K.; Northampton, MA, USA: Edward Elgar Pub., 2012), 18, where, Monateri, described the division of legal systems needs to be "seen for what they really are: biased, non-neutral political projects of governance supported by the use of the academic discipline of Comparative Law."

customary law; *Mixed legal system* such as the combination of Common law and Civil law such as Quebec in Canada or Louisiana in the USA.[61]

Church & Edwards[62] succinctly described the comparison at a *'micro level'*, where two jurisdictions within the same system of family are compared. On the other hand, political or legal philosophers can also compare two or more different systems at a *'macro level'*.

This book will involve looking at invisible factors and contexts including cases, statutes, codes from each jurisdiction, in particular, from the PRC and England & Wales at the micro level, but will also look at issues from the macro level to fully understand the issues – similarities and differences, gaps, protection of local businessmen in their jurisdictions. This will take into account the socio-economic aspects that underpin the relevant laws, codes, guidance, and practice directions at the macro level, including any debates that have taken place.

In order to compare the laws in the two separate jurisdictions, there is a need to deconstruct the laws, premises and justifications, as sometimes, many rules or laws in a particular jurisdiction are socially irrelevant and are just followed by practitioners and commercial men of that jurisdiction.[63]

Konrad and Kotz's *Functionality Method* takes into account the problems of the society/commercial men and these problems are stated in the *functional terms*.[64] The proposition in the functionality method is that every society in every jurisdiction faces essentially the same questions due to universal values in all legal systems;[65] they may even face equivalent problems, though the methods to resolve those problems might be different.[66]

---

[61]Refer to Figure 1- Families of Legal Systems.

[62]Scott, "The Comparative Method of Legal Research," 5, where he discussed a concept from Church and Edwards, "Comparative Law/Comparative Method," 1270.

[63]Monateri, "Intellectual Overview of Comparative Law," 23. However, this approach of Comparative law clashes with that of the norm and rule approach of jurisprudents from positivist school of thought.

[64]Zweigert, Kotz, and Weir, *Introduction to Comparative Law*, 31. See also, James Gordley, "The Functional Method," in *Methods of Comparative Law*, in *Methods of Comparative Law*, ed. Monateri. Pier G., Research Handbooks in Comparative Law. (Cheltenham, U.K.; Northampton, MA: Edward Elgar Pub., 2012), 117. *See also*, Ralf Michaels, "The Functional Method of Comparative Law," in *The Oxford Handbook of Comparative Law*, ed. Mathias Reimann and Reinhard Zimmermann (Oxford: Oxford University Press, 2008), 339-82.

[65]Gordley, "Functional Method," 118.

[66]Ibid., 117.

Figure 1: Families of Legal Systems

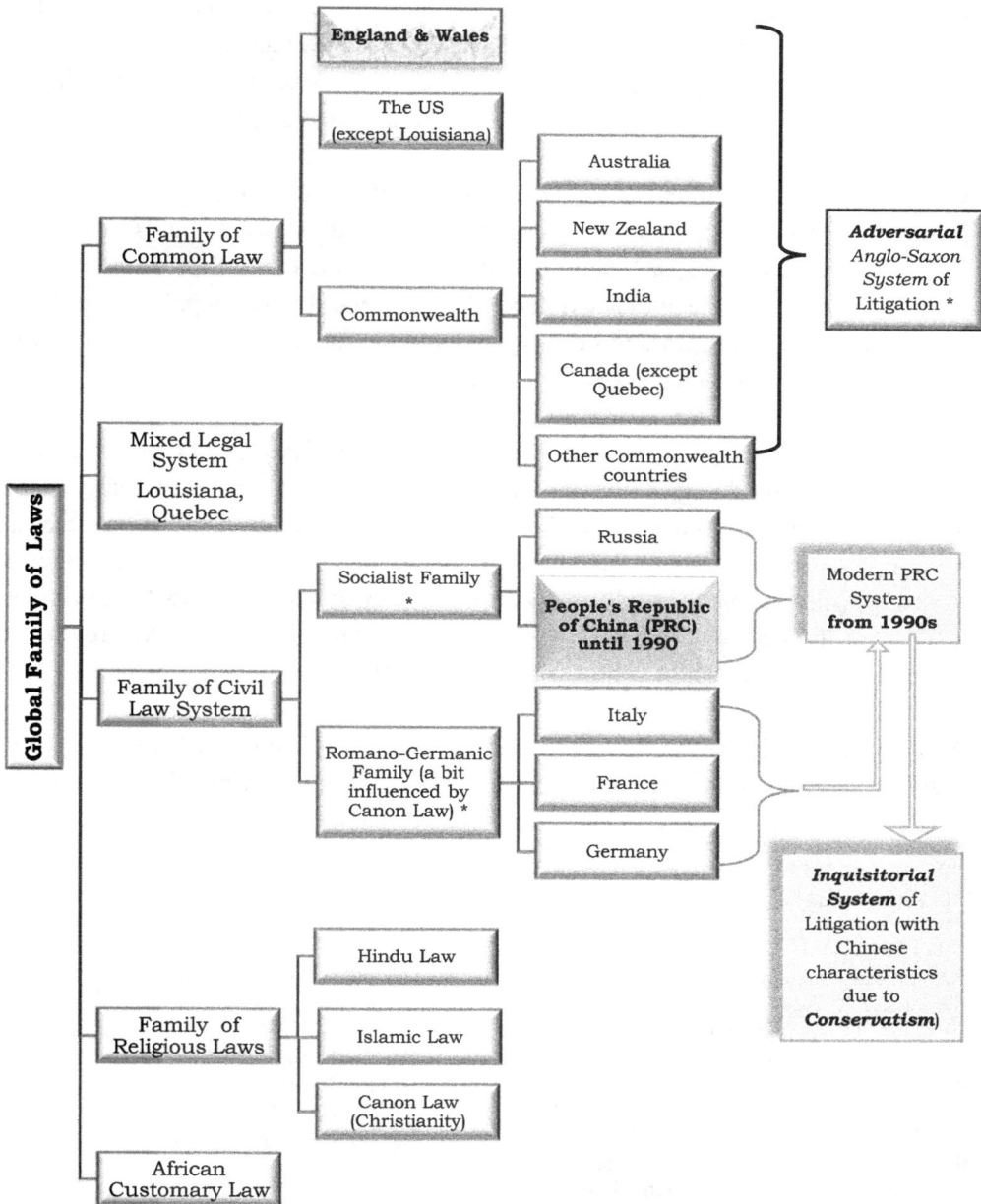

Global Family of Laws	Family of Common Law	England & Wales
		The US (except Louisiana)
		Commonwealth → Australia, New Zealand, India, Canada (except Quebec), Other Commonwealth countries
	Mixed Legal System Louisiana, Quebec	
	Family of Civil Law System	Socialist Family * → Russia, People's Republic of China (PRC) until 1990
		Romano-Germanic Family (a bit influenced by Canon Law) * → Italy, France, Germany
	Family of Religious Laws	Hindu Law, Islamic Law, Canon Law (Christianity)
	African Customary Law	

Adversarial Anglo-Saxon System of Litigation *

Modern PRC System **from 1990s**

Inquisitorial System of Litigation (with Chinese characteristics due to ***Conservatism***)

*Civil procedure systems of Romano-Germanic & Anglo-Saxon are together called *systems liberaux*. Socialist civil procedure system is different from Systems liberaux.

It is important to appreciate that even though rules can serve their purpose, it cannot be said with certainty that the purpose can be achieved by following the rules.[67] In addition, each legal system faces different problems due to invisible factors such as legal history and legal philosophy. In many jurisdictions, many rules may serve the purpose, and the purpose itself may not be limited to the application of rules, but they might be useful in maintaining overall legal order.[68] This methodology requires the author not only to study the *rules*, but also to try to understand the *concepts* behind the rules that have a specific *purpose* in a particular jurisdiction.[69]

In contrast to the Functional method, *the Contextual method* of Comparative law tries to find the reasons behind the law and ordinarily involves various fields of law. It is generally a difficult approach and will invariably broaden the scope of the research area. In this method, the author will have to go beyond the pure legal devices.[70] The approach will focus on finding the *'why'* behind the laws, but there is an issue with such an approach as such research can continue perpetually.[71]

Palmer has differentiated between *'methods'* and *'techniques'* in the context of comparative methodology.[72] Pursuant to this method any Comparative law scholar should consider the interactions of the laws of a particular jurisdiction with the philosophy, culture, language, and nuances in the same jurisdiction.[73] This is referred to as an *organic* method,[74] where every important element of law or doctrine is looked at through the prism of culture in detail; thus, an attempt is made to capture 'its essence as a unique manifestation of the community.'[75]

Another method is the *'factual method'* where each jurisdiction will find a solution based on the facts of the case, rather than the terminology.[76] Palmer divided the rules

---

[67]Ibid., 114.
[68]Ibid., 111.
[69]Ibid.
[70]Ibid., 35,38.
[71]Antonios Emmanuel Plastas, "Functional and the Dysfunctional in the Comparative Method of Law" (December 2008), 4.
[72]Palmer, "Comparative Law Methodology," 2.
[73]Eberle, "Methods of Comparative Law," 458. In this article, Eberle highlighted the concept of cultural immersion required of a researcher and as highlighted by comparativist Vivian Grosswald Curran. *See also*, Vivian Grosswald Curran, "Cultural Immersion, Difference and Categories in U.S. Comparative Law," *Am. J. Comp. L.* 46, no. 1 (1998): 43–92. http://www.jstor.org/stable/841076. Vivian highlighted that a comparativist needs to free themselves of "cognitive lock-in".
[74]Palmer, "Comparative Law Methodology," 7.
[75]Ibid. Palmer, "Comparative Law Methodology," 7.
[76]Palmer, "Comparative Law Methodology," 18, where an example is used to understand the factual approach in methodology. The example used is that of the concept of pure economic tort losses that are usually unrecoverable in most common law jurisdictions; if this is applied to the facts of a case, then the question posed to the civil law jurisdiction should not be whether such pure economic losses could be

into three levels - *Operative Rules, Descriptive Formants,* and *Metalegal Formants.* In Operative Rules, the judges will resolve conflicts based on judicial doctrine(s), and whether any exception has been created in finding solutions for specific types of problems. In Descriptive Formants, however reasons will be cited on the basis of procedural rules, constitutional doctrines fit within the scheme of legal arguments based on law, equity and so forth. Lastly, in Metalegal Formants, these are the *reasons for the other reasons* such as economic policy issues, other policy issues, historical evolution, jurisprudential reasons, contemporary social values and so forth. The author will attempt to find such *reasons for reasons* in both the jurisdictions.

Hosten's comparative method prompts the author to go through various *reference points*.[77] For example in England & Wales's jurisprudence, the focus is on *property rights*, while in jurisdictions such as the PRC, the focus or the reference point is *state ownership and society*; similarly the focus in many countries in Africa is on *community values*. Hosten underscores the importance of reference points, saying that "this aspect of a comparative study of laws enables jurists and statesman alike to better understand foreign attitudes to law and not mistake them for bad faith".[78] Reitz has also stressed on the same methodology, referring to the reference points as *'data points'*.

McEvoy's categories of Comparative law, as applied to this analysis in book, will involve, the following- (1) External I (Homogenous), where the author will include both *horizontal* and *synchronic comparisons* along with *diachronic comparisons* that include the historical development of the horizontal laws that are being compared; (2) External II (Heterogeneous), where the author has to consider v*ertical, synchronic* and *diachronic comparison* from various disciplines such as history, legal philosophy and so forth; (3) Internal (Homogenous) Comparative law will entail that a researcher includes *horizontal synchronic comparison* of procedural law along with the relevant substantive law with *diachronic comparisons*; and (4) Purposive categories such as harmonisation, anti-systemisation, cognitive explanation and polyphonisation.[79]

---

recovered in that civil law jurisdiction. The civil law jurisdiction traditionally has no concept of pure economic loss.

[77]WJ Hosten, "Romeinse Reg, Regsgeskeidenis en Regsvergelyking" (1962), 30.

[78]Scott, "The Comparative Method of Legal Research," 2, where he cited and translated the ideas of Hosten from WJ Hosten, "Romeinse Reg, Regsgeskeidenis en Regsvergelyking" (1962). *See also,* Eberle, "Methods of Comparative Law," 457, where it was discussed that a comparativist should "shed built-in, native bias".

[79]Sebastian McEvoy, "Descriptive and Purposive Categories of Comparative Law," in *Methods of Comparative Law,* ed. Pier G. Monateri (Cheltenham, U.K.; Northampton, MA: Edward Elgar Publishing, 2012), 148–52.

The author also needs to avoid cultural biases referred to as 'cognitive lock-in',[80] and avoid patronising views as to what 'should' happen instead of uncovering the law and practice. This advice has been kept in mind throughout the book. In addition, the author has adopted the best routes from the above comparative methodologies to guide the readers in this book.

1.5. The Practice and Procedure of Comparing Laws and Systems

During the last stage of Qing dynasty,[81] the civil law model of law as adopted, for example, in countries such as France or Germany. One of the reasons to adopt civil law traditions was the desire to preserve the legal traditions of ancient China. These traditions when adopted emphasised the primacy of central authority, thereby preventing judges from having flexibility and thus curbing their exercise of discretionary power. In addition, it was about keeping up with the tradition of the existing system's propensity for legal generalisation.

Furthermore, by then, Japan had already adopted the German civil code; therefore scholars from the Qing Dynasty could easily use their knowledge in the neighbouring country because of these similarities.[82] Similarly, in the author's view, there is always a need in any legal system to compare prevailing and popular legal systems; using various methodologies for comparisons will allow the development of legal reforms in order to reach desired outcomes that can stimulate trade and commercial transactions.

Merchants and businessmen in other countries are often told daunting stories by foreign lawyers and media about the legal and civil procedural system in the PRC; thus by word of mouth, transaction costs are increased for all parties. A few of the stories may be true, but in the author's view, no system is perfect. Anyone with an interest in the PRC, be they foreign lawyers, businessmen or research scholars, should have some awareness of the PRC legal system. However, the author is writing from the position of having personally encountered the justice system in the PRC.

As with any justice system, the PRC's system is not perfect. However, the author has observed a noticeable keenness and genuine desire on the part of judges, legal academicians and local PRC lawyers to improve the legal system. This, in the

---

[80]Curran, "Cultural Immersion".

[81]Refer to Table VIII of the book.

[82]Chen Lei, "Contextualizing Legal Transplant: China and Hong Kong," in *Methods of Comparative Law*, ed. Pier G. Monateri (Cheltenham, U.K.; Northampton, MA: Edward Elgar Pub., 2012), 196–97.

author's view, is a good foundation for any legal system to blossom. This is in sharp contrast to many common law jurisdictions, where the centuries-old tradition of uninterrupted development has led to an element of haughtiness and superiority creeping in. These unwanted elements are detrimental to the smooth evolution of law.

According to Plastas, the purpose of Comparative law studies is not only that they provide 'valid comparison but they serve some purpose.'[83] In the context of pure academic research, the purpose of Comparative law research is to gain 'knowledge'.[84] Plastas has described the process of comparison, and states that its purpose is law reforms in legislatures, while Zweigert, Kotz & Weir highlight that the aim of practising lawyers may be to obtain better legal solutions, which might be available in other jurisdictions. The current comparison will consider the astonishingly rapid development of the PRC's economy in the last two decades, and other issues that have become important for stakeholders since the 1980s.

This comparison of Common law v. Chinese law will become even more important in the coming years as there will be more cross-border transactions, and gradually corporations and businessmen, local and from around the world, will come to rely more on the PRC courts to protect their commercial interests. The question will further gain prominence due to the PRC's big-ticket projects like the '*Belt and Road Initiative*' and other similar international projects. The remedies available in the PRC legal system to protect the interests of the parties are essential for ensuring sustained economic growth in those jurisdictions, and for ensuring that businessmen and corporations, both local and foreign, continue to have faith in the PRC's legal system.

This book has been written for purely practical purposes, for example, to ensure that commerce can flourish, and that scholars, businessmen & those in commerce can supplement their knowledge about PRC laws, have realistic expectations, and understand how the local courts in the PRC can assist them.[85] A similar aim was also discussed by Scott, echoing Church and Edwards; he asserted that the purpose of Comparative law is to assist people in commerce learn about foreign laws and how these laws can affect them.[86] Scott gave further examples of many Comparative law

---

[83] Antonios Emmanuel Plastas, "Functional and the Dysfunctional in the Comparative Method of Law" (December 2008), 6.

[84] Konrad Zweigert and K. Kotz, trans., Tony Weir, *An Introduction to Comparative Law*, 3rd revised ed. (Oxford: Clarendon Press, 1998), 15. Kotz and Zweigert have described the purpose of Comparative law as a means to harvest and garner knowledge.

[85] It is the author's view that this is even more relevant during the times of apprehensions about trade under WTO, ongoing trade war between US & China starting from 2018.

[86] J Church and A.B. Edwards, "Comparative Law/Comparative Method," in *Introduction to South African Law and Legal Theory*, WJ Hosten, *et al.* (Durban: Butterworths, 1995), 1264. *See also,* T.J.

institutes that are in existence in France and Germany to assist regional businessmen and corporations.[87]

The author hopes that the readers will gain a good overview of the PRC legal system and the invisible factors affecting it. This will assist them to compare it against their own experience with the most common legal system of England and Wales, which follows the common law system.

Scott, "The Comparative Method of Legal Research," 3, http://italeem.iium.edu.my/2014, where Church and Edwards' ideas were discussed.

[87]Scott, "The Comparative Method of Legal Research," 2.

CHAPTER TWO — HISTORICAL ORIGINS OF SUBSTANTIVE AND PROCEDURAL LAW – COMMON LAW v. CHINESE LAW

2. Introduction to Chapter Two

In order to understand laws in any jurisdiction, it is important to consider the historical evolution of the substantive and procedural law. Without taking into account the origins, it is very difficult to understand the context of the laws and to speculate how a judge in a foreign jurisdiction will think. These are important *invisible factors* and provide *one of the contexts*, which businessmen and/or foreign lawyers need to appreciate before working with legal experts in a foreign jurisdiction. The author here discusses the historical origins of substantive and civil procedural law for both the common law of England & Wales and PRC law.

The author provides the readers with a comparison of the two jurisdictions in relation to historical evolution at the end of this Chapter. However, it is important that readers try to reach their own conclusions as to the comparison of the evolution of substantive and procedural law in both the jurisdictions.

2.1. Historical Origins of Substantive Law and Civil Procedural Law in England & Wales

In this book, historical analysis of the evolution of substantive law and civil procedure law provides context and is an essential invisible factor in understanding the relevant issues in each of the jurisdictions. The area covered by these factors is colossal; however, the author will try to convey the ideas succinctly to allow readers to comprehend the issues clearly.

2.1.1. Common Law & Equity – Substantive Law v. Civil Procedure Law

For many centuries in England, civil cases were litigated either in the common-law courts or the courts of equity. Each of these courts had different kinds of relief, and different procedural reliefs were granted to the litigants.

2.1.1.1. Common Law

There is a long history of substantive law in common law. For example, according to history, common law originated in 1066 CE, meaning that this body of law is nearly a thousand years old. However, according to Risinger, the earliest record of procedural law in England & Wales (with the division of laws into either substantive or procedural law) can only be traced to the eighteenth century:

> The dichotomy was fathered by Jeremy Bentham in a 1782 work entitled *Of Laws in General, sub norm* [emphasis in original] the distinction between substantive law and adjective law. Bentham there makes clear that he believes he is drawing a near distinction in the descriptive organization and analysis of the concept of law, and an examination of the leading pre-Bentham sources on English legal theory supports his claim.[88]

---

[88] Michael D. Risinger, "'Substance' and 'Procedure' Revisited: With Some Afterthoughts on the Constitutional Problems of 'Irrebuttable Presumptions'," *UCLA L. Rev.* 30, no. 2 (1982): 191 (footnotes omitted). Risinger was also quoted in Thomas O. Main, "The Procedural Foundation of Substantive Law," *Wash. U. L. Rev.* 87, no. 4 (2009): 4. http://ssrn/abstract=1113916. However, in the same article, Risinger has mentioned in footnote 3, that many ancient books by authors such as M. Bacon, *A New*

Figure 2: Historical Origins of Common Law and Civil Procedural Law in England & Wales

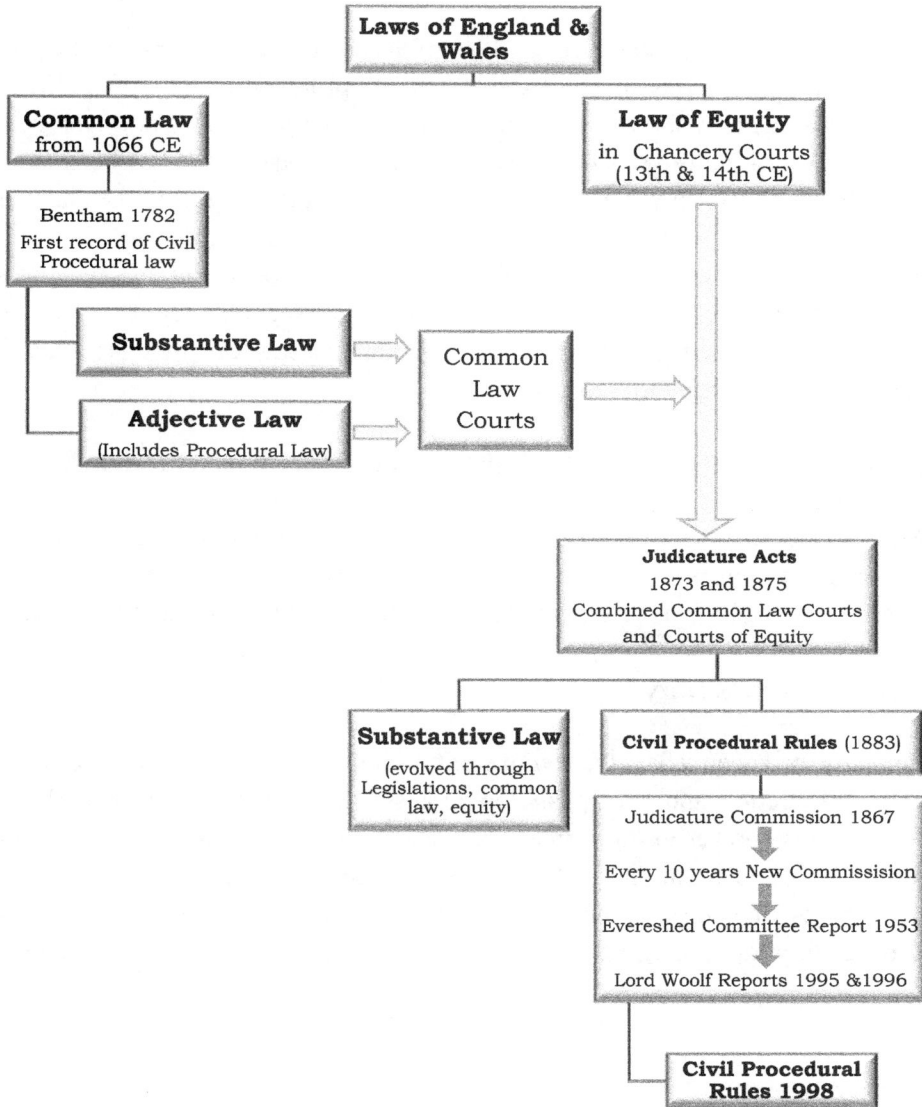

Abridgment of the Law (5th ed, 1798), and N. Blackstone, *Commentaries on Laws of England* (1765) that seemed to have made no distinction between the procedural and substantive law.

In the earlier years of the development of procedural law, it seems there was a difference between '*adjective law*' and '*procedural law*'. Risinger mentioned that procedural law was 'only a part, though a major part, of adjective law'.[89]

Later, it became common knowledge which of the adjective laws would be helpful to litigants, and thus the way in which the law would protect the rights of the litigants would be specified. In spite of the debate as to whether procedural law ever existed in a separate form before this development, this particular format has been used to bring actions in court for a long time, to pursue the claims or rights of the claimants.

There were also separate forms for different causes of action. Common law courts in England & Wales had experience in writs, forms, and pleadings for centuries.[90] It is important to note that in those years, common-law lawyers thought about the substantive law through these forms.

There would have been no remedy available through the courts for a civil dispute, if a form of a writ already fixed was not available.[91] In a few areas, where the substantive law was just evolving, such as in law of tort, lawyers used the forms and procedures to evaluate the merits of a case. Sir Henry Maine has said, "Substantive law has at first the look of being gradually secreted in the interstices of procedure."[92]

2.1.1.2. Law of Equity

Historically, and even today, the law of equity is famous for allowing for the exercise of judges' discretion, and its emphasis on fairness.[93] In jurisprudential terms, the term 'equity' means "power to do justice in a particular case by exercising discretion to mitigate the rigidity of strict legal rules."[94] Bray has discussed the special characteristics of equity, namely that it involves "case-specific judgment, moral reasoning, discretion, or anti-opportunism."[95] It seems that this distinction slowly is

---

[89]Risinger, "Substance and Procedure Revisited," n 11 at 191, where Risinger discussed Bentham's ideas on adjective law.

[90]Thomas O. Main, "Traditional Equity and Contemporary Procedure," *Wash. L. Rev.* 78, no. 2 (2003): 454.

[91]Rhee and Verkerk, "Civil Procedure," 3.

[92]Main, "Procedural Foundation of Substantive Law," 7, where Maine was quoted. *See also*, Henry S. Maine, *Dissertations on Early Law and Custom* (Delhi: B. R. Pub Corporation, 1985), 389.

[93]Samuel L. Bray, "The System of Equitable Remedies," *UCLA L. Rev.* 63, no. 3 (2016): 532.

[94]Kevin C. Kennedy, "Equitable Remedies and Principled Discretion: The Michigan Experience," *U. Det. Mercy L. Rev.* 74, no. 4 (1997): 609.

[95]Bray, "Equitable Remedies," 536.

blurring the lines between common law and the law of equity.[96] According to Bray, in law of equity, there are three categories of equitable remedies:[97]

- First category: injunctions, constructive trusts, accounting for profits and specific performance;

- Second category: equitable remedies such as contempt of power;

- Third category: equitable remedies such as defenses and equitable justifiability requirements.

The English courts of Equity, called Court of Chancery procedures, were based on the *Romano-canonical* European continental model of law, and no common-law method of writs was applicable in such courts.[98] The Romano-canonical model was itself based on Roman as well as medieval laws, namely "the law of northern Italian cities and papal decretals."[99] Equitable remedies were developed in this Court of Chancery. In the thirteenth and fourteenth centuries, the Chancery Court, which started as the administrative department, slowly took over the judicial role to resolve disputes.

The Chancery Court gradually developed its own procedure; at the turn of the sixteenth century, common-law lawyers began to be chosen as Chancellor instead of bishops, who had up till then been heading these courts.[100] Bit by bit, principles of equity started to develop in the Chancery courts. In the early nineteenth century, the court of equity was dissolved, but the principles of equity remained in the English legal system. This step is often talked of in terms of fusion of law & equity in England & Wales, or merger in the United States.[101] The fusion of common law and equity courts was finally accomplished in *Judicature Acts of 1873 – 1875* in England.[102]

---

[96]Ibid., 532.
[97]Ibid., 533–34.
[98]Rhee and Verkerk, "Civil Procedure," 3.
[99]Ibid.
[100]Bray, "Equitable Remedies," 537.
[101]Ibid.
[102]See *Supreme Court of Judicature Act 1873* ,36 & 37 Vict, c 66 and *Supreme Court of Judicature Act 1875*, 38 & 39 Vict, c 77.

When claimants made claims pursuant to equity, there were no forms, no special way of arguing a cause of action. The main yardsticks to decide the cases were the judge's discretion, fairness, and good conscience. These criteria do not match with the formal procedural requirements that were the hallmark of the common law courts. In the Court of equity, there were no procedural requirements such as pleadings or forms, and the focus, in particular, was on the substantive law to determine the relief in equity.

2.1.1.3. Evolution of Common Court of Common Law and Equity

The common courts that were developed in the twelfth century were largely procedural as to evidence and proof, but matters of facts were left for the jury selected from the community.[103] As the system of case precedents had not yet evolved during that time, it still represented a unified application of law.[104] In fact, in these earlier centuries, the substantive law was created in courts on arguments based on hypothetical facts.[105] The judges in these earlier times, while making law, were thinking in procedural terms rather than substantive terms.[106]

As seen in the above section, even though there were no procedural rules in courts of equity, these courts started making a few rules to assist the litigants. On the other hand, the common law courts started to adopt the good practices of the courts of equity by simplifying the process for resolving civil disputes. Gradually, over the years, the differences between these two courts were limited to procedure or mode of trial.

In the end, both the courts — Courts of common law and Courts of equity – were merged.[107] Across the Atlantic, the US was establishing a new court system modelled on the common law system but comprised of the dual system of state and federal courts. There were statutes that were drafted by US Congress that distinguished the substantive law from procedural law. These US courts in later years were to have a profound effect on civil procedure law in England & Wales. Therefore, the development of common law was enhanced by adopting good practices in similar common law systems.

---

[103]Gerald J. Postema, "Classical Common Law Jurisprudence (Part I)," *Oxford U. of Commw. L.J.* 2, no. 2 (2002): 160.
[104]Ibid.
[105]Ibid., 162.
[106]Ibid.
[107]Main, "Equity and Contemporary Procedure," 464.

As codification was gaining momentum in England & Wales, procedural laws and substantive law were slowly drifting apart, and common aspects between the two laws were slowly decreasing. As substantive law and procedural law were developing distinct identities, scholars slowly started to consider civil procedural law as inferior to substantive law. Even after many years of discussion by scholars, this tag of procedural law being inferior to substantive law has remained.

However, the definition of and divide between substantive law and procedural law have never been that clear. We can see from the examples below that it is difficult to state with certainty, whether something is procedural or substantive in nature:

- Issue of Time bar in context of claims – does this issue fall under substantive law, or does it come under procedural law?

- Issue of case law in relation to issuing and service of claim forms – whether such issues fall under substantive law, or procedural law?

- Issue of interim remedies, both pre-trial and post-trial – whether such issues are under substantive law or under procedural law?

- Issue of statutes dealing with Evidence and Burden of Proof – are they a matter of substantive law or procedural law?

The answers to the above questions are not clearly identifiable, nor can they be separated easily into substantive or procedural law.

In simple words, civil procedure law is a body of law that the English courts follow to adjudicate the litigation before them. It traditionally starts with the issuance of a claim form, its service on the opponents, pleadings such as Statement of Claim & Defence Submissions, various interim applications in courts & orders, legal aid and so forth. The main aim of any civil procedure, as in the common law grounded US legal system, is based on the 'liberal ethos',[108] where the main purpose of any civil

---

[108]Benjamin A. Spencer, "The Restrictive Ethos in Civil Procedure," *Geo. Wash. L. Rev.* 78, no. 2 (2010): 101. Benjamin used the term 'liberal ethos' to describe the *Federal civil procedure 1938* rules.

procedure is to ensure easy access to the justice system and to adjudicate disputes based on merit.[109]

Civil Procedure law, as discussed earlier, is a body of law that is not completely isolated from the various substantive laws. This body of law is usually drafted in all jurisdictions to facilitate the resolution of disputes in the courts, where substantive law(s) such as law of contract, tort, agency and so on are applicable to the matter of dispute.

When the litigants knock on the doors of the courts that are established by the Constitution of any country, then these courts represent the overall system that is present in that jurisdiction. This system is the combined product of the constitution, legal system, legal philosophy, legal culture, legal education and so forth of that jurisdiction; therefore, one selected element within a system cannot just be looked at in isolation. These are the invisible factors and contexts that the stakeholders cannot ignore.

2.1.2. Origins of the Current English Procedural System

When parties have a civil dispute, one of the oldest ways to resolve the dispute was by means of violence. However, as societies advanced up the ladder of sophistication, as businesses prospered and nations started to trade with each other, civil dispute resolution systems for and within the society began to be developed. Legal historians have also confirmed that civil litigation procedures in advanced societies replaced the rough justice of self -help, revenge, counter-reprisal and vendetta.[110]

Along similar lines, Couture described civil litigation as 'civilisation's substitute for vengeance'.[111] In a way, the civil procedural system replaced violence as the common means to resolve civil disputes. Consistency of decisions in the courts along with the way the system can make parties feel about the legal system, especially the weaker parties, are hallmarks of advanced societies. These markers will in turn ensure the legitimacy of the civil courts and in the broader context will ensure the application of the rule of law within a society.

---

[109]Spencer, "Restrictive Ethos of Civil Procedure," 101. *See also,* Main, "Procedural Foundation of Substantive Law," 5.
[110]See F. Pollock and F. Maitland, *The History of English Law Before the Time of Edward I, Volume 1 & 2* (Cambridge: Cambridge University Press, 1988).
[111]E.J. Couture, "The Nature of Judicial Process," *Tul. L. Rev.* 25, no. 1 (1950–51): 7.

There were demands for swift justice after the adoption of the *Magna Carta* in 1215 CE. However, over the years, in both the common law and the court of equity, litigants began to experience excessive delays. In the nineteenth century, even the novelist Charles Dickens highlighted the ills of the civil litigation system in England.[112] It was also highlighted in many lectures by jurists of the time.[113]

In the early twentieth century, due to the advent of *Judicature Acts of 1873 and 1875*,[114] the Chancery Courts and the common-law courts together became a Supreme Court. In addition, the new rules of the Supreme Court ("RSC") came into existence pursuant to *Supreme Court of Judicature Act 1875*. These rules themselves were replaced later by RSC 1883. Though these new rules brought in more litigants to access the civil courts, leading to more reliance upon the litigation system, over the years again, the civil courts found themselves in a state of crisis.[115]

There were thus two crises - one in the eighteenth and nineteenth centuries, and another in the late twentieth century. To deal with the first crisis, two commissions were appointed – first in 1828, and then again in 1850 with the appointment of the second common law commission. Both these commissions attempted to bring in reforms to cut expenses and delays in courts by making the civil process faster and less cumbersome. This was done by simplifying the civil procedures. The Chancery Court was given power of common law courts and was reformed as well. However, these structural and procedural simplifications could not resolve the ongoing crisis.

The *Judicature Commission* was appointed in 1867. This Commission argued to replace all courts by 'one single omnipresent Supreme Court',[116] meaning that just one system of procedure would be needed. That was a big simplification in itself as all procedure was to be found in just one *White Book* as edited by Thomas Snow in

---

[112]C. Dickens, *Bleak House* (Harmondsworth: Penguin, 1996). The issues of delay were also discussed in Anthony Clarke, "The Woolf Reforms: A Singular Event or an Ongoing Process," and in *The Civil Procedure Ten Years On*, ed. Déirdre Dwyer (Oxford: Oxford University Press, 2009), 33–49.

[113]W. B. Odgers, "Changes in Procedure and in the Law of Evidence," in *A Century of Law Reform: Twelve Lectures on the Changes in the Law of England During the Nineteenth Century* (London: The Macmillan Company, 1901), 212. In this article, Odger said "Sadly hampered in the year 1800 by cumbrous procedure and pedantic technicalities which caused the suitors expense, delay, vexation and disgust. It took years for a merchant to recover a debt due to him... [and even then] ... half the actions were decided not on their real merits, but on questions of forms and pleadings."

[114]See *Supreme Court of Judicature Act* 1873, 36 & 37 Vict, c 66 and *Supreme Court of Judicature Act 1875*, 38 & 39 Vict, c 77.

[115]C. Glasser, "Solving the Litigation Crisis," *The Litigator* (1994): 14. This article was discussed recently by Anthony Clarke in Clarke, "Woolf Reforms- Singular Event?" 39.

[116]Clarke, "Woolf Reforms- Singular Event?" 39.

later years.[117] It is important to note that similar reforms, where the common law and equity merged, were introduced in the United States by David Dudley Field through the *1848 Code of Procedure of the State of New York*.[118] Therefore, the necessary and relevant reforms in the common law grounded US legal system came even before those in the English Legal System, which was the founder of the common law legal system.

Thereafter, every ten years, new Procedural Reform Committees or Commissions[119] were appointed in England & Wales. All the Reports generated by such Committees and Commissions attempted to reduce cost and complexity, except for the *Peel Committee Report* in 1932. All such reports relied on the structural and procedural reforms within the court system in England & Wales. However, a fresh approach was recommended in the *Evershed Committee Report*.[120]

For the first time, there was discussion about the need for new features of case management using sanctions and summons for directions to limit legal costs, and issues to control costs for ordinary litigants. Some other minor recommendations were introduced in relation to the use of relevant documentary evidence instead of oral evidence. The most important of such reports was by Lord Woolf in 1995 and 1996.[121] It replaced Rules of Supreme Court ("RSC"), which were already 124 years old in 1999. In addition, it also replaced County Court Rules. County Courts are the lowest court in the hierarchy of the Court System in England & Wales. The details of the court systems in England and Wales will be discussed in Chapter Four of this book.

---

[117]Earlier there were multiple procedures such as described in Daniell's *Chancery Practice*, Stephen's *Pleading in Civil Actions*, Tidd's *Practice, a guide to common law process*, or Chitty's *Precedents in Pleading*; all of these were converted later into just one civil procedure book called the *White Book*.

[118]Rhee and Verkerk, "Civil Procedure," 3.

[119]For e.g., in 1908 *Gorell Committee*, in 1913 St. *Aldwyn Committee*, in 1922 *Swift Committee*, in 1932 *Hanworth Committee* and *Peel Commission*, in 1947 *Evershed Commission*, in 1968 *Win Committee*, in 1979 *Cantley Committee*, in 1988 *Civil Justice Review Report* followed by *Heilbron/Hodge* views in 1994 and Middleton's views in 1997.

[120]Lord Evershed, *Committee on Supreme Court Practice and Procedure, Final Report*, Cmd 8878 (1953). It was discussed in Clarke, "Woolf Reforms - Singular Event?" 40.

[121]See Lord Woolf, *Access to Justice: Interim Report to the Lord Chancellor on the Civil Justice System in England and Wales* (London: HMSO, 1995). *See also*, Lord Woolf, *Access to Justice: Final Report to the Lord Chancellor on the Civil Justice System in England and Wales* (London: HMSO, 1996). These reports highlighted the need for results in the court to be just, the need for fairness of the courts towards litigants, the need for appropriate procedures at a reasonable cost, the need to deal with cases with reasonable speed, the need to be understandable to those who use it, to be responsive to those who use it, to be responsive to the needs of litigants, to provide as much certainty as possible, and to ensure courts are effectively resourced and organized. *See also*, Déirdre Dwyer, ed., *The Civil Procedure Rules Ten Years On* (Oxford; New York: Oxford University Press, 2009), 2–3.

The *Woolf Reforms 1999* simplified procedural rules were simplified, and the use of old case precedents in civil procedure was done away with.[122] Rules were simplified in brand new Civil Procedural Rules ("*CPR 1998*").[123] These are regularly updated and amended based on the experience of the courts. It is the author's view a similar approach might be needed in many other common-law jurisdictions such as India, where delay in courts is legendary.

It is crucial to note that the first reforms introduced in England in the eighteenth and nineteenth centuries to deal with the crisis in the civil litigation system failed because the rules became more technical. In addition, the culture and mindset of litigation as practiced by the judges and lawyers of the times did not change. This resulted in the failure of the first set of reforms that were implemented to bring about improvements in the way civil litigation was conducted in the courts.

According to Lord Justice Clarke, the Woolf forms brought about changes in litigation culture in the following ways:

- By introduction of active case management that took the control of progress of claims from the hands of the parties (mainly their lawyers) and put it back in the hands of the Courts;[124]

- By introducing the overriding objective and secondary objectives;[125]

- By imposing duty on the litigants and their representatives to assist the courts in furthering the overriding objectives.[126]

Under the new *CPR 1998*, new judges are more active as compared to judges in the years before the reforms set in. Rhee and Verkerk are of the view that this

---

[122] The philosophy behind the new Rules is discussed a bit more in Chapter 4, §4.2.1.

[123] *Civil Procedural Rules 1998, SI 1998/3132 (as amended until August 2016).*

[124] Jack I.H. Jacob, *The Fabric of English Justice*, Hamlyn Lecture Series (London: Sweet & Maxwell, 1987), 7.

[125] For more discussion on this topic, refer to Chapter 4, §4.2.1.1. The importance of overriding objective was cited in A. Zuckerman, *Zuckerman on Civil Procedure: Principles of Practice*, 2nd ed. (London: Sweet and Maxwell, 2006), 3.

[126] See *CPR 1998* r.1.1(3); In this rule, the hope of previous Commissions' was converted into an obligation on the parties, as discussed in Clarke, "Woolf Reforms- Singular Event?" 45.

development in England & Wales in 1998 was influenced by the early twentieth century Austrian reformer Klein, who also advocated active judges in contrast to passive judges. The Klein model was adopted by many countries in continental Europe such as Germany and France.[127]

2.2. Historical Origins of Substantive Law and Civil Procedural Law in PRC

It is essential to first discuss the subtle difference between the substantive and procedural Law of the PRC. Thereafter, the author will discuss the historical origins of procedural law in traditional PRC and recent developments in the current PRC Civil Procedure Law (*"CPL 1991"*).

2.2.1. History of Substantive Law v. Civil Procedural Law in PRC

Throughout Chinese legal history, the main focus was on penal codes and the importance of family relationships.[128] However, surprisingly, within the context of the family relationship, details of inheritance, property and commerce in society are not as detailed as one would have expected in a civilized society.[129] Whatever rules were present in ancient China, such as for land use, regulation of debt and market transactions, were primarily concerned with maintenance of good order,[130] rather than with encouragement of commerce for wealth creation. Another reason cited by Chinese legal historians for the sparseness of rules was the Confucian concept of 'nourishing the people' (*yang min*) based on the concept of sharing of resources to keep the populace 'fed, housed and employed'.[131]

Possibly the lack of civil litigation within ancient Chinese society was also the result of Confucian thought about 'self-cultivation', which encouraged individuals to reflect on their conduct, and such reflection was treated as a mitigating factor.[132] Further, the Confucian school of thought led to distrust of lawyers and valuing education,[133] and in the author's view, stunted the growth of civil litigation over the centuries. There

---

[127]Rhee and Verkerk, "Civil Procedure," 4.
[128]Refer to Table VIII on Ancient Chinese Dynasties in Chapter 1.
[129]Geoffrey MacCormack, *The Spirit of Traditional Chinese Law*, The Spirit of the Laws (Athens; London: University of Georgia Press, 1996), 8.
[130]Ibid.
[131]Ibid., 9.
[132]Ibid., 9–11.
[133]Ibid., 10–11.

are extreme examples from its history, in which 'litigation tricksters' or 'pettifoggers' (*sung kun*) found promoting litigation were subjected to severe punishments.

A very similar concept to that of human rights, which has gained prominence in western jurisprudence in the last few decades, was available in ancient China; termed '*jen*', this concept was prized by neo-Confucians, [134] especially after the Song dynasty. [135] It was founded on the Confucian teaching that a ruler, in whose hands were placed all legislative powers, has to be benevolent and humane. However, the author's view is that this concept of '*jen*' was very particular to Chinese society and in reality, it cannot be compared with the current school of thought pertaining to human rights as available in western societies.

Chinese legal history and jurisprudence are famous for constructing a narrative that harmonious society should prevail over any conflict, and therefore, society needs to avoid any kind of litigation. [136] Tang dynasty Code not only discouraged, but actually put a prohibition on litigation. Wu, reflecting a complete change in attitude in the PRC in relation to litigation, said, "The prosperity of law and the development of legal spirit are all based on litigation. With no litigation, there will be no truth and justice." [137] In the author's view, this current thought process of scholars such as Wu is a significant departure from ancient thought processes and should not be treated lightly.

Historically, unlike the ancient Chinese Penal Codes (mostly for criminal offences) that were available during most dynasties, it has been very difficult for foreign historians even to decipher the historical administrative legal system and its principles that governed ancient China. This may be because there could have been a lack of human interest in any non-criminal laws; however, such legal principles are available sometimes from varied sources, including customary rules that can be assumed culturally or are occasionally discussed. [138]

Fortunately, after the fall of the Qing dynasty, there was an attempt to compile those principles that were not readily available in most provinces, and findings were even

---

[134]Ibid., 9.
[135]Refer to Chapter 1, Table VIII.
[136]Book of Changes, for "ten evils" provided by the Codes of Tang Dynasty and as discussed in Jing-Xiong Wu, *A Study of Legal Philosophy* (Shanghai: Shanghai Law Translation & Edition Press, 1933), 15; *See also*, Qinhua He, "The Birth and Growth of Modern Jurisprudence in China," *Frontiers of Law in China* 1, no. 4 (2006): 508, where the book was cited and discussed.
[137]Wu, *A Study of Legal Philosophy*, 24 as quoted and analysed in He, "Birth and Growth of Modern Jurisprudence," 508.
[138]MacCormack, *Spirit of Traditional Chinese Law*, 19–20.

published later by Kroker.[139] Two things were clear: first, that there was a system of delegation to manage the huge land mass of ancient China; and second, at the same time, there was an extensive and well-established system of supervision. Specially commissioned imperial investigators were trained for the role of supervisor, censor and so on. The system followed and adopted legalist jurisprudential thought as well.[140]

Figure 3: Historical Origins of Substantive and Civil Procedural Law in PRC

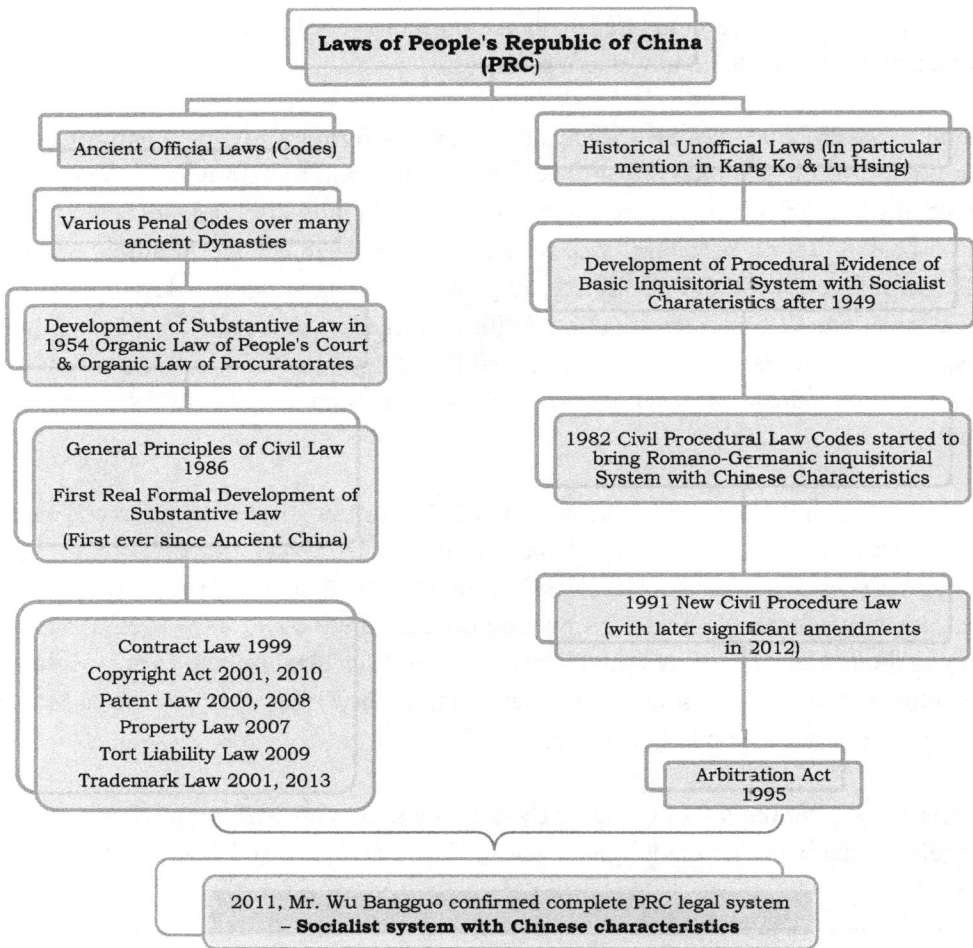

```
                    ┌──────────────────────────────────┐
                    │  Laws of People's Republic of China │
                    │              (PRC)                  │
                    └──────────────────────────────────┘
         ┌──────────────────────────┐        ┌──────────────────────────────────┐
         │ Ancient Official Laws     │        │ Historical Unofficial Laws (In    │
         │ (Codes)                   │        │ particular mention in Kang Ko &   │
         └──────────────────────────┘        │ Lu Hsing)                         │
                                             └──────────────────────────────────┘
         ┌──────────────────────────┐        ┌──────────────────────────────────┐
         │ Various Penal Codes over  │        │ Development of Procedural Evidence │
         │ many ancient Dynasties    │        │ of Basic Inquisitorial System with │
         └──────────────────────────┘        │ Socialist Charateristics after 1949│
                                             └──────────────────────────────────┘
         ┌──────────────────────────┐        ┌──────────────────────────────────┐
         │ Development of Substantive │       │ 1982 Civil Procedural Law Codes   │
         │ Law in 1954 Organic Law of │       │ started to bring Romano-Germanic  │
         │ People's Court & Organic   │       │ inquisitorial System with Chinese │
         │ Law of Procuratorates      │       │ Characteristics                   │
         └──────────────────────────┘        └──────────────────────────────────┘
         ┌──────────────────────────┐        ┌──────────────────────────────────┐
         │ General Principles of Civil │      │ 1991 New Civil Procedure Law      │
         │ Law 1986                   │       │ (with later significant amendments │
         │ First Real Formal          │       │ in 2012)                          │
         │ Development of Substantive │       └──────────────────────────────────┘
         │ Law                        │       
         │ (First ever since Ancient  │       
         │ China)                     │       
         └──────────────────────────┘        
         ┌──────────────────────────┐        ┌──────────────────────┐
         │ Contract Law 1999         │        │ Arbitration Act       │
         │ Copyright Act 2001, 2010  │        │ 1995                  │
         │ Patent Law 2000, 2008     │        └──────────────────────┘
         │ Property Law 2007         │        
         │ Tort Liability Law 2009   │        
         │ Trademark Law 2001, 2013  │        
         └──────────────────────────┘        
              ┌────────────────────────────────────────────────────────┐
              │ 2011, Mr. Wu Bangguo confirmed complete PRC legal system │
              │ – Socialist system with Chinese characteristics          │
              └────────────────────────────────────────────────────────┘
```

---

[139]MacCormack, *Spirit of Traditional Chinese Law*, 21, cited Kroker in an endnote on page 215 as in Kroker "rechtsgewohnheiten in der Provinz Shantung nach *Ming Shang shih hsi kuan tiao ch'a pao kao lu*" that was actually published in *Monumenta Serica* 14 (1949-55), 215-302.
[140]MacCormack, *Spirit of Traditional Chinese Law*, 21.

Most of the private or civil law in ancient Chinese legal history was contained in something equivalent to an *unofficial law*. The Emperor and his officials in various provinces adopted a 'hands-off' attitude.[141] The likely reason for this could be that many of the civil laws were actually included in the penal codes, as they assisted the authorities in maintaining law & order; for example, rules on debt or recovery or borrowing or pledging of property and even sales of goods were included in these penal codes (instead of having a separate civil code).

Another reason can be found in the prevailing philosophy and thought processes in ancient China, which maintained that the populace should remain well-fed and clothed and should have a share in the available resources. The hands-off attitude could also be due to concern for maintaining the harmony of society as a whole by avoiding civil litigation. Magistrates were discouraged from intervening due to their responsibility for maintaining order efficiently. Magistrates were also prevented from acting as arbiters in civil disputes.

However, there were contradictions: on one hand, there was a desire to maintain harmony, peace and order in ancient Chinese society, but on other hand, there seemed to be no available mechanisms for resolving civil disputes. However, in the Ming and Qing dynasties, older and more influential people were appointed through the perfectures to prevent and settle disputes. There is evidence in legal history that magistrates' help was indeed asked for in order to resolve such civil disputes, and these magistrates would then refer the matter back to the elders in the villages.

However, the civil court system available in the west at around that time, during the development of the common law system or the continental civil law system, was not established in ancient China. As discussed in preceding paragraphs, the legal profession was not so developed in ancient China, and lawyers were in fact looked down upon and in some cases were even punished.[142]

Lawyers in most jurisdictions play an important part in developing the legal system; this tradition in the author's view seems to be missing in ancient China. In contrast, one of the old books, *Ming shang shih hsi kuan tiao ch'a pao kao lu*, which means 'Reports on Investigation of Civil and Commercial Customs' had compiled lists of various customs used to deal with issues of that time. In this book, legal customs were arranged by province, under three main headings: "real rights and obligations, personal rights and obligations and rights and obligations arising from marriage,

---

[141]Ibid., 23.
[142]Ibid., 25–26.

adoption or inheritance."[143] However, further investigation of these customs indicates that not much thought went into important issues such as the relationship of those customs with the statutory law of that time. Further, a significant question asked by legal historians is whether it was completely an *'unofficial law'*?[144]

However, procedural justice in ancient China could be found as early as during the Zhao period through *Kang ko*, or a few centuries later in *Lu hsing*, which was the procedural manual for a ruler to order punishments. The processes were inquisitorial, and the magistrates would investigate the circumstances to find relevant facts.[145]

In contrast, in modern PRC, regulations were promulgated on 3 September, 1953, identifying principles for trials and systems, including open trial, circuit justice and jury system. These regulations also required the Procuratorate's involvement in civil litigation. Most socialist legal systems have a Procuratorate body to investigate and prosecute such issues. The regulations that were promulgated at all levels by the Central People's Government Committee were *Interim Organic Regulation of People's Courts, Interim Organic Regulation of the Supreme People's Procuratorate and Organic General Principles of People's Procuratorate*.[146]

Subsequently, in 1954, the PRC promulgated the *First Constitution* together with *Organic Law of People's Courts and Organic Law of People's Procuratorate*s, which further developed principles and systems concerning civil litigation and established trial organization, basic trial principles and systems of civil litigation.[147]

In October 1956, the Supreme People's Court (highest hierarchical PRC Court) summarized civil trial experience since the founding of the PRC and delivered a summary of the experiences associated with civil case handling procedure by various courts at various levels in the PRC. This *Summary* assisted in correcting mistakes in trial practices and thereby assisted in enhancing judicial efficiency.[148] The Summary was composed of seven parts: receiving cases, pre-trials, trial, adjudication, appeal, retrial, enforcement. In 1957, the Supreme Court changed the Summary into

---

[143]Ibid., 26.
[144]Ibid.
[145]Ibid., 27–31
[146]Jianfeng Pan, "Scientific Reforms of Civil Trial Procedure System in China - Reflection on the Civil Procedure and Its Relationship," *Tribune of Political Science and Law*, no. 5 (2012): 99–113.
[147]Jianfeng Pan, "On the Revision of Civil Procedure Law (2012)," *China Law* 5 (2012): 65-71. *See also*, Weijian Tang, "The Evolution of Civil Procedure System of China," *Frontiers L. China* 7, no. 2 (2012): 192–93.
[148]Pan, "Revision of PRC's CPL."

Provisions, and enacted the Procedure of Hearing Civil Cases (draft), which included eighty-four provisions.

Thereafter, in 1963, the national civil trial working meeting, the first of its kind, highlighted the principles of civil trial, which were to "investigate and study, resolve on site and *prioritize mediation* [emphasis added]."[149]

The introduction of the above principle in 1964 has been acknowledged as having a great impact on the development of civil procedure law in the PRC. [150] The establishment of these principles has had a profound impact on the PRC's civil trial activities in subsequent years.

However, the rapid pace of law reforms was halted in 1966, that is, from the start of the Cultural Revolution[151]; this also meant that the development of civil procedure law in the PRC was finally halted.[152] In February 1979, SPC issued the "*Supreme Court's Regulation Regarding the Institution of the Procedure of Civil Cases.*"

In recent years, the need for procedural law has arisen as a result of the rapid opening up of the PRC's economy. Before, any Civil Procedure Code could be enacted or put in place, it was necessary for the PRC to lay down some basic principles for different areas of civil law relating to substantive law matters such as contracts, business enterprises, land, intellectual property, marriage and succession. This resulted in the landmark *General Provision of Civil Law* (*Minfa tongze*) in 1986, which also marked the acceptance of Continental European traditions.[153] It should be appreciated that these were the first major Codes for substantive laws such as contract and property issues since ancient times in PRC.

2.2.2.   Origins of the PRC's current Civil Procedural System

---

[149]Ibid.

[150]Ibid.

[151]Chairman Mao, the supreme leader of the PRC, the leader of the communist revolution in 1949, in his last years in power (1966-76), fearing the Soviet Union's influence on the PRC and the dilution of the Communist revolution by those not believing in the principles of communism, started this great upheaval in the PRC. It was an era of constant changes in economic policies and affected the PRC as an entity in many ways.

[152]Tang, "Evolution of CPL in PRC," 193.

[153]Albert H. Y. Chen, "The Developing Chinese Law and the Civil Law Tradition," *China Rev.* (1996): 31. http://www.jstor.org/stable/23453139.

The PRC's current Civil Procedure System was introduced on a trial basis in 1982, and culminated in *Civil Procedure Law 1991* in its current form.[154] If we were to only compare the current law in force, then this Civil Procedure Law (*"CPL 1991"*) is older than the current *CPR 1998* applicable in England & Wales. However, the history of Civil Procedure System in England & Wales is relatively much older. There have been regular amendments to it over the years, compared to the PRC's Civil Procedure Law.[155]

CPL 1991 went from 205 articles in the 1982 version of *CPL* to 270 articles in its 1991 version. In 1991 the *CPL* for the first time introduced special provisions applicable to civil cases involving foreign cases, as more and more countries were investing in and doing business with the PRC. Additionally, the Supreme People's Court of PRC has issued the following pertinent guidelines, among many others that will be referred to throughout this chapter, that have the force of law:[156]

- Judicial Committee of the Supreme People's Court on July 14, 1992, issued guidelines in relation to the application of *Civil Procedure Act, Fa Fa [1992] No. 22.*[157]

- *Interpretation of the Supreme People's Court on the Application of The Civil Procedure Law of the People's Republic of China Fa Shi [2015] No.5*, January 30, 2015.[158]

- *Circular of the Supreme People's Court on the Issuance of the Document Samples for the Certain Rules for Evidence in Civil Procedures, Fa Fa [2003] No. 2*, September 1, 2003.

- *Guiding Opinions of the Supreme People's Court on Several Issues Concerning Trial of Cases on Disputes over Civil and*

---

[154]See as adopted at the Fourth Session of the Seventh National People's Congress on April 9, 1991 and promulgated by *Order No. 44 of the President of the People's Republic of China on April 9, 1991.*
[155]See as amended for the first time according to the *"Decision on Amending the 'Civil Procedure Law of the People's Republic of China '"* as adopted at the 30th Session of the Standing Committee of the 10th National People's Congress on *28, October, 2007* (came into effect on 1, April, 2008), and amended for the second time according to the *"Decision on Amending the 'Civil Procedure Law of the People's Republic of China'"* as adopted at the 28th Session of the Standing Committee of the 11th National People's Congress on *31 August 2012* (came into effect on 1, January, 2013).
[156]See *Provisions of the Supreme People's Court on the Work of Judicial Interpretations 2007*, Art. 5.
[157]See *Fa Fa [1992] No. 22*, as adopted at the 528th meeting of the Judicial Committee of the Supreme People's Court on July 14, *1992.*
[158]See *Interpretation of Application of Civil Procedure Law of PRC*, as adopted at the 1636th session of the Judicial Committee of the Supreme People's Court on December 18, 2014.

*Commercial Contracts in the Current Situation, Fa Fa [2009]
No. 40*, July 7, 2009.

- *Provisions of the Supreme People's Court on Several Issues
  concerning the Hearing of Cases by Circuit Courts, Fa Shi
  [2015]* No.3, January 28, 2015.

- On April 15, 2015, the Supreme People's Court released the
  *Opinions on the Implementation of the People's Courts of the
  Reform concerning the Case-filing Registration System (the
  "Opinions"), stipulating that regarding case filings, the
  current review system shall be changed into a registration
  system as of May 1, 2015.*

- *Circular of the Supreme People's Court on Promulgation of
  the Amended Regulations on Causes of Action in Civil Cases,
  Fa [2011] No.42*, February 18, 2011.

In the author's view, The *CPL 1991* is a major achievement for the PRC, which historically did not have any procedural rules in the context of civil litigation;[159] furthermore, according to Yikun, the PRC traditionally lacked the culture of rule of law.[160] However the PRC has, in the recent past, adopted the *Criminal Procedure Code on July 1, 1979, Administrative Litigation Law* of April 4, *1989, Organic Rules for People's Mediation Committees of 1989* and *Measures of Handling Disputes among the people of 1990.* Lately, the *Law on Arbitration of March 31, 1995* was also promulgated.

These are major achievements when seen from the prism that as late as 1979, there was no difference between the substantive law and procedural law in traditional Chinese law.[161] It is an even bigger achievement that in a small span of time, many new substantive laws have been promulgated and made effective in the PRC.

Without keeping the above in mind, any businessmen and/or foreign lawyers will approach the PRC with unrealistic hopes and expectations. The author's view is that

---

[159]Chen Weizuo, *Chinese Civil Procedure and the Conflict of Laws*, Tsinghua Chinese Law Series. (Beijing: Tsinghua University Press, 2011), 4.
[160]Yikun Zhu, *China's Procedural Law* (Beijing: Law Press China, 2003), 1. This issue of culture of lack of rule of law was also discussed in Weizuo, *Chinese Civil Procedure and the Conflict of Laws*, 3.
[161]Weizuo, *Chinese Civil Procedure and the Conflict of Laws*, 4.

one should avoid looking at the PRC legal system from the prism of western historical experience of civil litigation and/or from a similar experience in other common law jurisdictions and/or continental civil law systems. Rather, readers must appreciate that civil litigation in the PRC is of relatively recent origin as compared to common law systems and continental civil law systems.

Currently, in the PRC, the classification of law into procedural and substantive laws is similar to that in England & Wales. In the PRC, procedural law exists to enforce rights created by substantive laws such as contract or tort. Zhu Yikun has rightly said, *"Substantive law is concerned with what, while procedural law is concerned with how."*[162]

2.3. Comparison of Historical Evolution of Substantive and Procedural Law

Common Law has been in existence in England & Wales from around the middle of the eleventh century and has developed a large body of substantive law in these years.[163] This body of law was also enhanced by law of equity, which itself was later merged with the common law courts.[164] This body was further developed by the reasoning of judges in other common law jurisdictions such as the US, Australia, India, Singapore, Canada and so forth. Common law courts further developed adjective law, that included procedural law to assist litigants, but these procedures over the years had the tendency to become too formal. Such excessive formalities require separate forms for different causes of actions and accordingly the understanding of substantive law was through these forms.

On the other hand, the civil procedures lacked any formality in the courts of equity. In such courts, the focus was on moral reasoning and/or case-specific judgment and/or discretion of the judges and/or anti-opportunitism and/or good conscience.[165] The civil procedure system in a way developed after the advent of the *Magna Carta* in 1215 CE. However, as discussed above, it developed as a part of an adjective law, but slowly began to produce its own body of rules. However, too many rules were added in these courts over the years, resulting in the litigants facing increased complexity.

---

[162]Yikun Zhu, *Concise Chinese Law* (Beijing: Law Press, 2007).
[163]Refer, Chapter 2, § 2.1.1.1.
[164]Refer, Chapter 2, § 2.1.1.2.
[165]Refer, Chapter 2, § 2.1.1.2, and in particular, Bray's analysis on equitable remedies.

The complexities faced by litigants were even commented upon by some of the novelists of the eighteenth and nineteenth centuries in England. Legal costs and delays in the civil courts were increasing, which was quite contrary to the requirements of access to justice for civil litigants. After a century of many Commissions and Committees, the *Woolf Reforms of 1999* were bought in and introduced, *inter alia*:

- active case management that was quite similar to what judges are used to doing in the PRC;

- introduction of overriding objectives of civil procedure that provides the judges with enough flexibility; and

- imposition of penalties on the litigants for their conduct in order to further these overriding objectives.[166]

The other important feature than cannot be overlooked is that even though the civil procedure system in both common law and the PRC is about resolving private disputes; they still serve the public purpose of avoiding conflicts due to civil disputes. In addition, most civil disputes are not publicly funded.

On the other hand, even though ancient China was economically an advanced civilisation, the dominant focus was on penal codes, and any civil law that was needed for society was developed out of concern for maintaining public order.[167] Many reasons have been cited for this monumental neglect, foremost being the Confucian concept of '*Yang Min*', where the focus is on the sharing of resources between the people. Another reason cited was the ideology of '*sung kun*' bringing in distrust of litigation and lawyers, who were even considered as tricksters. Though there are examples of an ancient Chinese version of human rights in the form of '*jen*,' that required rulers to be kind and humane, it did not assist in bringing in the concept of access to justice for civil disputes.

All the above reasons cited for lack of civil procedure law were actually there to ensure a harmonious society by prohibiting litigation.[168] However, in the author's view, the route taken came at the expense of the development of a body of substantive

---

[166]Refer, Chapter 2, § 2.1.2.
[167]Refer, Chapter 2, § 2.2.1.
[168]Pursuant to Tang Code during Tang Dynasty (681-906 CE).

and procedural law, and basically denied access to justice; it actually let to suppression of the truth in civil cases. In addition, most of the ancient traditional laws were included as part of the *unofficial law*, and in civil cases, the administration would try to avoid any kind of involvement. The Ming and Qing dynasties commenced a *dispute resolution system* across ancient China that was to be *managed by seniors or elderly persons,* and there were no civil courts or procedures along the lines of *'Kang Ko'* or *'Lu hsing'*, which were the procedural manuals applying to penal codes.

It was not until 1954, with the promulgation of the *Organic Law*, that the trial system and principles of civil litigation were established. However, this development too was halted during the Cultural Revolution (1966-76). The first body of substantive law in the field of civil law (*Minfa tongze*) came about only in 1986, following which the *Civil Procedure Law* was introduced in 1991.[169]

Given the above, in the author's view, it is still too early in the PRC for a body of considerable procedural law that could assist litigants to have spread in the local courts. In addition, it was only in 2012 that *CPL 1991* was amended, and this body has yet to blossom in the PRC. However, even though the PRC has relatively new rules, in the author's view, this may actually confer on the PRC some procedural advantages, as the complexities that have been added in England & Wales through numerous case precedents can be avoided.

Foremost, PRC rules are not burdened by the set of rules that has been appended over the years, adding to complexity for the litigants. However, the reasons for inclusion of principles in courts in PRC, namely that public interest should always be maintained, have historical linkages. Historically, the focus, from ancient China to the current PRC, has always been on the maintenance of public order. However, whether this point is needed in Commercial Law or civil disputes is another question.

Substantive law in England & Wales as compared to the PRC has developed over centuries with debates in courts or advocates' arguments in the courts or discussed in Parliament. On the other hand, the origin of substantive law as civil law code in the PRC is just a few years old. As the economy has developed in the PRC, it has become clear that the body of substantive law such as law of contract, agency, tort, commercial law, restitution and so forth is not adequate to cater to new causes of actions, new economic activities, training of judges in the new substantive law and

---

[169]Ibid.

so forth. However, there is a great push from the top echelons of the political class of the PRC to improve the state of affairs in this respect.

However, in the author's view, it is easier to draft the laws, still easier to circulate them; the most difficult task is the training of judges, especially given the vast continental size of the PRC. It can be said that manufacturing hardware is easy, but the real challenge lies in developing the software for the hardware. This is the real challenge for the PRC.

2.4. Comparative Relationship between Substantive Law and Procedural Law

The relationship between substantive law and procedural law needs to be understood, before we can go further. It could be argued that procedural law exists because of substantive law. However, substantive law in the form of the best codes or legislations will be of no benefit without the support of good civil procedure rules.[170] The aims of procedural law rely on the relationship between substantive and procedural laws. There are, however, jurisdictions where the legal philosophy's aim is to focus on the aims of substantive law and remove procedural hurdles, for example, in Germany pursuant to the old civil procedure code.[171]

There are three broad theories in the context of the relationship of substantive law to procedural law:[172]

- The aim of civil procedural law is procedural and therefore, does not rest on substantive law;

- The aim of civil procedural law should emphasise and concentrate on the realisation of substantive law;

- The aim of civil procedural law should be on the realisation of individual rights, and on a broader level should be the maintenance of social harmony and rule of law.

---

[170] W. J. Habscheid, "The Fundamental Principles of the Law of Civil Procedure," *Comp. & Int'l L.J. S. Afr.* 17, no. 1 (1984): 4.www.jstor.org/stable/23246919.
[171] Ibid., 5.
[172] Ibid., 6.

At one extreme, a few scholars assert that the aim of civil procedural law should be to provide the requisite authority for judgment (*res judicata*), though other scholars are of the view that it may be the consequence of the civil procedure, but this cannot be the sole aim of the civil procedure.[173] A few scholars are of the view that the main aim of civil procedure should be formulating a judgment to end a dispute.[174] However, procedural law cannot be separated from substantive law. Habscheid said, "*The civil process is consequently a procedure in which the pre-existing substantive law is concretised in each decided case, or possibly settled* [emphasis in original]."[175] Without doubt, civil procedural law also protects the "objective private law."[176]

From the perspective of the English law, lots of substantive laws in the areas of contract, tort and restitution are developed after litigation has commenced in the courts. In fact, in common law systems, it is essential for disputes to go through the process in courts all the way up to the trials, and then for judgments to be passed for these substantive laws to develop.

Legal scholars are of the view that the aim of protecting *individual's rights* will lead to the adversarial system, and the importance of *protecting public interest* will lead to the inquisitorial system.[177] However, there are many disputes where both private and stakeholders' interests are at stake; in such a scenario, which system will be most appropriate is difficult to predict.

Civil procedural laws in most countries have developed independently of substantive law, but there are jurisdictions such as England & Wales, where in the past, precise forms were required to be filled for a specific cause of action. Therefore, the procedures were overly dependent on substantive law.[178] However, although civil procedural law has developed independently of substantive law in most other jurisdictions, the civil procedural law still complements the substantive law.[179] However, the procedural laws cannot develop properly without keeping the substantive laws in mind.

---

[173] Ibid.
[174] Ibid., 7.
[175] Ibid., 9.
[176] Ibid., 13.
[177] Ibid., 11. *Refer also*, Chapter 1, Figure 1 for Families of legal systems and resulting in adversarial system and inquisitorial systems.
[178] Ibid., 14.
[179] Ibid., 15.

The principle of *procedural justice* in the context of ensuring equality for all litigants before the courts, and the emphasis on the need for just and equitable judgement, has developed over the years in the field of civil procedural law independently of the substantive law. According to Habscheid and adopting to his thoughts, it includes *inter alia* the following issues:[180]

- Functional independence of the judges, who require no interference from the executive;

- Personal independence of the judges, so that they can have tenured positions; and a legal procedure for their removal (if required);

- Powers available through the courts to uphold the dignity and prevent the contempt of court; for example, in England & Wales such powers are supreme over other fundamental rights such as freedom of press, expression or speech;[181]

- Allocation of a judges to the cases (in socialist systems, the judges can be replaced easily by superior courts);

- Impartiality of the judges, including the recusal process to ensure impartiality and bias. It could be voluntary such as in England & Wales, or it could be written in the procedural codes;

- Issues of Access to justice such as form of pleadings, pre-trial and trial procedures, availability of legal aid to prevent the harshness of costs, and right to notice allowing a defendant to argue his case. Additionally, right to be heard available to litigants and parties affected by the litigation, where the judges and courts follow a fair procedure;

- Authority of the judges to determine a case, whereby parties alone can decide what actions are required to settle the dispute; but in many socialist countries and countries following civil

---

[180]Ibid., 15–30.
[181]See *Morris and Others v The Crown Office* [1970] 2 QB 114, where the issues around contempt of court were clarified.

law system, judges have been given power to investigate the facts, or to interfere actively. This happens in the PRC, where a public body such as *Procuratorate* has supervisory powers. Procuratorates has oversight over judges and judgments; this is unique to the PRC legal system. It is an organ of the PRC system, just like the People's Court and the government. It exists as an independent body to uphold the Communist party system and its leadership and also has its roots in *Marxism and conservatism.*[182] It is also important to appreciate that there is no concept of separation of power in the PRC. The judiciary is not independent in the PRC when seen through the prism of western concepts of independence. In England & Wales, there is usually much less interference in determining the facts, unless the parties have requested the courts specifically. This shows clearly the subtle differences between the common law and the inquisitorial system in relation to collation of evidence and investigation into the cases;

- Public nature of trials, including the need for oral or written arguments.

For the sake of completeness, after discussing the interrelationship between substantive and procedural law, it is important to appreciate that in commercial cases, procedural rules, including rules of evidence and Standards of Proof, may be according to the *lex fori,*[183] but the relevant substantive law may be as selected by the parties to the contract or a different substantive law may govern disputes over rights and obligations.

2.5. Comparative Analysis of Overview of Differences between Civil Procedure systems

The author is conscious of warnings from Chase and Varano, who said "There are as many differences among the civil law countries as there are between the English and the US model of procedure (which diverged especially after the virtual abolition of

---

[182]Refer to Chapter 3, §3.6 & §3.7.
[183]C. H. Van Rhee and R. Verkerk, "Civil Procedure," in *Elgar Encyclopedia of Comparative Law*, ed. J. M. Smits (Cheltenham: Edward Elgar Publishing, 2006), 121.

the jury in England [in civil litigation], and still further after the sweeping reform of the Civil Procedure Rules of 1998)."[184] Jolowicz highlighted the differences between the procedural systems more realistically when he said:

> ...a pure adversarial procedure is no more capable of existing in the real world than a purely inquisitorial one ...the most that can be said is that some systems are more adversarial —or more inquisitorial —than others.[185]

Oscar suggested that the civil process is a reflection of political, social, and legal reality in any jurisdiction, and any change in the political or moral or social side will be reflected during the operations of civil procedure in any jurisdiction.[186] In order to discuss comparative civil procedures, it is important to appreciate from the start the *cultural* dimensions of civil procedure as local practices even within a jurisdiction will affect the practice of procedural law in the courts. This factor is even more noticeable in the PRC due to its geographical size, as the practice of law in the local courts may vary from one province to another and the practice may vary even within various cities or villages within a province. The local courts, while applying the Civil Procedure Code that is applicable for the whole of the PRC, may also apply very local practices within the working of the courts.

It is very difficult to document culture, but it is a representation of collective personality for a group of people within a boundary.[187] Chase discussed the work of the Dutch socialist and organisational theorist Hofstede, who found that organisations are culturally bound; Chase includes the legal process as part of that culture.[188]

---

[184]Oscar G. Chase and Vincenzo Varano, "Comparative Civil Justice," in *The Cambridge Companion to Comparative Law*, ed. M. Bussani and U. Mattei (Cambridge; New York: Cambridge University Press, 2012), 213. *See also*, Neil Andrews, "Fundamental Principles of Civil Procedure: Order Out of Chaos," in *Civil Litigation in a Globalising World*, ed. X. E. Kramer and Rhee, H (The Hague: T.M.C. Asser Press, 2012), 22, 387.

[185]J. A. Jolowicz, "Adversarial and Inquisitorial Models of Civil Procedure," *I.C.L.Q.* 52, no. 2 (2003): 281. *See also*, Chase and Varano, "Comparative Civil Justice," 222, where Jolowicz was quoted.

[186]Oscar G. Chase, "Some Observations on the Cultural Dimension in Civil Procedure Reform," *Am. J. Comp. Law* 45, no. 4 (1997): 862. Oscar, in particular said those words while discussing the views of famous proceduralists Piero Calamandrei and Chiovenda.

[187]Oscar G. Chase, "Some Observations on the Cultural Dimension in Civil Procedure Reform," 863.

[188]Oscar G. Chase, "Some Observations on the Cultural Dimension in Civil Procedure Reform," 864–5. Hofstede's findings were published in a book in 1980 called *Cultural Consequences*; these findings were extended by Oscar in the context of legal processes.

At this stage, it is important to appreciate that the PRC has adopted the *inquisitorial system* as part of its civil procedure system, where a judge can investigate the facts. This system is different from the *common law adversarial system*. In common law courts, judges will decide on the basis of the case that is presented to them by each party to the dispute. From 1949 onwards, the PRC's civil law system was modelled after the Socialist legal system; however after the 1990s, with more relevant substantive law being drafted along with amendments to Civil Procedure Law containing codes, the PRC has slowly started to adopt the Romano-Germanic model.[189] It involves more formality, notarization, powers to judge to investigate facts and so forth.

The author will discuss the difference between the philosophies of civil litigation in common law and in the PRC in Chapter 4, the judges' power and discretionary power within this system in Chapter 5 and 6 respectively, and in the end will compare both the civil procedures of the common law and the PRC in context of judicial activities in Chapter 7.

---

[189] Refer Chapter 2, § 2.2.1 & § 2.2.2.

CHAPTER THREE — JURISPRUDENCE AND LEGAL SYSTEM – COMMON LAW v. CHINESE LAW

3.1   Jurisprudence Influencing the Judges in England & Wales and PRC

In Chapter one, the author analysed the need to evaluate the *Internal Law*, as any lawyer or researcher needs to analyse the *invisible factors* that influence the judges' judicial activities in any jurisdiction. It influences judges and stakeholders at a foundational level, even to the extent of influencing thought processes, such as asking relevant questions in the courtrooms. The author will start with the jurisprudential thoughts of Northrop:

> In Law, as in other things, we shall find that the only difference between a person "without philosophy" and someone with a philosophy is that the latter knows what his philosophy is, and is, therefore, more able to make clear and justify the premises that are implicit in his statement of the facts of his experience and his judgment about those facts.[190]

The above definition is from the perspective of philosophy; however, the author will now discuss the concept of jurisprudence in the context of judicial activities. Postema has described jurisprudence in the context of the judges' legal reasoning and their ability in this context as follows:

> This learned capacity for reflective judgment-*juris*prudence [emphasis in original], we might call it is a social capacity: the ability to reason from a body of shared experiences with normative significance to solutions for new practical problems.[191]

Jurisprudence in any jurisdiction is not the law of the particular subject area, but the law in general. In the author's view, even at the primary level of origins of humans, there is an essential jurisprudence that governs the actions, thinking and activities of all humans. However, a particular kind of thinking has assisted in the development of the legal system in each jurisdiction. This section of this Chapter will attempt to go into detail about the jurisdiction of England & Wales and the PRC, in the context of jurisprudence. Each and every judicial activity is part of jurisprudence.

Written jurisprudence attempts to unravel the unconscious way the judges, lawyers or even populace think, and attempts to clarify it in words.[192] *Legal theorists* are the scholars who

---

[190]F. S. C. Northrop, *The Complexity of Legal and Ethical Experience: Studies in the Method of Normative Subjects*, 1st ed. (Boston: Little, Brown, 1959), 6. This quote was also cited and discussed in James Penner, David Schiff, and Richard Nobles, "Approaches to Jurisprudence, Legal Theory, and the Philosophy of Law," in *Introduction to Jurisprudence and Legal Theory: Commentary and Materials*, Anne Barron, et al. (London: Butterworths, 2002), 4.
[191]Gerald J. Postema, "Classical Common Law Jurisprudence (Part II)," *Oxford U. of Commw. L.J.* 3, no. 1 (2003): 9.
[192]Penner, Schiff, and Nobles, "Approaches to Jurisprudence," 4.

ask the basic questions about the law, duties, obligations and governance, while *philosophers of law* have a narrower focus on one aspect of the law, such as nature of authority or obligation or freedom, etc. Philosophers of law share this aspect with other philosophers, such as political or economic philosophers. However, *jurisprudents* connect the various philosophies with the *practice of law and judicial activities.*

This Chapter will also connect with the previous Chapter in relation to the origins of the legal system in both common law and PRC jurisdictions. A word of warning: the invisible factors and contexts involved here are extensive, and the author has had to condense them to a single chapter. It is advised to study this area in greater detail through books on Jurisprudence, after grappling with the basic concepts used for comparative analysis in this Chapter.

3.2   Western Jurisprudence (in particular, England & Wales)

Jurisprudence can mean the critical analysis of a case in a particular court in a particular jurisdiction; for others it may mean law in general; and it can also mean the study of legal philosophy.[193] Jurisprudence as a subject in itself will not attempt to study a particular law. Instead, it will attempt to analyse the law at a broader level.[194] It may at a very specific level mean "what is implicit in a lawyer's understanding of law that forms the background assumptions or beliefs he or she has."[195] The author will proceed with the study of legal philosophies that are most appropriate to the subject matter of this book. These legal theories will be discussed more in context with the practice of law in both common law and civil law jurisdictions such as France and Germany.

For the sake of completeness, it is important to highlight that pure philosophers of law are different from jurisprudents as they don't concentrate on the practice of law or even consider that philosophy of law is necessary for everyday lawyers working in the legal system in any jurisdiction.[196] In this Chapter, the author will analyse first the legal philosophies, and thereafter how these philosophies are linked to the practice of law in the relevant jurisdictions.

The author will discuss the background to Classical English jurisprudence, before examining different types of legal philosophies, and jurisprudents' thought processes about law.

---

[193] Thomas Lundmark, *Charting the Divide between Common and Civil Law* (New York; Oxford: Oxford University Press, 2012), 89–90.
[194] Penner, Schiff, and Nobles, "Approaches to Jurisprudence," 3.
[195] Anne Barron, et al., *Introduction to Jurisprudence and Legal Theory: Commentary and Materials* (London: Butterworths, 2002), 4.
[196] Ibid., 5.

Figure 4: Jurisprudence Influencing Judges in England & Wales

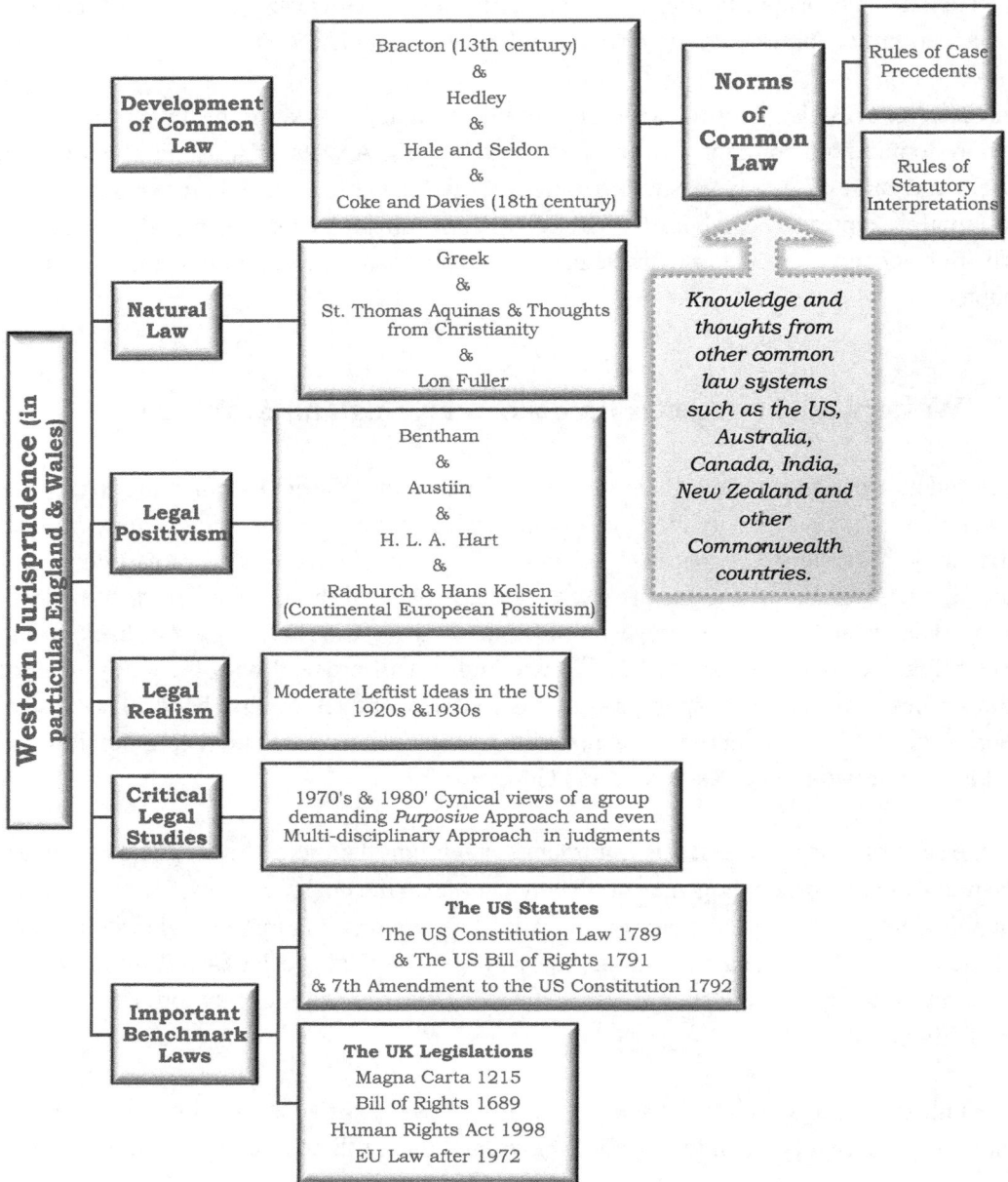

Western Jurisprudence (in particular England & Wales)

Development of Common Law
Bracton (13th century)
&
Hedley
&
Hale and Seldon
&
Coke and Davies (18th century)

→ **Norms of Common Law**
- Rules of Case Precedents
- Rules of Statutory Interpretations

Natural Law
Greek
&
St. Thomas Aquinas & Thoughts from Christianity
&
Lon Fuller

Legal Positivism
Bentham
&
Austiin
&
H. L. A. Hart
&
Radburch & Hans Kelsen
(Continental Europeean Positivism)

Legal Realism
Moderate Leftist Ideas in the US 1920s &1930s

Critical Legal Studies
1970's & 1980' Cynical views of a group demanding *Purposive* Approach and even Multi-disciplinary Approach in judgments

Important Benchmark Laws

The US Statutes
The US Constitiution Law 1789
& The US Bill of Rights 1791
& 7th Amendment to the US Constitution 1792

The UK Legislations
Magna Carta 1215
Bill of Rights 1689
Human Rights Act 1998
EU Law after 1972

Knowledge and thoughts from other common law systems such as the US, Australia, Canada, India, New Zealand and other Commonwealth countries.

3.2.1 Background to Classical English Jurisprudence

Henry II, the twelfth century English king, created a system whereby laws and customs for the whole of England were administered by a centralized court system.[197] A permanent court was established at Westminster, and justices would travel from there around the country, in this way harmonising the different laws of local areas within England.[198] By the thirteenth century, Bracton was able to compile the laws and customs of England. Regional and local customs were instrumental in the development of a law common throughout England.[199] This led to the emergence of common customs in the whole of England.

It developed as an oral tradition, but slowly records began to be kept; for example, case decisions that were made, were cited later in other cases, and thus started to act as *case precedents*. This led to the development of year books containing judgments and pleadings. In other words, *the law in action* was recorded by those yearbooks containing pleadings, arguments and decisions of courts.[200] The arguments developed in the judges' reasoning in their judgments were given prominence, as compared to the actual decisions, which could be fact-sensitive. The legal arguments before the court based on hypothetical facts seemed to create the laws that would eventually decide the matter on the actual facts about the case.[201] The role of the jury developed, and the role of lawyers, in the beginning, was merely to interpret and to explain the story containing facts to the jury under the guidance of the judges.

Legislations would often correct the anomalies and would fill the gaps in decisions emanating from the common law courts, thus starting the relationship between the legal system and legislature. The courts would develop legal rules out of the legislation that fit with the common-law reasoning in the cases. The common law system slowly became an institution in itself by the seventeenth century. Therefore, the common law was "body or practices and patterns of practical thinking,"[202] that has been developed over years by customs, its application through reasons and through experience of the courts and stakeholders. The common law arose out of the customs (local or merchants) shared assumptions, though some scholars in the past distinguished common law from customs and traditions.[203] Legal theories were developed around common law as a product of customs, or normative force of customs that were part of the common law or as a product of rules that were recorded.[204]

---

[197]Gerald J. Postema, "Classical Common Law Jurisprudence (Part I)," *Oxford U. of Commw. L.J.* 2, no. 2 (2002): 157.
[198]Ibid., 158.
[199]Ibid., 159.
[200]Ibid., 161.
[201]Ibid., 162.
[202]Ibid., 167.
[203]Ibid., 168.
[204]Ibid., 169.

A few scholars, such as Coke and Davies in the eighteenth century, argued that the common law was made up of customs which were affected by conquerors such as Romans, and that these customs had not changed since then. The other reason that they cited for its wide acceptance was that it was antique in nature, and was therefore accepted by the populace.[205] Other scholars argued that the real issue was the effect of natural law on the common law, and not that the common law had its origins in past customs. The author will discuss the theory of natural law in a later part of this Chapter. However, no scholars deny that the common law is made up of rules, norms, doctrines and customs, and has slowly become very technical in nature over centuries of development.

St German in the sixteenth century argued that the *maxims* that were only known to the courts and the learned professionals can actually be distinguished from the general customs.[206] Maxims are the specialised rules and principles that govern the working of judicial activities, but are "congruent with the ordinary customs of people."[207] Thomas Hedley in the seventeenth century was of the view that though common law was not synonymous with customs, its source could be traced back to customs.[208] Thus, there were enormous debates amongst scholars about the philosophical origins of the common law.

Seldon in the seventeenth century had a view quite different from Hedley; he commented that the common law was affected by many cultures as a result of successive invasions of England, and accordingly common law has its own distinctive features. In any event, according to Seldon, the source of the common law could be traced all the way to the fundamental nature of humans that had remained unchanged even after many interpretations and adjustments of law.[209] According to the scholars of this school of thought, even the legislated laws had left imprints in the common law, even if they had been amended or repealed over time. Hale suggested validity of *a* norm, rather than the rules that are followed by the populace, is crucial to the existence of common law.[210] Therefore, for scholars such as Seldon, the source of rules was not important, but what was important was incorporation of such rules over the years.[211]

It was gradually accepted by many scholars that common *reasons* have a great role to play in the common law.[212] However, the source of reasons cannot be natural law, as it can be too general in nature. These reasons must be rooted in the experience and reasons of the

---

[205]Ibid., 169–71.
[206]Ibid., 172.
[207]Ibid.
[208]Ibid.
[209]Ibid., 173.
[210]Ibid., 174.
[211]Ibid.
[212]Ibid., 177–78.

judges.[213] Hale argued the essential feature of these reasons was "consistency and its constancy".[214] Hale was of the view that natural law was not the source of rules in common law, but it assisted in ensuring that the populace followed the common law.[215] Over time, rules of interpretation and rules in context as to how the judges were required to fill the gaps in common law came into existence. Hale was of the view that with any such rules, it was not the discretion exercised by the judges, but rather the process by which they found the solutions within cases, that was critical. Judges' reasons are ordinarily called artificial reasons by jurists as they bear no resemblance to any one thread of philosophy. However, the judges' reasons are pragmatic and practical, and have many unique qualities. A few such qualities as postulated by Postema are as follows:[216]

♦ *Practical* and common law reasoning by which the judges in the courts tend to solve the real particular and specific problems before the courts by going deeper into the issues of law and facts;

♦ *Contextual* as the common-law judges have learned legal skills over many years by immersing themselves in the legal profession. The reasons of such common-law judges are mostly analogical, where difference and similarities are found using all resources that are available to them in their capacity as judges in the common law courts;

♦ *Public mission*, where common-law lawyers and judges' skills such as public reasoning, deliberation, judgement and oratory are essential elements to solve even cases with particular and specific facts;

♦ *Non-systematic* as common-law lawyers and judges are trained to utilise all available means to provide justice as long as their reasons are *locally* congruent with the other parts of law in their own jurisdiction, as compared to the need to have global congruence. The common law can appear chaotic to continental civil law lawyers, and sometimes even to early common-law lawyers. As a result, many lawyers who are trained outside of common law jurisdictions are usually puzzled by the multitude of resources and lack of a list of ready-made doctrines to solve problems. A few common-law lawyers, like the scholar Bacon in the seventeenth century, tried to find relevant doctrines on similar lines, but found it impossible to list

---

[213]Postema, "Classical Common Law Jurisprudence - II," 2.
[214]Postema, "Classical Common Law Jurisprudence - I," 178.
[215]Ibid.
[216]Postema, "Classical Common Law Jurisprudence - II," 3–8.

all the doctrines that can impact specific cases. This is also an area where many clever PRC lawyers or students from the PRC studying in the common law system have struggled with or not appreciated the uniqueness of the common law system. The most general issue has been trying to understand the common law system through the prism of the PRC system or civil law system;

◆ *Discoursive* as legal reasons are developed during oral arguments and debates in the court rooms. The skills of oral advocacy are very important for the common law's development; as legal arguments are debated in front of the public to increase the legitimacy of the courts. In the author's view, this is crucial, especially when there are gaps in legislation, and common law is being developed in the courts by these legal arguments to resolve a particular problem;

◆ *Common reasons* that come out in the open courts through arguments from various stakeholders, rather than discovery of reasons by philosophers. These reasons are congruent, compatible and consistent with the law as a whole in a common law jurisdiction and accordingly will become part of the shared experience that is acceptable to the populace living in that common law jurisdiction, such as England & Wales.

For the common-law judges and lawyers, the moral acceptability of reasons is not a requirement, as long as there is a coherence of reasons, and pragmatic solutions to problems in the disputes are available. Any case law itself is not supposed to bind future cases, but illustrates the common law's underlying principles, or a view that it is a "...practised framework of practical reasoning and this practised framework constitutes a form of social ordering."[217]

In common law, legal reasoning from past cases provides a benchmark for future reasoning, and it gives judges a framework to keep in mind for the case at hand. In common law, technically speaking, even statutes legislated in Parliament need to be incorporated into practice by judges in order to become part of the common law. In addition, in later years, more and more rules have been devised by the judges based on interpretation of the statutes in the courts. This has also become part of the common law.

3.2.2   Natural Law – Greeks, St. Thomas Aquinas to Lon Fuller

---

[217]Ibid., 14.

The author has discussed the issues of customs, rules and so forth in the common law in the previous section. One such issue was the effect of natural law, from the time of the origins of humans, on the development of common law. The focus of such theories is not on the creator of the law, but rather on their acceptance by the populace. If an immoral or unethical law is accepted by the populace, it is likely out of fear, and that is tantamount to a threat. According to such theories, *morality* is an important consideration in the content of the law. Under this legal philosophy, any law devoid of morality is mere pronouncements.[218] Justice is the ultimate aim of any law under this legal philosophy or under similar philosophies. These concepts are ancient in origin, and it can be traced in western jurisprudence to the formation of the Greek cities, and specifically to Plato.[219]

With the formation of empires, such as the Greek or Roman empires, it was realized that the community law or a particular custom from the conqueror's land, cannot be held supreme in conquered lands. There must therefore be something universal, a 'common legal order' that was superior, called *jus naturale*, along with secondary customs, such as those that facilitate trade, called *jus gentium*.[220] In the thirteenth century, St. Thomas Aquinas combined Christianity with natural law and distinguished such natural law from human-made law. Morality is a science that needs to be learned by most, according to Aquinas.

Such theories presume that even though humans are not perfect, they have a sense of justice, a sort of inbuilt compass based on morality. According to scholars in this field, if in any country there are no declarations as to human rights as a result of not signing any International Conventions or local legislations, it does not necessarily mean the populace does not have such rights. It merely means that such rights are denied by the institutions. Thomas Jefferson wrote in the *US Declaration of Independence 1776* that "We hold these truths to be self-evident, that all men are created equal, that they are endowed by their Creator with certain unalienable rights that among these are Life, Liberty and the pursuit of Happiness."[221] It appears that by using word 'Creator' in the previous statement, Jefferson, a lawyer, would seem to believe in such philosophies. Common law jurisdictions, however, are more in favor of the legal philosophy of natural law.

A very important sub-set of the theories in this section was propounded by Lon Fuller. His natural law theories were based upon the concept that a social contract exists between the government and the populace that is governed.[222] He concentrated on procedural aspects of any law, saying for example that there is a need for laws to be understood, and they can

---

[218]Lundmark, *Divide between Common and Civil Law*, 94.

[219]Plato thought of law as the embodiment of justice, beauty and ethics. In addition, Plato gave prominence to these theories even above customs or conventions. For details, see Richards Nobles and David Schiff, "The Evolution of Natural Law," in *Introduction to Jurisprudence and Legal Theory: Commentary and Materials*, by Anne Barron, et al. (London: Butterworths, 2002), 39.

[220]Richards Nobles and David Schiff, "Natural Law," 41.

[221]Preamble of *The United States Declaration of Independence*, 4, July, 1776.

[222]Richards Nobles and David Schiff, "Natural Law," 44.

only be understood by governance of rules.[223] The rules will allow for the laws to be published enabling the governed to understand and thereafter show 'fidelity' to those laws. This philosophy was also an attempt to distinguish them from theories of Legal Positivism (to be discussed later in this Chapter) because it still draws attention to elements of ethics and content of the law. Nonetheless this school of thought is more relevant to the practice of law.[224] Fuller succinctly described the difference between *"what law is"* as described by the jurisprudents of the positivist school of thought, and *"what law ought to be."*[225]

3.2.3   Legal Positivism – Bentham, Austin, H. L. A. Hart, Radburch, Kelson

Positivists believe there must be a creator (man-made) of some rules or *customary rules* that are given legal sanctity. Such rules are clear and usually described in detail to prevent as much as possible the intrusion of subjectivity and unnecessary exercise of discretion. Such rules are created by a 'sovereign' and are habitually followed by the populace. These aspects of the rules were interpreted by the analytical branch of positivism as the difference between real and mystical matters.[226]

Bentham argued that English Law was not the product of natural law,[227] and he criticised other lawyers arguing otherwise. However, rules or laws will have to be interpreted by judges at a later stage, and therefore, the jurisprudents of natural theories have pointed this out as a shortcoming.[228] There is a need for some institution to suggest that a particular custom is to be treated as a law; only then will all the populace and business organisations consider that particular custom as a law within that jurisdiction.

John Austin, a famous positivist, has explained that a law needs a creator, and once the law has been created, it will require a declaration. Austin's scheme of things includes the science of making good laws. An element of coercion in the form of sanctions is also necessary. Rules that have been created are *formally valid*; whether at a later stage the stakeholders *like* such rules is not important or even relevant in this school of thought. In this author's view, however, this top-down approach will not work where the government is elected by the people and there is a vibrant democracy. The requirement for formal validity, with rules needing to be declared as law, was criticised by Ronald Dworkin, who refers to it as a 'pedigree thesis' of positivism.[229]

---

[223]Richards Nobles and David Schiff, "Natural Law," 44. It was also discussed in Lon L. Fuller, *The Law in Quest of Itself* (Boston, Mass.: Beacon Press, 1940), 33–42.
[224]Refer §3.2.1 & §3.2.3.
[225]Fuller, *The Law in Quest of Itself*, 5–11.
[226]See the discussion on Bentham's analytical jurisprudence in Richard Nobles and David Schiff, "Debating with Natural Law; the Emergence of the Legal Positivism," in *Introduction to Jurisprudence and Legal Theory: Commentary and Materials*, Anne Barron, et al. (London: Butterworths, 2002), 92.
[227]Richard Nobles and David Schiff, "Legal Positivism," 93–94.
[228]Fuller, *The Law in Quest of Itself*, 5–11.
[229]Lundmark provides a succinct discussion of Positivism in *Divide between Common and Civil Law*, 92.

The famous twentieth-century jurisprudent H. L. A. Hart has classed as '*primary rules*' laws such as criminal law, that governs the behaviour of the populace or the powers of the population to make contracts; and as '*secondary rules*', laws such as constitutional law or contract law that assists in identification of the primary rules, and acts as a guide to interpret them.[230] The legal rules lead to obligations, and authority comes from a set of recognised criteria such as statutes or judicial precedents. According to Hart, the secondary rules can be classed as *rules of recognition*,[231] which are necessary in order to identify a system or to consider whether a particular primary rule is valid or not; and *rules of adjudication*, that are used to interpret and apply such rules.[232] A legal system can only be understood as an entity once it has the above set of rules in place.

However, apart from the '*external aspects*' of these rules, there are also the '*internal aspects*' that are used akin to reasons or as a benchmark for behaviour of the populace in relation to the external law. In the words of Hart "...wide range of normative language is used...."[233] to describe the internal rules, in contrast to external behaviour, of the populace. "There is no contradiction in saying that people accept certain rules but experience no such feelings of compulsion."[234]

Thus, while Austin's theory sees the law as the command of a sovereign, Hart's ideas and system of rules are more suited for democracies, secular and pluralistic societies. Hart agreed that any power associated with a sovereign cannot be unlimited, and in view of that, he discussed bills of rights and constitutional laws that bind the sovereign.[235] Hart explained the difference between the rules that are sanction-oriented and the rules that can empower the populace to conduct their day-to-day business, such as contract or family laws.[236]

Very fundamentally, Hart believed that the populace follows the law not just because they are worried about any sanctions consequent on *not* following the law, but also because the laws serve as a benchmark that can be seen as providing a reason for their actions. Further, Hart was of the view that officials also need to have such an attitude towards their own legal system's rules, thereby bringing a form of democracy within the rule-based system.[237]

---

[230]H. L. A. Hart, *The Concept of Law*, 2nd ed. (Oxford: Oxford University Press, 1994), 79, for further discussion on 'primary rules' and 'secondary rules'. See also, Nicola Lacey, "Modern Positivism: H. L. A. Hart and Analytical Jurisprudence," in *Introduction to Jurisprudence and Legal Theory: Commentary and Materials*, by Anne Barron, et al. (London: Butterworths, 2002), 157.
[231]Hart, *The Concept of Law*, 105–10.
[232]Lacey, "Modern Positivism," 164–65 for the detailed discussion on Hart's classification of secondary rules.
[233]Hart, *The Concept of Law*, 56–57.
[234]Ibid., 57.
[235]Ibid., 68.
[236]Hart, *The Concept of Law*, 84. *See also*, Lacey, "Modern Positivism," 161–62 for further discussion and analysis on the same issues in the context of Hart's jurisprudence.
[237]Hart, *The Concept of Law*, 116. *See also*, Lacey, "Modern Positivism," 166 for further discussion on the same issues.

Hart was an analytical positivist; however, he did not negate the use of natural law to fill the gaps in law during adjudication. Hart acknowledged that judges had to exercise their discretionary power during the process of adjudication in the courts, and he further conceded that there were elements of natural law in most laws. However, Hart was clear that natural law did not guide the judges or populace.

While the author has discussed the school of positivism that developed in common law jurisdictions, there was also a parallel development of this concept in civil law jurisdictions. This was also quite influential in the development of jurisprudential thought. The author will also discuss two jurisprudents from the civil law jurisdictions found in continental Europe — Hans Kelsen and Radbruch – who share a similar school of thought. The populace can adhere to these rules out of respect for the institution that is the creator of such rules, and/ or respect for the laws, and/or out of custom, and/or out of pure submission to the authorities. However, the main reasons are irrelevant.

Hans Kelsen, a positivist in the continental European tradition, commented in the context of law that "any desired content can be the law."[238] Pursuant to this school of thought, it is immaterial whether the contents of the rules are good or bad or capricious, immoral, unethical, racist or vulgar and so forth, as all these factors are irrelevant to its validity. During the years of enlightenment in Europe, law was more like a science and as a result, any consideration of morality or human rights was considered part of political thinking.

While it was common to view the law from the angle of morality or human rights, these issues themselves could be seen as quite separate matters and were very subjective in nature. This is popularly called the 'separation thesis' within the theory of positivism.[239] Kelsen's main idea was to search for the fundamental character of law, and according to him, it was to be found in what the law was rather than what the law ought to have been.[240]

Kelsen notably seemed to distinguish societal foundations from foundations of law. Kelson firmly believed in keeping politics or morality out of the concept of law and was a proponent of the *pure theory of law*. A particular act passing through a chain of legal norms can be provided with a *legal normative meaning*; norms give meaning to an act. This school of thought suggests that behaviour resulting in that act is due to the fact that the behaviour was "commanded or permitted or authorised."[241] Norms are also related to other norms in a hierarchical chain and are necessary to validate the relatively lower norms.

---

[238]Lundmark, *Divide between Common and Civil Law*, 92.
[239]Ibid., 93.
[240]David Schiff, "Modern Positivism: Kelsen's Pure Theory of Law," in *Introduction to Jurisprudence and Legal Theory: Commentary and Materials*, Anne Barron, et al. (London: Butterworths, 2002), 191.
[241]Lacey, "Modern Positivism," 195.

However, Kelsen agreed that in this chain of legal norms, the highest norm, for example, the US Constitution, will be an exception, and accordingly it will not require another superior legal norm for it to be classed as valid. This is an exception which is allowed in this chain of legal norms. Additionally, such norms together form a legal system, and as a result they demonstrate the systematic nature of norms within a legal system. These norms are followed by the populace. These norms need to be understood from a particular point of view and not necessarily from the point of view of morality. Kelson also highlighted the concept of *coercion* in this positivist theory based on norms.[242]

However, continental legal philosophers such as Radbruch were very vocal in suggesting that not all laws declared by institutions should be seen as formally valid and therefore suitable to be called law. In his view, such laws can be ignored by judges.[243] Radbruch suggested that issues of morality and ethics cannot be separated from the issue of validity of law. In Radburch's view, the declaration of such law, when missing vital ingredients of morality and ethics, renders it unsuitable to be classed as law.

3.2.4 Legal Realism (1920s & 1930s onwards) and Critical Legal Studies (1970s and 1980s)

In the common law jurisdiction of the US, the school of thought of Legal Realism (also called '*socio-legal*' studies),[244] had gained so much popularity in 1920s and 1930s that it even affected other common law jurisdictions such as England & Wales. In the US, legislations and cases have to conform to the *US Constitution Law 1789*, especially the *Bill of Rights 1791*, which includes the principles of liberty, equality, and freedom of speech; these principles result in political or social issues such as privacy, that are ultimately resolved by the courts.

The US Courts were applying the general principles enshrined in the framework of the *US Constitution 1789*, and therefore, were exercising broader discretion, and in that way, were going much further than the formal processes that were envisaged in the first place. Thus the US Courts themselves raised the issue of the legitimacy of judicial decisions, as well as questions about the judicial reasons coming out of the courts.[245] It raised fears that US judges, who were not elected through a democratic process by citizens of the US, were putting across their own subjective political affiliations in their judgments, on the pretext that their judgments conformed with the *Bill of Rights 1791* enshrined in the US constitution.

---

[242]Ibid., 196.

[243]Lundmark, *Divide between Common and Civil Law*, 93.

[244]Hugh Collins, "Law as Politics: Progressive American Perspectives," in *Introduction to Jurisprudence and Legal Theory: Commentary and Materials*, Anne Barron, et al. (London: Butterworths, 2002), 281.

[245]Ibid., 279.

This school of thought was developed by the moderate leftist parties in the USA, who challenged the established rules and even institutions of the US. This naturally provoked fierce reaction from the other side of the fence.[246] According to believers of this philosophy, the protection of private rights, privacy and similar concepts obstructs social welfare policies. Therefore, the developers and followers of this school of thought believe that the law is actually used in practice as an instrument of the government and this was the primary reason for the development of this school of thought.[247]

Some scholars who can be considered '*rules sceptic*' and '*facts sceptic*', feel that the law and society is in constant flux, and they therefore look at the process of adjudication.[248] According to scholars from this school of thought, no rules could be drafted in such detail as to cover all aspects and issues from the start. The scholars therefore recommended including inter-disciplinary approaches to the law and suggested that subjects such as sociology and economics should also be considered for the study of law. Scholars of this school of thought believed in '*law in action*' and analysed the law as practised in court rooms.

The believers in this school of thought advocated the progressive interpretation of statutes and case laws in court rooms. This would have to include arguments about justice and morality to ensure that judges adapt to the rapid changes experienced in society.[249] According to these scholars, law and politics cannot be separated, and they were therefore more interested in what they called '*law in action*'.[250]

Even though Hart, the famous English jurisprudent,[251] agreed that any judiciary can encounter and fill gaps during the application of law by inclusion of natural law principles, he disagreed with the notion that there are gaps that need to be actively filled. According to Hart, the judges are constrained by "rule-governed operations over the vast, central areas of the law".[252] It is here that the 'rule sceptic' scholars in the common law argue that the main reasons given by judges in their judgments are actually their own rationalisations based on their subjective political affiliations. Therefore, to analyse the judgments, according to realists, researchers have to go deeper into the political opinions of the judges to dissect their own subjectivity and political affiliations.

---

[246]Ibid., 280.
[247]Ibid., 281.
[248]Thomas Lundmark, *Charting the Divide Between Common and Civil Law* (New York; Oxford: Oxford University Press, 2012), 96. *See also*, Collins, "American Perspectives," 281, where legal realism is further discussed.
[249]Lundmark, *Divide between Common and Civil Law*, 96. *See also*, for further discussion, Karl Llewellyn, "Some Realism About Realism- Responding to Dean Pound," *Harv. L. Rev.* 44, no. 8 (1931): 1222.
[250]Collins, "American Perspectives," 281.
[251]Refer above §3.2.3.
[252]Hart, *The Concept of Law*, 154.

The author's view is that even Supreme Court judges are approved by politicians based on such affiliations, and therefore, this subjectivity is not something secret. This argument has been taken further forward by the 'fact sceptics', who suggested that even facts were rationalised by the judges and interpreted subjectively to arrive at their judgments.[253] This has been frequently discussed by lawyers in almost every jurisdiction; for example, many state that there is a need for the judges to be selected from wider sections of society, as the judges themselves are required to have the ability to relate to the disputes that come to the courts.

The realist scholars favoured a *'purposive approach'* to law, which can guide judges and courts using research in 'policy science' that has its roots firmly founded in social sciences.[254] This argument has actually in a way been adopted by judges in England & Wales as 'purposive interpretation of statutes'. It means that now, the interpretation of statutes in England & Wales is based on this inter-disciplinary approach, and the legal reasons in any judgment clearly reflect this approach.

Realists in relation to the philosophy of natural law argued that morality is usually fixed by the dominant groups within a society, and there was actually no fundamental and universal moral truth. It appears they have borrowed this argument from the 'pragmatic' school of thought.[255]

Natural Law scholars were worried at the thought of realists rejecting the concept of morality and undermining the legal system, and they were basically appalled by the realists' notion that the legal system exists to meet social ends. The natural law scholars were worried that this approach by realist scholars might open the doors for totalitarian systems, where legal systems are used without any constraints.

The jurisdiction of England & Wales, though affected by the currents of the realist school flowing across the Atlantic Ocean, was in fact not willing to examine the political orientation of its judges. However, it did incrementally adopt the purposive approach in relation to the interpretation of statutes in the subsequent years. At the same time, a few studies on political orientation have been done in the recent past, and results are not very different from the US' studies on the same subject.[256] The application of *Human Rights Act*

---

[253]An example was cited where the description of event was judged in a particular way in the Court of Appeal but was reversed on an appeal in House of Lords, which described the very same event in a different way to arrive at different judgement. For details, see Collins, "American Perspectives," 283.

[254]Collins, "American Perspectives," 284.

[255]Discussion on pragmatism was carried out in Collins, "American Perspectives," 284, Pragmatism as a school of thought was developed by scholars such as John Dewey and William James.

[256]For more detail, see J. A. G. Griffith, *The Politics of the Judiciary*, 5th ed. (London: Harper Collins, 1997), 337. *See also*, Collins, "American Perspectives," 285–6.

1998 has recently increased the opportunity for judges in England & Wales to display their political orientations.[257]

At the other extreme end are the scholars of Critical Legal Studies (1970s and 1980s), who attempted to demonstrate that legal reasoning in most judgments was just a hoax, and many principles in the context of interpretation of statues, reasoning provided in common law judgments, and even the basic principles used in these judgments, were actually contradictory.[258] They attempted to bring about social change by attacking the legal system. However, judges and lawyers across the Atlantic Ocean reacted furiously even at the suggestion that they were 'making sense out of nonsense' in the context of common law. Many legal professionals were furious that their commitment to the profession in their lives was questioned in such a manner.[259]

3.3 Jurisprudence in context of Practice by Judges and Lawyers in English Courts

In the previous section, the author has discussed various theories in jurisprudence that have been developed over the last few centuries. The author has observed that currently in England & Wales, judges use policy reasons in their judgments to justify a stand taken in cases. The main arguments that have been raised over the years are in relation to the use of policy reasons by the judges. These arguments were raised by scholars as according to them, these judges are not even elected by the populace, and therefore they should leave the setting out of policy to legislatures. A recent study comparing the English jurisdiction to other jurisdictions confirmed that the English jurisdiction is gradually focusing more on interdisciplinary areas such as economics, sociology and so forth in legal practice.[260]

For centuries, legal scholars accepted that it was due to the concept of consent that the relevant parties, including monarchs, had agreed to be bound by the Constitution or Acts of Parliament.[261] Consent is developed by long usage of the common law and this could be classed as the normative foundation of common law. In the author's view, a few snapshots from English legal history such as the *Bill of Rights 1689*, as discussed later, can suitably demonstrate these foundations.

---

[257]A further discussion on application of *Human Rights Act 1998* is carried out in §7.2.1.6 & §7.2.1.6.1.
[258]Collins, "American Perspectives," 318–20.
[259]See the defence of common law in D. Howarth, "Making Sense out of Nonsense," in *Jurisprudence: Cambridge Essays*, ed. Hyman Gross and Ross Harrison (Oxford: Clarendon Press, 1992), 29–53. *See also*, Collins, "American Perspectives," 323 for further discussion on Howarth.
[260]Lundmark, *Divide between Common and Civil Law*, 110.
[261]Postema, "Classical Common Law Jurisprudence - II," 23–4.

It is impossible to understand even English civil & criminal procedural law without citing and appreciating the *Bill of Rights,*[262] which was instituted in the year 1689. It limited the power of the monarchs. In the United Kingdom, the *Bill of Rights 1689* was accompanied by the famous declarations *Magna Carta 1215, Petition of Right* 1628,[263] and *Habeas Corpus Act 1679.*[264]

The purpose of all these ancient laws was to curtail the arbitrary powers of the state in various areas that directly affect the populace. There is a need to know and appreciate this basic foundation of English law, and the mere mention of declarations or statutes will not fulfil that purpose.

Lord Denning, a famous jurist, described the *Magna Carta 1215* as "the greatest constitutional document of all times — the foundation of the freedom of the individual against the arbitrary authority of the despot."[265] After nearly 850 years, the *Magna Carta* is still an important symbol of liberty in the western world and India, and most lawyers need to understand its significance even to appreciate procedural rules.

The *Magna Carta* limited arbitrary powers to illegally imprison a subject, or to impose arbitrary taxes, and ensured swift justice; most importantly all the principles enshrined in it are in the context of common men. In the author's view, its significance is under appreciated in the younger generation.

Therefore, even the hard-core lawyers specializing in commercial law or intellectual property law, who are interested in contract and commercial laws, cannot afford to lose sight of this powerful document that has formed the core of jurisprudence and even percolates through the civil procedure rules in the form of words such as 'just', 'fairness', 'equality of arms,' and so forth.

3.4   Classical Chinese Jurisprudence

It is important to appreciate that due to the PRC's long history and its position as a civilisation state like India, the study of its jurisprudence needs to be divided into different periods: classical Chinese Jurisprudence, jurisprudence in later centuries until the end of the Qing Dynasty, and modern jurisprudence in the later years.

---

[262]*1 William and Mary Sess 2 c 2.*
[263]*3 Car 1 c 1.*
[264]31 Cha. 2. 2.
[265]Danny Danziger and John Gillingham, *1215: The Year of Magna Carta* (New York: Simon & Schuster, 2004), 268.

The author will try to discuss each of these briefly within the confines of this chapter. However, readers are advised to study specialised texts if they want to study any particular jurisprudence in detail.

Classic Chinese Jurisprudence will be analysed in the context of ancient history, when many kingdoms were spread around in the geographical area of the present PRC. The author will refer to *Table VIII* in Chapter 1 in this book for the detailed and relevant chronology of the ancient history of China. The author here inserts a warning that a few of the dates in the Table are not exact, as they seem to vary slightly in different legal history articles.

The Western Zhou Kingdom (1046–771 BCE) in ancient China established their royal authority over peripheral kingdoms through heavy reliance upon lineage affiliations and kinship hierarchies.[266] In ancient China, in order to maintain cohesion affected by demands from other kingdoms for more autonomy, an institution called *ba*, or hegemony system, was designed to re-establish inter kingdom cohesion.[267]

However, gradually, Zhou rulers were weakened, and there were societal changes. Accordingly, there was a demand for different kinds of institutions that included written scripts, new ceremonies and rites. This was the advent of written codes and along with these codes, a period of debate commenced. As a result of such debates, various jurisprudential thoughts occupied the intellectual space.

3.4.1 Background to Classical Chinese Jurisprudence

Before discussing Classical Chinese jurisprudence, it is important to appreciate that its main concepts will be different, as compared with the western concepts or modern concepts that are available in Jurisprudence.[268] In addition, it will again be erroneous to divide ancient Classical Legal Jurisprudence into modern sub-divisions of law.[269] It is important to highlight the words of Zeng and Ma before looking at classical Chinese jurisprudence:

> In traditional Chinese law, *"fa"* usually refers to an institutional dimension, especially after Qin and Han dynasties, whereas *li*, especially *li yi* (moral basis for rites and ceremonies), is where the value and spirit of traditional Chinese law can be found [emphasis added].[270]

---

[266]In particular, ruler Wu of the Western Zhou dynasty overthrew the Shang dynasty (1600–1045 BCE).
[267]Ernest Caldwell, "Social Change and Written Law in Early Chinese Legal Thought," *L. and History Rev.* 32, no. 1 (2014): 7.
[268]Xianyi Zeng and Xiaohong Ma, "A Dialectic Study of the Structure and Basic Concept of Traditional Chinese Law and an Analysis of the Relationship between Li (Ceremony) and Fa (Law)," *Frontiers of Law in China* 1, no. 1 (2006): 35.
[269]Ibid., 52.
[270]Ibid., 34.

Figure 5: Jurisprudence Influencing Judges in PRC

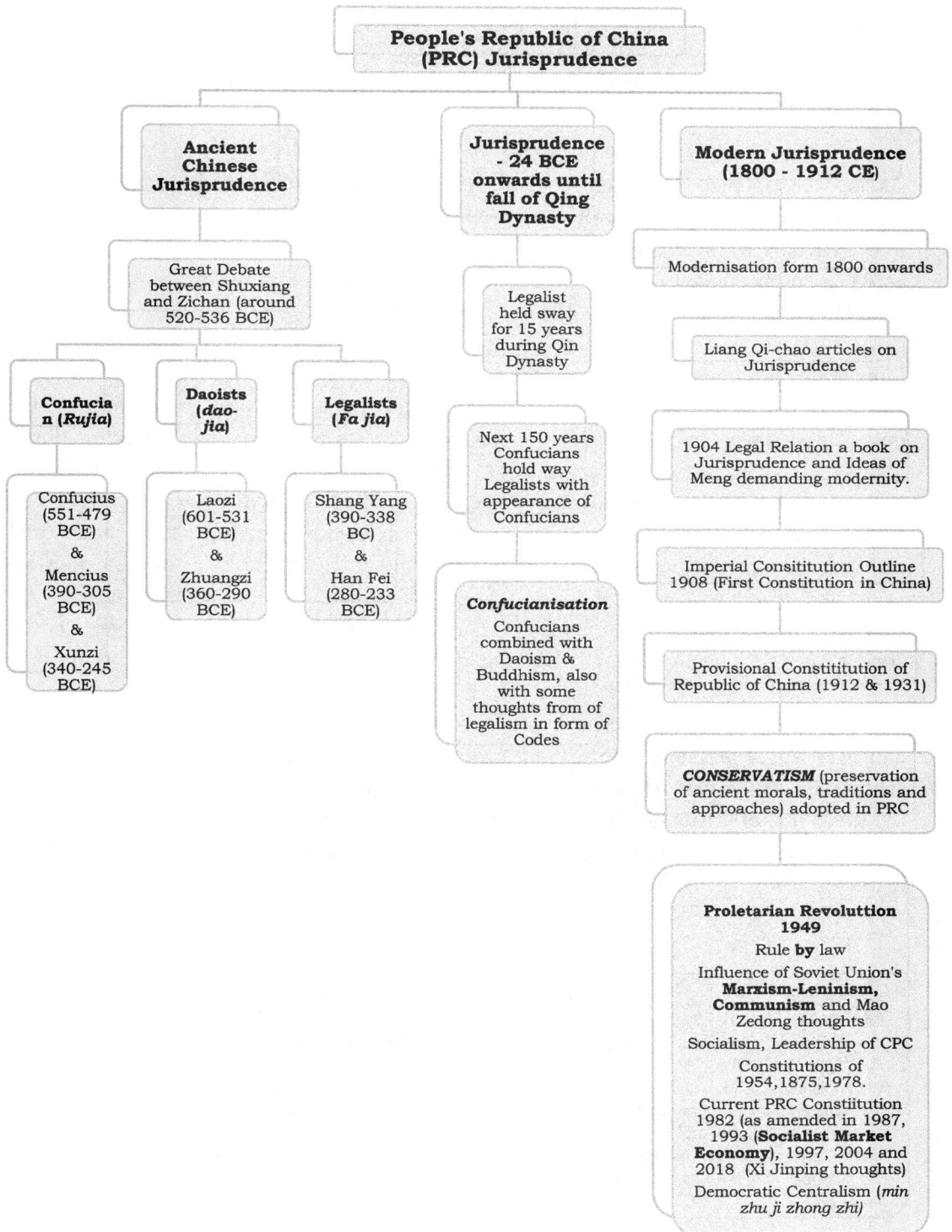

People's Republic of China (PRC) Jurisprudence

Ancient Chinese Jurisprudence

Great Debate between Shuxiang and Zichan (around 520-536 BCE)

Confucian (*Rujia*)
Confucius (551-479 BCE)
&
Mencius (390-305 BCE)
&
Xunzi (340-245 BCE)

Daoists (*dao-jia*)
Laozi (601-531 BCE)
&
Zhuangzi (360-290 BCE)

Legalists (*Fa jia*)
Shang Yang (390-338 BC)
&
Han Fei (280-233 BCE)

Jurisprudence - 24 BCE onwards until fall of Qing Dynasty

Legalist held sway for 15 years during Qin Dynasty

Next 150 years Confucians hold way Legalists with appearance of Confucians

Confucianisation
Confucians combined with Daoism & Buddhism, also with some thoughts from of legalism in form of Codes

Modern Jurisprudence (1800 - 1912 CE)

Modernisation form 1800 onwards

Liang Qi-chao articles on Jurisprudence

1904 Legal Relation a book on Jurisprudence and Ideas of Meng demanding modernity.

Imperial Constitution Outline 1908 (First Constitution in China)

Provisional Constititution of Republic of China (1912 & 1931)

CONSERVATISM (preservation of ancient morals, traditions and approaches) adopted in PRC

Proletarian Revoluttion 1949

Rule **by** law

Influence of Soviet Union's **Marxism-Leninism, Communism** and Mao Zedong thoughts

Socialism, Leadership of CPC

Constitutions of 1954,1875,1978.

Current PRC Constiitution 1982 (as amended in 1987, 1993 (**Socialist Market Economy**), 1997, 2004 and 2018 (Xi Jinping thoughts)

Democratic Centralism (*min zhu ji zhong zhi*)

There were already established social and political norms – '*li*' (the rites), which were the social norms and behaviour for the aristocrats, and '*fa*' (the law), which was for the commoners and slaves, and governed anti-social behaviour in ancient China. For example, same aspects in relation to the above can be analysed across several dynasties, in particular, during Xia (2300-1800 BCE), Shang (1800-1200 BCE) and Zhou (1122-255 BCE) dynasties.[271]

As the economy picked up in ancient China, there was a need for the relationships between the ruler and commoners, as well as the relationship of the commoners with the aristocrats, to be managed. There was a need for rules to be drafted clearly for commoners, so that they could comprehend them easily. This resulted in a statue with criminal law provisions being installed by the provincial chief, Zichan, in 536 BCE.[272]

Shuxiang, a prominent statesman of the state of Jin, argued that if the rules were too clear and specific, then people might find loopholes, and might even think that these were the only rules that were to be obeyed.[273] The populace therefore in theory could commit crimes that were not even written in the edicts, possibly leading to an increase in the number of cases, and corruption in the judiciary. According to Shuxiang, crime can be controlled by setting an example for people to follow from the top, leading the people to be orderly and peaceful. However, Zichan argued that he could only control the present bad state of crime in the area of Zeng;[274] he agreed in principle with Shuxiang's view, seeing it as ideal for long-term improvement in the law and order situation in his Kingdom. However, he was short of the talent needed to implement the ideals proposed by Shuxiang.

Shuxiang preferred to practice *xi xian-wang yi-shi yi zhi bu wei xing-pi.*, where those in authority would give direction without making use of any kind of edict or rule.[275] A few scholars have highlighted that Shuxiang's main aim in his school of thought was to maintain the status quo of aristocratic power.[276] It also highlights "the traditional tension in ancient China between **rule-by-man and rule-by-law** [emphasis added] notions of political legitimacy."[277]

---

[271]Wejen Chang, "Classical Chinese Jurisprudence and Development of Chinese Legal System" (2009–10), 210.
[272]Ibid., 211.
[273]Wejen Chang, "Classical Chinese Jurisprudence and Development of Chinese Legal System," *Tsinghua China L. Rev.* 2, no. 2 (2010): 211.
[274]Wejen Chang, "Classical Chinese Jurisprudence and Development of Chinese Legal System," 211, where they discussed James Legge, trans., *The Ch'un Ts'ew with the Tso Cheun in 5 the Chinese 609,* Taiwan (ROC) (1883) (Oxford: Clarendon Press, 1971), 610.
[275] See Caldwell, "Early Chinese Legal Thought," 15. *See also*, Wejen Chang, "Classical Chinese Jurisprudence," 210, where they discussed James Legge, trans., *Thet Ch'un Ts'ew with the Tso Cheun in 5 the Chinese 609,* Taiwan (ROC) (1883) (Oxford: Clarendon Press, 1971).
[276]Caldwell, "Early Chinese Legal Thought," 16.
[277]Ibid.

However, over the years, other rulers seemed to prefer Zichan's view and even in Shuxiang's kingdom of Jin, rules were made and instituted. Shuxiang was not there anymore to argue against the practice. However, in 513 BCE, Confucius argued on similar lines as Shuxiang and was of the view that people would now only follow the rules instead of respecting the authority. This was the start of jurisprudential theories in ancient China. The author has looked at this acknowledgment of the need to manage societal change. In addition, this issue has been acknowledged by legal historians studying from the point of history.[278]

These basic ideas were turned into two important jurisprudential themes of Classical Chinese jurisprudence – one, the arguments of Zichan, known as *Fajia,* the legalist branch of jurisprudence; and the other, the approach of Shuxiang, supported by Confucius' views, which formed a branch called the Confucian branch of jurisprudence, or *Rujia.[279]*

Although the thought processes in the two branches are different, there is a common thread, namely the belief that humans can resolve issues themselves. However, a third branch of jurisprudence was also being established in ancient China, which criticised institutions, rules, and regulations, and advocated a simple form of life following the way of nature; this branch was called *Daojia* or Daoists.[280]

3.4.1.1   Confucians (Rujia) – Confucius, Mencius & Xunzi

Confucian jurisprudential thought was initiated by Confucius but was further developed by many scholars in later centuries. The key features under this stream of jurisprudence as developed by important scholars are discussed below.

3.4.1.1.1   Confucius

This was the start of classical theories; Confucius was the first to propound certain theories in detail.[281] Primarily, he looked at the rules of behaviour (*li*) and the principles behind them (*ru*). Two other scholars and philosophers, Mencius and Xunzi, who were from the period before the Qin dynasty (221-205 BCE), then further enhanced and diffused the teachings of Confucius. Instead of focusing on heavens (*tian*), Confucius focused more on earthly affairs and believed humans could regulate their own affairs.

---

[278]Ibid., 17.
[279]Wejen Chang, "Classical Chinese Jurisprudence and Development of Chinese Legal System," 212.
[280]Ibid.
[281]*Shu-jing, The Book of Historical Documents,* (a collection of proclamations of rulers), *Shi-jing (The Book of Poetry,* a selection of verses from folk songs), and *Yi-jing,* (The Book of Changes*)* all observed a set of rules of refined behaviour known as *li* (the rites) and studied the principles behind them (*ru*) (as cited in Wejen Chang, "Classical Chinese Jurisprudence and Development of Chinese Legal System," 212.)

Confucius recommended two principles – a positive one that recommended humans to help each other to reach their goals and another negative principle that recommended humans to avoid doing things that they did not want others to do to them.[282] This was Confucius' way of explaining that man is capable of reason and compassion, and this led to the formation of the rules of social interaction as follows:

> In *Lun-yu* (*The Analects*) they appeared in four groups: *de* (moral principles), *li* (the rites), *zheng* (government decrees), and *xing* (penal laws). Among the moral principles, the primary one was *ren* (humaneness). Basically, *ren* denoted that people should treat fellow human beings with empathy, care and respect. From this principle Confucius derived more specific moral rules, including *xiao* (filial piety), *ti* (brotherly love), *zhong* (loyalty), *xin* (faithfulness), *qian-rang* (modesty and yielding), *gong-jing* (humility and respect), *hui* (kindness and generosity), *shu* (understanding and forgiving), *yi* (rectitude and justice) and *zhi* (straightforwardness, honesty, truthfulness, uprightness) [emphasis in original].[283]

One of the important aspects of Confucius' approach to jurisprudence was *li*, behaviour by which humans restrain themselves. Adoption of such behavior by a society can create a *harmonious* society and *li* was therefore considered very important. Confucius did not discuss government decrees and laws in detail as his preference was for modifying human behaviour. According to Confucius, humans might know that some acts can lead to punishment, but this in itself will not change their behaviour or make them aim for higher standards. Among all his principles, he reserved the top rank for the notion of moral principles of humaneness.

Penal laws, according to Confucius, had a systemic issue – they were drafted by people lacking in wisdom, or they were arbitrary in nature. He suggested that the right people had to be selected to draft penal laws, and the ultimate authority should always be vested in the king or the feudal lord. According to him, the king or the feudal lord must also follow the rules of behaviour. According to Confucius, the only way people will respect the king or law is through the concept of moral authority and not because of penal laws or codes, which Confucius thought were inferior in his ranking system.[284] Pursuant to this school of thought, the most effective form of education was not preaching but "teaching by example" (*shen-jiao*).[285]

---

[282]Wejen Chang, "Classical Chinese Jurisprudence and Development of Chinese Legal System," 213.
[283]Wejen Chang, "Classical Chinese Jurisprudence and Development of Chinese Legal System," 214. Please note that the Chinese characters have been removed from the quote.
[284]Caldwell, "Early Chinese Legal Thought," 20.
[285]Wejen Chang, "Classical Chinese Jurisprudence and Development of Chinese Legal System," 217.

Scholars agreed with an adage in *Yi-jing* that litigation always ends in disaster *(song-ze zhong-xiong)* and should be avoided in society.[286] According to Confucius, punishments were needed, but in fact, this very act of punishment signified the failure of society. According to him, 'rightness' or 'justice' was not an absolute concept; it could have different meanings in different contexts, but the moral duty of humans is always supreme.[287] In addition, a relationship between a ruler and his subjects is based on mutual benefit.

In summary, according to him, the state through a ruler should use both persuasion and coercion to enforce the moral values that need to be inculcated in the people.[288]

3.4.1.1.2   Mencius

Mencius (390-305 BCE), who was a believer in the Confucian branch of jurisprudence, in his work *Mengzi* discussed that all humans share the following qualities:

> ➢ Heart of compassion *(ce-yin zhi xin)* leads to humanness;

> ➢ Heart of shame (*xiu-e zhi xin*) leads to rightness;

> ➢ Heart of right and wrong *(shi-fei zhi xin)* leads to wisdom;

> ➢ Heart of humility (*ci-rang zhi xin*) leads to the concept of propriety.[289]

According to Confucius, it was impossible for people to be unable to distinguish right from wrong; this apparent inability was because of the influence of evil forces. Mencius, however, was of the view that a few people cannot distinguish between right and wrong. Mencius suggested there were four groups of norms, as noted by Chang: "for self-cultivation, personal interactions, government action and the relationship between the individual and the authorities; and in each group he saw the norms in different ranks."[290]

---

[286]Ibid.
[287]Ibid., 219.
[288]Geoffrey MacCormack, *The Spirit of Traditional Chinese Law*, The Spirit of the Laws (Athens; London: University of Georgia Press, 1996), 7.
[289]Wejen Chang, "Classical Chinese Jurisprudence and Development of Chinese Legal System," 221–22.
[290]Wejen Chang, "Classical Chinese Jurisprudence," 223.

Mencius did not discuss the origins of law and its enforcement; presumably it does not come from the hearts of the ordinary people. However, he did refer to *ren-zheng*,[291] which meant the benevolent policies of the government. These policies aimed to provide education so that people could learn from the good things; they could then make a decent living, and profits could be shared. Mencius highlighted the need for division of labour in society and a need for good government officials.

These views were rejected by many people due to their own experiences with bad rulers and local leaders.[292] However Mencius was of the view that good rulers were required to implement rules, and as long as there was legitimacy in the selection of the successors of such rulers, the system was credible. According to him, the people were the most important, followed by the state and then the rulers, who were the least important in terms of ranking within a society. Chang clarifies this point in relation to Mencius' statement about ranking within society:

> …the people were the most important, the "altars of the gods of earth and grain" (*she-ji*, the state) was the next, the ruler the least. Therefore, when a ruler was cruel and abusive, the people were justified to revolt and exterminate him, and, in Mencius's view, executing a tyrant (*zhu yi-fu*) was different from murdering an ordinary ruler, it was not regicide. (*shi-jun*) [emphasis in original]. [293]

Mencius did not give a lot of attention to the law/codes, or its development; in fact, to the author, it appears that he ignored it, even in comparison to Confucius.

3.4.1.1.3 Xunzi

The last classical jurisprudent in the Confucian school of thought was Xunzi (340-245 BCE), before the advent of Qin dynasty (that unified many provinces of ancient China). His legal jurisprudence was based on reason. According to him, humans liked living in groups, and had fairly similar needs leading to common likes and dislikes. With limited resources, however, humans were competing with each other and therefore, in general, human nature was bad, *'e,*[294] or the humans could get be swayed by their bad nature. Therefore, norms were needed to regulate humans. Mencius thought norms could be found in their hearts, but

---

[291]Konrad Zweigert, Hein Kotz, and Tony Weir, trans., *An Introduction to Comparative Law: Volume I: The Framework*, 2nd Revised ed. (Oxford: Clarendon Press, 1987), 224.

[292]Xu Xing, an agriculture leader, alleged that a good ruler should live just like his subjects as discussed in Wejen Chang, "Classical Chinese Jurisprudence and Development of Chinese Legal System," 225.

[293]Wejen Chang, "Classical Chinese Jurisprudence and Development of Chinese Legal System," 228. Please note that the author has removed the Chinese characters, which were within the quote.

[294]Wejen Chang, "Classical Chinese Jurisprudence and Development of Chinese Legal System," 230.

Xunzi disagreed with that view. He suggested that such norms had originated from learned people such as sages, but ordinary people would not be capable of coming up with such norms.

Xunzi was of the view that there were two principles which could lead any person – compassion *(ren)* and righteousness *(yi)*. Additionally, Xunzi suggested that in order to achieve these two principles, the sages in ancient lands created rites *(li)*, music *(yu)* for noble persons, and law *(fa)* for the commoners.[295] He was of the view that there must have been reasons for the ancient dynasties such as Zhou or Xia to have established institutions *(zhi)* and detailed procedures *(ming)* for the enforcement of those principles.[296]

Xunzi was of the view that such institutions and procedures were artificial and believed that humans were impressionable. He believed, therefore, that humans could be taught compassion. According to him, moral principles deserved to be ranked higher as compared to other principles. He would rank the laws made by previous rulers more highly in comparison to the laws made by the later rulers. Although he believed that rites should be placed at a lower level as compared to morals, he still felt that rites can be taught to people. Importantly, Xunzi discussed the problem of social equality in greater depth than Confucius and Mencius. According to him, individuals who were trying to learn and to move up the social ladder should be rewarded accordingly. Xunzi seemed to have been encouraging social mobility within ancient China, rather than preserving the aristocrat's power and rank within society.

He maintained that 'where there is law it should be followed *(you fa zhe yi fa xing)*'.[297] However, laws were below the rank of norms as he felt that human behaviour was too varied and complicated for laws to be able to cover all contingencies; furthermore, they were not sufficient to manage all aspects of human behaviour.[298] According to him, the laws on their own were also not sufficient to motivate people to follow them. Additionally, in the author's view, Xunzi seems to have suggested a solution similar to the doctrine of precedent in common law: where there was no applicable law, the judges should place the case in a category of similar cases, drawing an analogy *(yi leiju)* and deliberating *(yi)* on an appropriate solution.[299]

Xunzi believed deliberation *(yi)* was needed when handling cases, and the relevant person should not only know the law from the texts *(shu)*, but also should know the intention *(yi)* behind it. Xunzi described the intention as 'the spirit of law' *(yi)*; he had also put forward

---

[295]Ibid., 231.
[296]Ibid.
[297]Ibid., 233.
[298]Ibid., 234.
[299]Ibid., 235.

interesting questions as to the purpose of all laws.[300] In summary, according to him, a good ruler with good conduct could establish a set of concrete rules for good conduct, while the rites and laws could be strengthened to make them more efficient and harmonious. Xunzi's ultimate objective was for human society to be 'greatly transformed and absolutely unified (*da hua zhi y*i)'.[301] He could, in fact, be considered as the bridge between pure Confucians and Legalists in Chinese jurisprudential theory.

3.4.1.2 Daoists (dao-jia) – Laozi, Zhuangzi

Confucians propounded theories based on society and recommended societal solutions, especially for rulers to follow. However, Laozi and Zhuangzi disagreed with those solutions and were very pessimistic about the state of affairs during their time. These two scholars were therefore perceived as great expounders of 'the Way' (*dao*) and were later labelled as the founders of the 'Daoist school' (*dao-jia*). These theories were built on a healthy cynicism about the authorities, a critical view of the man-made rules that governed the populace, and belief that the common folk's conscience could make them stand up to the authorities. They could be said to have brought in the concept of equality among all men before the authorities.

3.4.1.2.1 Laozi

Laozi was a contemporary of Confucius and alleged that there was a set of rules, which operated constantly and affected everything. He explained by giving the example of the rain, which would naturally stop after a while. He explained that, similarly, physical laws also governed human behaviour. According to him, there was a natural, universal valid law, *the way*, and the way was 'natural' (*zi-ran*).[302] Laozi was of the view that harmony with the universe was affected by unlimited desires, and especially by the teachings of so-called learned men called sages. According to him, such teachings were artificial and thus imperfect, and therefore caused more problems.[303] According to him, when morality failed, the rulers would end up making laws to protect the special interests.[304]

In summary, he advocated discarding morality and laws and exterminating the false 'sages' (*jue-sheng*). His view on governance seems to be against authority, but there were contradictions as noted by scholars of Chinese jurisprudence, and at times he appeared to be advocating governance by extreme authoritarianism.[305] In the author's view, the most

---

[300]Ibid.

[301]Ibid., 236.

[302]Ibid., 241.

[303]Ibid., 242.

[304]In the author's view, this is remarkable as these views were expressed a few thousand years ago. And yet the practice exists in most current systems, where lobbying of legislators by interest groups is common practice. It affects the drafting of laws, which work to protect such special interest groups.

[305]Wejen Chang, "Classical Chinese Jurisprudence and Development of Chinese Legal System," 245.

controversial aspect of his philosophy was the view that a sage or authority should take care of the common population like well-cared-for infants, and this well-cared-for population should be devoid of knowledge and desire *(wu-zhi wu-yu)*.[306]

3.4.1.2.2 Zhuangzi

Unlike Laozi, Zhuangzi (360-290 BCE) was of the view that there could be many, indeed infinite *ways* and the sages should attempt to guide people by any means, including deceit.[307] The rules that people followed naturally were better than any morals suggested by any sage or philosopher. Interestingly, even though this was a few thousand years ago, he referred to the possibility of technological inventions leading to strife and competition; he felt that tough laws and rules would be needed and therefore, should have been drafted. He was of the view that with the increase in talk of morality from sages, there would be a corresponding increase in issues of law and order.

Zhuangzi's views on the relationship between the ruler and his subjects were based on the idea that the ruler should remain aloof, which he referred to as *hang ru biao-zhi, min ru ye-lu*. What this meant was that ruler and subjects should have as little as possible to do with each other; this could be achieved by avoiding each other.[308] It seems to be the case that he distrusted the authorities and valued freedom. His advice was that the common people should not become 'upside-down people' *(daozhi zhi min)* at any cost as freedom was the most valuable commodity.[309]

3.4.1.3 Legalists (Fa-Jia) – Shang Yang, Han Fei

Even in ancient China, it has been observed that there were incidents of ministers protecting *xiangwei* or *bianshu* or *Mozi* in order to protect the compilations of written laws, or using iron pillars to communicate the law to the populace within the state.[310] Therefore, it can be seen that it was customary to have some form of written edicts or policies emanating from the rulers.

Legalists placed a great deal of emphasis on law, which slowly gained prominence just before the Qin Dynasty (221-206 BCE), which unified China nearly two thousand years ago. Shang Yang (390-338 BCE) and Han Fei (280-233 BCE), produced two substantial works – *Shangjun shu* and *Han Feizi* respectively. During their time, both Confucian and Daoist schools of thought were popular. It was a period of turmoil, known as 'a time of great strife' *(da-zheng zhi shi)*, also termed as the warring period, from 467-221 BCE.[311]

---

[306]Ibid., 244.
[307]Ibid., 246.
[308]Ibid., 248.
[309]Ibid., 249.
[310]Caldwell, "Early Chinese Legal Thought," 23–24.
[311]Wejen Chang, "Classical Chinese Jurisprudence and Development of Chinese Legal System," 250.

After 221 BCE, the State of Qin defeated all of its rivals and created a unified country that was made up of many regions and provinces, very similar to the present-day PRC. During the Warring Period, strict rules were required; they would come from the top that is the ruler or Emperor. These rules were drafted for the subjects and contained no discussion of morals or rites. In any event, these morals were impractical, given the great strife which occurred during the Warring Period. It was also a time when different schools of thought had their own followers such as Daoists and Confucians. Many rulers of the region aspired to establish something similar but were thoroughly confused as to which one of the schools of thought was more relevant for the times.

3.4.1.3.1 Han Fei

Han Fei (280-233 BCE) felt that the Confucians' views were ideal, as loving all and maintaining harmony within society were good concepts, but according to him, these concepts were not practical under the circumstances of his time. *Compassion and benevolence* (*ci-ren, guo zhi mu ye*), the two qualities favoured by all the philosophers, were actually harming the cause of rulers as they were proving to be too lenient in punishing criminals or were too lavish in bestowing benefits on underlings. In addition, as a result of being influenced by the concepts of compassion and benevolence, these rulers were acting like common men, and as a result were losing the respect and awe of their subjects. He was of the view that these qualities could bring about disaster for the rulers, and consequently the states would suffer.

Han Fei was of the view that humans by nature are wicked and are competing for scarce resources. Therefore, punishment and reward were important tools for rulers who had to manage people who were perhaps not very clever. For Han Fei, law was a coercive device, similar to a timber straightening machine (*bang-qing*), or a hammer and an anvil *(zhui-duan)*; the system of punishment and reward functioned as 'two handles' (*er-bing*) for the rulers to control the common people, as they were not intelligent enough to appreciate what was important to the state as a whole.[312] He recommended heavy punishment even for minor offences, as it caused to people to fear. This fear according to him had prevented them from committing even minor crimes. In his eyes, all sections of society were required to be punished before the law, but his views on whether the rulers were also answerable to the laws were not apparent in his jurisprudence.

According to him, the role of the rulers was to guide people away from the self-destruction. Therefore, the persona of the rulers was very important for Han Fei.[313] He was of the view that if the ruler were the upholder of laws, they needed to be of strong character, and then

---

[312]Ibid., 255.
[313]Arabella Lyon, "Rhetorical Authority in Athenian Democracy and the Chinese Legalism of Han Fei," *Philosophy & Rhetoric* 41, no. 1 (2008): 58.

the likelihood of their states being strong was higher. Additionally, he felt that power cannot reside in two places.[314] It is arguable whether he placed the authority in the upholder of law (an institution), or the person who was actually the upholder of law as an individual. Han Fei advocated that the rulers should lead through a method of *wuwei*, translated as 'the ruler should do nothing or take no action'.[315]

Han Fei did not believe in embracing diversity, but rather wanted to establish unity and stability in the state through law or order (*fa*), strategic method (*shu*), and position/power of the ruler (*shi*).[316] Han Fei's views are very persuasive even in the current PRC.[317]

3.4.1.3.2   Shang Yang

Shang Yang (390-338 BCE), who came earlier than Han Fei, nonetheless had similar views about compassion and benevolence being recipes for disaster. He condemned kindness and benevolence as 'the mother of transgressions' (*ci-ren, guo zhi mu ye*) and rites and music as 'the symptoms of excess and license' (*liyue, yin-yi zhi zheng ye*); he also disapproved of various other moral principles such as filial piety, brotherly love, sincerity, faithfulness, and so on. He condemned the Confucian classics that highlighted the virtues as "Six Parasites" *(liu-shi*).[318] Shang Yang was also not kind to the advocates of Confucian schools of thought, calling them 'insects' (*ming te qu zhu*).[319] He worked from the belief that people were always looking for personal gains in the form of fame and profit (*ming li*).

He wanted efficiency within the state to be the hallmark of any state that aspires to become prosperous. Accordingly, he wanted the rulers to reward people involved in agriculture and military service. Additionally, he wanted all doors to other professions to be closed by the imposition of taxes and prohibitions. He recommended doing that by promulgating laws and thereafter by the strict enforcement of those laws within the states.

In order to enforce those laws, even petty crimes or deviations would have to be punished, with the goal that this would prevent any crimes in the future due to the fear of the law. He referred to this as 'using punishments to eliminate punishment' (*yi xing qu xing*).[320] According to him, all sections were answerable to the law; however, he also felt that the ruler and his heirs were not answerable. He and other legalists suggested that rulers needed to be a 'brilliant master' (*ming-zhu*), a 'sage' (*sheng-ren*), a '*sagacious lord*' (*sheng-zhu*), or a 'bright ruler' (*ming-jun*).[321]

---

[314]Ibid., 59.
[315]Ibid., 62.
[316]Ibid., 56.
[317]Ibid., 57.
[318]Wejen Chang, "Classical Chinese Jurisprudence and Development of Chinese Legal System," 253–54.
[319]Ibid., 254.
[320]Ibid., 255.
[321]Ibid., 260.

3.4.1.4 Comparison of Classical Chinese Jurisprudence

Legalist views were very similar to Daoist thinking, with ruthless implementation of the laws for the common people, and the belief that there was no need for respect for the common people. Unlike Confucians, the rules of the legalists were more quickly implemented and were uniform. Confucians' views were more suitable for achieving long-term peace, and this was perhaps not applicable in a society that was changing rapidly during the Warring Period. In addition, Confucians' ranking of rites and norms were seen as having the potential to create confusion among the masses.

In Daoist philosophy, a Daoist sage has an absolute understanding about the world; and the ruler in the template of the Legalist traditions had the absolute authority as an upholder of laws.[322] Concentration of power in the hands of a ruler who was above the law was good for stability and success in the short-term. In the long run, however, the problems that the concentration of power in one person could create within a society were manifold – and the Confucians foresaw this. Drafters of law, according to the legalist scholars, had to be very clever, with multiple skills that a single person could not have all at the same time.

For Confucians, the ruler could be a wise and educated person. Legalists, however, expected rulers to be clever people born with the skills to draft the most intelligent laws. Legalists believed if they were not able to find such a clever man as a ruler then it would lead to the drafting of arbitrary rules, and the arbitrary enforcement of these rules would then lead to break down of the state. It seems clear that the legalist solution was just a quick-fix solution and completely neglected the long-term approach of Confucians.[323]

One thing that was noticeable in the legalist tradition was that self-interest and distrust among stakeholders within a society was assumed; therefore, debate and reasoning were not valued because it was assumed that people were scheming and self-interested. Their arguments were therefore distrusted.[324] In the author's view, these concepts have had profound effects on the thinking of drafters and stakeholders in the legal system even 2000 years later.

Furthermore, it is to be noted that the retreat from virtue-based Confucian governance towards laws that even the general populace could understand would have had a profound societal change. This move meant a change from laws being the province of governing rulers and noble families, to a position where even ordinary people could know the origins of law. However, the written laws in the legalist template could just have been a way to

---

[322] Lyon, "Chinese Legalism and Athenian Democracy," 63.
[323] Wejen Chang, "Classical Chinese Jurisprudence and Development of Chinese Legal System," 261.
[324] Lyon, "Chinese Legalism and Athenian Democracy," 66.

perpetuate the power and control of the competing nobles in ancient China.[325] There was another function of the drafted laws, that is, to communicate authority and thereby convey the policy decisions of rulers.[326]

3.5 History of Chinese Jurisprudence over Later Years/Centuries

The legalists won the war of thoughts, when the unifier of all regions of ancient China, the Qin, seemingly in ruthless Daoist traditions, removed traces of Confucian thought and scholarship. However, this success was short-lived, lasting only fifteen years before the arrival of the Han dynasty (260-24 BCE). The Han dynasty followed Zhuangzi by not taking active part in the sphere of disputes (*hang ru biao-zhi, min ru ye-lu*); it also enacted many laws in the form of penal codes.

However, in the next 150 years after the fall of this dynasty, Confucians made a slow return to mainstream political and legal thought, even though the legalists remained in power. One reason for the return of the Confucians was that they had rules to prevent the excesses experienced by the populace in the previous dynasties and the Warring period. In later years, many legalists survived but they appeared to emulate the Confucians (*yang-ru yin-fa*).[327] Initial attempts by Confucians in the subsequent years to dilute the harshness of the criminal code drafted by legalists were unsuccessful, but gradually, over the years, the process of 'Confucianization' started.[328]

This Confucianization brought with it the dilution of penalties for offences. It also attempted to create more trust within society with the following steps–

◆ removing the duty to report others;

◆ commencing the development of procedural law;

◆ allowing the use of evidence to some extent;

◆ commencing the system of punishment according to the level of crime, and so on.

---

[325]Caldwell, "Early Chinese Legal Thought," 26.
[326]Ibid., 27.
[327]Wejen Chang, "Classical Chinese Jurisprudence and Development of Chinese Legal System," 263.
[328]Ibid.

Confucianization also brought in the concept that laws are never complete, and that principles of morality are therefore needed to interpret them. In addition, the application of laws was slowly eased to avoid harshness, thus bringing the concept of compassion into society.

Slowly, the effects of Confucianization had an effect on the common people, allowing them to avoid the authorities. It also assisted in the formation of local government and informal civil codes, which co-existed with the formal code. There were seeds of change and subsequent improvements in the idea of a harmonious society, but Confucianization within Chinese society also led to a decline in legal training in comparison with the time when legalists were dominant.

Drafters of law were sarcastically called 'petty clerks' (*dao-bi-li*), and those who provided legal services to private individuals were called litigation tricksters (*song-gun*). Even the civil examination system that commenced during the Tang dynasty (618-906 CE) focused more on Confucian ideas rather than knowledge about laws. Slowly, judicial assistants trained in law did emerge, but they were still much lower in the ranks, unless they had passed the civil service exams.

Fixed laws tend to provide only one solution, that is, only one party is correct and the other party is wrong. This motivated the populace to develop close-knit communities that could find their own solutions to disputes without resorting to the use of laws. This resulted in the development of a system of community mediation in ancient China that is still followed centuries later in many parts of modern PRC.

During the same time, there was a movement towards Daoism being followed as a religion, in conjunction with ancient Chinese beliefs that there was an interaction of god and spirits with humans, with rewards for good deeds. It also coincided with the arrival of Buddhism from present day India/Nepal into various regions of ancient China. Buddhism became popular with the common people, especially the concept that justice will eventually be done, if not in their current lives, then in their after-life.

There was no concept of 'rights' in any of the classical models of Chinese jurisprudence, but a concept of share (*fen*) in the resources for an individual's effort developed in ancient China.[329] Additionally, the Confucian view that one should avoid doing anything that they don't want others to do to them, and that one should assist others in achieving their objectives, was the nearest that ancient Chinese jurisprudence came to the concept of human rights.[330]

---

[329]Ibid., 269.
[330]Ibid.

Traditionally, ancient Chinese Society was also lacking in respect for the laws. Many articles suggest that the lack of procedural laws was one of the many reasons for this, not to mention the lack of culture of debate, which was actually abhorred in ancient China.

It is important to note that in order to understand modern PRC jurisprudence, it is also necessary to look beyond the dichotomy between Confucians and Legalists, and therefore there is also a need to analyse the earlier drafted codes from the viewpoint of the socio-political role the same codes had played in various dynasties.[331] It is important to highlight the words of Caldwell in the context of Chinese Legal history:

> The early Chinese, therefore, seem to espouse a positive belief that by writing down laws and making them publically [sic] known, they can provide a visible, written standard of conduct for all levels of society.[332]

3.6 Jurisprudence and Legal History in the Modern Chinese/PRC Legal System

Classical Chinese jurisprudence has formed the basis of modern jurisprudence, but in a real sense, the advent of modern Chinese jurisprudence started after the economy was opened up.[333]

However, the actual process of modernisation started around one hundred and fifty years before that. In the last Qing dynasty, the Chinese legal system interacted with the western legal system through the work of missionaries, such as Prussian missionary Gutzlaff (1803-1851), who established the *Monthly Digest of Oriental and Occidental Studies* in Guangzhou in July, 1833; and the American missionary Yong John Allen (1836-1907), who began a journal originally named *New Church News*, 1868, which was later changed to *International News* in September, 1874.

The latter Journal discussed concepts such as separation of powers, or how laws were legislated in the US Congress, including jurisprudential studies.[334] After that, a project involving the revision of the existing laws by the Qing government in 1901 brought a lot of western ideas into China. This task was also assisted by scholars from abroad, as well as

---

[331]Caldwell, "Early Chinese Legal Thought," 28.
[332]Ibid., 30.
[333]Qinhua He, "The Birth and Growth of Modern Jurisprudence in China," *Frontiers of Law in China* 1, no. 4 (2006): 487.
[334]Ibid.

Chinese students who returned to China after studying law in foreign countries such as the US and various European countries.

A prominent scholar, Liang Qi-chao, published a famous series of long articles on jurisprudence, such as *China should Pursue the Study Of Law* in 1896.[335] From the late Qing dynasty to 1949, China saw the publication of approximately 424 works on jurisprudence[336] Many scholars emerged from this development in Chinese jurisprudence.[337]

A real need to bring the Chinese legal system in line with the International legal system arose, when there was an abuse of the extra-territorial system of justice delivered by the United States and other foreign powers, who managed to gain the right from the Qing Dynasty to govern their own citizens according to their own laws, in China. Various treaties with the western imperial powers coerced the then Emperor Guangxu to reform the existing legal system, as this was the condition set by the foreign powers for relinquishing the extra-territorial right to adjudicate the crimes of their nationals according to their own country's laws in China.[338] Shen Jiaben was tasked by the Emperor Guangxu to bring about the necessary reforms within the existing legal system.[339]

A book on jurisprudence, *Legal Relations*, for the first time in Chinese legal history talked of rights in 1904, and was even used by Peking University to guide officials.[340] Liang, a legalist, wanted the assistance of new legislations to develop a strong state and in his papers discussed the reasons behind the failure of earlier legalists in previous dynasties. He cited the main reasons as being opposition to legalists, and the fact that law affairs were actually managed by low-ranking officials.[341]

---

[335]Ibid., 488.

[336]He, "Birth and Growth of Modern Jurisprudence," 490, where he discussed the publications and cited *General Catalogue of Law Books in China* (compiled by the library of China University of Political Science and Law, China University of Political Science and Law Press, 1991), *General Catalogue of Kuomintang Government - Law* (compiled by the National Library, and published by Catalogue and Bibliography Press, 1990), and those collected from the National Library, Library of Peking University, Shanghai Library and Library of Shanghai Academy of Social Sciences.

[337]Scholars such as Liang Qi-chao, Yan Fu, Xiong Yuan-han, Meng Sen, Wang Chuan-bi, Wu Jing-xiong, Qiu Han-ping, Ruan Yi-cheng, Zhang Ruo-yuan, Mei Ru-ao etc as cited in He, "Birth and Growth of Modern Jurisprudence," 495–6.

[338]See Article 12 of the *Treaty of Commerce and Navigation Renewed between China and Britain (also called Mackay Treaty), September, 5, 1902,* that provided that "China having expressed a strong desire to reform her judicial system and to bring it into accord with that of the Western nations, Great Britain agrees to give every assistance to such reform, and she will also be prepared to relinquish her extra-territorial rights when she is satisfied that the state of the Chinese laws, the arrangement for their administration, and other considerations warrant her in so doing." Cf. Shiming Zhang, "Re-Examination of Abolishing Consular Jurisdiction," *Frontiers L. China* 10, no. 2 (2015): 344–45.

[339]*Decree for Law Reform*, March 11, 1902.

[340]He, "Birth and Growth of Modern Jurisprudence," 496.

[341]He, "Birth and Growth of Modern Jurisprudence," 498, where He cited Qi Chao Liang, *The Collection of Yin Bing Shi, Vol. 5* (Shanghai: Shanghai China Bookstore, 1936), 43.

Another scholar, Meng believed that the law should not be the product of history, but instead should represent the current place, time, and social aspirations; he represented the *idealistic school* of thought.[342] Wu Jing-Xiong rejected the excessive focus on morality, which suppresses creativity and tries to artificially produce a harmonious society.[343] Meng encouraged litigation in society to bring out the truth and even went on to say, "true peace comes from litigation."[344]

After various discussions on western jurisprudential ideas, the Qing government finally and formally adopted the *Imperial Constitution Outline 1908*,[345] which could be called the first Constitution ever in China. It was to represent the meaning of *xian fa*. Thereafter, subsequent to the Wuhan uprising, the *Provisional Constitution of Republic of China (Zhōnghuá Mínguó línshí yuēfǎ) 1912* and then in 1931, the *Provisional Constitution of Titulary Period of Republic of China 1931* were promulgated.

In the middle period of the Kuomintang government, major concepts that were available in Western jurisprudence, such as rights and obligations, efficiency of litigation in the civil society, separation of powers, rule of law, international law, and so forth had arrived in China. Discussions among the then Chinese scholars later developed into the definition of law, essence of law, role of law, functions of law, forms of law, and so forth. Nonetheless, even after the development of scholarly debates and translation of western jurisprudence ideas, it was observed by the scholars that there was still disconnect between the theory and practice of law.[346]

During the proletarian revolution, the Soviet Union's philosophy of Marxism and Communism was dominant. It led to the *First Common Programme of the Chinese People's Political Consultative Congress*, which was promulgated in 1949 and officially adopted in 1954. It contained both the essential principles of Constitution guided by *Marxism – Leninism*, and the *thoughts of Mao Zedong*.[347] It mainly reflected the will of the dominant class. It was moderated by different classes based on their changing relationships.[348] It was marked by Lenin's own ideas:

---

[342]He, "Birth and Growth of Modern Jurisprudence," 503, where He discussed Meng's ideas as in Sen Meng, *New Introduction to Jurisprudence* (Shanghai: Shanghai Commercial Press,1911),23.

[343]He, "Birth and Growth of Modern Jurisprudence," 508, where He discussed Wu's ideas pursuant to Jiang-Xiong Wu, *A Study of Legal Philosophy* (Shanghai: Shanghai Law Translation & Edition Press, 1933), 15.

[344]He, "Birth and Growth of Modern Jurisprudence," 508, where quoted Meng and also discussed Jing-Xiong Wu, *A Study of Legal Philosophy* (Shanghai: Shanghai Law Translation & Edition Press, 1933), 26.

[345]*Qinding Xianfa Dagang 1908*.

[346]He, "Birth and Growth of Modern Jurisprudence," 512.

[347]Guobin Zhu, "Constitution Law and State Structure," in *Chinese Law*, ed. Wang Guiguo and John Mo (The Hague, London, Boston: Kluwer Law International, 1999), 25. *See also*, Albert H. Y. Chen, "The Developing Chinese Law and the Civil Law Tradition," *China Rev.* (1996): 30. http://www.jstor.org/stable/23453139.

[348]Guobin Zhu, "Constitution Law and State Structure," 25. *See also*, Jialin Wu, *Xian Fa Xue ('Constitutional Law')* (Beijing: The Press of Central Radio and TV University, 1985).

> The crux of constitution lies in: all basic laws of the state and laws relating to the power of election of the representative institutions and to the competence of the latter to express a contrast of all forces in class struggle.[349]

Marx's model of law was based on ideas in relation to the need for structural reforms that can make the working class's struggle successful. Law according to Marx has symbolic and practical dimensions.[350] The new thought of Mao Zedong followed Confucianism to an extent, but feudalistic thoughts within it were filtered out to help achieve the Communist utopian society. Confucian thought about loyalty to family was converted to loyalty to the Chinese Communist Party ("CPC") and the state.

In the Maoist school of thought, any written law was eschewed in favor of general principles, resulting in there being no written laws in the 1970s. Elements of Legalism were also borrowed in the Maoist school of thought, particularly the idea that the state can only determine what is right and what is wrong with the exclusion of religion-related morality.

The four Constitutions were adopted in 1954, 1975, 1978 and 1982 along with 1949 Common Programme. The *1954 Constitution* emphasised the concept of 'the socialist legality'.[351] The *1975 Constitution* was less focused on law, but instead preferred to focus on the class struggle.

In 1978, it was affirmed that the *proletarian revolution* for class struggle had succeeded in China, and thereafter a new Constitution was promulgated. Finally, a new Constitution was promulgated in 1982; this Constitution is still in use in the PRC, and has four principles as set out in its Preamble:

- ◆ The socialist road;

- ◆ The people's democratic dictatorship;

- ◆ The leadership of the CPC; and

---

[349]Guobin Zhu, "Constitution Law and State Structure," 25, where Zhu discussed Jialin Wu, *Xian Fa Xue ('Constitutional Law')* (Beijing: The Press of Central Radio and TV University, 1985), 36.

[350]Robert Reiner, "Classical Social Theory and Law," in *Introduction to Jurisprudence and Legal Theory: Commentary and Materials*, in *Jurisprudence and Legal Theory: Commentary and Materials*, Anne Barron, et al. (London: Butterworths, 2002), 246.

[351]See Guobin Zhu, "Constitution Law and State Structure," 30 for further discussion on this concept.

◆   The guidance of Marxism - Leninism and Maoist thought.[352]

It was the first time in Chinese history that the rulers were also to be governed by the Constitution, as the Constitution was declared supreme.[353] The Constitution of 1982 has been amended in 1987, 1993 and 1997, 2004 and most recently in 2018. This is the Constitution that is applicable currently in the PRC.

However, the disconnect between the theory and practice of real jurisprudence, and its purpose in modern China continued until the *Third Plenary Session of the Eleventh Central Committee of the Communist Party of China*.[354] The route of making amendments to Constitution is usually taken to allow for policy changes as determined by the CPC. The 1993 amendment to *PRC Constitution 1982* introduced the concept of '*socialist market economy*'.

According to the ranking from top to bottom, the major legislative documents are – Constitution of the PRC (as amended), basic laws such as civil law by National People's Congress ("NPC"), laws, resolutions and decisions by NPC Standing Committee, Administrative laws and regulations and normative documents made by State Council, and local rules and regulations of Local People's Congress & Local People's Government at the provincial level. The rapid development of the economy has, however, led to supervisory issues over the local rules and regulations.[355]

3.7 Jurisprudence in context of Practice by Judges and Lawyers in Modern China

Jerome Cohen, as far back as 1980, wrote:

> ... both in basic assumptions and in institutions and practices, judicial administration in contemporary China displays some striking resemblances to its predecessor under the Chinese empire.[356]

---

[352]Guobin Zhu, "Constitution Law and State Structure," 31; the principles were restated in General programme of the *Constitution of (Communist Party of China) CPC 1997.*

[353]See *Constitution of PRC 1982*, Art. 5.

[354]He, "Birth and Growth of Modern Jurisprudence," 512; this session was held from 18 - 22 December 1978 and is famous for 'reform and opening' policy of China; more attention was paid to the economy and the push to make 'China a strong powerful socialist country.'

[355]Guobin Zhu, "Constitution Law and State Structure," 47.

[356]Jerome Cohen, ed., *Essays in China's Legal Tradition* (Princeton: Princeton University Press, 1980), 4, as quoted in Roderick O'Brien, "The Survival of Traditional Chinese Law in the People's Republic of China," *Hong Kong L. J.* 40, no. 1 (2010): 165.

The above statement is not surprising given that the seventh century Tang Code was similar to the twentieth century Qing Code in respect of the penal codes.[357] The influence of the many ancient jurisprudential theories is still there on the current legal system, and can still be observed by legal researchers, and therefore in the author's view, Cohen's statement is correct. This is the right time to bring in the words of scholars from the Qing Dynasty, Wang Kuo-Wei and Ching-I Tu, who discussed the concept of *conservatism*:

> [T]he essence of conservatism is "preservation of the ancient moral traditions of humanity." A conservative has a great respect for the wisdom of his ancestors and is somehow dubious of sweeping change. He regards society as "a spiritual reality, possessing an eternal life, but a delicate constitution: it cannot be scrapped and recast as if it were a machine." Most important is the conservative's belief that a civilized society "requires order" and the "tradition and sound prejudice can provide checks upon man's anarchic impulse," especially in a revolutionary age.[358]

Conservatism has had a profound effect upon the development of law in the PRC, even on the procedural aspects, and its effects are still relevant. For the sake of completeness, even though the above were major jurisprudential thoughts, it is important to appreciate at this stage that between the period of the Han dynasty in 206 BCE until the fall of the Qing dynasty in 1911, the dominant doctrines about morals were from Confucian thought. However, there were some emperors and dynasties which were also swayed by Buddhist and Daoist schools of thought and some elements of these are also reflected in current legal practice.

After the proletarian revolution that culminated in 1949, the PRC followed the concept of *'rule by law'*, where the Communist party of China through institutions ruled the populace by rule by law, instead of *'rule of law'*.[359] In the Confucian model also the purpose of law was to control the masses, and it appears that this tradition had continued after the 1949

---

[357]MacCormack, *Spirit of Traditional Chinese Law*, 3.

[358]Ching-I Tu, "Conservatism in a Constructive Forum: The Case of Wang Kuowei (1877–1927)," *Monumenta Serica 28* (1969): 188, as quoted in MacCormack, *Spirit of Traditional Chinese Law*, 32.

[359]O'Brien, "Survival of Traditional Chinese Law," N.7 on 166, where he distinguished the meaning as "Jurists distinguish between rule by law, and rule of law. The essence of the distinction is that in the former case, the ruler rules by means of law, but is not subject to the law, while in the latter the ruler is subject to the law. At best, China presently has a system of rule by law. However, in English, the terminology carries many assumptions. In order to avoid these, the author has chosen to use the neutral term "ruling according to law".

revolution.[360] This feature has affected all forms of legal institutions. However, it appears that with more senior officials being convicted for corruption in the last few years (2012 onwards), this implies, according to the author, a slow movement towards *rule of law*. In addition, jurists have been debating whether China has been following 'rule by ethics'. The *socialist legality* model of Chinese law which followed after 1949 slowly started moving into the realms of the *Romano-Germanic* family of law in the 1990s with various procedure codes that were promulgated.[361]

In 2000, scholars viewed the governing philosophy as '*rule by ethics*'; this was actually socialism in ethical form. However, it appears that 'rule by ethics' disappeared by 2003 in official circles, remaining only in academic discussion.[362]

Another similarity to Confucians in the current system is that in the initial years of the PRC, few laws were published by the authorities. However, this has changed in recent years. The PRC's accession to the World Trade Organization ("WTO") brought about profound changes in many published legislations in order to satisfy external and domestic stakeholders.[363] However, in practice, at local levels, many officials and official machinery are still in the Confucian mode and still believe that more dissipation of law and knowledge means more demands from the populace and could cause social unrest.[364] It is the author's view that the motive for drafting and publishing many legislations was more due to international stakeholders in the PRC's economy and society.

The bureaucrats are again all too powerful in the PRC today; in this way, it is very similar to the traditional Chinese system which relied on the administrative system with penal laws to manage the administration through powerful bureaucrats.[365] The PRC bureaucratic system is similar to such systems anywhere in the world, in which the bureaucracy prefers to manage problems rather than solve them. This means availability of only general guidelines in the absence of concise laws or may be the availability of multiple laws on same topic, will only assist bureaucracy to become all powerful in PRC. This will affect the practice of governance and even the practice of law in the PRC.[366] In the author's view, it may be one of the reasons why there is a gulf between theory and the actual practice of law in the PRC. This particular feature is one of the major reasons for the consternation noticed in external stakeholders.

---

[360]Roderick O'Brien, "Survival of Traditional Chinese Law in the People's Republic of China," *40 Hong Kong L.J.165* (2010): 167. *See also*, Ann D. Jordan, "Lost in Translation: Two Legal Cultures, Common Law Judiciary and the Basic Law of Hong Kong Special Administrative Region," *Cornell Int'l L. J.* 30, no. 2 (1997): 338.
[361]Albert H. Y. Chen, "Developing PRC's Civil Tradition," 30.
[362]O'Brien, "Survival of Traditional Chinese Law," 167.
[363]Ibid., 169.
[364]Ibid., 170.
[365]Ibid., 171.
[366]Ibid.

The traditional magistracy in ancient China used to operate both as the investigator and as the judge. Additionally, there was no requirement in ancient Chinese society for the magistrate to be perceived as impartial and distant when compared with the adversarial system of common law. Zhu is of the view that the *inquisitorial system* was also followed in the modern PRC's courts due to traditional Chinese practices, and not due to the classification of the legal system into civil or common law system as one might have expected.[367]

From the above discussion, it seems that in the current practice of law in the PRC, there are many elements from traditional jurisprudence that are still applicable to modern jurisprudence and practice. However, there are views within the academic community that the customary laws were not incorporated fully into the PRC system.[368] Nonetheless, a few scholars would disagree with the notion that, in practice, more laws, clarifications and certainty need to be incorporated into the current legal system.

With the advent of the Internet, apps like Wechat, and mobile technology, it is very difficult to keep any policy, rules or local regulations away from the populace. The demands of the populace will only increase in the coming months and years, and in the author's view, the PRC's legal system, in practice, should be prepared for this eventuality. This is particularly true in the practice of adjudication of civil disputes between persons or businesses, especially when they might have cross-border elements.

Additionally, the PRC has demonstrated a desire to learn from and be influenced by foreign systems; for example, tax laws from the US and industrial property laws from Germany have influenced corresponding laws in the PRC. However, the PRC has still resisted the phenomenon of wholesale copying and transplantation.[369] The major changes introduced in the legal system were due to PRC's accession to World Trade Organisation ("WTO"), and the PRC's planned transition towards the socialist market economy. These changes brought profound changes in Commercial law and set the basic foundations of Civil law in the PRC. They also brought a profound understanding of the essence of law from the point of view of Marxist ideology. It was described in *China Grand Encyclopedia* (1984) as:

---

[367]Yikun Zhu, *Concise Chinese Law* (Beijing: Law Press, 2007), 3, and as discussed in O'Brien, "Survival of Traditional Chinese Law," 172.

[368]Jianfu Chen, "Civil Codification and Foreign Influence in China - Towards China's Own Civil Code," *Culture, Law and Order: Chinese and Western Traditions, Macao Ricci Institute* (2004): 221, and as discussed in O'Brien, "Survival of Traditional Chinese Law," 172.

[369]Wang Guiguo, "The Legal System of China," in *Chinese Law*, ed. Wang Guiguo and John Mo (The Hague, London, Boston: Kluwer Law International, 1999), 3.

[T]otal sum of the codes of behaviour enacted or approved by the State to be implemented with the guarantee of the State's power of enforcement in accordance with interest and will of the ruling class.[370]

Nonetheless, in the later years, PRC scholars changed the meaning of essence of law by adding qualifications:

[T]he nature of law is a reflection of the will of the ruling class, whose contents are decided by material conditions of the society.... while making the law the ruling class must take into account the endurance and strength of the ruled or the non-ruling class.[371]

However, from the 1990's the stamp of continental European tradition has been clearly visible in PRC law, and in the author's view, has surely affected jurisprudence. The scholars Ping and Jian summarize the point succinctly:

As two stages in the history of the development of Chinese law, the law of the Kuomintang period and the present law of the People's Republic of China have a necessary historical and cultural connection. This is an objective manifestation of the national character and continuity of Chinese legal development in the contemporary age.

It is true that for long periods after 1949, particularly in the 1960s, Chinese legislative work and the legal system could not undergo normal development. But since the 1980s, the legislative work and legal system of contemporary China have been able to develop rapidly and to perfect themselves step by step, even though there have existed many deficiencies in this process. It may now be predicted that the rapid progress of the Chinese legal system in future is an irreversible trend of history. And in this process, the characteristics of the Civil Law tradition [emphasis added] will continue to stamp themselves upon the Chinese legal system.[372]

3.8 Various Comparisons

---

[370]Ibid., 5.

[371]Guiguo, "Legal System," 5–6, where Guiguo quoted Shen from Zongling Shen, ed., *Jurisprudence (Fa Li Xue)*, 3rd ed. (Taipei: Beijing University Press, 2009), 28.

[372]Albert H. Y. Chen, "Developing PRC's Civil Tradition," 53, where Chen quoted Jiang and Mi from Ping Jiang and Jian Mi, "The Civil Law Tradition and Contemporary Chinese Law [Part II]. (Lun Minfa Chuantong Yu Dangdai Zhangguo Falii (Xia))," *The Tribune of Political Science and Law (Zhengfa Luntan)*, no. 3 (1993): 7.

The author will carry out various comparisons between the two jurisdictions in following paragraphs.

3.8.1 Comparison of Jurisprudence – Common Law v PRC

Ancient Chinese classic thinkers Zichan and Shuxiang put forward two classic arguments around 536 BCE:

- Laws need to be publicized for the people to have clear instructions to follow;

- Law alone without societal norms will not be able to bring lasting change in the populace.

These arguments were later fleshed out in detail by later Chinese thinkers a few thousand years ago and settled into two groups: *Fajia* (the Legalists, who believed in the former argument), and *Rujia* (the second argument, followed by the Confucians) respectively. The first thread of rules, as discussed earlier,[373] is not very different from what common law jurisprudent Lon Fuller said in 1940 about the need for making public the procedural aspects of jurisprudence to allow the public to understand. The second argument later divided broadly into two groups under the questions '*what law is*' and '*what law ought to be?*'. These were called *positivism* and *natural law* respectively in western jurisprudence.[374]

There was a third group of jurisprudents, who argued in ancient China that any norms or laws or man-made rules or man-made institutions were the real cause of misery for the people and advocated a simpler way of life more in conformity with the way of nature, or *dao* (the Way). They were called *Daojia* or Daoists.[375] In modern times, in western jurisprudence, realists in the USA (of the 1920s and 1930s) and from the CLS movement of the 1970s and 1980s had similar views about the institutions and judges in the US, and advocated the *purposive approach* to the law.[376] Xunzi also raised questions about the purposive approach to the law.

The written law of Zichan also had the undesired effect of shaking the foundations of the aristocratic pillars of ancient Chinese society, who for centuries had maintained a monopoly over legal authority. It altered the perception of the populace toward authority and brought

---

[373]Refer, Chapter 3, §3.4.1 and §3.4.1.1.
[374]Refer, Chapter 3, §3.2.1 and §3.2.2 & §3.2.3.
[375]Refer, Chapter 3, §3.4.1.2.
[376]Refer, Chapter 3, §3.2.4 for Legal Realism and Critical Legal Studies.

in benchmarks in judgment. Written laws such as this were preferred only during times of chaos and social disorder. As a positivist Austin, many centuries later, was no different; he focused on making good laws and stated that the coercion of sanction was necessary. The positivist point of view of civil law tradition, as propounded by Kelson, states that any custom will need validation by the authority or through a higher norm (ending at the highest). Hart described these norms as *secondary rules* that are needed to identify the primary rules.

The focus of Confucians was on regulating human behaviour by principles that lead to a good society. It was generally thought that litigation (*song*), that by nature is adversarial, can only bring catastrophe (*song-ze zhong-xiong*). This in turn removed the focus from civil litigation, and turned it to finding solutions based on compassion, good social interactions and norms that were always higher than the written law. The focus of Confucian though on the need for authorities to cultivate themselves (*xiu-ji*) and ensure impeccable conduct by improving themselves (*zhengqi-shen*) means that high standards of conduct, integrity, fairness were demanded of authorities when dealing with subjects, though again the focus was not on the law but on good human behaviour.

Mencius, on the other hand, did refer to *ren-zheng* and the importance of educating the populace and human nature, but he did not emphasise the development of law. According to the author, Xunzi was the first Confucian to have come out with a theory on the development of law, albeit only for the commoners, with moral principles occupying the highest rank. This can be arguably compared with ancient Greek jurisprudence, with its focus on universal morality in the form of *jus naturale*, and its belief that people were capable of having a sense of justice based on this natural law.

Xunzi suggested a solution similar to the doctrine of precedents in the common law, whereby the judges could place the case in a category of similar cases, drawing an analogy (*yi leiju*) and deliberating (*yi*) on an appropriate solution. It was a remarkable view considering it was formed nearly 2400 years ago. Xunzi was a bridge between the pure Confucians and the Legalists in Chinese jurisprudential theory, as he stressed the importance of morals, but also developed a legal theory about the legal system and laws. Xunzi even raised questions about the purposive approach to the law. Hart also, in spite of being a positivist, stressed the *internal aspects to the law* which are used by the authorities and populace to accept the external rules that are there to govern them, in spite of the fact they are not compelled to follow them.

However, this is different from the hardcore Confucian view where the behaviour (*li*) of the populace is targeted, but it was governed by moral principles. In English jurisprudence, moral principles would be used only to fill the gap in the legislations and there is usually no role for them.

Daoists, on the other hand, had some similarity with the US' CLS movement of the 1970s and 80s. However, Daoists believed in authoritarianism, which put forward the belief that the common population should be deliberately deprived of knowledge. The followers of CLS and the Realist movement from the US seem to bring about a subtle purposive approach in secondary rules as proposed by Hart. According to these schools of thought, this purposive approach was to be followed by the judges during the interpretation of the legislations.

In summary, English jurisprudence has focused more on technicalities of secondary rules, of norms to validate the primary rules; morals have no place in the laws, though they can be used at times to fill in gaps in the law. In principle, populations following the Western common law jurisprudence were not coerced to follow any rule but should have an internal desire to respect the rules to maintain order. This summary is still valid in the current practice of English Law.

However, classical jurisprudence in ancient China predominantly was in the Legalist frame but with a Confucian touch. Even though there were many Codes, the stress on behaviour, vesting of all authority in the Emperor (*shi*), the domination of morality, and dislike for litigation prevailed, and persuasion & coercion were both used. However, in history, when the legalists, or legalists cloaked as Confucians, (*yang-ru yin-fa*) were dominant in most dynasties, the political elites would reject reason or deliberations because of their distrust of scheming, self-interested people. However, *compassion and benevolence* (*ci-ren, guo zhi mu ye*) had an important place. It also led to there being no concept of 'rights' in any of the ancient Chinese schools of jurisprudence, but a concept of having a share (*fen*) in resources for individual effort developed over time in ancient China.

The reference point is society rather than individuals' rights, as deduced from classical Chinese jurisprudence, in contrast to the excessive focus on individual rights in the English jurisdiction.[377] This led to a system of deliberations and debates in the English system and jurisprudence, while in ancient China, devotion to authority and strictly following the drafted codes became the norm; in the author's experience this is followed even today in the PRC courts.

At the level of practice by the judges in the courts in any jurisdiction, there are constant instances of the judges trying to find rules in the form of statutes, legislations, and case law, and subsequently exercising their *discretion*. But there are also regular instances in difficult cases, where no appropriate law is available. In those scenarios, the judges then proceed to apply general principles utilising the history of application of law in a similar set of circumstances. Many scholars describe the steps in relation to the application of law and

---

[377]Refer, Chapter 1, § 1.4.3 for Hosten's reference points in context to know the clear focus for carrying out Comparative law studies in different cultures.

filling in of the gaps by the judges as if these judges were rejecting the established rules.[378] Surprisingly, some of the principles that the judges employ to alter the established rules of the positivist model are actually based on justice, morality or natural law and so forth in the same way Xunzi and Hart suggested.

These steps of the judges create problems for positivists (in England & Wales) and legalists (in the PRC), whose focus exclusively is on the concept of '*what the law is?*', and it is painful for them to see that the judges are actually applying these principles at an adjudication level. The positivists and legalists are further shocked by the judges overturning the law established by valid norms pursuant to the positivists' jurisprudence.[379] Some positivists such as Hart could not ignore this fact in the practice of law in courts, where the judges' discretion is used regularly such as in the field of interim applications.

Hart argued that judicial practice is based on *judicial customary practice* that has been accepted by the law over the years. The guidelines established by the judges in various cases assist the courts in knowing the issues that affect the stakeholders, but in the PRC only the highest court can issue the guidelines, though there are instances of the local courts' guidance as well in the PRC. In the author's view, in commercial law and business, where speed is the key, more power being made available to the judges may be the key in any jurisdiction.

The focus of Confucians was on regulating human behaviour by principles and discarding litigation (*song*) to avoid catastrophe (*song-ze zhong-xiong*); because of this, the Confucians abhorred civil litigation. This had a profound effect in practice for receiving legal remedies in the PRC, as the overriding focus remains on finding solutions based on compassion, good social interactions and public interests. In the author's view it seems these norms, if we were to look from the point of view of English Jurisprudence, appears to be always higher than the written law. The external stakeholders with business interest can be puzzled by the application of such norms in PRC.

The Supreme People's Court's of China (SPC's) guidance and *CPL 1991 (as amended in 2012)*, in the author's view, are drafted on the lines of cultivating the judges and authorities (*xiu-ji*) and also affecting the behaviour (*li*) of the populace. The populace, and the judges have little room to exercise their own discretion for the cases before them. On the other hand, in England & Wales, Hart's theory of internal aspects to the law is used in the practice of law, so that the populace and more importantly the judges have to mandatorily follow the case precedents, laws as a reason or a benchmark, leaving the door wide open for the

---

[378]Ronald Dworkin, *Taking Rights Seriously* (London: Duckworth, 1977), 37. Dworkin was also discussed in detail in James Penner, "Law and Adjudication: Dworkin's Critique of Positivism," in *Introduction to Jurisprudence and Legal Theory: Commentary and Materials*, by Anne Barron, et al. (London: Butterworths, 2002), 346–51.
[379]Penner, "Law and Adjudication," 346–50.

judges to exercise discretion during the cases. The effect of this philosophy can be widely seen from the way in which procedural remedies in the English Courts have evolved, because the judges have exercised wide discretion.

Many remedies in English & Welsh courts have been developed using the arguments submitted to the judges by commercial lawyers, and it assisted greatly in ensuring that balance of interests among the parties is maintained not only when the orders are granted, but also for the necessary duration due to the effects of the orders. In the author's view, debate is required between the parties and even to challenge the judges in the PRC, especially in commercial law, as the stakeholders are working every day in that environment; therefore, in the author's view, it will not be catastrophic (*song-se zhong -xiong*) for the PRC legal system.

The author is mindful of the fact that debates are allowed in the PRC courts, but excessive reverence for the hierarchical authorities is not conducive for such open debates and can stymie the development of law in PRC. From 1986 onward, there has been a development of *General Principles of Civil law*, development of substantive law in various areas of law, and *CPL 1991*, thereby bringing in the legalist approach (*Faijia*). This has assisted the stakeholders, both local and external to be made aware of what the law is.

However, in the author's view and experience, the challenge lies in ensuring that court orders are respected not only because the populace has to follow it, but because it is in the interests of society and the development of trade and commerce, along the lines of Hart's internal aspects of the law. The continental size of the PRC is a major hurdle in ensuring uniformity throughout the legal system in all provinces. Uniformity is, in the author's view, what is needed to sustain the momentum of the astronomical growth of the PRC's economy, and to build the trust of stakeholders with commercial interests in the PRC courts. In commercial matters, especially international trade, this is also a matter of ensuring comity of nations is maintained, as most commercial courts throughout the world would tend to follow the path of reciprocity of availability of remedies in other jurisdictions.

This aspect will be further analysed in the context of general legal thought for the practice of law at an *adjudication level* and the issue of exercise of judge's discretion in the adjudication process. If the judges can alter the established rule, then no law can be considered safe at the level of practice of law in the courts, and this holds relevance in the context of the practice of civil litigation before the courts. Some limitations on the judge's discretionary power in English Courts and to some extent PRC courts are the rules that have been developed within the areas of deference to legislation, doctrine of precedent, courts' customs. This will have to be analysed from the jurisprudential aspect in forthcoming Chapters. These are other invisible factors that need comparing between common law and PRC law.

3.8.2   Comparison of Current Jurisprudence and its influence

As discussed above in §3,8.1, the focus on developing principles of justice that led to the development of procedural justice came out of the above jurisprudential processes. These thought processes also led to declarations such as the *Magna Carta 1215, Petition of Right 1628, Habeas Corpus Act 1679,* and these set-in motions further development of rights for individuals in the English common law legal system. *Procedural justice* was an extension of the above concepts as enshrined in the above Acts such as concepts of fairness, justice, equality of arms. These concepts are common to both common law and PRC legal system.

The jurisprudential theories of Hart in England & Wales and the influence of realist movements are still valid in the current legal system in the same way they were valid a few hundred years ago. These days the concepts of morality or policy reasons are often alluded to by judges to fill in the gaps in the law, following the purposive approach. The law in practice in the common law system is also taking on ideas from other disciplines regularly.

In England & Wales, the focus on the adversarial system to protect with all might the individuals' rights led to development of concepts along these lines, as well as principles within civil procedures such as judicial independence, access to justice and so forth. However, issues over the years in the English common law are becoming more complex due to intricate principles that are emerging out of the judgments. In addition, it has led to debates about whether the civil litigation system has been hijacked by adversarial lawyers and affected due to systemic procedural inefficiencies and so forth.

On the other hand, thousands of years of legal jurisprudence in ancient China have not led to the development of litigation culture, or led to culture of debates & deliberation, or allowed the current courts to focus strongly on individuals' rights. Through the concept of *conservatism*, old traditions are preserved even to this day to ensure order and have deeply affected even current jurisprudence in the PRC.

There are striking resemblances in the current legal system to the ancient power structure where the *rule by law* was favoured over *rule of law*; where the focus was on authorities, who were presumed to be brilliant masters (*ming-zhu*); where the focus was on virtue-based governance modeled on Confucian concepts; where the written law was to serve as a common benchmark for conduct for society; where the focus was on morals, concepts such as teaching by example (*shen-jio*), behaviour training and so forth.

These influences from ancient jurisprudence carried from the past into the present were also affected by the proletarian revolution, import of western ideas during Qing Dynasty, effect of socialism according to Marxism - Leninism and Mao Zedong's thoughts, resulting in the requirement for devotion to the CPC and the state, where religion was separated from the concept of morality. These concepts are preserved in Article 5 of *Constitution of PRC 1982*.[380]

Law is not supposed to be a means to control the masses, and this had a profound effect on development of civil litigation and civil law until *CPL 1991* was promulgated in the PRC. It also affected concepts such as judicial independence, judicial neutrality, supervisory systems such as that of procuratorates, administrative supervisory powers and so forth.

The above concepts and rules, though ideal for resolving the usual civil disputes in the PRC, are not adequate and flexible in the context of the advent of the socialist market economy after the 1993 amendment to *Constitution of PRC 1982*, as economic stakeholders are independent and autonomous and they require rule of law.[381] The need for market-friendly PRC courts has been further increased by the PRC's accession to WTO. It affects the issue of procedural injustice in any aspect of civil litigation as a result of lack of social justice.[382]

Many laws are enforced by administrative organs that are prone to arbitrariness and at times recklessness, and also raise the issues of impartial administration of justice along with principles of *judicial independence* and *judicial neutrality*.[383] These are the issues that are least needed in commercial litigation by the stakeholders.

The stakeholders require many remedies for the PRC courts, and a few of these remedies require exercise of discretion of the judges. But discretion does not mean arbitrariness, as experienced by stakeholders in the local PRC courts. On the other hand, in the common law system of England & Wales, access to justice is affected due to the escalating costs of solicitors and barristers, courts fees, and other costs. These systemic issues have over the years become serious issues for most common law jurisdictions and as discussed earlier, these legal systems seem at times to have been hijacked by vested interests.

3.8.3 Comparison of Origins of current Legal System and Philosophical Development

In the common law system, a framework for the legal system originated around the twelfth century, leading to the development of local customs; records were also compiled. The legal reasoning provided by the judges in their judgments was important for the development of

---

[380]Article 5 of *PRC Constitution 1982* provides: "The state upholds the uniformity and dignity of the socialist legal system. No law or administrative or local rules and regulations shall contravene the constitution. All state organs, the armed forces, all political parties and public organizations and all enterprises and undertakings must abide by the Constitution and the law. All acts in violation of the Constitution and the law must be investigated. No organization or individual may enjoy the privilege of being above the Constitution and the law."
[381]Huang Lie, "Rule of Law in China: Ideal and Reality," in *Constitutionalism and China*, in *Constitutionalism and China*, Buuyun Li (Beijing: Law Press, 2006), 189.
[382]Ibid., 179.
[383]Ibid., 183–84.

law. This was accompanied by developments such as jury trials, and legislations enacted to fill the gaps that remained after judgments. The emergent common law was thus made up of rules, doctrines, customs, norms and, later, maxims that were relevant to the working of judicial activities in the courts.

The emerging common law was also affected by natural law or the influence of foreign culture, but the most important thing for its sustainability as a whole was the *rules, doctrines, customs,* and *norms that were incorporated regularly in the future cases* in the courts. Their future use was also based on reasons that were consistent, constant, practical, contextual, and congruent with other parts of law. Additionally, these rules, doctrines, customs, norms and so forth were made after considerable debate & deliberation.

Eventually, common reasons came out of debates and oral arguments during trials in the common law system, which were coherent and not necessarily governed by the rules of morality. This brings into focus the issue of *culture of training of lawyers, the judges, and the legal clerks;* the soft aspects of training had to keep up with the development of law. In summary, there was an internal aspect of law that developed where the populace will respect the law, but this respect from the populace was not out of compulsion or coercion from the authorities.

Traditionally, the effect of the Confucian mode was that there were formal codes to govern the populace, but there also existed informal codes in society. There was also hardly any training in law, and even drafters of law were called 'petty clerks' (*dao-bi-li*). This was even repeated in the civil examinations which started during the Tang Dynasty (AD 618 – 906).

The focus of the thoughts and jurisprudence in ancient China was more on sharing the resources (*fen*) and there was no specific focus on individual rights. Traditionally, respect towards the law was missing in Chinese society. The only focus of law was limited to penal codes. However, with the arrival of western thought during the Qing dynasty and the arrival of imperial powers and the drafting of commercial treaties with them, there was compulsion to reform the legal system of China.

The resulting interaction of Chinese scholars with western scholars also acted as a catalyst to reform the legal system during the Qing dynasty. In the middle period of the Kuomintang government after the fall of the Qing dynasty, many principles from western jurisprudence arrived on Chinese shores.

Nevertheless, there was disconnect between theory and practice, and to certain extent it is still felt by many. The focus on training of lawyers and judges is a relatively new phenomenon in the PRC. In addition, bureaucrats, who were traditionally powerful in ancient China, were again all too powerful. This phenomenon was not very different to the traditional Chinese system's emphasis on an efficient administrative system managing the penal laws. The PRC also adopted the *inquisitorial system*, which is still followed in the modern PRC's courts, more due to principles of *conservatism*. The requirements for additional formalities such as *notarisation* or *legalisation* of evidence and other documents stems from the historical development of law in the PRC, but it definitely affects access to justice in relation to urgent applications.

General Principles of Civil law were finally introduced in the PRC in preparation for accession to WTO in 1986. In addition, the recent growth in the economy combined with the new focus on law means it will still take some time before the full legal system blossoms, especially in respect of training of lawyers and judges in continental-size PRC.

In summary, the legal system in the PRC is relatively new as compared to England & Wales, but it has picked up the pace in the last three decades by incorporating customs from ancient China and a few thoughts & influences from the Western legal systems. PRC law has managed to absorb foreign influences, while maintaining strict Chinese characteristics. However, whether these characteristics are adequate with the rise of the PRC as an economic superpower is not easy to answer.

The author's view is that the PRC might have to give up a few special Chinese characteristics in the realm of commercial law and civil procedure as more foreign & external stakeholders will come to rely on the PRC's legal system in the near future. This need for reforms will further increase with the PRC's '*Belt and Road Initiative*' and as the PRC continues to increase its share in global exports and imports.

From the 1990's, the PRC's legal system has shown the influence of continental Romano-Germanic civil traditions in contrast to the common law adversarial system. This aspect definitely has its own unique effects on PRC's procedural law. These effects are compounded by the availability of modest substantive law in PRC, along with the limited avenues of judicial and legal training in many provinces of the PRC. Most of the substantive law in the PRC was drafted as recently as the 1990s.

CHAPTER FOUR — LEGAL PHILOSOPHY OF CIVIL LITIGATION – COMMON LAW v. CHINESE LAW

4.1   Basic Introduction to Civil Litigation - England & Wales and PRC

In this Chapter the author will discuss briefly the structures of the courts in England & Wales as well as in the PRC. The basic steps of civil litigation in both jurisdictions will also be discussed. The author will introduce the relevant terminology used in both jurisdictions as well. In the later part of the Chapter, the legal philosophy behind civil litigation in both jurisdictions is discussed and then compared using comparative analysis. The distinction between the civil law involving general tort, contract or similar cases and commercial law involving bigger disputes about projects, company laws and so forth in both jurisdictions is also discussed. It is important to appreciate the comparative analysis in this Chapter to fully fathom the analysis going forward in Chapters 5, 6 and 7.

4.1.1 Court Structure in England & Wales

Briefly, the Court structure and related terminologies in England and Wales are as follows:[384]

- *The UK Supreme Court* – This is the highest court, and it hears appeals on points of law in cases of major public importance. In this Court, the judgments are given by Justices of the Supreme Court. The Supreme Court hears appeals from the Court of Appeal and in exceptional circumstances can hear appeals from the High Court. These appeals are normally heard by five Justices (formerly Lords of Appeal in Ordinary, or Law Lords), but there can be as many as nine such Justices.

- *The Civil Division of* Court *of Appeal* – It hears appeals on points of law in civil cases from all the courts. The Civil Division of the Court of Appeal hears appeals from all Divisions of the High Court and, in some instances from the County Courts and certain tribunals. The judgments are given by the Lord Chief Justice, Heads of this division, and Court of Appeal judges. The Civil Division is presided over by the Master of the Rolls. Bringing an appeal is subject to obtaining *'permission'*, which may be granted by the court below or, more usually, by the Court of Appeal itself. Applications for permission to appeal are commonly determined by a single Lord Justice, and full appeals are heard by two or three judges. The Civil Division of the Court of Appeal also deals with family cases.

- *The High Court* – It hears complex or important civil cases and appeals from the County courts. High Court judges use

---

[384]The author has prepared a basic Court system in a flowchart in Chapter 4, §4.1.1.

the title in office of *Justice.* The head office of the High Court is in London. The High Court consists of three divisions:

o *Queen's Bench Division ("QBD")* – where all commercial, common law cases of contract and tort & similar cases, and judicial review applications are dealt with.

o *Family Division* – where matrimonial cases are dealt with.

o *Chancery Division ("Ch D")* – all matters of insolvency, intellectual property, trusts, probate, deeds, company law, mortgages, and land-related issues are handled in this court. As discussed in Chapter 2, § 2.1.1.2 and § 2.1.1.3, it was originally the Court of Equity before it was merged with common-law courts between1872-75.

o There are *specialist courts* as well within the High Court such as Admiralty, Technology & Construction courts, Patent Court.

■ *County Courts* hear a wide range of civil actions, including small claims and family cases. They are located around each district in England & Wales. There are also Magistrates Courts, but they have limited jurisdiction in civil matters. *District judges* are full-time judges who deal with the majority of cases before the county courts of England and Wales.

■ *The Enforcement of Judgments Offices* enforces civil judgments. For the sake of completeness, it should be mentioned that there are a number of other tribunals outside of this court structure (for example, School Exclusion Panels, Employment Tribunals) which are equally important within the legal system – their supporting legislations explain their individual appeal routes.

Most civil cases are tried in courts that do not have a system of jury trial. The only exceptions are for cases involving libel and slander trials. In all the above courts, very briefly, the judges hear these cases on their own, deciding them by first finding relevant facts, then applying the relevant law to those facts – and there may be considerable arguments about what that law actually is – and finally giving reasoned judgments. The judges also decide on all matters of procedure which may arise during a hearing. The reasons cited by the judges in the cases are important for the development of common law as discussed in Chapter 3 of this book.

After their judgments, the judges then go on to decide the fees of any lawyers, court fees to be paid out by the parties involved, fees of expert witnesses, allowances that may be allowed to the litigants who have acted in person (without lawyers), earnings that have been lost by the litigants, and travelling & other expenses incurred by the parties and their witnesses. The general rule in relation to legal costs is that the unsuccessful party will have to pay the successful party's costs, but the judges have a wide discretion to depart from this rule under the *Civil Procedure Rules 1998*.

4.1.2   Procedural Steps in Civil Litigation in England & Wales

The author had also briefly discussed procedural steps in any civil litigation in Chapter 1. In more detail, the various procedural steps in civil litigation in England & Wales are as follows:[385]

- A claimant formally notifies the appropriate court (depending on nature and value of claim) by '*issuing*' a claim form;

- A defendant receives a notification of the claim through '*service*' of a copy of the claim form; service of the claim form must be made within the first four months of issue;

- *Acknowledgement* of the service of the claim form is filed with the court by the Defendant;

---

[385]Susan Blake, *A Practical Approach to Effective Litigation*, 8th ed. (Oxford: Oxford University Press, 2015), 107–29. *See also*, in detail, *Civil Procedural Rules 1998, SI 1998/3132 (as amended until August 2016)*. See also, "Civil Procedure: White Book Volume 1 & 2" (2015). *See also*, "Civil Procedure: White Book Volume 1 & 2" (2016). *Refer also*, Chapter 4, §4.1.2, where the author has prepared a basic step in civil litigation in England & Wales.

Figure 6: Structures of Courts in England & Wales

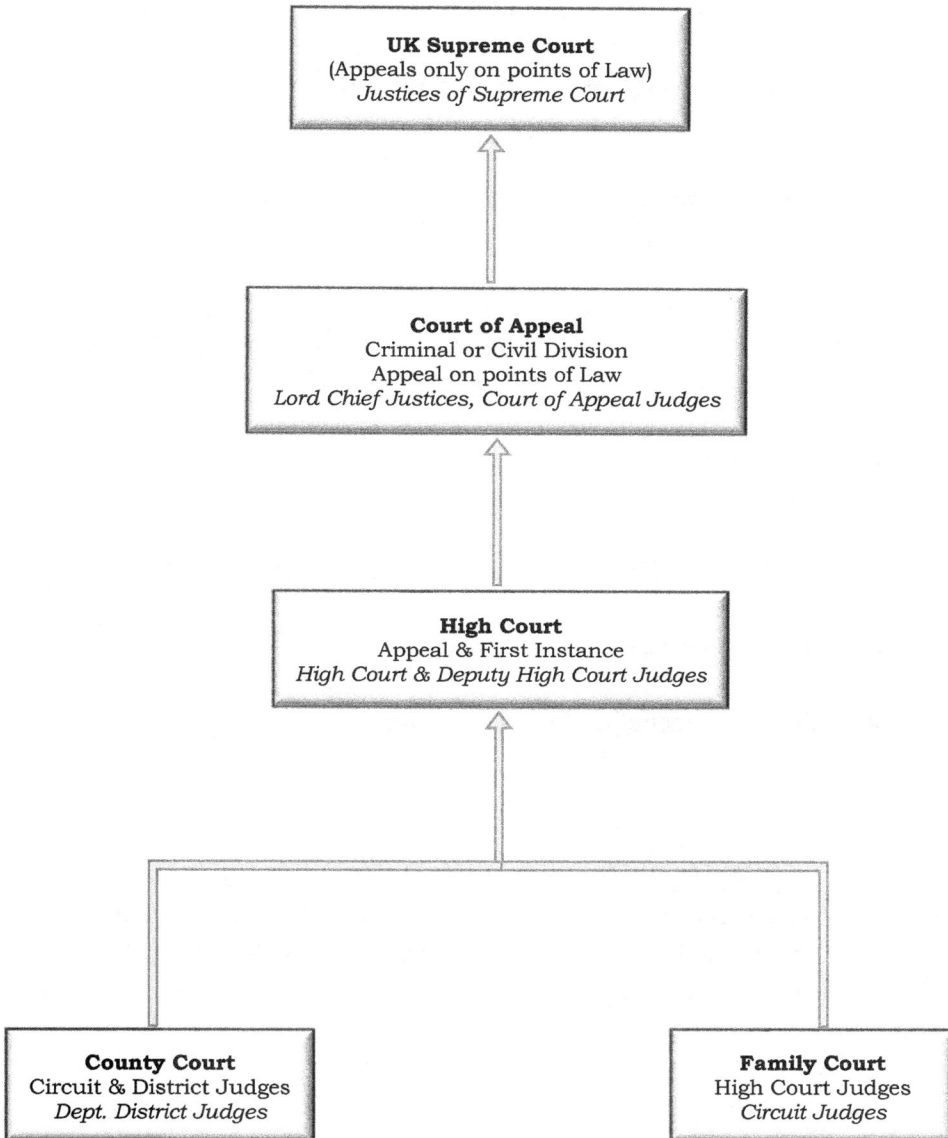

```
                    ┌─────────────────────────────────┐
                    │        UK Supreme Court          │
                    │  (Appeals only on points of Law) │
                    │    Justices of Supreme Court     │
                    └─────────────────────────────────┘
                                   ▲
                                   │
                    ┌─────────────────────────────────┐
                    │         Court of Appeal          │
                    │     Criminal or Civil Division   │
                    │      Appeal on points of Law     │
                    │ Lord Chief Justices, Court of    │
                    │        Appeal Judges             │
                    └─────────────────────────────────┘
                                   ▲
                                   │
                    ┌─────────────────────────────────┐
                    │           High Court             │
                    │      Appeal & First Instance     │
                    │ High Court & Deputy High Court   │
                    │            Judges                │
                    └─────────────────────────────────┘
                                   ▲
                                   │
              ┌────────────────────┴────────────────────┐
              │                                          │
  ┌────────────────────────┐              ┌────────────────────────┐
  │     County Court       │              │      Family Court       │
  │ Circuit & District     │              │  High Court Judges      │
  │      Judges            │              │    Circuit Judges       │
  │  Dept. District Judges │              │                         │
  └────────────────────────┘              └────────────────────────┘
```

- The Claimant provides sufficient details of the claim, normally in *Particulars of claim*. This is followed by a *Defence and Counterclaim* from the Defendant; thereafter the Claimant can file a *Reply and Defence to the Counter Claim*;

- Additional party(ies) can be jointed to the main parties by an additional CPR *Part 20 procedure*;

- *Case management questionnaires* are filed by the parties to the civil litigation;

- *Case Management Conference* is held, where Case Management and allocation of the case are done by a Judge according to the complexity of the case;

- *Disclosure of evidence* (including what is not favourable) by each party;[386]

- *Exchange of Witness Statements and Expert Report*s;

- *Trial* of the case;

- *Judgment* including *Cost orders*; and

- Appeal

Interim applications can be made any time by any party in the civil litigation. In the usual course of things, interim applications are made at the Case Management Conference, unless there are urgent issues or tactical applications before the courts are needed.

---

[386]This is the step that is considered as most controversial by PRC lawyers about the common law system. PRC lawyers or even parties from the PRC fail to understand why they must disclose evidence that is unfavourable to them. These scenarios arise when parties are running their case in the common law system, such as in many shipping law cases that have the English jurisdiction clause.

Figure 7: Steps for Civil Litigation Pursuant to CPR 1998 (England & Wales)

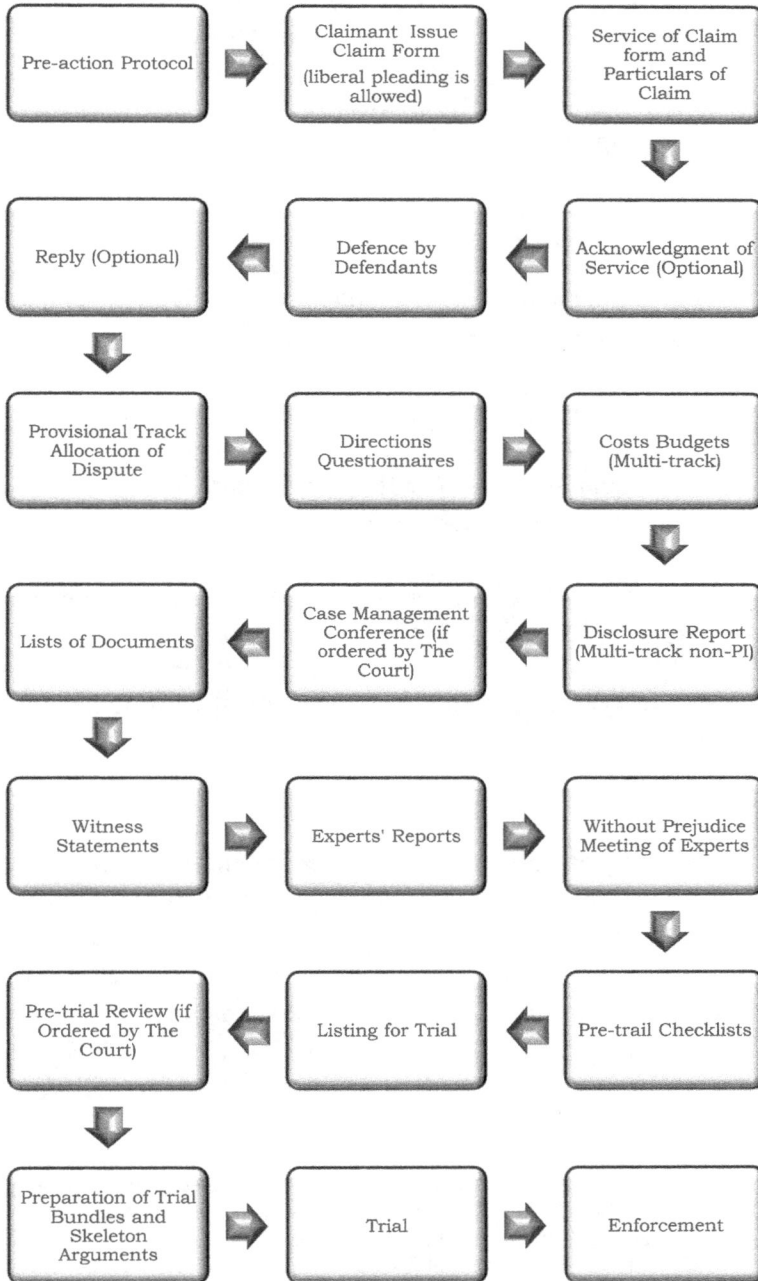

Pre-action Protocol	→	Claimant Issue Claim Form (liberal pleading is allowed)	→	Service of Claim form and Particulars of Claim
Reply (Optional)	←	Defence by Defendants	←	Acknowledgment of Service (Optional)
Provisional Track Allocation of Dispute	→	Directions Questionnaires	→	Costs Budgets (Multi-track)
Lists of Documents	←	Case Management Conference (if ordered by The Court)	←	Disclosure Report (Multi-track non-PI)
Witness Statements	→	Experts' Reports	→	Without Prejudice Meeting of Experts
Pre-trial Review (if Ordered by The Court)	←	Listing for Trial	←	Pre-trail Checklists
Preparation of Trial Bundles and Skeleton Arguments	→	Trial	→	Enforcement

4.1.3 Court Structure in PRC

There are many aspects of civil litigation in any jurisdiction. In this section, the basic court structure and procedural steps in civil litigation in the PRC will be briefly discussed.

The structure of the PRC's Court system is characterised by four levels and two instances of trial:[387]

- National Supreme People's Court based in Beijing, including Circuit Courts in the various provinces;[388]

- High People's Courts at the provincial level;

- Intermediate People's Courts (at prefecture level), usually in the capitals of provinces in the PRC;

- Basic People's Courts at country level, including People's Tribunals;

- There are also special courts such as Military Courts, Maritime Courts, Forest Courts and Railway Courts.[389]

The PRC follows the principle of *two instances*: as the first instance, the trial is carried out, and any subsequent appeal from the first instance takes place in the Intermediate People's Court and the High People's Court. The case may also be transferred from the lower court to the higher courts. The jurisdictions of the courts are decided both hierarchically and geographically. Intermediate People's Courts have jurisdiction as the courts of first instance over cases involving foreign

---

[387]See Art. 2 of *Organic Law of People's Courts of PRC 1979 (as amended in 1983)*. See also *Organic Law of People's Courts of People's Republic of China 1979 (as amended in 1983)*, Art. 2. *Refer also*, to flowchart highlighting the court structure in PRC, another flow chart to highlight the status of courts within the PRC as they must report to National People's Congress and the last flow chart relates to the Procuratorate system in the PRC that is the supervisory system.

[388]Circuit courts are a crucial step in China's judicial reform. They are meant to facilitate the filing of inter-provincial cases and prevent local-government intervention, thus freeing Beijing headquarters from complex cases and policy issues in relation to the judicial system.

[389]Arts. 2 and 18 of *Organic Law of People's Court of PRC 1979 (as amended in 1983)*.

elements.[390] Civil cases of first instance are tried in Basic People's Courts by a collegial bench consisting of both judges and assessors, or of judges alone. Assessors have the same rights and obligation as judges. Civil cases to which summary procedure is applied shall be tried by a single judge.[391]

In the PRC, the Procuratorate system works in a similar way to the Court system, and it has similar hierarchies to the PRC court system. The Procuratorate supervises the functioning of the courts, in particular, trials in criminal and civil courts at all levels of the courts within the legal system. This organ within the Constitution of the PRC even has investigative powers within the legal system. It also has another role within the PRC system, that is to ensure public interests are maintained.

4.1.4 Procedural Steps in Civil Litigation in PRC

An overview of procedural steps in civil litigation in PRC courts is important in the common law versus PRC debate. The important procedural steps in the PRC's civil litigation process are as follows:[392]

◆ Filing and accepting lawsuits with *Motion of complaint* and satisfying all the requirements of *CPL 1991*.[393] It has been observed by many stakeholders that many times the claimants could not pass the hurdle of satisfying the court officials of his case, and his applications are not accepted. This aspect is discussed in relation to the Standard of Proof in context of evidence that is required by the court officials even at this stage of the process. Such evidence must accompany the application;

◆ *Mediation* should be attempted by the parties before the case is passed through the courts;[394]

---

[390]See Art. 18 of *CPL 1991 (as amended in 2012)*.
[391]See Art. 39 of *CPL 1991 (as amended in 2012)*.
[392]See the flow chart in this section of the book, where all the procedural steps in the civil litigation in PRC legal system can be seen for easy reference of the readers.
[393]See Arts. 119, 120, 121 of *CPL 1991(as amended in 2012)*.
[394]See Art. 122 of *CPL 1991(as amended in 2012)*.

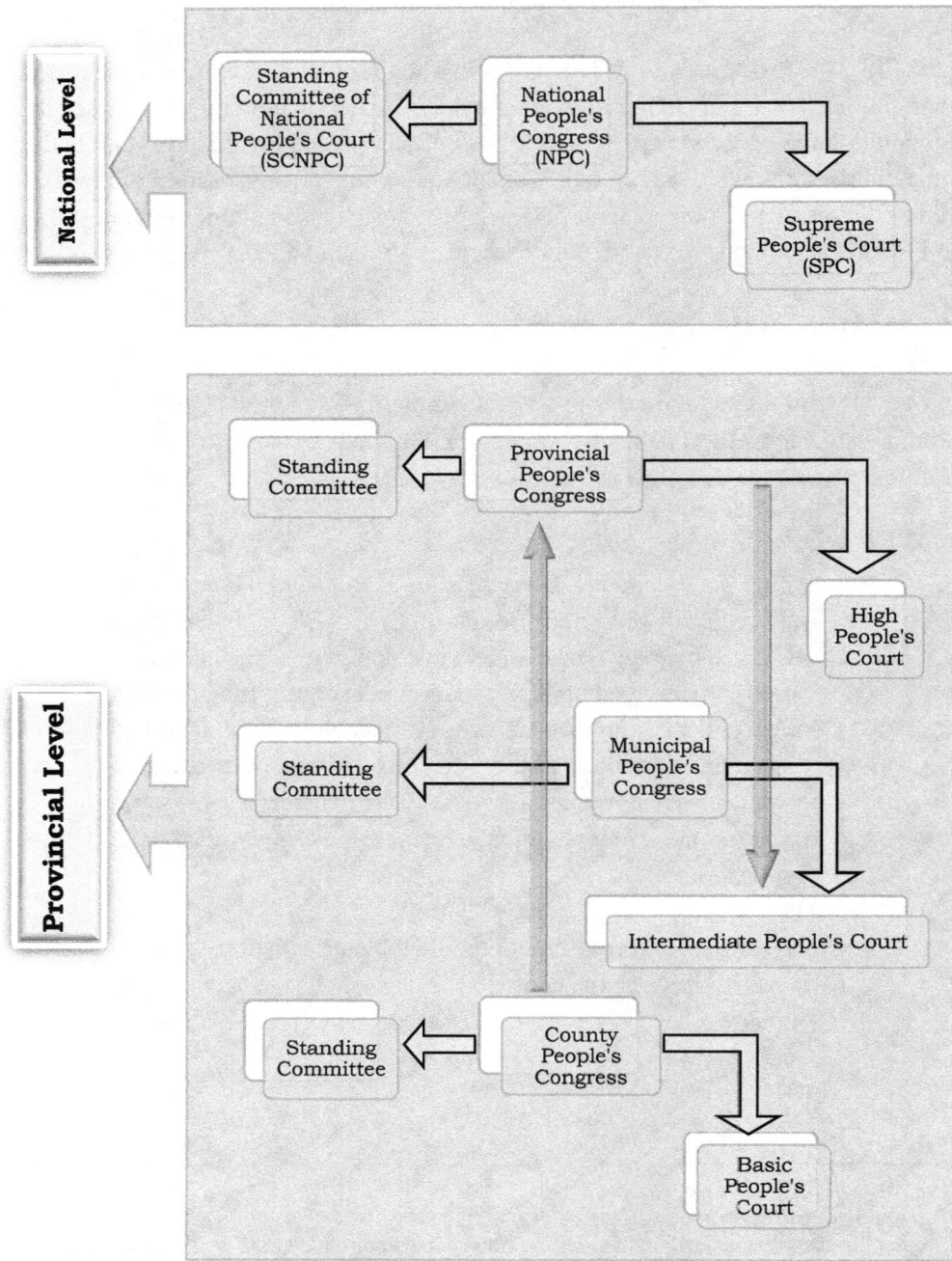

Figure 8: Relationship of Courts with Legislature and Governing body: Highlighting no separation of power

Figure 9: Structures of Courts in People's Republic of China's (PRC)

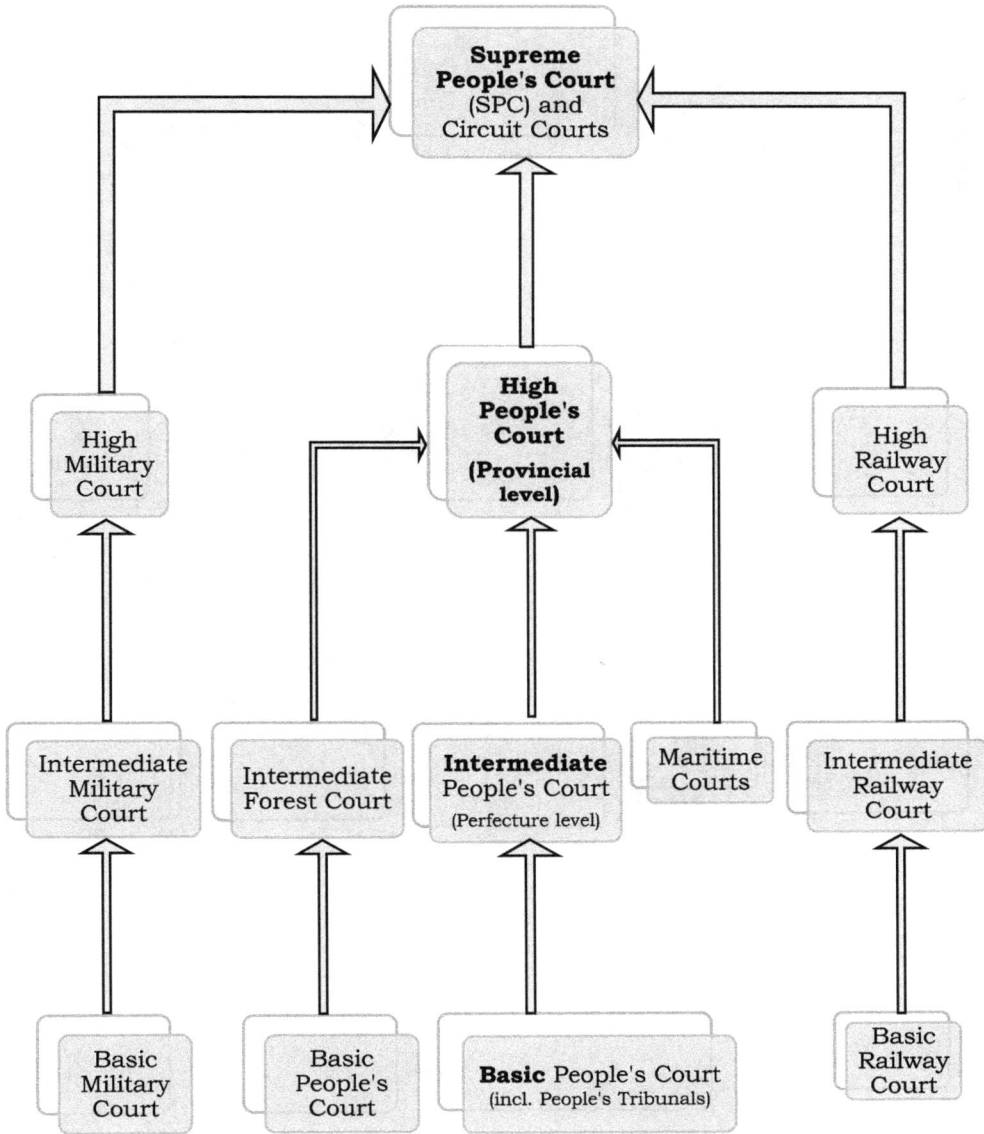

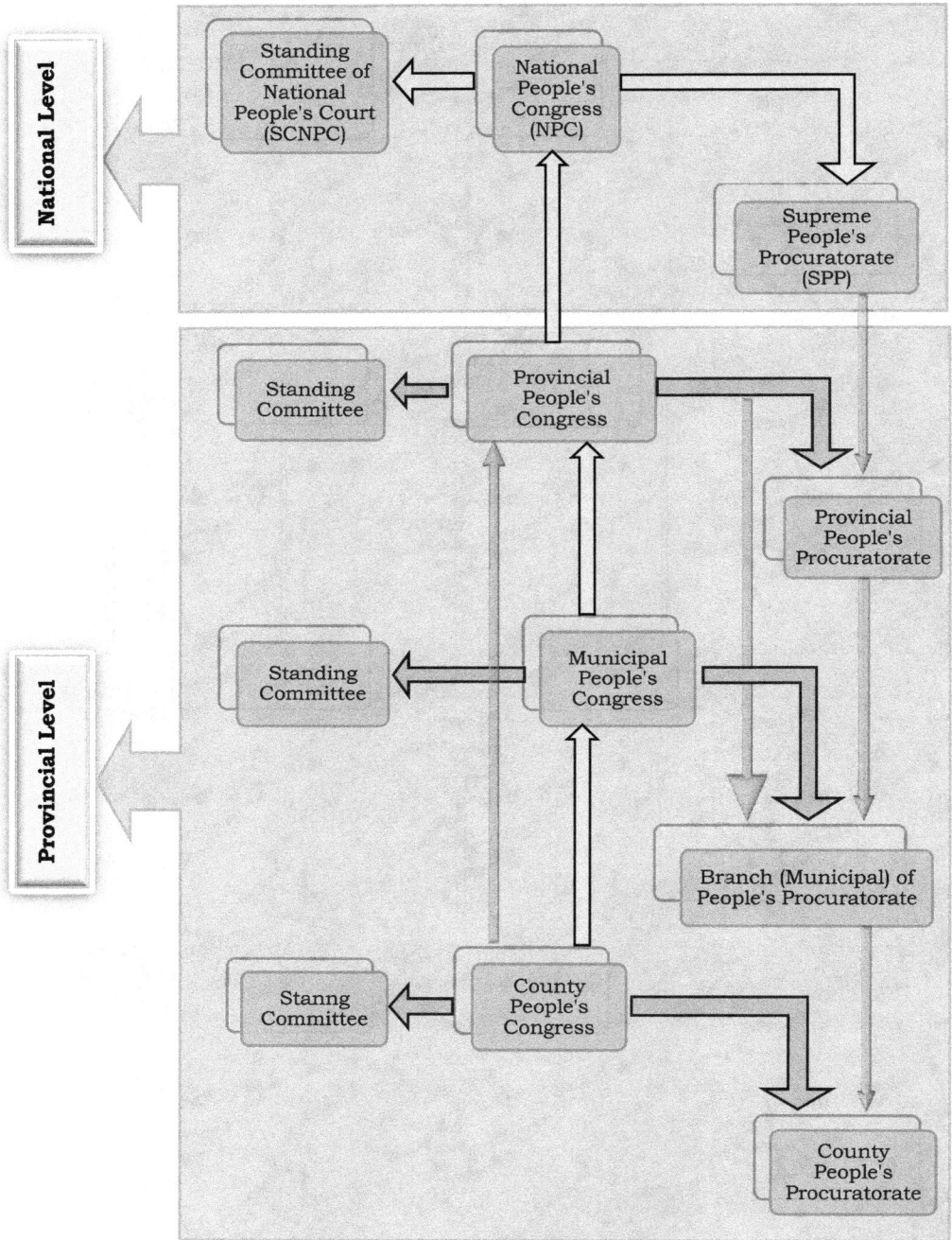

Figure 10: Procuratorates System (Supervisory System) in PRC: Supervises Courts and Decisions

National Level

Standing Committee of National People's Court (SCNPC)

National People's Congress (NPC)

Supreme People's Procuratorate (SPP)

Provincial Level

Standing Committee

Provincial People's Congress

Provincial People's Procuratorate

Standing Committee

Municipal People's Congress

Branch (Municipal) of People's Procuratorate

Stanng Committee

County People's Congress

County People's Procuratorate

◆ Pre-trial preparation with the claim passed to the defendant in five days. Defendant has fifteen days to present the defence satisfying the conditions of the courts;[395]

◆ Courts inform the parties about their rights and obligations going forward;[396]

◆ Argument as to the jurisdiction (if any) is dealt with, and collegiate bench is established. Thereafter, the parties are informed within three days of its constitution;[397]

◆ Investigation by the courts as to the dispute by entrusting an adjudicating person at the courts or other courts in another jurisdiction within the PRC;[398]

◆ Courts can decide the process relevant to the dispute – (1) Where the parties concerned have no dispute and the requirements of the procedure for hastening debt recovery are met; such procedure may be initiated by the court ; (2) Where mediation may be conducted before trial, mediation shall be conducted in a timely manner to solve the dispute; (3) The summary procedures or ordinary procedures may be applied according to the specific conditions of the case; and (4) Where a court session is needed, the focus on the dispute may be clarified through requiring the parties concerned to swap evidence or by other means;[399]

◆ Summary procedure can be decided by the courts according to the facts of the case;[400]

◆ Trial is conducted in open courts, including opening statements, exchange of evidence and experts' reports, adducing new evidence, and cross-examination, including debate between the litigants;[401]

---

[395]See Art. 125 of *CPL 1991(as amended in 2012)*.
[396]See Art. 126 of *CPL 1991(as amended in 2012)*.
[397]See Arts. 127 & 128 of *CPL 1991(as amended in 2012)*.
[398]See Arts. 129, 130 & 131 of *CPL 1991 (as amended in 2012)*.
[399]See Art. 133 of *CPL 1991 (as amended in 2012)*.
[400]See Art. 157 of *CPL 1991 (as amended in 2012)*.
[401]See Arts. 139, 140, 141 of *CPL 1991 (as amended in 2012)*.

- ♦ Mediation can be tried again if the parties agree before the judgment;[402]

- ♦ Judgment is usually given within six months of case filing date;[403]

- ♦ Motion of appeal by any party to the litigation, if any, within fifteen days after the judgment;[404]

4.2 Legal Philosophy of Civil Litigation Influencing the Judges

The author has discussed earlier in this book that the civil litigation system is an alternative to the self-help system that often led to violence in the past.[405] However, participation in civil litigation is also voluntary, which means parties are not compelled to come to the legal system to seek help to resolve their dispute. Civil Litigation has a close relationship with the substantive law in any legal system but has also developed many principles independently of the substantive law.[406]

Civil Litigation serves a public purpose even though private disputes are resolved through it. Many third parties such as family of an injured person, and/or local or central government, and/or other stakeholders in commercial disputes and so forth have stakes in such litigation in courts. In most jurisdictions it is not a dispute resolution center that is fully publicly funded. However, civil litigation definitely has a public purpose, as stated by the Chief Justice of New South Wales, Australia, another common law jurisdiction similar to England & Wales:

> The enforcement of legal rights and obligations, the articulation and development of the law, the resolution of private disputes by a public affirmation of who is right and who is wrong, the denunciation of conduct in both criminal and civil trials, the deterrence of conduct by public process with public outcomes — these are all public purposes served by the courts, [emphasis added] even in the resolution of private disputes. An economist might call

---

[402]See Art. 142 of *CPL 1991(as amended in 2012)*.
[403]See Art. 149 of *CPL (as amended in 2012)*.
[404]See Art. 164 of *CPL 1991(as amended in 2012)*.
[405]Refer, Chapter 2, §2.1.2, Origins of English Procedural System.
[406]Refer, Chapter 2, §2.4, Comparative Relationship between Substantive & Procedural Law.

them 'externalities'. They constitute, collectively, a core function of government.[407]

Habscheid also said:

> Since the state embodies the social system, procedural law reflects the ethical, ideological and political ideas which characterise a society. In consequence, the law of civil procedure must not be considered in isolation, but rather as an integral part of the ideas and conceptions which are expressed in the constitutional order.[408]

Therefore, when anyone studies any issue in civil litigation, every aspect of the legal system, its jurisprudence, associated political thoughts, its stage of economic development and so on must be analysed. Civil procedure systems have been divided into two major types in the comparative studies –Romano-Germanic & Anglo-Saxon systems (together called *systemes liberaux*), and socialist systems.[409]

In socialist systems of civil procedure systems, an individual that is a subject of litigation is a member of a society and of a class. Therefore, all legal philosophy will rotate around this concept. This has a considerable bearing on the role of the courts and their approach during litigation in courts. An inquisitorial regime is common in socialist systems. In western legal systems, the concept of procedural rights is inherent in an individual and not conferred on the litigant; this is an important distinction from socialist systems.[410] As a result, the legal philosophy in western systems, even in civil systems such as in Germany, is more in tune with the adversarial concept (*principe de contradiction*), and there is no room for outside third-party interference,[411] or any retrial without the request of the litigants. It is important to appreciate from the start what is considered as a matter that can be considered as 'civil' and can be brought to the civil courts. In England & Wales,

---

[407] J. Spigelman, "Judicial Accountability and Performance Indicators," *Civil Justice Quarterly* 21 (2002): 26. www.http://ssrn.com/abstract=1802176 as quoted in J. A. Jolowicz, "Civil Litigation: What's it For?" in *The Civil Procedure Ten Years On*, ed. Déirdre Dwyer (Oxford: Oxford University Press, 2009), 60.

[408] W. J. Habscheid, "The Fundamental Principles of the Law of Civil Procedure," *Comp. & Int'l L.J. S. Afr.* 17, no. 1 (1984): 2.www.jstor.org/stable/23246919.

[409] Habscheid, "Fundamental Principles of Civil Procedure," 2. Habscheid has clearly distinguished the civil litigation process in western liberal democracies from the socialist systems.

[410] Habscheid, "Fundamental Principles of Civil Procedure," 3.

[411] Ibid., 3–4.

Figure 11: Civil Litigation Steps Pursuant to CPL 1991 in People's Republic of China (PRC) (as amended in 2012)

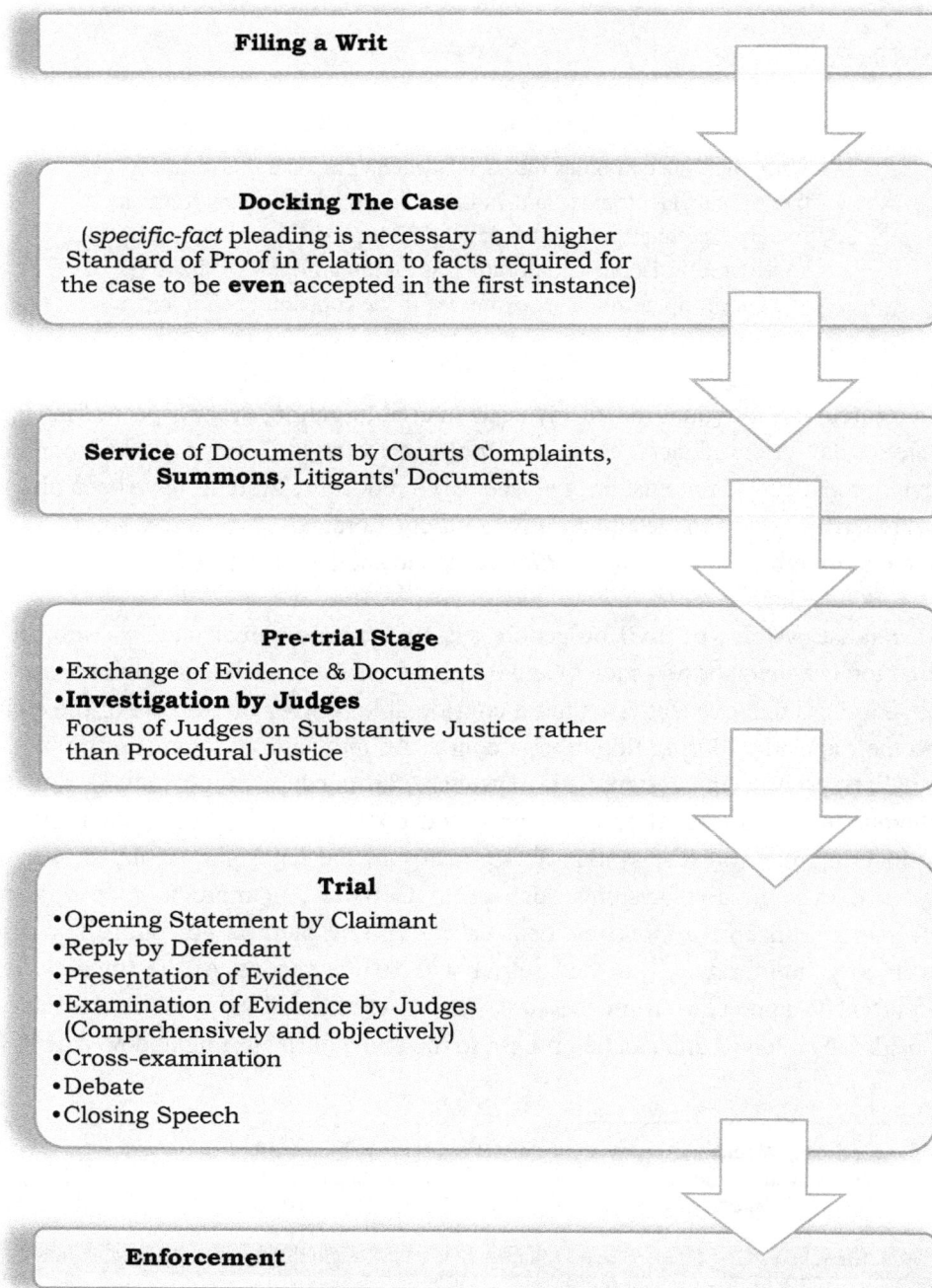

Filing a Writ

Docking The Case

(*specific-fact* pleading is necessary and higher Standard of Proof in relation to facts required for the case to be **even** accepted in the first instance)

Service of Documents by Courts Complaints, **Summons**, Litigants' Documents

Pre-trial Stage
- Exchange of Evidence & Documents
- **Investigation by Judges**
  Focus of Judges on Substantive Justice rather than Procedural Justice

Trial
- Opening Statement by Claimant
- Reply by Defendant
- Presentation of Evidence
- Examination of Evidence by Judges (Comprehensively and objectively)
- Cross-examination
- Debate
- Closing Speech

Enforcement

anything that is not governed by the criminal law is a civil matter and civil procedure rules will apply.[412] On the other hand in most continental countries, the deciding factor is the difference between private and public law.[413]

Legal philosophy of the civil courts has been influenced by political thought such as the *Seventh Amendment to the US Constitution 1792* that allows for the litigant's right to jury trial, or codification of principles in continental civil procedures, [414] International conventions such as Article 6 of *European Court of Human Rights 1998*, c 42 that provides for the right to a fair and public hearing, and, similarly, Article 14(1) of the *International Convention on Civil and Political rights of the United Nations 1966*.[415]

4.2.1 Legal Philosophy of English Civil Courts

It is often said in the English courts that the best judge to resolve the matter is an 'uninformed judge'. This means that the judge's decision is based entirely on the pleadings, evidence and arguments by the litigants or parties. It is common knowledge that pleadings are based on issues as decided by the parties themselves, which are formulated into those pleadings and presented to the civil courts. It means that the court's role (or judge's role in the common law system) is not to find the truth, but to decide upon the basis of what is in front of him, that is, pleadings, evidence and arguments.

In the case of *Air Canada v Secretary of State for Trade (No 2)*[416], where an International airline had a dispute with the Secretary of State for Trade that concerned landing charges at Heathrow Airport in London, the case went all the way up to the House of Lords. A few other airlines also decided to be included as the parties in the same case. This very interesting case came before the High Court; Bingham J at the High Court, in order to find the truth, wanted to see particular documents that were with the defendants. The claimants (airlines) could not state with certainty whether such disclosure would be useful or would damage their case. The Court of Appeal

---

[412]See dicta of Lord Goff in *Re State of Norway's Application (Nos 1 and 2) [1991]* 1 AC 723, where he clarified that all commercial matters can be considered as part of proceedings in civil matters. *See also*, *Evidence (Proceedings in other Jurisdictions) Act 1975*, c 34.

[413]C. H. Van Rhee and R. Verkerk, "Civil Procedure," in *Elgar Encyclopaedia of Comparative Law*, ed. J. M. Smits (Cheltenham: Edward Elgar Publishing, 2006), 120.

[414]See Principes Directeurs du proces in the first Chapter of *French Code of Civil Procedure 2007*.

[415]Rhee and Verkerk, "Civil Procedure," 4–5.

[416]2 AC 394 (HL).

and House of Lords disagreed with Bingham J. on important facets of jurisprudential issues on which the English civil procedure is founded.

Two statements from the House of Lords, need to be analysed deeply in order to understand the jurisprudential issue. Lord Edmund Davies bluntly said:

> to urge that, on principle, justice is most likely to be done if free access is had to all relevant documents is pointless, for it carries no weight in our adversarial system of law [emphasis added].[417]

Lord Wilberforce explained the jurisprudential position on English law in the same case as follows:

> Yet if the decision has been in accordance with the available evidence and with the law, justice will have been fairly done. It is in aid of justice in this sense that discovery may be ordered, and it is so ordered upon the application of one of the parties who must make out his case for it. If he is not able to do so, that is the end of the matter. There is no independent power in the court to say that, nevertheless, it would like to inspect the documents with a view to possible production for its own assistance [emphasis added].[418]

However, within the community of judges in England & Wales, this analysis is controversial. The argued that no party would ever come to the courts if the judges' role were not to find the truth of matter using procedures. Sir John Donaldson MR argued this point vehemently:

> Litigation is not a war or even a game. It is designed to do real justice between opposing parties and if the court does not have _all the relevant information_ [emphasis added and italics in original], it cannot achieve this object.[419]

---

[417]Ibid., 441 (Lord Edmund Davies).
[418]Ibid., 438 (Lord Wilberforce).
[419]See _Davies v Eli Lilly & Co_ [1987] 1 WLR 428,431(Sir John Donaldson MR).

Another judge, Denning LJ, in the High Court said the judges' objective in the courts is "above all to find out the truth [emphasis added] and to do justice according to law."[420] However, with the advent of the new *CPR 1998*, relatively more written evidence is now available to the judges; the old idea of the uninformed judge has slowly been replaced by judges who have a wealth of information, well in advance of a civil trial. Therefore, the old issues that existed pre-*CPR 1998* do not exist anymore with new *CPR 1998* and its case management principles.

Old issues which are no longer relevant with the new *CPR 1998* are: a) whether judges in the English courts should adjourn the case hearing for more evidence, or b) whether, according to jurisprudence, in principle, the judges really have power to adjourn the hearing to seek more evidence, or c) whether it is too late for the judges to adjourn due to the need for additional evidence in the middle of the hearing.[421]

Therefore, the question that could be asked by the author is whether, in the English procedural law, the English judges are under an obligation to find the truth in any case before him and whether this standpoint in English jurisprudence has finally arrived on the lines of continental civil law traditions? Jolowicz,[422] in order to answer this question, compared English civil procedure with French jurisprudence as a result of an amendment to the then-existing French civil procedural system in 1972 that provided:

> Everyone is bound to co-operate with the administration of justice
> with a view to revelation of truth.[423]

According to Jolowicz, the position in the English civil procedure is still different from the French law, and the case of *Air Canada* still retains jurisprudential authority in the courts. The main principle that still remains is in relation to the resolution of disputes, as emphasized in Sir Peter Middleton's report:

> Justice - by which I mean the satisfactory resolution of disputes -
> is part of the service sector of the economy.[424]

---

[420]See *Jones v National Coal Board [1957]* 2 QB 55, 63 (Denning LJ).
[421]J. A. Jolowicz, "Civil Litigation - Purpose?" 56.
[422]J. A. Jolowicz, "Civil Litigation: What's it For?" *Camb. L.J.* 67, no. 3 (2008): 56–58.
[423]See *Code de procedure civile 1806*, art 11, al 1.
[424]Peter Middleton, *Review of Civil Justice and Legal Aid*, Report to the Lord Chancellor (London: Lord Chancellor's Department, 1997), Chapter 1.

In order to understand the application and practice before the courts, the administrative purpose of civil procedure needs to be analysed closely. According to Lord Woolf, it is important to note that the goal of the civil procedure system is to ensure that fewer cases should pass through the filter, so that full-fledged civil trials can be avoided in most cases; he said, "My approach to civil justice is that disputes should, whenever possible, be resolved without litigation."[425] However, Fiss puts forward a dissenting opinion from across the Atlantic, which is very much against the policy of encouraging settlement:

> [T]hat settlement as generic practice is preferable to judgment... should be treated instead as a highly problematic technique for streamlining dockets.... Like plea bargaining, settlement is a capitulation to the conditions of mass society and should be neither encouraged nor praised.[426]

The author's view is that Fiss's statement, though true from the point of view of jurisprudence of a pure adversarial process, does not take into account the administrative burden that is required to manage the huge case load of such civil disputes at the executive level of any state. At times, the clients' objectives are in fact fulfilled by mechanisms available at the courts that ensure settlements, rather than encouraging the parties to be adversarial and request civil trials at the courts.

With the advent of new *CPR 1998*, the case management powers of the courts have been considerably increased; it is the author's view that it is no longer the case of the 'uninformed judge' in civil law cases. If the powers that are available to the courts are used effectively by the judges, then it will be the case of very informed judge.

A number of legal philosophers, then, argue not only that the fairness of the process is desirable, but also that the civil process should ensure that the decisions are arrived at by the courts after using all tools available to the judges, pursuant to civil procedural code. These include tools available to the judges to find the truth in

---

[425]Lord Woolf, *Access to Justice: Final Report to the Lord Chancellor on the Civil Justice System in England and Wales* (London: HMSO, 1996), 107. This Report was discussed in J. A. Jolowicz, "Civil Litigation - Purpose?" 58.
[426]Owen M. Fiss, "'Against Settlement'," *Yale L.J.* 93, no. 6 (1984): 1073–92.

disputes. Therefore, in this context, it is argued by the scholars that judgments should not be confused with settlements or amicable solutions reached through Alternative Dispute Resolution mechanisms.

Judges should no longer rely only on the *Statements of the parties*;[427] and further, no judges should believe that such statements of parties are gospel truth in the context of the cases put forward by them. Without any doubt, in any litigation, one of the parties must be saying the truth or must be relying on the result of *cross-examination*.[428] Jolowicz discussed Wigmore's statement[429] that cross-examination is the greatest ever legal engine invented for the discovery of truth, from which various inferences could be drawn.

In the author's experience, no matter how competent and skillful a lawyer is when cross-examining a witness, there are seldom any witnesses who will readily agree that they have breached a contract or have been a participant in conduct that could be penalized in the law. Ultimately, the result will be based on inferences, guesswork and speculation. However, it is the author's view that the new case management powers under the new *CPR 1998* have given ample ammunition to the judges to at least try to find the truth, while maintaining the adversarial nature of litigation in English courts.

4.2.1.1 Overriding Objectives and Secondary objectives of English Civil Procedural Code

It is important to introduce and highlight in full the first rule, *CPR 1998* r. 1.1 that provides as follows:

> (1) These Rules are a new procedural code with the **overriding objective** [emphasis added] of enabling the court to deal with cases justly and at proportionate cost.
>
> (2) Dealing with a <u>case justly and at proportionate cost</u> [emphasis added] includes, so far as is practicable –
>
> (a) ensuring that the parties are on an equal footing;

---

[427] See *Ex p Lloyd (1822) Mont 70*, where Lord Eldon was reported to have said, "[T]ruth is best discovered by powerful statements on both sides of the questions."

[428] John Henry Wigmore, *A Treatise on the Anglo-American System of Evidence in Trials at Common Law -V3* (Whitefish: Literary Licensing, 2012), 1367.

[429] J. A. Jolowicz, "Civil Litigation," 508. Jolowicz discussed Wigmore in context of cross-examination.

(b) saving expense;

(c) dealing with the case in ways which are proportionate –

(i) to the amount of money involved;

(ii) to the importance of the case;

(iii) to the complexity of the issues; and

(iv) to the financial position of each party;

(d) ensuring that it is dealt with expeditiously and fairly;

(e) allotting to it an appropriate share of the court's resources, while taking into account the need to allot resources to other cases; and

(f) enforcing compliance with rules, practice directions and orders.

The *CPR 1998* r. 1.1(1) is referred to as the *primary* objectives of *CPR 1998*, while *CPR 1998* r. 1.1(2) is referred to as the *secondary* objectives of Civil Procedure Rules of England & Wales.

The most important terminology from *CPR 1998* r. 1.1(1) are the words as '*overriding objective*'. The meaning of the word 'overriding', according to the Oxford English Dictionary, is 'able to overtake or supersede another authority, or taking precedence over all other subjects, or considerations, or predominant and primary'. In many legislations, before the advent of the new *CPR 1998*, the concepts of a few statutes having an 'overriding' effect was only understood by legal stakeholders.[430]

However, the moot question that is asked by legal scholars has been whether this overriding objective can trump anything else. To answer this question, the evolution of the new *CPR 1998*, a part of which was discussed in Chapter 2 of this book, needs to be discussed in detail.[431] However, from the jurisprudential point of view, it is important to trace the arguments in legal philosophy leading up to the new civil procedural code. In the various Lord Woolf Reform Reports, different meanings were provided for this concept of '*overriding objective*'. In the *Interim Report*,[432] the

---

[430] A few examples such as s 70(1)(g) *Land Registration Act 1925 (repealed)* c 21 ,15 and 16 Geo 5, whereby certain interests in registered land can override the entry on the register & s 1 *(repealed)* of the *Employment Act 1989*, c 19, which can have similar effects. Even within the new *Civil Procedural Rules r. 35.3* titled 'experts', an expert has an overriding duty to the court, where the expert's duty to court will override any duty even to his own client, who has appointed the expert; s 42 of *Access to Justice Act 1999*, c 22, where advocates have duties to act with complete independence in court when exercising rights of audience were also discussed in Déirdre Dwyer, "What is the Meaning of CPR r 1.1(1)," in *The Civil Procedure Rules Ten Years On*, Déirdre Dwyer (Oxford: Oxford University Press, 2009), 72.

[431] Refer, Chapter 2, §2.1.2, where the origin of New English Procedure Code was discussed in detail.

[432] Lord Woolf, *Access to Justice: Interim Report to the Lord Chancellor on the Civil Justice System in England and Wales* (London: HMSO, 1995).

overriding objective was itself called '*general objective*', and even in the *Final Report*,[433] leading up the Civil Procedure Code, it came under the heading of '*overall objective*'.

Therefore, while it seems that the judges and the courts could utilize the concept of overriding objective to trump other rules, in fact, the meaning of the concept of 'overriding objective' is in fact much broader. This concept of overriding objective encompasses the concept that lawyers and judges should also keep the overriding objectives in mind when analysing the other rules of new *CPR 1998*.

It was further stated, that the judges should not rely on the cases concerning civil procedure as a matter of precedence, but instead should use these cases to ensure that there is consistency in application of the new *Civil Procedure Code*.[434] This is known as the *purposive approach* and even Lord Woolf's Final Report, which was prepared before the Civil Procedural Rules came into existence, seems to be suggest that this is the best approach. In the Report, the idea of '*purposive construction*'[435] was highlighted:

> Although the rules can offer detailed directions for the technical steps to be taken, the effectiveness of those steps depends upon the spirit in which they are carried out. That in turn depends on an understanding of the fundamental purpose of the rules and of the underlying system of procedure... Rule 1 ... provides a compass to guide courts and litigants and legal advisers as to their general course.[436]

However, in a case,[437] where the default judgment was given against a party that was not the correct defendant and subsequently the civil court justified this decision on the basis that it could not be set aside due to the operation of the concept of overriding objective to prevent escalating costs. The judge in this case was not willing to allow the procedural errors to be corrected. This justification by the civil court was severely criticised by lawyers, academics and judges. Even a few other jurisdictions that

---

[433]Lord Woolf, *Access to Justice: Final Report to the Lord Chancellor on the Civil Justice System in England and Wales*.

[434]Dwyer, "Overriding Objective," 73.

[435]Refer Chapter 3, §3.2.4, where scholars of Legal Realism school of thought laid emphasis on a demand for purposive construction during judicial activities.

[436]Lord Woolf, *Access to Justice: Final Report to the Lord Chancellor on the Civil Justice System in England and Wales*, n2 [20.10]. Quoted in Dwyer, "Overriding Objective," 70.

[437]See *Law v St Margarets Insurance Ltd [2001] EWCA Civ 30, 18 January 2001*.

usually follow the English courts also rejected the overriding approach of the English courts in this particular case; for example, Hong Kong (part of the PRC but operating under the banner of 'one country two systems') had similar concerns about such a powerful tool being put in the hands of inexperienced judges.[438]

In the author's view, the fact that the authorities gave such a powerful tool to English judges means that they believe in their competence and training, and in fact empowered them by doing so. This can be contrasted with the PRC system where, far from empowering judges, there is a supervision system to keep an eye on judges, in the form of the Procuratorate System.

It is important to note that there are jurisdictions such as the US, where a similar purposive approach was used in their own *Federal Rules of Civil Procedure 1938*;[439] later, a similar approach was followed in South Australia via section 2 of the *Supreme Court Rules 1987*. In fact, they were the pioneers in the purposive approach to the interpretation of the civil procedure rules. However, it is important to note that civil law jurisdictions such as the *German Zivilprozessordnung 1877* and French *Nouveau Code De Procedure Civile 1975*, both of which are famous for introducing the case management approach, did not take the similar approach based on the concept of overriding objectives, as was done in common law jurisdictions.

4.2.1.2 Quasi-Public nature of English Civil Procedure Code

Many traditional jurisprudential philosophers, who are firm believers in the traditional adversarial system of English Law, are generally not pleased that there is a 'quasi-public'[440] aspect to disputes, even if the cases are between private parties. This is in complete contrast with civil law jurisdictions, in particular the PRC jurisdiction as discussed in Chapter 1, where judges must consider public purpose to civil litigation involving private commercial disputes according to the PRC Code.[441]

---

[438]Civil Justice Reform (Hong Kong), *Final Report of the Working Party on Civil Justice Reform* (Hong Kong, 2004). http://www.civiljustice.gov.hk/eng/archives_fr.html, as cited in Dwyer, "Overriding Objective," 71.

[439]See *r.* 1 of *Federal Rules of Civil Procedure 1938 (US)* provides that "These rules govern the procedure in all civil actions and proceedings in the United States district courts...They should be construed and administered to secure the just, speedy, and inexpensive determination of every action and proceeding." *See also,* s 2 of *Supreme Court Rules 1987 (Australia)* that was superseded by *Supreme Court Civil Rules 2006.* See also, Dwyer, "Overriding Objective," 70.

[440]A term used in J. A. Jolowicz, "Civil Litigation."

[441]Refer, Chapter 1, §1.2.

To demonstrate the quasi-public nature of disputes, it is necessary to discuss a particular case from English Law.[442] In this case, the dispute was between one of the Councils in London (Bromley London Borough Council ("LBC")) and the overall London Administrative Council ("LAC"). The LAC had decided to reduce the fares for the local buses and trains by 25%, but that reduction had to be paid for by various Local Councils in London. One such local Council, LBC, rejected the proposal, and sued the LAC (on behalf of the Bromley residents) on the grounds that everyone who lived in Bromley would have to pay for the fare reduction through increased taxes. Even though the case was between the two parties, there were many stakeholders, for example, the local taxpayers living within the tax jurisdiction of Bromley and all commuters using the local trains and buses within London.

In the above case, the taxpayers of Bromley prevailed over the LAC, and as a result any tax increase arising out of fare reduction was ruled as unlawful. This means that the LAC will have to consult all local Councils in future before taking any similar decisions.

In such cases, as discussed above, there are instances of repercussions and conflicts of interest. In many jurisdictions such as France, these types of cases will not even be considered as a part of civil litigation procedure but will rather be the part of *administrative jurisdiction.* Similarly, there are other cases that are in the field of law of tort which also have many stakeholders. This itself will generate lots of conflicts of interest.

Therefore, in the author's view, the increased efficiency in case management after the advent of *CPR 1998* means that disputes between parties are being resolved; but the courts will always be mindful of public interests even in private disputes.

4.2.2   Legal Philosophy of the PRC Civil Court

In the English civil procedural system, along with most continental civil procedural systems founded on western jurisprudence, there is an emphasis on ensuring *procedural rights.*[443] However, in the PRC system there is an emphasis on securing *substantive justice.*[444] In the modern PRC Civil courts, ancient Chinese traditions

---

[442]See *Bromley LBC v Greater London Council [1983] 1 AC 768.*
[443] Kristie Thomas, "Dynamism in China's Civil Procedure Law: Civil Justice with Chinese Characteristics," in *The Dynamism of Civil Procedure – Global Trends and Developments*, ed. C. Picker and G. Seidman (London: Springer, 2015), 2.
[444]Margaret Y. K. Woo and Mary E. Gallagher, eds., *Chinese Justice: Civil Dispute Resolution in Contemporary China* (Cambridge: Cambridge University Press, 2011), 13. Woo has discussed that

have been combined with new ideas to draft a modern civil procedural law that sits pretty well within the ideas of *democratic centralism (min zhu ji zhong zhi)* and socialism, which is one of the fundamental principles of the Constitution of the PRC. Huo is of the view that the modern PRC civil procedure law, which is relatively new, adheres to the following principles:[445]

- ■ Principle of Right to debate;

- ■ Principle of right of action and various procedures in accordance with litigation theory;

- ■ Principle of maintaining a balance between procedural justice and substantive truth using theory of evidence;

- ■ Principle of the role of binding arbitration, mediation and adjudication and related adjudication theories and their combination with Judgment;

- ■ Principle of supervision and retrial theory.

For the first principle, the starting point is Article 12 of the *CPL 1991 (as amended)* that provides:

> When adjudicating civil cases by the people's court, the parties shall have the <u>right to engage in argument</u> [emphasis added].[446]

According to Chai and Chang,[447] the principle of right to debate is essential in litigation, to ensure the parties' positions can be preserved by debating both orally and in the written form. The right to debate is also part of the democratic rights

---

populations with experience with the courts have relatively more negative experience with the legal system. In addition, *distribution of justice* was preferred over *procedural justice*.

[445]Haihong Huo, "Chinese Expression or Theory of Civil Procedure Law," *Legal System and Social Development*, no. 4 (2013): 3–9.

[446]See Art. 12 of *CPL 1991 (as amended in 2012)*.

[447]Huo, "Chinese Expression in CPL" where he cited Yi Chang, Chief Editor, *The Civil Procedure Law* (Beijing: China University of Law and Political Science and Law Press, 1996), 69–70. Huo also cited Fabang Chai, *New Civil Procedure* (Beijing: Law Press, 1992), 96–97.

provided to its citizens. Even though in Article 12 of *CPL 1991* the right to debate is not specifically guaranteed, courts will ensure that litigants are provided the opportunity for right to debate.[448] If any civil procedure court deprives a litigant of such a right, then there are provisions for retrial in the *CPL 1991*.[449]

The principle of right to debate provided in the PRC system is a non-binding debate system, so that courts are not constrained by the facts presented by the parties, but the courts can choose to actively investigate. This system of debate is different from the continental civil law systems, where the principle of debate is binding in nature.[450] However, over the years, there have been demands from scholars such as Jiang Wei to adopt some of the principles of the continental civil law system. In the author's view, the demand is appropriate as the judges' power to investigate on their own pursuant to *CPL 1991* gives too much discretionary power to the judges. The discretionary power of judges is further discussed in Chapter 6.[451]

The second principle of civil procedure in *CPL 1991* is the *right to action*, which is based on the Soviet Union's binary theory right of action, which is based on procedural right and substantive right.[452] In theory, the courts should not prevent the right of action as long as the procedural requirements specified in *CPL 1991* are clearly satisfied.

However, in practice, there have been occasions where the judges have refused to accept cases on the grounds that adequate evidence and facts are not presented with the applications. In many instances, PRC judges have failed to distinguish between procedural rights, & the substantive rights that are essential at the judgment stage of the matter, and not when the matter is just at the initial right of action stage. In the author's view, this is also the result of inconsistent training of judges, and difficulty in maintaining consistency in all courts due to the continental size of the PRC. It could be argued that since the public interest is so important in PRC law, the authorities can filter out problematic applications from litigants at this early stage. This is a major issue that certainly needs rectification, in particular for foreign stakeholders in the PRC's economy.

---

[448]Huo, "Chinese Expression in CPL".
[449]See Art. 200(9) of *CPL 1991 (as amended in 2012)*.
[450] Huo, "Chinese Expression in CPL" where he cited Weiping Zhang, "Restatement of China's Principles of Debate in Civil Litigation," *Legal Research* (1996).
[451]Refer, Chapter 6, §6.3.3 in context of PRC judges' discretionary power.
[452]Huo, "Chinese Expression in CPL."

There is recognition amongst PRC scholars that the right of action in civil courts is related to various other issues such as human rights, constitutional rights and so forth.[453] Another issue that is relevant in the above context is the test of Standards of Proof in relation to the evidence that has to be filed with the claim forms. In addition, it is argued that the principle of right of action should exist alongside the abuse of such right of action by frivolous litigation wasting judicial resources.[454] *CPL 1991* has preserved the right to litigate for litigants.[455] However, in the author's experience, *CPL 1991* still requires a considerable amount of detail in the pleadings from litigants, before a court will even accept a case; the Standard of Proof at this stage is also a bit higher. Therefore, in the author's view, while in common law systems such as in the US or in England & Wales, where liberal pleadings are allowed to start a claim,[456] it is very different in PRC, where *specific-fact pleading* is required.[457]

In the third principle of civil procedure in *CPL 1991*, the delicate balance between substantive and procedural justice is maintained by appropriate Standards of Proof and theory of evidence. This concept is founded on Soviet jurisprudence, whereby there is a need to find the *objective truth* is favoured. This may be because traditionally the populace has preferred substantive justice over procedural justice.[458] Scholars in the PRC from 1990 onwards have commented on the issue of lower Standards of Proof for civil litigation as compared to the higher Standard of Proof for criminal litigation.[459] The topic of Standards of Proof is analysed further in Chapter 7.[460]

Pursuant to *CPL 1991*, PRC judges have to examine evidence '*comprehensively and objectively*'.[461] The Standards of Proof required in the PRC courts are higher than in common law courts, and maintain a delicate balance to satisfy scholars, who emphasise the need to find the '*objective truth*'. In order to balance the need for substantive justice with procedural justice, judges in the PRC have been given discretionary powers that are discussed in detail in the Chapter Six of this book.[462]

---

[453]Ibid.
[454]Huo, "Chinese Expression in CPL" where he discussed Ming Shao, "Abuse of Civil Litigation Law and Regulation," *Tribune of Political Science and Law*, no. 6 (2011): 175–80.
[455]See Art. 123 of *CPL 1991 (as amended in 2012)*.
[456]Scott Dodson, "The Challenge of Comparative Civil Procedure," *Ala. L. Rev.* 60, no. 1 (2008): 144.
[457]See Art. 121 of *CPL 1991 (as amended by 2012)*.
[458]Huo, "Chinese Expression in CPL" where he cited and discussed Zhixiang Wang and Zengrun Wang, trans., *Soviet Civil Procedure* (Beijing: Law Press, 1957), 65.
[459]Huo, "Chinese Expression in CPL."
[460]Refer, Chapter 7, §7.4.
[461]See Art. 64 of *CPL 1991 (as amended in 2012)*.
[462]Refer, Chapter 6, §6.3.

An important issue in relation to this principle is that it has a huge effect on what can be considered appropriate training for judges.[463]

Additionally, the concept of adverse consequences for the party that was unable to adduce evidence was introduced through the Opinions of Supreme Court.[464] By adopting the German system, judges in the PRC have been given the authority to allocate the Burden of Proof based on principles of fairness and honesty.[465] Gradually, more rules are being developed within the field of evidence, for example, the adaptation of rules about the acknowledgment of facts in the statements of others which can assist judges in their judicial activities.[466] Huo has discussed, in his article, these aspects in the context of the new developments that have assisted judicial activities.[467]

As to the fourth principle, the PRC has modified a system where mediation was given prominence in *Civil Procedure Code (trial basis)*,[468] as compared to the contemporary view, where parties can opt for mediation based on legal principles and can voluntarily agree to go through mediation.[469] In the current scenario, the trial is at the core of the adjudication system. In 2010, *Supreme People's Court on Issuing Several Opinions on Further Implementing the Work Principle of "Giving Priority to Mediation and Combining Mediation with Judgment"* clearly highlighted the role of mediation in the adjudication system.[470]

The policy reasons that have been cited for the existence of such principles in the context of mediation are, first, that this is based on Chinese characteristics; and, second, to ensure that personal and business relationships will remain intact. In addition, there is an important need to maintain social harmony despite rapid economic expansion.[471] Over the years, reforms have been made in this area, so that

---

[463]Huo, "Chinese Expression in CPL."

[464]See, Art. 2 of *Some Provisions of Supreme People's Court on Evidence in Civil Procedures [No. 33 of 2001] (as revised in 2008)*. It provides: "Where any party cannot produce evidence or the evidences produced cannot support the facts on which the allegations are based, the party concerned that bears the burden of proof shall undertake unfavourable consequences."

[465]See, Art. 7 of *Some Provisions of Supreme People's Court on Evidence in Civil Procedures [No. 33 of 2001] (as Revised in 2008)*.

[466]See *Some Provisions of Supreme People's Court on Evidence in Civil Procedures [No. 33 of 2001] (as Revised in 2008)*.

[467]Huo, "Chinese Expression in CPL" for further discussions.

[468]See Art. 6 of *Civil Procedure Law (Trial Implementation) 1982*.

[469]See Art. 93 of *CPL 1991 (as amended in 2012)*.

[470]*Supreme People's Court on Issuing Several Opinions on Further Implementing the Work Principle of "Giving Priority to Mediation and Combining Mediation with Judgment" (No.16 [2010] of Supreme People's Court)*.

[471]Ibid.

the separation of mediation and litigation within the court system has improved vastly. As a result of these reforms, litigants are given enhanced autonomy to resolve their disputes by mediation.[472]

The fifth principle of civil litigation is based on the process of trial supervision adopted from the Soviet Union's supervision procedure under their civil procedure law.[473] In countries practicing continental civil law system, the process of retrial is distinct from the 'retrial supervision procedure' that is available in the PRC. For example, according to section 578 of the *German Code of Civil Procedure*, retrial will be triggered when the judgment was based on false evidence, or if there were serious procedural violations. However, in the PRC, the motion for retrial supervision can be done *sua sponte* at the behest of the courts without it being triggered by the litigants.[474]

Finally, there is one more important principle that governs civil litigation in the PRC. Article 13 of *CPL 1991 (as amended in 2012)* provides:

> Parties shall follow the principle of honesty and good faith.[475]

4.2.2.1 Aims of PRC Procedural Code

Article 2 of *CPL 1991 (as amended in 2012)* details its aims as follows:

> to protect the exercise of the litigation rights of the parties;[476]
> to ensure the ascertaining of facts by the People's courts; distinguish right from wrong; apply the law correctly, try civil cases promptly;
> to affirm civil rights and obligations, impose sanctions for civil wrongs, protect the lawful rights and interests of the parties, educate citizens to voluntarily abide by the law;
> to maintain the social and economic order;
> to guarantee the smooth progress of the socialist construction.

---

[472]Huo, "Chinese Expression in CPL."
[473]Ibid.
[474]See Art. 198 of *CPL 1991 (as amended in 2012)*.
[475]See Art. 13 of *CPL 1991 (as amended in 2012)*.
[476]See also, Arts. 13 & 33 of *Constitution of PRC 1982*.

These aims as drafted within *CPL 1991* are similar to overriding objectives of *CPR 1991* in England & Wales. However, the aims as provided in *CPL 1991* are relatively less detailed in articles as compared with the English *Civil procedural code*. This may be due the fact that English courts have extensive experience of adversarial litigation. The above objectives in the PRC civil procedural system are supplemented as discussed earlier by important principles aimed at achieving the overriding objectives. In the author's view, a few of these principles are as follows:

◆ In the PRC, the principle of equal treatment and the principle of reciprocity are fundamental aims of *CPL 1991*.[477] It is important to appreciate that the principle of equal treatment depends on the principles that are available in the foreign courts for assistance being applied in the PRC courts for foreign nationals. Similarly, the *principle of reciprocity*, which is called the *principle of retaliation* in *CPL 1991*, ensures equality between countries.[478]

◆ According to Tang, the *principle of equal litigation* in *CPL 1991* has two meanings – first, the parties to litigation enjoy equal rights and obligations according to *CPL 1991*; and second, in judicial practice, the courts must safeguard the parties' litigation rights, and accordingly must treat the parties equally when applying the articles of *CPL 1991*.[479] Similarly, the aim of providing *equal opportunity* to parties is enshrined in *CPL 1991* in order to enable them to argue their case in PRC courts. [480] This principle of providing equal opportunity is provided alongside the *principle of disposition* of *CPL 1991*;[481] it means that the parties can exercise their civil rights and litigation rights within the scope of the law.[482]

---

[477]See Art. 5 of *CPL 1991 (as amended in 2012)*. *See also*, the discussion on Art. 5 in Weijian Tang, "The Evolution of Civil Procedure System of China," *Frontiers L. China* 7, no. 2 (2012): 205.
[478]See discussion on Art. 5 in Tang, "Evolution of CPL in PRC," 205. *See also, Civil Procedure Law 1991 (as amended in 2012)*, Art. 5.
[479]Tang, "Evolution of CPL in PRC," 205.
[480]See Art. 12 of *CPL 1991 (as amended in 2012)*.
[481]*Civil Procedure Law 1991 (as amended in 2012)*.
[482]Tang, "Evolution of CPL in PRC," 204–5 for further discussions on aims and principles.

Scholars in the PRC have acknowledged that even though these principles are enshrined in the law, there is a huge gap in the execution of such principles in the courts, pursuant to *CPL 1991*.[483] Scholars have recommended a separate legislation in order to fill this gap but it is a controversial topic and beyond the scope of the book.[484] This issue of a separate legislation has in fact raised demands for increased judicial supervision and separation of mediation under the civil procedure.[485] In the author's view what is missing is consistency in both the application of the rules throughout the local courts in the PRC, and also in the training of judges. As Tang says in relation to the principles of *CPL 1991*:

> In my view, there are two defining standards for the principles of the Civil Procedure Law: (a)implementing [these standards] throughout the [civil litigation] process; (b)serving the [purpose of providing] normative and guidance to the legislation, judicial and law obeying to the Civil Procedure Law.[486]

4.3 Historical Comparative Civil Procedure

Before the author starts to compare different aspects of the civil procedure of the two jurisdictions, it is important to look at comparative civil procedure in a historical context. As far back as in 1889, the Japanese government adopted the *German Code of Civil Procedure of 1877*[487] because of their belief that Germany was a successful developed nation, without doing a thorough comparative analysis of the then-existing codes in Japan.[488]

Another example of the adoption of the code of a different jurisdiction was the *Greek Civil Code of 1834*, which was a combination of the French and German codes, and came into existence without any comparative analysis.[489] However, there are instances where foreign influence upon the civil procedure systems was rejected, for example, in the USA, when it was suggested by a few US scholars that a few advantages of German civil procedure could be adopted in the US.

---

[483] Tang, "Evolution of CPL in PRC," 207–8.
[484] Ibid., 207.
[485] Ibid., 208.
[486] Ibid., 206.
[487] Gottwald, "Comparative Civil Procedure," 24–5.
[488] Gottwald, "Comparative Civil Procedure," 24, where he discussed the historical context H. Nakamura's 1971 article - "Die Rezeption Des Deutschen Rechts in Japan".
[489] Gottwald, "Comparative Civil Procedure," 24.

Gottwald's view is that even the German Civil procedure code is a mix of "German, Roman, Italian, French, Dutch, English and American influence".[490] Since the 1950, the World Congress of Procedural Law has been organised to study the comparative law process, with noble aims such as harmonisation and reforms of procedural systems. However, the research scholars that have attempted comparison of the civil procedures seem to have actually been comparing the legal systems in full, as the focus of early comparativists was only on comparisons of substantive laws in different jurisdictions.[491]

In the nineteenth century & immediately after the Second World War, civil procedure went through the stage of codification in many jurisdictions. However nowadays the focus of comparativists in this field has moved to transplantations of one procedural system into another jurisdiction's procedural system. It is only recently that attempts have been made by scholars to harmonise civil procedure laws, as can be seen in many research papers.[492]

4.3.1 Unpopularity of Comparative Civil Procedure

Scholars have cited various issues to suggest why comparativists have shown less interest in comparing civil procedure rather than other areas of laws from various jurisdictions. Gottwald, for e.g., has highlighted four reasons that the author will discuss here, one by one:[493]

First, Gottwald discussed the issue of *Lex fori*, where if a civil dispute is to be litigated between two parties from two countries, then the most utilised concepts are the conflict of law rules, as at times a foreign substantive law can govern a dispute in another jurisdiction. However, whichever jurisdiction the civil disputes were to be litigated in, local civil procedural rules will be applied by the local courts. Often, in such cases, the local lawyers and judges in the local courts have no interest in knowing the foreign procedural rules. However, in the author's view and experience where a party is dealing with the foreign country's civil procedural rules, those rules may or may not provide necessary comfort to the foreign litigants. For example, with

---

[490]Ibid., 25.
[491]James R. Maxeiner, "Legal Methods as a Point of Reference for Comparative Studies of Procedural Law," *XIIIth World Congress on Procedural Law, Salvador-Bahia, 16 to 22 September 2007* (2007): 1, http://ssrn.com/abstract=1232579.
[492]Ibid., 2.
[493]Gottwald, "Comparative Civil Procedure," 26.

the PRC's projects in Africa and SE Asia, the PRC companies and businessmen may have to litigate disputes in unfamiliar foreign jurisdictions.

With the increasingly globalised economy, more and more foreign litigants are experiencing commercial disputes and litigation in another country. There is no doubt that such litigants expect that the remedies available in the foreign jurisdiction pursuant to that system's rules will not be completely different from those of their own jurisdiction, and that the, foreign jurisdiction will be able to protect their interests. However, if the procedural rules in the foreign jurisdiction are not robust, then it can leave a bad taste in the mouths of foreign litigants, and consequently, can affect commercial trade and investments going forward. The only other area where comparative analysis in the field of civil procedure is usually pursued by research scholars is in the area of recognition and enforcement of foreign judgments and comparison of service rules, which allows them to obtain proofs using instruments of international judicial assistance.[494]

Another reason as to why comparative civil procedure has not been so popular is due to *divergent court practice*s, [495] and also due to difficulty in comparing civil procedures (rather than substantive law) between two jurisdictions. It will be difficult to measure and compare the exercise of discretion by judges (including availability of discretionary power to the judges) in the courts. In the author's view, as discussed earlier, in a country such as the PRC, which is as big as a continent, the local courts' practices also differ from one province to another province. Court procedure in one court in one province of the PRC cannot be treated as representative procedure in all local courts of the PRC. A similar observation to this effect was made by Murray, who said that one local court in Freiberg was not representative of all the courts in Germany.[496]

The courts are a symbol of constitution, where the relationships between the state and citizens are tested. The purpose of numerous courts in many jurisdictions is not only to render correct justice, but also to ensure the justice is delivered swiftly by making

---

[494]Ibid., 27.

[495]The term 'divergent court practice' was coined in Gottwald, "Comparative Civil Procedure," 27. It was used in the context of highlighting why comparative civil procedure has not become popular as compared to many topics in substantive law that have been compared by comparativists.

[496]Peter L. Murray, "A Morning at the Amtsgericht: German Civil Justice in Practice," in *Law and Justice in Multistate World: Essays in Honor of Arthur T. von Mehren*, James Nafziger and Symeon Symeonides (New York: Transnational Publishers, 2002), 779–92.

efficient utilisation of court resources,[497] to maintain the legitimacy of the courts and therefore, by extension the legitimacy of the state power.

In many jurisdictions, such as England & Wales, there is an application of human rights to the legal proceedings, and this can affect the proceedings and outcome. Clearly, any comparative analysis of civil procedure even within one jurisdiction is not a straightforward matter, but a product of many facts and influences. Due to these challenges, the field of comparative civil procedure has not been popular. Nevertheless, researchers (such as the author) are coming into this area of law gradually to solve common problems that are faced by litigants in almost all jurisdictions, especially in light of rapid globalisation.

Only in the last few years, due to the popularity of forum shopping, and the concept of *procedural advantages,*[498] have practising lawyers from one jurisdiction begun analysing key aspects of civil procedures from another jurisdiction, to be able to take advantage of a particular jurisdiction for their clients. However, as discussed above, there is a difference between knowing the procedural law in texts, and procedural law that is *actually experienced in practice* that a litigant might experience in a foreign jurisdiction.[499] The actual practice in the courts can make all the difference for litigants in civil disputes.

4.3.2   Purposes of Comparative Civil Procedure

Comparing the civil procedure of two jurisdictions can provide knowledge,[500] which can also be useful for practitioners in the area of *forum shopping*, or in cases where clients of a lawyer or businessmen have no choice, and therefore have to rely on civil procedural law in courts in another country's jurisdiction. A good comparative analysis can offer guidance about pitfalls and procedural advantages in another

---

[497]The concept of proportional use of court's resources as discussed in A. Zuckerman, *Civil Procedure: Principles of Practice*, 2nd Revised ed. (London: Sweet & Maxwell, 2006), 3. *See also*, Gottwald, "Comparative Civil Procedure," 28, where Zukerman was cited.

[498]See O. G. Chase, "American 'Exceptionalism' and Comparative Procedure," *Am. J. Comp. L.* 50, no. 2 (2002): 277, where issues such as pre-trial discovery and the possibility of liberal damages being awarded to the claimant were discussed to highlight the procedural advantages of the US as a jurisdiction where disputes can be litigated. The US as a jurisdiction is usually selected by parties via the forum clause in their contracts.

[499]Gottwald, "Comparative Civil Procedure," 27, where distinction between "law in the books" and "law in action" was described in the context of specific problems of comparative procedural law. *See also*, P. Gilles, "Eigenheiten der Prozessrechtsvergleichung" (1998), which was discussed by Gottwald in his paper.

[500]Gottwald succinctly said, "Comparative ...civil procedure in particular is working like a wonderful mirror: It opens your mind. The comparison increases your knowledge and wisdom." *See also*, Gottwald, "Comparative Civil Procedure," 35.

jurisdiction's civil procedures and rules to these practitioners. This will allow practitioners to assist their clients by being well-prepared, and thus avoiding nasty and costly surprises in that other jurisdiction.

The comparative civil procedure is also utilised within the context of law reforms, possibilities of legal transplants, harmonisation, unification of laws such as in the European Union, drafting new regulations, and drafting model codes that can be adopted by other countries. One such example is *UNICTRAL Model Law on Arbitration of 1985*, which has been immensely successful and popular in most jurisdictions.

4.3.3 Methodology of Comparative Civil Procedural Law

The author has discussed in Chapter 1 the functional approach that is becoming increasingly popular and is often adopted by comparativists.[501] However, such functional comparative methods are usually utilised by the comparativists in the context of comparison of substantive laws. This method of functionalism has been discussed in popular books on comparative law which compare German and the US civil procedural rules. In order to compare civil procedure, one must find the *invisible factors* that influence the external law. The invisible factors are usually the factors that are taken for granted by lawyers in their home jurisdiction.[502] Once again, in the author's view, the factors that a lawyer takes for granted are more relevant to the context of the substantive law.

Comparativists have taken the above concepts further and have discussed the use of the above methodology within the context of civil procedural rules. Chase has described the court procedures as follows: "[C]ourt procedures reflect the fundamental values, sensibilities and beliefs (the 'culture') of the collectivity that employs them."[503] Maxeiner suggests that the two approaches of *functionalism* and *culturalism* represent the similarities and differences respectively among civil procedural systems.[504] This means that in order to analyse the similarities and differences between English civil procedural laws and PRC procedural law, the

---

[501] See Chapter 1, §1.4.3, Konrad and Hein Functionality Method; according to this method, the researcher should focus on the problem, which must be stated in functional terms.

[502] Refer, Chapter 1, §1.4.3 and invisible factors such as custom, sub-customs, history including legal history, religion, ethics, geography, language, philosophy, caste, creed, foreign invasion or interpretation or translation or foreign influence.

[503] O. G. Chase, "American Exceptionalism," 278. Chase was also quoted in Maxeiner, "Legal Methods in Comparative Procedural Law," 2. Maxeiner has described this issue as 'culturalism'.

[504] Maxeiner, "Legal Methods in Comparative Procedural Law," 2. The discussion of 'culturalism' in context of comparative civil procedure is in many ways the same concept that involves analysing the invisible factors and contexts in general comparative law.

author must first take a functional approach to find similarities and then look through the prism of culture and invisible factors to find differences. The second step is a difficult one for any researcher or foreign lawyer, and even at times for lawyers within the same jurisdiction.

It is the amalgamation of jurists' opinions that form law and legal doctrines, and in the words of Maxeiner represent the "technical tool for organising society and those who see it as an historical development of the people's consciousness."[505]

In procedural law, it is very difficult to dissect varying functions in one element of procedural law,[506] and therefore, according to Maxeiner, various functions have to be analysed together. Maxeiner proposed a study of *legal methods* that govern how the procedural system will work in any jurisdiction. However, the purpose of civil procedure may differ in different jurisdictions, and highlights Fuller's question as whether the rules or the courts come first.[507]

In the civil law system, such as in the PRC, the rules come first and the court has to apply the rules. In the common law system, where the courts will come first, procedures take the primacy and norms must take the back seat. This is an important distinction one must appreciate.

The starting point of any legal methodology will include the whole process of creation of the pertinent laws and rules in legislature, interpretation of statutes and case precedents, and subsequently applying the laws to the relevant problems. *Legal methodology* is therefore, the application of the laws, thereafter the facts are collated and analysis of facts is completed within the framework of law that has been legislated. Maxeiner highlighted the use of legal methodology by comparing the two legal systems of the US law (a common law system), and the German law (a civil law system). The US system is predominantly a common law system based on case precedents, while the German law is based upon the civil law system, where there is extensive codification that is usually fleshed-out in detail.

In German courts, the legal rules are given prominence and facts of the cases are subsumed in the rules, whereas in the US courts, the norms are used, but they are not that prominent in deciding the issues between the parties. There is a maxim in German courts, famously called *Iura novit curia,* which in English means 'the courts know

---

[505]Maxeiner, "Legal Methods in Comparative Procedural Law," 2.
[506]Ibid., 6.
[507]Lon Fuller, "The Forms and Limits of Adjudication," *Harv. L. Rev.* 92, no. 2 (1978): 353–409. This was discussed by Maxeiner in "Legal Methods in Comparative Procedural Law," 6.

the law.'[508] Most German law is drafted with precision, and excessive thought is given to ensuring proper quality control of the statutes during drafting stage. This is then followed by an attempt to find the most objective judgment based upon deductive reasoning.[509]

On the other hand, Subrin was of the view that the highest goal for the US courts (a common law system) appears to be that these courts will attempt not to apply the law to the facts of the disputes.[510] In addition, the US system seems to indicate a bit of indifference to the norms as compared with the German courts. Matters linked with the US procedural system are further complicated by vibrant democracy of the US, where legislation is drafted and agreed upon by competing lobbies. Solum state that there are two competing models in the US - the *accuracy model,*[511] and the *participation model.*

In the traditional accuracy model, the aim of civil dispute resolution is to apply accurately the relevant laws to the facts, which in the author's view is very similar to the German procedural law. However, the goal of the participation model, according to Solum, is that the correct outcome should be a function of a process that guarantees fair and equal participation. He further added that it is "…the process itself and not the outcome that defines **procedural justice** [emphasis added]."[512]

As discussed earlier,[513] the functional comparative method has limitations in the context of civil procedures. To add to this complexity, in some procedural systems the purpose is to ensure that *'private rights'* are protected like in the US,[514] whereas in many other civil jurisdictions, the *'public purpose'* is to resolve private disputes.[515]

---

[508]Maxeiner, "Legal Methods in Comparative Procedural Law," 5.

[509]Reinhard Zimmermann, "An Introduction to German Legal Culture," in *Introduction to German Law*, ed. Werner F. Ebke and Matthew W. Finkin (Hague, Boston: Kluwer Law International, 1996), 1,13.

[510]Stephen N. Subrin, "How Equity Conquered Common Law: The Federal Rules of Civil Procedure in Historical Perspective," *U. Pa. L. Rev.* 135, no. 4 (1987): 989.www.jstor.org/stable/3312053. It was further discussed in Maxeiner, "Legal Methods in Comparative Procedural Law," 5.

[511]Lawrence B. Solum, "Procedural Justice," *S. Cal. L. Rev.* 78, no. 1 (2004): 191. Solum's accuracy model was also discussed in Maxeiner, "Legal Methods in Comparative Procedural Law," 6.

[512]Solum, "Procedural Justice," 243. This was quoted in Maxeiner, "Legal Methods in Comparative Procedural Law," 6.

[513]Refer, Chapter 1, §1.4.3 on Konrad and Hein Functionality Method.

[514]P. L. Murray and Rolf H. Sturner, "German Civil Justice," in *German Civil Justice* (Durham, N.C.: Carolina Academic Press, 2004), 575. *See also*, the discussion on Murray and Sturner in Maxeiner, "Legal Methods in Comparative Procedural Law," 7.

[515]David J. Gerber, "Comparing Procedural Systems: Towards an Analytical Framework," in *Law and Justice in Multistate World: Essays in Honor of Arthur T. von. Mehren*, James A. R. Nafziger and Symeon C. Symeonides (2002), supra note 3, at 666, http://ssrn.com/abstract=12342579. The focus of procedural systems on private rights, as contrasted with Gerber's view of public purpose in resolving private disputes was discussed in Maxeiner, "Legal Methods in Comparative Procedural Law," 7.

Therefore, there are arguments about whether justice is what happens in German Courts favouring the legal order by finding legal truth, or if it is the procedural justice of the US courts. In the US courts, the norms as derived from legal methods take a step back relatively to the procedural rules because the focus is on procedural justice. English courts, being common law courts, follow the US model to a great extent, while the PRC court follows the German courts but with Chinese characteristics.

4.3.4   Relevant Functions to Compare in Civil Procedural Systems

The starting point of this discussion is Maxeiner's statement that "[p]rocedural law can only accomplish those tasks which the legal methods are capable."[516] However, in the author's view, Maxeiner's statement and these concepts are more applicable in the context of substantive law. Whatever methods are available in substantive law will also be available for procedural law. There could be different causes of action in substantive law, but if there were to also be different requirements pertaining to procedural law for each of cause of action, then in the author's view it would be an administrative nightmare. It could be argued that there could even be a possibility of the legal methods in a procedural system being incompatible with the legal methods of the substantive law in a few jurisdictions.

In addition, there are models of procedural law as discussed above,[517] where procedural rules will be played out in the courts according to the philosophical approaches of the systems, i.e. having a public purpose or not having such public purpose when resolving private disputes in the courts. The PRC system does have the public purpose in mind even in private disputes as per their *Civil Procedure Code 1991 (as amended in 2012)* as discussed earlier in Chapter 1, §1.2 and also §4.2.2.

The question arises as to the utility of comparative civil procedure: what can we compare in civil procedural laws or rules? The comparativists have tried to explain this, once more in functional terms, taking into account the philosophical approach of the US courts, where the courts come first. In this case, the norms of substantive law are inferior to those of procedures, but on the other hand, in the German courts, the norms are superior to the procedures before the courts.

This point has been further explained in the terminology used by Maxeiner, who refers to *internal and external functions of the civil procedure.*[518] The internal function refers to the protection of the private rights of the parties, while external

---

[516]Maxeiner, "Legal Methods in Comparative Procedural Law," 6.
[517]Refer, discussion above in §4.3.3.
[518]Maxeiner, "Legal Methods in Comparative Procedural Law," 8.

function of the civil procedure law in any jurisdiction refers to function of procedural law in resolving civil and commercial disputes within the context of whole legal system.

A very pertinent example is the European Union project of harmonising provisional and interim measures; it has adopted the functional approach to these provisional remedies. The working paper provides that "The particular measure should be identified not by looking at the measures existing formally in the laws of different European states, but rather at the purposes/functions that they serve."[519] In this working paper, the EU working group analysed the various functions of interim remedies, and then for each function, they analysed various measures that could be taken to fulfil that function. Thereafter, they analysed different measures and the relevant terminology in each of the EU's contracting states.

4.3.4.1 External Function of Civil Procedural Rules

The author will begin this section with Subrin's description of external functions of the civil procedural rules from the point of view of the US legal system. Subrin has listed these functions in the context of the US procedural system, as follows:[520]

♦ Resolving and ending disputes peacefully;

♦ Efficiency of the court system;

♦ Fulfilling societal norms through application of law

♦ Accurate ascertainment of facts;

♦ Predictability;

♦ Enhancing human dignity;

♦ Adding legitimacy and stability to government and society;

---

[519]European Law Institute - Working Group on Provisional and Protective Measures, "First Report, November 2014," *Transnational Civil Procedure - Formulation of Regional Rules ELI - UNIDROIT Rules of Transnational Civil Procedure, Steering Committee and Working Groups Joint Meeting, Rome, 27–28 November 2014* UNIDROIT/ELI 2014, Study LXXVIA-Doc. 1 (2014): 5.

[520]Stephen N. Subrin, "On Thinking about a Description of a Country's Civil Procedure," *Tul. J. Int'l & Comp. L.* 7 (1999): supra note 12,140. *See also*, Maxeiner, "Legal Methods in Comparative Procedural Law," 9, where Subrin's view of internal functions was also discussed.

- Permitting citizens to partake in governance;

- Aiding the growth and improvement of law;

- Restraining or enhancing power

On the other hand, Murray and Sturner have listed the following external functions, taking a cue from transnational principles in the context of US procedural law:[521]

- Maintaining the independence and credibility of judicial institutions;

- Providing litigants with high-quality determinations of facts and law;

- Guaranteeing litigants procedural and systematic fairness;

- Producing final enforceable decisions without undue delay and at reasonable cost;

- Affording litigants reasonably free access to justice;

- Contributing positively to the development and explication of the law;

- Generating among litigants and overall population confidence and satisfaction in civil justice and rule of law;

- Public regulation of economic and social actors (peculiar only to the US procedural system);

- Public education (peculiar only to the US civil procedural system).

---

[521]Murray and Sturner, "German Civil Justice," supra note 4, at 574. *See also*, Maxeiner, "Legal Methods in Comparative Procedural Law,"9, where it was discussed that these functions seem to have been derived from 31 principles from *Transnational civil procedure.*

The functions, therefore, can be grouped as:

- ◆ Norm-based functions such as method of finding facts and their accurate determination;

- ◆ Process-based functions such as systematic fairness;

- ◆ Litigant-focused functions such as free justice, high-quality determination of dispute;

- ◆ Legal system-focused functions such as development of law, independence of judiciary, etc.

4.3.4.2 Internal Function of Civil Procedural Rules

In the context of jurisdictions where there is a primacy of public purpose in resolving private disputes, Gerber's selection of functions of procedural law is as follows:[522]

- ◆ Commencing litigation;

- ◆ Acquiring data;

- ◆ Shaping the facts;

- ◆ Establishing the facts;

- ◆ Law knowing: the background knowledge set;

- ◆ Structuring law for the cases;

- ◆ Law determination: deciding on law for the cases;

---

[522]Gerber "Comparing Procedural Systems," supra note 3, at 666. *See also*, Maxeiner, "Legal Methods in Comparative Procedural Law," 10, where he discussed Gerber in detail.

- ◆ Decoding the outcome: fact-law interaction;

- ◆ Termination issues: appeals, etc.

It is important to note that the foregoing desired functions of procedural law are very norms-based, and it tend to relegate procedural justice to the margins. The above functions should be contrasted with the focus of the US system on finding the pertinent facts and allowing the litigants their "day-in-court."[523] Therefore, the focus of the PRC system would be less on procedural justice as compared to the common law system.

If the author were to analyse the internal functions suggested by Gerber in relation to German Civil Procedural System, it is clear the focus is clearly on norms in order to find the legal truth and accordingly decide the case. This aspect the author has discussed earlier in this chapter in relation to the legal philosophy of the civil jurisdictions. PRC would therefore focus on the finding the legal truth like any civil law system instead of focusing on procedural justice in any common law system.

4.3.4.3 Conclusions for Theoretical Comparative Civil Procedure

Many scholars have cited different functions within the context of the focus and priorities of different legal systems. The view of the author based on the above findings, is that the functions need to be compared carefully in relation to civil procedure. It would therefore be a comparison of functions that are common between the jurisdictions.

However, there is a need to take into account factors that can be classed as *exceptions* within a particular jurisdiction, or cultural factors affecting those jurisdictions. **These exceptional factors can also be discussed in the context of invisible factors or cultural factors that are also not constant in any jurisdiction.** For example, Chase has identified four features that are very relevant to the US procedural law that he considers as 'American procedural exceptionalism':[524]

- ◆ The civil jury;

---

[523]Maxeiner, "Legal Methods in Comparative Procedural Law," 10.
[524]O. G. Chase, "American Exceptionalism," 287. *See also*, Maxeiner, "Legal Methods in Comparative Procedural Law," 11, where Chase was discussed at great length.

- ◆ The use of party-controlled pre-trial investigation;

- ◆ The relatively passive role of the judge at the trials or hearings;

- ◆ The method of obtaining and using expert opinions on technical matters.

Even though *culturalism* or *exceptionalism* must be taken into account for the comparative project in the context of English and PRC civil procedure law, the initial research for the comparative exercise will have be on the common functions and how the civil procedure law differs in relation to those familiar functions. This is an appropriate time to bring in *UNIDROIT Principles of Transnational Civil Procedure*, prepared by a joint American Law Institute / UNIDROIT Study Group and adopted in 2004 by the Governing Council of UNIDROIT.

The thirty-one principles/functions of transnational civil procedure of UNIDROIT[525] were adopted by the International Institute for the Unification of Private Law (UNIDROIT) in April 2004, and by the American Law Institute (ALI) in May 2004. The principles were adopted for the guidance of nations that were in the middle of drafting civil procedural codes for their own national systems. Many scholars within the field of comparative research in the context of civil procedural law regularly utilize these principles or functions to compare civil procedure systems or codes from different jurisdictions. The scholars find these more than thirty-one principles to be extremely useful.

Last but not least, the author will be mindful of the fact that every jurisdiction has its own notion of civil justice with its own corresponding principles of civil justice. A few of the principles of civil justice are given prominence over other principles within a jurisdiction based on ideological or philosophical grounds or pursuant to the constitution governing that jurisdiction. Even though the principles are clear and might have been devised upon the basis of both common law and civil law, it is still useful to group them in such a way as to keep this issue clear-cut and plain. Prof. Andrews has noted this need, in relation to increasingly complicated sets of rules in each jurisdiction:

---

[525]UNIDROIT (as adopted and promulgated by), "Principles of Transnational Civil Procedure." www. Unidroit.org/instruments/transnational-civil-procedure.

Another value of emphasising general principles is that they are an antidote to the numbing and bewildering complexity, detail, and technicality, which characterise many national procedural rule books. Finally, international scholarly discussion thrives on the fundamental principle.[526]

Andrews, following the path of fundamental principles, has sub-grouped the principles of civil justice into four groups to avoid too much complexity. These four groups and key principles within these groups are as follows:[527]

♦ Regulating access to courts and justice –

➢ Access to Justice;
➢ Right to Choose a Lawyer;
➢ Confidential Legal Consultation;
➢ Protection against Spurious Claims and Defences;
➢ Promoting Settlement and Facilitating Resort to Alternative Forms of Dispute Resolution, notably Mediation and Arbitration.

♦ Ensuring the fairness of the process –

➢ Judicial Independence;
➢ Judicial Impartiality;
➢ Publicity or Open Justice;
➢ Procedural Equality (equal respect for the parties);
➢ Fair Play between the Parties;
➢ Judicial Duty to Avoid Surprise: The Principle of Due Notice;
➢ Equal Access to Information, including Disclosure of Information between Parties.

♦ Maintaining a speedy and efficient process –

---

[526]Andrews, "Fundamental Principles of CPR," 19. Andrews analysed the American Law Institute and UNIDROIT ('International Institute for Unification of Private law') common project that started in 2004 called 'Principles and Rules of transnational civil procedure'. This project combined the best practices of common law and civil law systems. Andrew noted that there were significant differences within the common law systems as well as differences between the civil law and common law systems.
[527]Andrews, "Fundamental Principles of CPR," 33–34.

> Judicial Control of the Civil Process to Ensure Focus and Proportionality (tempered, where appropriate, by principle of procedural equity; the process is not to be administered in an oppressive manner);
> Avoidance of Undue Delay.

♦ Achieving just and effective outcomes –

> Judicial Duty to Give Reasons;
> Accuracy of Decision-making;
> Effectiveness (provision of protective relief and enforcement of judgments);
> Finality

4.4   Comparison of Legal Philosophy of Civil Litigation

The concept of procedural rights as *inherent in individuals* rather than *conferred* upon the litigants is an important feature in western civil procedures, in particular, common law systems. On the other hand, the PRC has adopted the *socialist* system where an individual is a member of a society, and all legal philosophies will rotate around the concept of society or public interests. PRC courts, as discussed, are required to maintain social and economic order and are in fact mandated to guarantee the smooth progress of the socialist construct.

Issues of public interest could create concerns in commercial litigation, in particular where foreign corporations have reasonable commercial interests to protect in the PRC. Foreign lawyers acting for these foreign corporations may be in a bind as to how to advise their clients and what actually are issues of public interest in the PRC. Any clear-cut guidance from the local PRC lawyer would probably not be clear with regard to these issues.

In fact, in relation to commercial litigation, looking at profits or competition from the socialist angle can be quite contradictory in any market economy. Furthermore, the gradual transition of the PRC through the 1980s to a *socialist market economy* is not, in the author's view, reflected in the PRC's civil procedure codes. For local businessmen and in particular foreign businessmen, when dealing with an economic powerhouse such as the world's second largest economy, there ought to be a reasonable expectation that other issues such as public interest can be filtered out of the pure business interests. Due to these arguments, many PRC scholars could critique the author for apparently seeing the issues from the prism of capitalism. However, given that PRC international trade volumes are so huge and the level of commercial activities so gigantic, then it is difficult to accept such arguments.

In the English civil procedural system and in most continental civil procedural systems founded on western jurisprudence, there is an emphasis on ensuring *procedural rights*. But in the PRC system, there is an emphasis on securing *substantive justice*. This difference in philosophy has a considerable bearing upon the role of courts, and their respective approaches to civil litigation. In addition, in the PRC as well as in foreign civil law system, an inquisitorial system during civil trials is followed. Many aspects in continental civil law systems still have concepts such as adversarial debates (*principe de contradiction*) in civil trials, and there is no room for outside third-party interference, or any retrial without the request of the litigants. This is akin to the adversarial system as seen in common law based civil procedure systems.

The PRC seems to have been following continental civil traditions from the 1990s onwards, but in the author's view, it has only borrowed a few aspects of the continental system. In fact, by adopting the concepts of re-trial and supervision, the PRC has adopted *democratic centralism* (*min zhu ji zhong zhi*) and *socialism*, and there is a subtle balance maintained between procedural justice, and substantive truth using theory of evidence. This balance between substantive and procedural rights is due to the influence of the Soviet Union's theory of *binary theory right of action*. The PRC has adopted the right to debate in *CPL 1991*, thus bringing the system nearer to the continental civil procedural system, but Article 12 of *CPL 1991* has not guaranteed such a right.

Unlike in the English procedural system, the principle to debate as provided in the PRC's *CPL 1991* is a *non-binding debate system*, as a result of which the PRC courts are not constrained by the facts presented by the parties. PRC courts are more likely to actively investigate the case themselves. This is also an example of the wide discretionary power given to judges, in particular, in relation to investigations.

The English civil procedural system promotes active case management and a process of disclosure, but the main obligation to present the case to the judge is on the parties. However, the PRC procedural system uses the '*discovery model led by the judges*'.

From the time an application is submitted, the system requires a high Standard of Proof in relation to the evidence; this includes *specific-fact pleading*.[528]

In the PRC system, there are more formal requirements as to the form of evidence that is acceptable to the courts. In addition, at the level of practice of law in courts, requirements as to the evidence vary considerably in the local courts. In a way, the PRC's civil procedure system believes in the state's responsibility, carried out through the judges, to investigate what the parties have not even said in their pleadings. This is an important difference between the two jurisdictions, and it has a profound effect on procedural justice and outcomes. How far English judges can investigate any case on their own is highly debated among academics and practicing lawyers.

Any non-criminal matter, including commercial cases, can be brought to English civil courts, while in continental countries, it is usually the difference between public and private law that matters. On the other hand, in the PRC, there is a subtle distinction between commercial and civil cases, even though commercial cases can be brought in civil courts. In the PRC, there is no separate commercial code; rather, it seems to be scattered in various individual codes meant for different areas of law related to commerce such as partnership law, insurance law and so forth. In the PRC, the principles of civil law is absorbed in commercial law, but the key point to note that is even in commercial litigation, parties are supposed to be equal, and any litigation to be conducted in PRC courts will eventually follow the *concept of fairness*.

The concepts of *honesty* and *credibility* are brought into areas of commercial litigation. *General Principles of Civil Law 1986* acts likes an ethics clause, and it seems to impact commercial litigation, which was designed for common civil disputes and is clearly unsuitable for dealing with issues of commerce & trade, where there is already intense competition between the parties. However, in the author's view, while the concept of socialist market economy pursuant to the 1993 amendment to the *Constitution of PRC 1982* is slowly impacting commercial litigation, in practice, there are divergences that have been observed in the local PRC courts due to the fact that there is no precise and straightforward distinction between civil and commercial litigation in PRC codes.

---

[528]See *Provisions of the Supreme People's Court on Several Issues concerning the Registration-based Filing of Cases by People's Courts, Fa Shi* [2015] No. 8, effective from 1 May 2015. These Provisions in a way attempt to improve the system but it is a relatively new system. However, the philosophical approach of the PRC civil procedure system is a major impediment, as higher Standards of Proof are usually required even at the time of filing of these cases.

4.5 Comparison of Objectives in Civil Litigation

Prior to the advent of the new *CPR 1998* in England & Wales (even before the effects from continental jurisdictions were visible), the concepts of a few statutes having an 'overriding' effect was known to legal stakeholders, but under this new approach, the meaning of the concept of overriding objective is much broader. *Overriding objective* encompasses the concept that lawyers and judges should also keep the overriding objectives in mind when analysing the other rules of the new *CPR 1998*. The *purposive construction* of *CPR 1998* was mooted to ensure the spirit of civil procedure is maintained within the courts, and it was the main reason for the advent of the new rules in 1998, replacing old rules. While discussing the overriding objectives, the *secondary objectives* such as ensuring that cases are dealt with justly and that costs are proportionate could also not be disregarded in this new spirit of *CPR 1998*.

Therefore, with increased efficiency due to proper case management, disputes are resolved between the parties, but the courts will always be mindful of the public interests in private disputes, although in western jurisprudence, the main reference point is individuals' rights and by extension the rights of businesses. In the author's view, there is also no denying that there are public dimensions to civil litigation in England & Wales – firstly, due to the administrative burden of civil litigation and a need for the executive to manage it effectively; and secondly, because the stakeholder approach cannot be neglected by the courts in many cases. The second approach may be argued to some extent to be similar to the PRC's approach, even though this approach, in the context of taking into account public interest, is more visible in the PRC. The issue of public interest being taken into account is also likely to affect the outcome of any litigation in the PRC.

In the PRC, in *CPL 1991*, the principles and aims are mentioned at the beginning through its various articles detailing the *principles of equality, disposition, litigation rights of debate and argument, of mediation, of supervision and so forth.*[529] They are meant to be applicable throughout the civil process. According to PRC scholars, even the meaning of various articles needs be interpreted through the prism of the above principles. However, are these principles inherent in nature? If they are indeed inherent in nature, what was the need to list these principles out in the *CPL 1991*? This again, in the author's view, highlights where the theory diverges from the

---

[529]Refer to Chapter 4, §4.2.2.1.

practice of law in the PRC. In defence of the PRC's civil procedural system and law, it is relatively new in comparison to *CPR 1998*.

In one way, because the *CPR 1998* in England & Wales has introduced case management powers for judges, it is now somewhat equivalent to the approach of judges in the PRC. However, *CPR 1998* also introduced in England & Wales the unique concept of overriding objective. This concept is unique to common law systems and brings elements of *procedural justice* into elements of *substantive justice*. This approach of the judges also serves the larger purpose within the English civil procedure system to ensure that stakeholders are aware of the need to act fairly to avoid using excessive judicial resources.

The subtle difference between the PRC's aim to obtain substantive justice as compared to the English courts' focus to maintain the delicate balance between procedural and substantive justice,[530] is highlighted by Sorabjee's view on the overriding objectives in *CPR 1998,* which also highlights, in the author's view, the contrast with the PRC civil procedural system:

> (1) it does not contain a singular commitment to substantive justice's achievement; on the contrary it contains an <u>equal commitment to both substantive and procedural justice</u> [emphasis added];
> (2) it does not treat economy and efficiency as means for securing substantive justice through the legal process; instead it regards economy and efficiency as principles which place a limit on the civil process' commitment to securing substantive justice; and
> (3) it requires a rigorous approach by courts to litigants who fail to comply with procedural obligations, and who thus fail to make proper use of a fair process provided so that they can pursue substantive justice.[531]

4.6 Comparison between Civil Litigation and Commercial Litigation

---

[530]John Sorabji, Andenas Mads, et al., "The Road to New Street Station: Fact, Fiction and Overriding Objective," in *Legal Studies Research Paper Series: Paper No. 21/2011* (Cambridge, 2011), 18.
[531]Ibid., 17.

In England & Wales, there is no difference between civil litigation and commercial litigation due to the adversarial nature of the system followed in litigation. However, in the PRC, first there is no separate commercial code, so civil law and commercial law would appear to be same. However, in practice, commercial litigation in the same civil justice system that also runs ordinary civil disputes would create hurdles as by operation of *General Principles of Civil Law 1986*, principles of honesty, fairness and public law enter the arena of commercial disputes and litigation by the backdoor. These principles operate in commercial law litigation even when these disputes are very private in nature and focus on earning profits.

These principles will have a major impact on the course of any commercial litigation, as many cases find that public law and public interests affect the very private commercial disputes. The advent of the socialist market economy is a recent phenomenon dating from the 1990s it would appear that this aspect is not yet fully integrated in commercial litigation in PRC. This feature of PRC jurisdiction is very different from England & Wales, and it is a factor for the difference in how commercial litigation is run in the civil justice system in both jurisdictions.[532]

---

[532]Refer, Chapter 4, §4.4, §4.5 & §4.6.

CHAPTER FIVE – LAW IN ACTION – JUDGES' POWER AND REASONING – COMMON LAW v. CHINESE LAW

5.1 Judges' Role in Accepting & Dealing with Cases – England & Wales and PRC

In the previous Chapters, the author has discussed issues from jurisprudence and philosophy, but in this Chapter, the author will discuss their influence on *law in action* in courts. Very briefly, unlike in the PRC, where due to the inquisitorial system judges play an important role in whether to accept applications into the courts, English judges have no such role in the adversarial common law system. The differing role of the judge due to philosophical underpinnings has profound effects: due to their investigative powers in the inquisitorial system, judges in the PRC can even decline applications at an early stage. This issue is also discussed in Chapter Seven, when analysing issues from the perspective of Standards of Proof.[533] As discussed earlier, the claimants are required to adduce enough evidence even at the stage of submitting applications to the PRC courts to satisfy the judges manning the *case filing division*.

5.2 Judges – Common Law, Civil Law, PRC

Judges are often seen as the representation of power within any state. However, in modern society, with the separation of power between executive, legislature and judiciary, judges are independent from intervention by the executive or legislative branch in democracies. However, the judges could, a long time ago, be dismissed at the whims of monarchs or the executive in most jurisdictions. Over the years, this arbitrary power of the monarchs and later the executive was curtailed and accordingly, the situation began to improve in England & Wales. The legislature started to legislate to ensure that judges could not be dismissed at the whims and fancies of executives and/or monarchs; however, judges can be dismissed under well-defined circumstances.

The above developments led to the concept of '*personal independence of a judge*' and was an important factor for ensuring '*judicial independence*'. It is important to note that in the PRC, the judiciary remains answerable to the National People's Congress ("NPC").[534] There is a case where a judge found one of the statutes of Local Congress at the provincial level not fit, and therefore declared that provincial legislation void. According to Wang, this judicial action led to the impeachment of that judge by the Local Congress.[535] The reporting structure of the judiciary to legislature, supervised by the Procuratorate System, is clearly a distinct system unique to the PRC.[536]

The judges work within the structure and organisation of the court system. The author has briefly discussed the structure and organisation of courts in both England & Wales and the PRC in Chapter Four.[537] Historically, in the later years, as the monarch

---

[533]Refer, Chapter 7, §7.4.

[534]See, Art. 67(6) of *Constitution of PRC 1982*, by which SPC is answerable to NPC. *See also*, Art. 104 of *Constitution of PRC 1982* pursuant to which People's Court is answerable to Local People's Congress at provincial level in PRC. *Refer also,* to Figure 8 in Chapter 4 that highlights the reporting structure for the PRC courts.

[535]Liming Wang, "The Achievements and Prospects of Court Reforms in China," *Frontiers L. China* 1, no. 1 (2006): 11.

[536]Refer Chapter 4, Figures 8, 9 &10.

[537]Refer to the discussion of structure and organisation of the courts in England & Wales in Chapter 4, §4.1.1, and for the PRC in Chapter 4, §4.1.3.

was subject to the laws of England, this political feature ensured that the judges remained independent and were paid a salary. In one instance, between AD 1685-1688, a Monarch dismissed a few judges as they were not willing to grant that Monarch the requisite power to repeal Acts which were legislated in Parliament. Subsequently, in the eighteenth century, a piece of legislation called *Act of Settlement 1701*,[538] pursuant to which judges were appointed for life, helped to curtail the influence of monarchs on judges.[539]

The eligibility requirements to become judges are stated in *Tribunals, Courts and Enforcement Act 2007*.[540] This Act has vastly expanded the opportunity for people from a much larger section of society to become judges. Possible candidates are now not required to come from the exclusive club of barristers, but they can even be law scholars from the Universities. This has the effect of creating social mobility with regard to the selection of judges.

The ratio of judge to population in 2009 in a common law jurisdiction of England & Wales was around 1 to 39,506 inhabitants, whereas in the civil jurisdictions of Germany it was one judge per 4080 inhabitants in 2008, and one judge per 6368 in Sweden in the same period.[541] It seems there are more judges per inhabitants in the civil law jurisdictions in comparison to common law jurisdictions.

On the other hand, as discussed earlier, the legal system is relatively new in the PRC. *Law on Judges 1995* was introduced in the PRC to improve the quality of judges and thereby improve overall judicial activities within PRC courts. Following that, after years of flux in the legal system, 1999 heralded a massive attempt at reform, after which the centralised court reform blueprint was published.[542] In 2001, the NPC amended three laws —— *The Law on Judges, The Law on Procurators* and *The Law on Lawyers*.[543] In 2001, the Supreme Court of the PRC issued guidelines on ethics to

---

[538]12 and 13 Will 3 c. 2.

[539]Thomas Lundmark, *Charting the Divide between Common and Civil Law* (New York; Oxford: Oxford University Press, 2012), 204.

[540]2007, c 15.

[541]Lundmark, *Divide between Common and Civil Law*, 204–07.

[542]See *Outline of Five-year Reform* (referred to here as *Five-year Outline)*, Document Issued by the Supreme People's Court, No. [1999] 28, October, 20, 1999.

[543]See *The Law on Judges*, passed through the 12th Convention of the Standing Committee of the 8th National People's Congress on February, 28, 1995, and amended by the 22nd Convention of the 9th National People's Congress on June 30, 2001; *The Law on Procurators*, passed through the 12th Convention of the Standing Committee of the 8th National People's Congress on February, 28th, 1995, and amended by the 22nd Convention of the 9th National People's Congress on June, 30th, 2001; *The Law on Lawyers,* passed through the 19th Convention of the Standing Committee of the 8th National People's Congress on May.15th, 1996, and amended by the 25th Convention of the Standing Committee of the

enable judges to implement both procedural and substantive justice.[544] Gradually, there was a focus on developing teams of judges, including assistants. There were plans put in place for their continuous training.

Common-law judges depend on the advocates running the cases for their clients, while in civil law jurisdictions the focus is usually on one expert judge guiding everyone else in the panel. It would not be inaccurate to say that active judges in civil law jurisdictions also at times guide the parties' lawyers. It is important to note that the judge to population ratio is also higher in civil law jurisdictions in comparison to common law jurisdictions.

The author wishes to highlight the advances made in cognitive science that highlight "that patterns of acting and thinking [of any human] are not governed by reason, but rather are ingrained, unconscious, or triggered by our automatic nervous system."[545] The author's view is that the effects of education, history, cultural values, predominant jurisprudence, and political philosophy are all bound to dominate thoughts and assumptions in all areas of the judicial process. These are exactly the invisible factors and contexts the author has been speaking about from the start of the book. Such factors have a profound effect even on judicial activities within the courts. This dominance of assumptions and cultural habits in the minds of judges can lead them to take mental shortcuts called "'heuristics' or 'schemas' to make complex decisions."[546] All the above factors affecting the judges can lead them to have *cognitive illusions*.

In western jurisprudence, there is a focus on emotional detachment from the cases so that judges can remain rational. However, the cognitive sciences seem to suggest it is impossible for any human being to have complete emotional detachment.[547] Accordingly, taking into account the fact that a complete emotional detachment is not possible for any judge, then it may be could be called as a realist version of jurisprudence that impinges on judicial decision making.

5.2.1 Jurisprudence and Law in context of Judges in Adversarial System versus Inquisitorial System

---

Ninth National People's Congress at its 25th Meeting on December 29, 2001, and revised at the 30th Meeting of the Standing Committee of the Tenth National People's Congress on October 28, 2007.
[544]See *Basic Professional Ethics for Judges,* document issued by the Supreme People's Court of China, on October,18, 2001.
[545]Nicole E. Negowetti, "Judicial Decisionmaking, Empathy, and the Limits of Perception," *Akron L. Rev.* 47, no. 3 (2015): 694.
[546]Ibid.
[547]Ibid., 698.

We have seen in Chapter Three that jurisprudents had various viewpoints in most jurisdictions. Nevertheless, whatever may be the schools of thought as to the concept of law, it ultimately boils down to the elementary fact that eventually the judges will have to adjudicate disputes in the courts through an interpretive process as to the function of practice of law.

Comparativists, who prefer the continental system over the common law system, feel that the common-law judges' way of finding the appropriate law for the problem is unsystematic. It is even said that "continental lawyers think systematically; common lawyers think casuistically."[548] The mental process that a judge goes through to find the relevant law is nearly the same in almost all jurisdictions. The attack on the incoherence of legal reasoning in common law, as discussed in Chapter Three, was accelerated in the USA by Legal realists.[549] The realists' argument was that there is incoherence not only because of inconsistent statutory interpretation, but also with reference to the legal reasoning emerging out of common law cases.[550] In fact, in the author's experience, many Chinese students who go to the US, the UK and other common law jurisdictions to study law, struggle to come to terms with the common law system.

The civil justice system comprises two kinds of systems — the adversarial system associated with common law systems such as in England & Wales, and the inquisitorial system such as in the PRC and continental Europe. Every system has its own set of procedures to ensure that justice is seen to be done and done eventually. The main difference between the two systems lies in which party is in control of the process; for example, in the inquisitorial system, the judges control the litigation process, whereas in the common law, the litigation is controlled by the parties to the dispute. The role of judges is more passive in the common law system, relative to the inquisitorial system.[551]

Hodgson has discussed the jurisprudential difference in the way the two systems work in practice. She was of the view that the inquisitorial system works on the concept

---

[548]Lundmark, *Divide between Common and Civil Law*, 263, where he quoted Rene and Brierley. *See also*, Rene David and John E. C. Brierley, *Major Legal Systems in the World Today*, 3rd ed. (London: Sweet & Maxwell, 1985), 94.

[549]Refer, Chapter 3, §3.2.4 in context of Legal Realism and Critical Legal Studies.

[550]*Introduction to Jurisprudence and Legal Theory: Commentary and Materials*, Anne Barron, et al. (London: Butterworths, 2002), 287, where Hugh Collins, "Law as Politics: Progressive American Perspectives" was discussed.

[551]Fabien Gélinas, et al., *Foundations of Civil Justice: Toward a Value-Based Framework for Reform* (Heidelberg; New York; Dordrecht; London: Springer, 2015), 65. *See also,* Antony Duff, et al., *The Trial on Trial: Volume I: Truth and Due Process* (Oxford: Hart Publishing, 2004), 223.

that in litigation, it is the State's responsibility to "recreate what the parties do not say." The State's role, she notes, was also to balance any inequality between the parties. In the adversarial system available under the common law, it is assumed that all parties are equal and therefore, they must try their best to bring out the truth.[552] Shin, in the context of arbitrations, argued for the advantages of the adversarial system in finding the truth.[553]

Over the year's lot of research has been done by scholars on the advantages of one system over the other system. Block and his fellow scholars found that either of the two systems cannot assert their hold over the truth or efficiency. However, they found that efficiency, including hidden facts coming to the fore during litigation as well as accuracy of decision, depends "significantly upon the information structure of the case."[554] If there is no way any hidden information can be revealed, then it was found that inquisitorial system is better. However, if both the parties have access to the information, then Gélinas et al are of the view that the adversarial system is better for efficiency and accuracy of the decision.[555]

However, there are scholars such as Shin, who have done research in the context of arbitration carried out in the common law tradition, have concluded that the common-law adversarial system is better than the inquisitorial system as Burden of Proof can be allocated more efficiently, and the common law system has more inherent ability to "extract maximal informational content from seemingly inconclusive results."[556] Shin states that this is due to "the discretion [emphasis added] of the arbitrator to exercise the appropriate degree of skepticism and to react in a sophisticated way to the self-interested reporting strategies of the two opposing parties."[557]

The author's view is that though there is truth to the statement that there is an assumption in the common law system that every party is equal, the system is also aware of the reality of the matter in relation to the issue of whether a party can bear the legal costs. It is pertinent to note that in the most prominent common law

---

[552]Jacqueline Hodgson, "Conceptions of the Trial in Inquisitorial and Adversarial Procedure," in *The Trial on Trial: Judgment and Calling to Account*, A. Duff, Farmer, S. Marshall, and V. Tadros (Oxford; Portland; Or: Hart, 2004), 240n1. This was also discussed and quoted in Gélinas et al., *Foundations of Civil Justice*, 66.

[553]H. S. Shin, "Adversarial and Inquisitorial Procedure in Arbitration," *Rand J. Economics* 29, no. 2 (1998): 378–405.

[554]M. K. Block, et al., "An Experimental Comparison of Adversarial Versus Inquisitorial Procedural Regimes," *AM. L. & Econ. Rev.* 2, no. 1 (2000): 170–94. This article was also discussed in Gélinas, et al., *Foundations of Civil Justice*, 66.

[555]Gélinas, et al., *Foundations of Civil Justice*, 65–75.

[556]Ibid., 66.

[557]Shin, "Adversarial or Inquisitorial," 395. This was also quoted in Gélinas, et al., *Foundations of Civil Justice*, 66.

jurisdictions such as England & Wales, there has been a system of disclosure of information by every party to the litigation to other parties. For example, *CPR 1998* r. 31.6 in relation to *Standard disclosure* requires a party to disclose only –

a. the documents on which he relies; and
b. the documents which –
c. adversely affect his own case [emphasis added];
d. adversely affect another party's case; or
e. support another party's case; and
f. the documents which he is required to disclose by a relevant practice direction.

It is noteworthy that a party is required to disclose even those documents that can adversely affect his own case as well, which is not usually the case in the inquisitorial system. In the inquisitorial system, it is incumbent upon the judges to find the relevant adverse facts.

In the common law system, the arguments are usually presented in a partisan way, and the roles of the judges and advocates are clearly defined in this system. One key remark by Fuller was that the inquisitorial procedure has pre-trial efficiency but is in fact not prepared for unpredictable events during the trial. Fuller's view was that the early decision-making by a judge in the inquisitorial system was unsuitable to deal with the unpredictable events that can happen during the trial. Therefore, the civil system carries the risk of not having fully ascertained the weight of all the evidence. Pound also criticised the adversarial system as "contentious procedure, which turns litigation into a game" and "gives a false notion of the purpose and the end of law."[558]

In spite of the differences between the two systems, however, it is clear that both have the same objective. The underlying values or principles of the legal systems are, therefore, crucial to the discretionary power of any judge in either system.[559] A few of the examples of values or principles that are common to both systems are: "fairness, accuracy, humanity, and coherence with liberal-democratic values."[560]

---

[558]R. Pound, "The Causes of Popular Dissatisfaction with the Administration of Justice," *Reports of the American Bar Association* 29 (1906): 395.
[559]See § 5.3 of this Chapter.
[560] Gélinas et al., *Foundations of Civil Justice*, 67.

5.2.1.1 Key Defining Characteristics of Adversarial and Inquisitorial Systems

A few defining goals of the two systems are: finding the truth, discovery and disclosure to find the truth, cross-examination to find the truth, and economic equality in finding truth in the adjudication. The author will discuss these goals later in this Chapter.

5.2.1.1.1 Finding the truth

This aspect has been discussed in the preceding chapter under the section of Legal Philosophy.[561]

5.2.1.1.2 Discovery and Disclosure Process in Finding the Truth – England & Wales and PRC

Many movies show scenes where new evidence suddenly appears from one party in the middle of litigation. However, civil litigation does not work like this in the adversarial system. The approach of the lawyers to keep their cards close to the chest has been displaced by openness, with the onus now on parties to put their cards on the table, thus potentially encouraging settlement and saving ever-increasing litigation costs. This aspect of the common law system was discussed when analysing the overriding objective of *CPR 1998* in the context of England & Wales. The author has discussed earlier in this Chapter,[562] that pursuant to the obligations of *standard disclosure*, the parties to litigation need to disclose evidence even when such evidence would undermine their own case. This system works in the English courts, where the passive judge has no power to collate evidence, and each party is responsible for their own case.[563]

In the US, another prominent common law system, the process of discovery in its adversarial system is even more elaborate. In the discovery process, information is gathered formally from the parties through written questions by a process called *'interrogatories'*. In this process, requests for copies of documents and for admission, which the opponents are free to admit or deny, can be made. However, a special method by which civil litigation is carried out in the US is through the process of

---

[561]Refer, Chapter 4, §4.2 & earlier §5.2.
[562]Refer, *CPR 1998* r. 31.6 and its discussion in §5.2.1.
[563]Susan Blake, *A Practical Approach to Effective Litigation*, 7th ed. (Oxford: Oxford University Press, 2009), 378–9.

'depositions'.[564] In this process, prior to the trial, witnesses are questioned under oath by the parties' attorneys, and the witnesses' answers are recorded by a court reporter; these recorded statements can be used in a future trial.

However, in the inquisitorial system, most of the collection of evidence is left to the judges; to some extent the Standard of Proof to even commence a claim is higher, so considerable relevant evidence will have to be provided to the courts by the parties to the litigation.

In the PRC's *CPL 1991*, there is no separate law for any equivalent disclosure or discovery process. However, *CPL 1991* regulates a system in relation to Chapter VI of *CPL 1991*. *CPL 1991* provides that the claimants must provide evidence to prove their allegations. The courts will examine the evidence *comprehensively and objectively*.[565] In addition, in the PRC, evidence must be attached to the claimants' claims or defendants' counterclaims.[566]

The PRC courts will examine whether the evidence is relevant to the complaints alleged in the fact-specific pleadings.[567] A lawyer acting for a client has the right to investigate the claim.[568] The lawyer will investigate it by sending the questions to the other side. However, there is no obligation pursuant to *CPL 1991* to persuade the opponents to answer those questions, and in many cases, it is observed that the opponent simply ignores the requests. The relevant law for the lawyers also allows them to investigate materials held by others, provided the lawyer duly presents his professional qualification to the third parties.[569]

---

[564]See *Federal Rule of Civil Procedure 1938,* Rule 30.

[565]See Art. 64 of *CPL 1991 (as amended in 2012). See also,* Art. 105 of *Interpretations of the Supreme People's Court on Applicability of the Civil Procedure Law of the PRC, Zhu Shi [2015] No. 5 (hereinafter "SPC's Interpretation of CPL 2015")* that provides: "A people's court shall, under statutory procedures, conduct *comprehensive and objective examination* [emphasis added] of evidence, and according to provisions of law, judge whether a piece of evidence has probative force and the extent of its probative force, by *logical reasoning and daily life experience* [emphasis added], and then make public the reasons for, and the results of, such judgment.".

[566]See Art. 121(4) of *CPL 1991 (as amended in 2012).*

[567]See Art. 64 of *CPL 1991 (as amended in 2012)*

[568]See Art. 61 of *CPL 1991(as amended in 2012)* which provides: "Lawyers who serve as litigation representatives or other litigation representatives shall have the right to investigate and collect evidence and may consult relevant materials to the case. The scopes and measures of consulting relevant materials to a case shall be regulated by the Supreme People's Court."

[569]See *Lawyers Law of PRC 2008,* Art. 35, that provides: "When a lawyer investigates to collect evidence for a case on his own, he may, on the strength of his lawyer's practice certificate and the papers issued by his law firm, inquire of the unit or individual concerned about the legal matters which he has undertaken to handle."

It is a common practice by PRC lawyers to question witnesses present at the relevant scene, or any witnesses who are relevant; thereafter, the lawyers can offer a notarized witness testimony record to the PRC courts.[570] It has been noted by many lawyers and scholars, that the PRC courts often prefer documentary evidence over other evidence.[571]

Lawyers can even utilise the notaries to record, photograph, and interview witnesses.[572] The author's view, after discussions with other PRC lawyers, is that credibility of such evidence is relatively higher in the PRC courts. This utilisation of services of the notaries is very similar to the notary system found in other civil law systems. In the PRC there are strict formal requirements for any evidence to be accepted in the PRC courts, and many common lawyers find these requirements frustrating.

Instead of the system of discovery or disclosure as seen in the adversarial system, in the PRC, there is a duty on the judges to investigate in any case before them, particularly when the evidence is not clear.[573] PRC judges can exercise the right of explanation and clarification, and therefore can urge the parties to improve their evidence in such cases.[574] Additionally, there is a positive duty on the PRC judges to investigate and collect evidence.[575] In practice, the parties can also petition the courts requesting to collate the evidence, especially if the evidence is in the possession of the third party.[576]

The PRC courts employ trial personnel to maintain written records of the inspection and examination, which leads to the production of transcripts of inspection and examination.[577] Such transcripts are acceptable by law and can be used as evidence. The trial personnel must conduct an examination on-site for facts and assist the courts,

---

[570]Elizabeth Fahey and Zhirong Tao, "The Pretrial Discovery Process in Civil Cases: A Comparison of Evidence Discovery between China and the United States," *B.C. Int'l & Comp. L. Rev.* 37, no. 2 (2014): 284.

[571]Richard W. Wigley and Jing Xu, "Evidence Collection and Alternatives to Discovery in PRC Litigation," 1. www.chinalawinsight.com/2011/04/articles/dispute-resolution/evidence-collection-and-alternatives-to-discovery-in-prc-litigation.

[572]See Art. 11 of *Notarization Law of PRC 2005*.

[573]The relevant part of Art. 64 of *CPL 1991(as amended in 2012)* provides "...if the people's court considers the evidence necessary for the trial of the case, the People's Court *shall* [emphasis added] investigate and collect it."

[574]Wigley and Xu, "Evidence Collection and Alternatives to Discovery in PRC Litigation."

[575]See Art. 65 of *CPL 1991 (as amended in 2012)*.

[576]Wigley and Xu, "Evidence Collection and Alternatives to Discovery in PRC Litigation," 288.

[577]See Art. 63(7) of *CPL 1991(as amended in 2012)*. *See also*, Art. 80 of *CPL 1991 (as amended in 2012)*.

as some evidence is not easy to bring to the courts.[578] It is important to note that there is a provision in *CPL 1991* that resembles the exchange of evidence in Art. 133(4) of *CPL 1991*.[579] However, in practice, litigants in the PRC are not fully aware of it, and this provision is yet to be fully implemented in practice.[580] Trial courts can schedule the exchange of evidence by the parties.

Unlike the common law system where the discovery/disclosure is led by the parties and their lawyers, in the PRC system it is led by the judges and can therefore be called "discovery model led by judges."[581] One of the advantages of this model is that the discovery process is less time consuming, which is important as there are time limits for each process in the civil trial.[582] In the author's view, it is relevant to practice in the PRC, and at the same time maintains balance in the context of the economic inequality prevailing within the society. It will also assist the PRC judges to avoid irrelevant evidence.

The author's view is that the PRC judges do not spend too much time analysing the facts, but instead utilise their precious time in collecting the relevant evidence for the parties to the disputes. There is some question as to whether PRC judges can later rule on the evidence collected by them, if there were to be a rebuttal to the evidence from one of the parties to the dispute. The answer is not yet well-defined.

Although PRC lawyers have the right, enshrined in *CPL 1991*, to collect evidence,[583] the process by which they can investigate and collect evidence is also not well-defined. This issue is of relevance, as in any inquisitorial system, any evidence so collected should be acceptable to the PRC courts even at the later stage of the civil

---

[578]See Art. 80 of *CPL 1991 (as amended in 2012)*.

[579]See Art. 133(4) of *CPL 1991 (as amended in 2012)* which provides: "Where a court session is needed, the focus of the dispute may be clarified through requiring the parties concerned to swap evidence or by other means."

[580]Fahey and Tao, "The Pretrial Discovery Process in Civil Cases: A Comparison of Evidence Discovery Between China and the United States," 291–2. *See also,* Peggy McInerny, "Modern Legal Profession in China Is Only 35 Years Old", UCLA Int'l Institute, http://web.international.ucla.edu/Institute/Article/136768, where McInerny in her article explored the evolution of legal awareness and implementation of laws for ordinary PRC residents. The author accessed this website on April, 12, 2016.

[581]Fahey and Tao, "The Pretrial Discovery Process in Civil Cases: A Comparison of Evidence Discovery Between China and the United States," 292.

[582]See Art. 149 & Art. 161 of *CPL 1991 (as amended in 2012)*. Art. 149 provides: "A People's Court shall complete the adjudication of a case to which ordinary procedure is applied *within six months* [emphasis added] after the case is accepted. Where an extension of the term is necessary for special circumstances, a six-month extension may be given upon the approval of the president of the court. Any further extension shall be reported to the People's Court at a higher level for approval." On the other hand, Art. 161 provides: "The People's Court shall complete the adjudication of a case to which the summary procedure is applied within three months after the case is accepted."

[583]See Arts. 49 and 61 of *CPL 1991 (as amended in 2012)*.

trial. In practice, private investigators that can assist the parties to collect evidence have increased in number, but the regulations are not clear-cut in relation to these private agencies.[584] There is no provision for third-party orders where the courts can compel the third parties to assist with ongoing litigation in PRC courts.

A similar situation exists in the context of investigation orders, where one party is refusing to provide the relevant evidence. In such circumstances, the judges take the investigative role upon themselves. The author's view is that the ability of litigants to introduce new evidence at any time during the process of litigation, or to ask for an extension, is a major drawback in the PRC litigation system.[585] In practice, many litigants present new evidence on appeal, and in such cases, the PRC courts do not widely use the provision of fines in *CPL 1991*.[586] There is no concept of perjury in cases of presenting wrong certificates or misrepresentation in the courts, including when contradicting testimonies are involved.[587]

For the sake of completeness, it should be noted that there are other inquisitorial systems such as Germany and Japan that also have the parties-led discovery system.[588] On the other hand, as discussed above, the discovery model relevant to the PRC system is led by judges, and these judges are supervised by the Procuratorate system to maintain social harmony and public interests.

5.2.1.1.3   Finding the Truth and Cross-examination

In the PRC, the parties may cross-examine witnesses, expert witnesses, and inspectors with permission from the courts.[589] The author's view is that permission will still be required to cross-examine; it appears that this is not available as a right. However, a party in England & Wales has the right to cross-examine all the witnesses presented through witness statements submitted by the opponents, to forward their own case. It

---

[584]Fahey and Tao, "The Pretrial Discovery Process in Civil Cases: A Comparison of Evidence Discovery between China and the United States," 299–300.

[585]See, Art. 65 of *CPL 1991(as amended in 2012)*. In particular, it provides: ".... Where a party has difficulty in providing evidence within such time limit, *it may apply to the People's court for an extension of the time limit* [emphasis added] and the people's court may extend the time limit appropriately according to the application of the party...." *See also, Art. 139 of CPL 1991(as amended in 2012)* in the context of the parties' ability to present the evidence any time.

[586]See Art. 65 of *CPL 1991(as amended in 2012)*.

[587]See Art. 305 of the *Criminal Law of the People's Republic of China 1997*, which is not applicable to civil proceedings and only applicable to perjury committed during a criminal proceeding. It also does not seem to be included and applicable in cases pursuant to Art.110 of *CPL 1991 (as amended 2012)* which provides for criminal liabilities for disruptions, threats etc.

[588]Fahey and Tao, "The Pretrial Discovery Process in Civil Cases: A Comparison of Evidence Discovery Between China and the United States," 299.

[589]Art. 139 of *CPL 1991(as amended in 2012)*.

is an important element of the trial process in the common law adversarial system. Lawyers are trained over many years in cross-examination skills.

The main purpose of cross-examining a witness is to put forward a case, to try to discredit witnesses and the related witness statements that have been exchanged with the opponents, and ultimately to undermine the strength of the evidence. [590] Nonetheless, the purpose is definitely not to trick or attack the witnesses. Cross-examination is an exercise in skill, and it assists in finding the truth, especially in the common law systems. Leading questions are put to the witnesses during the cross-examination, following the proper order of the questions according to the case theory.

However, scholars have criticised the excessive focus on cross-examination in adversarial systems, as they are of the view that there is not enough time for any of the witnesses to reflect upon or deliberate, as compared to the ample time available to witnesses in the inquisitorial system. This lack of time, according to Kessler, may inhibit truth seeking.[591] Instead in the PRC, there is a system called *zhizheng* evidence, which examines all types of evidence that has been submitted on record in the PRC courts, and includes the process to confront it. [592] This process of Chinese style confrontation of evidence (*zhizheng*) appears to be much broader, and cross-examining witnesses is only part of that process.[593] The author is not sure whether any hidden information can emerge from *zhizheng*.

5.2.1.1.4 Finding the Truth and Economic Equality

It is no secret that the onus is on the parties to investigate and collate evidence, and cross-examine the opponents' witnesses, but this can be properly executed only by accomplished and experienced lawyers. Wealthy parties can afford good lawyers, and this can create inequality between the parties. Because of this, the system sometimes fails in achieving the primary goal of seeking the truth. In fact, in practice, in the author's experience, the procedural rules have been used by well-off parties in the adversarial system to deny substantive justice. In the inquisitorial legal system, the

---

[590]Blake, *Practical Approach to Effective Litigation*, 602.

[591]A. D. Kessler, "Our Inquisitorial Tradition: Equity Procedure, Due Process, and the Search for an Alternative to the Adversarial," *Cornell L. Rev.* 90, no. 5 (2005): 1216. Kessler was also discussed in Gélinas, et al., *Foundations of Civil Justice*, 70.

[592]Art. 49 of *Some Provisions of Supreme People's Court on Evidence in Civil Procedures [No.33 of 2001] (as revised in 2008)*, (hereinafter 'SPC Provisions on Evidence *2001*). Art. 49 provides "When documentary evidence, material evidence or audio-visual materials are cross-examined...." It appears from this section that a party can cross-examine the opponent on all types of evidence.

[593]Paul J. Schmidt, "A Review of China's New Civil Evidence Law," *Pacific Rim L. & Pol. J.* 12, no. 2 (2003): 309.

judges' deep involvement in investigating the case may neutralise some of the negative effects of economic equality; however, the issue does still persist.

5.3 Judges and Legal Reasoning – Common law and Inquisitorial, in particular, England & Wales and PRC

The author will discuss now one by one the issue of the judges' legal reasoning in both jurisdictions. Even though England & Wales belong to the common law system and the PRC belongs to the civil law jurisdiction, it is quite possible that they may have a few unique features of their own, either due to overriding philosophy due to their constitution, or the underlying influence of jurisprudence. This aspect will be analysed as well in the forthcoming paragraphs.

5.3.1 Judges and Legal Reasoning – Common Law

It is the author's view, which is also acknowledged generally, that the legal reasons included in judgments by judges provide a legitimate motivation for the populace to follow the rules. However, in many empires and dynasties, there have been instances where giving reasons "would jeopardize rather than further the power and legitimacy of the courts."[594] The judges' reasons also ensure that individuals and society as a unit become more tolerant of contrary and dissimilar views within a society. It is, however, debatable whether common-law judges are under a duty to provide reasons,[595] unless it is expressly provided under the statutes, or it is imposed by procedural requirements. In contrast, it is common in inquisitorial systems that judges are under an obligation by statutes, often called affirmative duty,[596] to provide justifications in a particular format for decisions or judgments made in their courts.[597]

In spite of the fact that common law judges are under no obligation to provide reasons, it is a fact that common law judgments are famous for including reasons in detail; therefore, these judgments impart education to other judges and lawyers. In practice,

---

[594]Mathilde Cohen, "When Judges Have Reasons not to Give Reasons: A Comparative Law Approach," *Wash. & Lee L. Rev.* 72, no. 2 (2015): 487. Cohen discussed Philippe Godding's jurisprudence in the context of Italians in the twelfth and thirteenth centuries. Another reason that was cited in the paper was 'judicial secrecy'.

[595]Cohen, "Judges' Reasons."

[596]Ibid., 557–8.

[597]In France, after the revolution of 1790, the judges' reasons in their judgment were monitored to prevent them from becoming corrupt, or to restrict their arbitrary/discretionary power. For further discussion on this aspect, *see* Cohen, "Judges' Reasons," 558. In France, it can be seen that even though the courts have an obligation to give reasons, the judgments are in fact very brief. Further, though under an obligation to follow statutes, Cohen observed that the courts have lately been involved in law-making of their own through these very brief judgments. *See also*, Cohen, "Judges' Reasons," 561.

reason-giving by judges is generally affected by the case-load of the courts and the judges in common law courts exercise their *discretion* to furnish either brief or detailed reasons.[598]

According to Rawls' *jurisprudence of justice*, in a democratic liberal society, providing the public with detailed reasons for the opinion of the judges is their moral duty, and therefore, philosophically, it is very important for the judiciary's continued existence. [599] Another jurisprudent, Dworkin, viewed the necessity of judicial discourse in the courts as essential for enhancing the participation of the populace. Dworkin viewed the courts themselves as an important element in the integrity of the whole system, as they employ fair methods accepted by the populace. In Dworkin's school of thought, judges are constrained by their previous decisions.[600]

Judicial reasoning encourages participation within the society, ensures losing parties in cases do not ruminate over loss due to any bias towards them, and lastly assists society to determine that judicial decisions were not arbitrary decisions. In addition, judicial decisions should take into account the facts and relevant law that the parties have put forward to the judges. [601] Cohen, while discussing social psychology, suggested that added participation in the form of arguments in front of judges also leads to consensus agreements.[602]

In addition, judgments containing detailed reasons ensure that the judges remain accountable, as their opinions can be read by the higher courts and the general public.[603] With fully reasoned opinions, any appeal or intervention by the higher courts will appear to be arbitrary. Thus, the opinions of the judges will enhance rule of law by providing transparency in the whole process of adjudication for litigants and lawyers, other judges and above all the general public. Legal reasoning enhances accuracy by imposing self-discipline on the judges, by avoiding speculation, avoiding irrelevant information, and avoiding deficiency due to inadequate research, etc.[604]

---

[598]See "Judges' Reasons," 563 for a discussion in the context of judges in the US, Cohen.

[599]See *The Law of Peoples* (Cambridge, Mass.: Harvard University Press, 1999) for a discussion on legal reasoning by judges and issue of public reasons in John Rawls. *See also*, Cohen, "Judges' Reasons," 498–9, for further discussion about Rawls' jurisprudence.

[600]See Ronald Dworkin, *Law's Empire (Legal Theory)*, New ed. (Oxford: Hart Publishing, 1998) for discussions on various aspects of law, institutions etc. *See also*, Cohen, "Judges' Reasons," 500–1, for further discussion on Dworkin's views.

[601]Cohen, "Judges' Reasons," 504.

[602]Ibid., 506.

[603]Ibid., 507.

[604]Ibid., 408.

No doubt the populace living in any jurisdiction expects the judges to do their best in an honest way to adjudicate the issues before the courts. However, is it a valid expectation from the populace that all the judgments will be of high cognitive standard? This is also the question many jurisprudents have asked over the years when considering the role of judges.[605] Incoherence in legal reasoning in various judgments, and in statutory interpretation, has been observed quite frequently. However, as in any profession, some incoherence may be encountered from time to time and is part and parcel of any job. In the author's view, it is to be expected that there will be mistakes. However, a system of appeal and checks and balances within the judicial system exists to provide legitimacy to the whole process.

However, there are jurisdictions where the political philosophy is *totalitarian*, where the political bosses insist on having very high expectations of the judges, and there is a reasonable expectation that these judges will conform to the major political philosophy.[606] Judicial systems that are not independent are definitely susceptible to demands from political bosses. Jurisprudents such as Dworkin were of the view that just as government officials are subject to pressure to conform to the philosophy of their political bosses, in a similar way, judges are also subject to this doctrine of political responsibility. It is even said that the judges are like critiques in the newspapers in various subject areas and are trying to find the best law applicable in the circumstances. The moot question then is whether the issue of legal reasoning is that simple?

In jurisprudential terms, legal reasoning refers to the arguments that judges give in their judgments/decisions on various cases in the courts. These arguments consist of the reasons behind their decisions, and these reasons are intended as *justifications* for the decisions.[607] The justifications can be through the exercise of precedents and/or through the interpretation of statutes. Legal reasoning in common law cases is in the form of *modus ponens*, which MacCormick has described as follows: "whenever certain *operative facts* [emphasis added] occur, a given legal consequences follows."[608] MacCormick further was of the view that this meant that all legal rules

---

[605] James Penner, "Law and Adjudication: Dworkin's Critique of Positivism," in *Introduction to Jurisprudence and Legal Theory: Commentary and Materials*, by Anne Barron, et al. (London: Butterworths, 2002), 382.

[606] Ibid., 377.

[607] David M. Gooden and Douglas Walton, "Defeasibility in Judicial Opinion - Logical or Procedural," *Informal Logic* 28, no. 1 (2008): 7n1. In this paper, Gooden & Waldon has discussed Golding's definition of legal reasoning.

[608] Neil MacCormick, *Legal Reasoning and Legal Theory*, Clarendon Law Series (Oxford: Clarendon Press, 1978), 67. MacCormick was also discussed by Gooden & Waldon in Gooden and Walton, "Judicial Opinion -Logical or Procedural," 8. *Modus ponens* is the principle in the area of logic that whenever a conditional statement and its antecedent are given to be true its consequent may be validly

are only *"ordinarily necessary and presumptively sufficient."*[609] This will determine the legal rules to apply in any particular case. However, there may be exceptions within the judgments, which would mean that the result might not follow the facts governing the dispute. Gooden & Walton were of the view that because of this, the legal rules can be *undercut* or *undermined.*[610]

However, legal cases are not straight forward, and strait-jacket deductive reasoning cannot be applied universally, as it may lead to application of conflicting rules. In those scenarios, as discussed in Chapter Three,[611] and in this context, such conflicts are resolved by application of principles such as fairness, equality, justice, and so forth. It means that at times, legal arguments are overridden or rebutted by the stronger arguments of the judges.[612]

It can by no means be said that all legal rules, such as case precedents or interpretations of statutes, or even statutes themselves, are perfect. Therefore, judges cannot just apply them in all factual scenarios; judges are supposed to be aware of all exclusions. At times, as common-law lawyers have found when looking for relevant legal rule(s) in a judgment, they cannot find the main operative fact(s) leading to that legal rule(s). Therefore, it is likely that such facts were omitted in the judgment. As said earlier, the concept of the legal rule in itself is far from being perfect. Additionally, such legal rules can be undermined by principles of natural justice, and/or can be outmaneuvered, undercut, overridden, or rebutted.

The judges operate in an environment of uncertainty. Hart said, "Fact situations do not await us neatly labeled, creased, and folded, nor is their legal classification written on them to be simply read off by the judge."[613] This succinctly emphasises that fact situations are not straightforward; therefore it can be said that MacCormick's *operative facts* are also not well-defined, and this could lead the judges to search for necessary legal rules to apply in new cases. From this analysis, it can be highlighted that the reasoning cannot be simply deductive. *Deductive reasoning* is where the reasoning moves from general premises to the particular and is circular in nature. In

---

inferred, for example, *if it is the author this must be Harry,* and *it is Harry, so this must be the author.* This principle is important in light of case precedents and statutes that are used as deductive reasoning as part of justifications.

[609]Gooden and Walton, "Judicial Opinion — Logical or Procedural," 8. In this article, these authors took a quote from MacCormick, *Legal Reasoning and Legal Theory,* 103.

[610]Gooden and Walton, "Judicial Opinion — Logical or Procedural," 8.

[611]Refer to Chapter 3, §3.2.3, where positivists such as Hart, though not agreeing that natural law concepts should be applied, acknowledged that in a few cases, to fill the gaps in law, principles of natural justice such as fairness and equality can be used by judges to provide justifications.

[612]Gooden and Walton, "Judicial Opinion —Logical or Procedural," 8.

[613]H. L. A. Hart, "Positivism and Separation of Law and Morals," *Harvard L. Rev.* 71, no. 4 (1958): 607.

addition, for the conclusion to be true, it is important that the premises (major or minor) are true.[614] This uncertainty leads to indeterminacy and the result is conceptual rule-indeterminacy.[615] MacCormick, on the other hand, considers this uncertainty as an issue of interpretation and not rule-indeterminacy.[616]

For judges equipped with many legal rules learned/obtained from cases, customs, and statutes, the main issue is whether modification as a result of new facts or information in a case from case precedents or previous interpretation of statute(s) can change the premises. This issue will have an impact on another issue, that is, whether the conclusions taken as legal rules from previous cases are applicable to the facts of the new case. These are a few scenarios that make the legal rules compelling but yet defeasible, as discussed by Gooden and Walton.[617]

In any event, most judgments can be appealed to the next stage, if the judges had failed to apply or had misapplied the legal rule; or used a legal rule other than the one which ought to have been applied; or failed to follow a correct procedure before the courts. Judges must be careful when applying legal rules derived from the previous cases, where they might have been based on mistaken findings of operative fact(s) or missing or ignored evidence, or due to mistakes arising from faulty analysis of the link between premise and conclusion in judgments. The mistakes of the judges could include a scenario where they failed to give enough weight to the arguments of lawyers who were acting in the previous cases.

In order to avoid the pitfalls of indeterminacy of legal reasoning, or excessive appeals, there are procedural requirements. Further, the judges themselves are aware of the challenges they face in the courts and the associated risks in reaching conclusions in their judicial decisions. One such guideline for judges in the PRC is provided in Article 152 of *CPL 1991*; it provides features that are required in any judgment from the judges in the PRC:[618]

> A judgment shall state the outcome of the judgment and causes, and shall
> include the following content:
> (1) The cause of action, claims, and the facts and reasons of disputes;

---

[614]Lundmark, *Divide between Common and Civil Law*, 281.
[615]Gooden and Walton, "Judicial Opinion — Logical or Procedural," 10.
[616]MacCormick, *Legal Reasoning and Legal Theory*, 65–68. MacCormick's theory was also discussed in Gooden and Walton, "Judicial Opinion - Logical or Procedural," 10.
[617]Gooden and Walton, "Judicial Opinion — Logical or Procedural," 10.
[618]Art. 152 of *CPL 1991 (as amended in 2012)*.

(2) The facts and causes affirmed by the judgment, applicable laws and causes.

(3) The consequences of a judgment and the obligation of litigation costs; and

(4) The time limit for filing an appeal and the appellate court with which the appeal shall be filed.

The judgment shall be signed by the adjudicating personnel and the court clerk, and the seal of the people's court shall be affixed to it.

In England and Wales, even though there are formal requirements in *CPR 1998* r. 40.2 for a judgment to be in a particular format, for example bearing date and seal of the courts, there are no requirements similar to those expressly stated in the PRC's Article 152 of *CPL 1991*. However, in most common law traditions, the cases will provide succinct, detailed reasons and justifications, which offer a great education to legal professionals.

Generally speaking, on analysis, judgments provided in England & Wales are detailed, as they should be in the common law system. In the PRC, however, they are not so detailed as to include or consider each and every fact and every element of law that was applicable before the judgement was reached.

However, in common law itself, there is a school of thought that giving detailed judgments with reasons can itself cause disputes, reduce judicial efficiency, and create opportunities for divisions within society.[619] Cohen even emphasised that having dissenting views from a multi-judge tribunal is frowned upon by this school of thought as such dissenting arguments have the potential to reduce the institutional legitimacy [of judiciary].[620] Another school of thought from psychology also is not in favor of excessive justifications for judgment as they are of the view either that reasoning is usually motivated to prove one side of the story based on cultural or subjective preference, or that justifications are provided in a strategic way, instead of these justifications being founded solely on evidence presented to the courts.[621] Cohen even said:

---

[619]Cohen, "Judges' Reasons," 515.
[620]Ibid., 516–17.
[621]Cohen, "Judges' Reasons," 519, where Cohen discussed "motivated cognition "issues"".

Imposing strict reason-giving requirements on judges may yield insincerity and artificiality in judicial discourse, rather than promoting accountability and transparency.[622]

5.3.2 Judges in the Civil Law Tradition

As seen from the above analysis,[623] in the common law system the role or function of its judges is not to pro-actively seek the truth. In order to present a client's case to the judges, it is the duty of the lawyers, pursuant to Rules of Professional Conduct, that they cannot invent facts to assist their client's case.[624]

The above can be contrasted with the approach of the Court of Appeal in England and Wales, that has said that excessive intervention by trial judges during the course of a trial is prohibited, because it would be wrong for a judge to 'arrogate to himself a quasi-inquisitorial role,' this being something which is 'entirely at odds with the adversarial system'.[625] However for many years, the selection of judges in England and Wales was more like an election into an exclusive club. The current transparent process through application for the post of judge only started in 1997 for the High Court and in 1994 for sub-ordinate posts.

These issues with selection of judges have been criticised by practitioners and social scientists alike in England & Wales as one of the hurdles to finding the truth in many cases. Therefore, the role of judges in the civil law system would likely not have been appreciated by common-law judges.

5.3.2.1 In context of PRC Law (within civil law system)

Historically, judges in ancient China were famous for making judgments with the model of legal reasoning as seen in the eighteenth and nineteenth centuries in the

---

[622]Cohen, "Judges' Reasons," 522.

[623]Chapter 5, §5.2.1.1.1

[624]See *Medcalf v Mardell, Weatherill* [2002] UKHL 27, [2002] 3 All ER 731, [2003] 1 AC 120, [2002] NPC 89, [2002] PNLR 43, [2002] 3 WLR 172, [2002] CP Rep 70, [2002] CPLR 647, [2002] 3 Costs LR 428. In this case, judges were of the view that the conduct of lawyers who make allegations of dishonesty without adequate grounds would amount to improper conduct.

[625]See *Southwark LBC v Maamefowaa Koadu* [2006] EWCA Civ 281, [148]. *See also,* the discussion on this case in Neil Andrews, "Fundamental Principles of Civil Procedure: Order out of Chaos," in *Civil Litigation in a Globalising World*, ed. X. E. Kramer and Rhee, H (The Hague: T.M.C. Asser Press, 2012), 29, 387.

Board of Punishments.[626] As discussed earlier,[627] in ancient sources such as *Kang kao and Lu hsing*, the procedure adopted was inquisitorial and no legal representation of any kind whatsoever was allowed by those judges.

Once the facts were ascertained, popularly called 'finding the truth', relevant rules from Codes were investigated and to them were applied the relevant facts that were ascertained in the finding the truth process.

However, this procedure was limited to criminal procedure and to some civil issues that were made part of the Code. In the Tang Code, during the Tang Dynasty (601-981 CE), there was a possibility of scenarios where truth cannot be ascertained completely. To deal with this, a relatively small number of rules were drafted so that they could be used in combination, in different circumstances & for different scenarios and offences. To achieve this, a key term in a particular set of rules was utilised to prevent the creation of lengthy codes.[628]

In later dynasties, torture was allowed to overcome the difficulty of excessive processes in the Codes; the priority was to extract quick confessions. This process of extraction of confessions by torture is deemed by western scholars as a failure of rationality.[629]

According to these scholars, the system ought to ascertain the facts clearly without legitimising torture, even in a milder form. Usually in ancient China, the Board of Punishments would discuss and analyse the procedure and findings and would sometimes send the case back to the magistrates.

The PRC still uses the inquisitorial system in its courts, where the judge's role is to find the truth, and the formal requirements and Standards of Proof are very high. However, in theory, the judges' power is limited, as will be discussed later in this Chapter.

5.4 Judges' Role in Accomplishing Various Functions in the Courts - Concept of Judge's Power

---

[626]Geoffrey MacCormack, *The Spirit of Traditional Chinese Law*, The Spirit of the Laws (Athens: London: University of Georgia Press, 1996), 16.
[627]Refer, Chapter 2, §2.2.1.
[628]MacCormack, *The Spirit of Traditional Chinese Law*, 15.
[629]Ibid., 148.

There are various functions that judges are asked to accomplish in relation to adjudication; some, as described by Katyal in the context of the US common law, are as follows:[630]

- *Clarifications* of a statute or law;

- *Personification*, whereby they guide the role of government organs;

- *Self-Alienation,* whereby the judiciary itself limits its role in a particular matter;

- *Exemplification*, whereby judges can strike down an act as unconstitutional;

- *Demarcation*, whereby an act is deemed unconstitutional but with examples of similar unconstitutional ones;

- *Prescription*, whereby the judges give policy advice to the executive based on their experience;

- *Penalization*, whereby the judges may ask the legislature to look at the acts as they are not serving the purpose.

A lot of scholarly space has been devoted to *doctrines of separation* and *judicial independence*, which are important for ensuring judicial effectiveness. However, this concept of *doctrine of separation* is very deeply rooted in western jurisprudence. Traditionally, in countries where the judiciary has not been independent, these concepts could be alien. However, in the author's view, legal cultures can be different, and so this should not be treated as if it is an insurmountable obstacle.

Gillespie has discussed that there are no distinct economic benefits in copying western concepts in Far Eastern legal systems, and that therefore, the courts should be structured differently in these countries.[631] However, Gillespie's key finding was that *judicial effectiveness* is actually enhanced by judicial power much more than

---

[630]Neal Kumar Katyal, "Judge as Advicegivers," *Stan. L. Rev.* 50, no. 6 (1998): 1722.

[631]John Gillespie, "Rethinking the Role of Judicial Independence in Socialist-Transforming East Asia," *I.C.L.Q.* 56, no. 4 (2007): 840.

judicial independence, as in the early stages the judiciary itself needs protection.[632] Judicial power can be seen within the context of jurisdiction to handle disputes, and discretionary power to manage different types of disputes and to grant general and specific remedies. Judicial power can also be seen within the context of their ability to give binding judgments that can be enforced later by the same courts.

Historically, the advent and evolution of legal judicial reasoning in the English courts ensured that the concept of judicial independence evolved to insulate the courts from external influences such as "clientelism, nepotism, hierarchical status and political cronyism."[633] In addition, legal reasoning that has emerged because of judges employing their discretionary power was used in England & Wales to find a way to resolve political interference before formal concepts of constitutional safeguards came into existence.[634]

This ability of the courts proved very useful in resolving economic disputes, especially when England & Wales was an economic superpower in the nineteenth century. It is the author's view that in legal systems where codes are new and still developing, such as in the PRC, judges need to have *discretionary power* to apply such codes appropriately to the facts of the cases. However, while judges might have such discretionary power, the capability and desire of the judges to exercise them are an altogether different issue. This issue is only sparingly touched on in the PRC. Such discretionary power is also exercised by the judges in civil law countries such as France.[635]

However, judicial discretion can be eroded easily, for example:[636]

- By guidance of senior courts' judges (outside of appeal process);

- By directive from a local or central leadership or ideology leadership;

- By formulating creative decision to protect interests of state;

---

[632]Gillespie, "Judicial Independence in East Asia.", where the main theme of his paper was that judicial power enhances judicial effectiveness.
[633]Ibid., 848.
[634]Ibid., 849.
[635]Ibid.
[636]Ibid., 851–3.

- By relying heavily on state's organs for guidance on commercial cases.

At times, the judges' discretionary power is exhibited by employing sentiment, or local norms such as morality and sentimental value in the courts to gain legitimacy; this may itself lead to the erosion of the judges' discretionary power.[637] In many jurisdictions, discretion is employed so widely by the judges that any law, if it were to be an impediment to the state's interest, would be considered as irrelevant to the facts of the dispute. As a consequence, the textual narrative of codes or statutes is sometimes overlooked, eroding not only the discretionary power, but also the legitimacy of the courts.

For discretionary power to be put into practice, judges in courts are usually encouraged to engage in legal discourse that assists in development of legal reasoning. Judges are further encouraged to exercise their discretionary power in a way that can assist the judges "to transpose political, moral and economic precepts into legally judicable questions."[638]

5.5 Judicial Decision-making Process

After the above discussion on judges' power, particularly in relation to discretionary power, it is important for the author to discuss the whole process of decision-making by the judges in any jurisdiction. Whether it is the common law system or civil law inquisitorial system, the judges in their decision making are affected by "anchoring, hindsight bias, self-serving bias"[639] and that can have an effect on a final judgment in any case.

The above factors affect the full judicial process, including the analysis of facts. The danger is even more pronounced when the judges are exercising their discretionary power. Therefore, any remedy that is dependent on the discretionary power of judges, for example interim applications, is affected by such factors.

---

[637]Ibid., 855.
[638]Ibid., 864.
[639]Negowetti, "Judicial Decisionmaking," 715.

Negowetti has said that "'Discretion-free" judging, bereft of the influence of one's own identity or experiences, is far-fetched in a profession populated by human beings, and not machines."[640] It is natural for judges to bring their assumptions, biases, intuitions, experience, religion, values, age, gender, political beliefs, sexual orientation and own sense of justice to bear. Complete emotional detachment of the judges from a case is impossible; they may well process only information that conforms to their world-view. Therefore, the theme of this book is that invisible factors do affect judges, and therefore law in action is affected by such invisible factors in various ways.

Globally, judges have started to acknowledge the above vulnerability, and are sceptical about their own intuition because of this vulnerability. However, it is still a work in progress. This *unconscious influence* can be mitigated by the judges by acknowledging them and developing the skill of *empathy*, where the judges will start to take into account the perspective of every party in their courts.[641] Empathy is different from compassion and is the cognitive capacity to understand others' point of view. It is a skill that can be developed by acknowledging and then overpowering one's own biases, prejudices and loyalties.[642] Empathy assists judges to understand disputes better, including the motivations and intentions of the litigants before the courts.

The role of empathy remains very important for handling applications in civil courts; as it is a fact that most of these applications require the judges to exercise their discretionary power. Many of the objective standards, test of reasonableness, and Standards of Proof in civil litigation can only succeed, if there is an impartial view of the facts. This is only possible if the litigators and judicial decision-makers are aware of their own personal biases.

The above issue also exposes the issue of selection of judges in England & Wales from only a narrow section of the society, which in the practice of law could cloud social realities. This in turn could affect the outcome in any civil litigation. Similarly, in the PRC, the ideological training in the philosophy of communism, socialism, Marxism and various thoughts highlighted in *PRC Constitution 1982* (as amended) again could cloud the judges' views about disputes before them.

---

[640]Ibid., 717.
[641]Ibid., 724.
[642]Ibid., 727.

CHAPTER SIX — JUDGES' DISCRETIONARY POWER – COMMON LAW v. CHINESE LAW

6.1   Judges' Discretionary Power

In the previous Chapter, the author discussed jurisprudence of justice in the context of *law in action*, in particular judges' roles, their powers, biases, decision making processes, their role in relation to evidence and so forth. In the previous Chapter, the author also touched upon the issue of judicial discretion and how it can be eroded due to interference from the executive and preservers of ideology. These issues were discussed from the point of view of both the common law system of England & Wales and PRC law. The author will now analyse judges' discretionary power in the context of legal philosophy, traditions in the historical context, and most importantly the current practice in courts.

There is a need in any legal system to have certainty in the application of law and to curb the arbitrary power of judges. However, no statute or case law can be perfect or can imagine all scenarios that might emerge in the future, to which such statute or case law might be applied. There is a great deal of uncertainty surrounding facts, law, customs, procedures in court, issues related to third parties that can be affected by any judgment, issues of economic equality between the parties and policy and so forth. Faced with this uncertainty, learned judges in any jurisdiction will have to exercise their discretionary power. The main issues that arise in both the jurisdictions are:

- Whether the judges in England & Wales and PRC jurisdiction are equipped with such power? and

- If they are equipped with such power, are the judges willing to exercise such discretionary power? and

- If the judges are willing to exercise that power, are there any impediments in relation to such exercise of discretionary power?

6.2 Principles and Philosophy in Current Legal System in English Law

In traditional England, the concept of *rule of law* needs to be applied to all types of judicial activities. This strand of jurisprudence gained further popularity with Rawls' concept of *formal justice* where justice demands that there is impartial application of the rules.[643] In order to uniformly apply the rules, the judges will have to give up their 'personal' discretionary power that is available to all humans at the personal level, so that all trials, hearings, procedures in the courts and rules in relation to evidence are constant.[644]

This uniform application of law will also be applicable to the executive and legislative branch in that society, and therefore, the rules will have primacy over all institutions, with the sole aim of curbing the arbitrary powers of officials. This leads to what Dicey has called "supremacy or predominance of regular law as opposed to influence of arbitrary power."[645]

However, there are scenarios where there is no consensus in a legislature to draft new law on a particular subject and therefore, there is no law on that subject. This results in a scenario where policy from the legislature is kept deliberately ambiguous and the only way for judges to resolve disputes in court is to employ their judicial resources.

---

[643]John Rawls, *A Theory of Justice*, 2nd ed. (Cambridge, Mass: Belknap Press of Harvard University Press, 1999), 235.
[644]Margaret Y. K. Woo, "Law and Discretion in the Contemporary Chinese Courts," *Pac. Rim L. and Pol'y J.* 8, no. 3 (1999): 583.
[645]A. V. Dicey, *Introduction to the Study of the Law of Constitution* (London; New York: Macmillan, 1902), 202–3.

Hawkins argued that there are functional benefits to the judges having discretionary power, such as avoiding costly formalities, or filling gaps in law or policy.[646]

On one hand, there is a need to enhance the legitimacy of the courts by providing certainty from the beginning; but on the other hand, there is also a need to do justice in the particular circumstances of a dispute. In ancient western jurisprudence, the Greek jurisprudent Aristotle was of the view that fair-minded judges could ensure justice was done for litigants in their courts.[647] In the historical English Legal system, as discussed earlier,[648] the role of certainty provided by formal rules in common law was balanced by courts of *equity* that granted discretionary power to provide justice to litigants. Now that both these courts are merged in the current legal system,[649] the judges' discretionary power is fully anchored in the system and is no longer considered an arbitrary power.

Dworkin has noted that the judges' power can be used in various ways in the context of common law:[650]

- Discretion is used in a weaker sense, meaning that judges cannot apply the rules or statutes mechanically, but will use their judgment based upon their training and experience;

- Another weaker sense in which discretionary power can be used is that the judges highest up in a hierarchy have the final say on the dispute, and their decisions cannot be reviewed or reversed;

- Discretion in the stronger sense (hereinafter '*third sense*' is most relevant in scenarios when the judges are not bound by the limits of law (statutes, case precedent, customary rules) but with exceptions. However, any discretion employed by the

---

[646]Keith Hawkins, "Use of Legal Discretion: Perspectives from Law and Social Science" (1992), 37. Hawking is also discussed in Woo, "Discretion in Contemporary Chinese Courts," 584n16.

[647]Woo, "Discretion in Contemporary Chinese Courts," 584n12, where Aristotle was discussed in relation to the concept of a fair-minded judge. Woo referred to Aristotle and J. A. K. Thomson, trans., *The Ethics of Aristotle: The Nicomachean Ethics*, Reprinted ed. (London: Penguin, 1961), 146–47.

[648]Refer, Chapter 2, §2.1.1.2, where the role of the Courts of Equity was discussed.

[649]Refer, Chapter 2, §2.1.1.3 and the discussion of the merger of parallel court systems in England.

[650]Ronald Dworkin, *Taking Rights Seriously* (London: Duckworth, 1977), 29–36. Dworkin's views were also discussed in Penner, "Law and Adjudication" 342–43.

judges contains in it the principles of rationality, fairness, effectiveness, etc.

Positivists like H. L. A. Hart in England & Wales agree with the concept of discretionary power being employed by judges. According to Hart, employment of discretionary power is based on the 'court's principles'. However, one school of thought argues that the judges having such discretionary power itself means that the judges are disregarding the rules; having such discretion in itself also means that there are no limits on the power of the judges.[651] The usual circumstances in which judges exercise their discretionary power are in scenarios where a dispute is complex and there is no law or policy for them to consider. The judges' discretionary power can be also being seen in the context of obligation or duty: the judges are morally obliged, or the courts are institutionally obligated, or it is a part of the judges' work to apply such principles when adjudicating disputes in court.

There is jurisprudential debate as to whether such *principles* are 'part of law' or, pursuant to Dworkin's argument, whether they play the role of extra-legal standards that the courts often employ in order to reach decisions.[652] However, in the positivists' view, it is very difficult to count the principles that the judges usually employ in their discretion as part of the law. However, careful reading and analysis show that Dworkin considers these principles as part of law. Therefore, when judges employ such principles when adjudicating disputes, it can be read as if they have no discretionary power, and/or may not actually be considered as their exercising discretionary power.

Raz explained in relation to Dworkin's view that when rules or law are read together with principles, there is no room for any vagueness. Therefore it seems clear to Raz that there is no need for the judges to have any discretionary power.[653] The only way to demonstrate that principles exist in the context of judges' discretionary powers is by appealing to 'community practices and understandings' along with the history of judicial practice, cases and legislations.[654] At the same time, however, Dworkin highlighted that the soundness of employment of discretionary power cannot be tested in exactly the same way, as the discretionary power of any other officials is incapable

---

[651]Ronald Dworkin, *Taking Rights Seriously*, 29–36. *See also*, discussion on Dworkin in Penner, "Law and Adjudication" 344.

[652]Ronald Dworkin, *Taking Rights Seriously*, 29–36.

[653]J. Raz, "Legal Principles and the Limits of Law," *Yale L.J.* 81, no. 5 (1972): 838–47. Raz's ideas were discussed in Penner, "Law and Adjudication" 357.

[654]Ronald Dworkin, *Taking Rights Seriously*, 36. See for further discussion on Dworkin, Penner, "Law and Adjudication" 345.

of being tested for soundness. Any other reasonable and educated person may very well disagree with the results after the exercise of discretionary power by the judges in courts.[655]

Raz took the analysis and the debate further in the context of principles that judges often employ. He was of the view that there was a difference between rules that are very specific in nature and could be found by judges in the law, in statutes or cases, and principles that are not specific enough, such as concept of justice or reasonableness or similar principles. In addition, the principles are relatively vague and less certain, but general goals and values can be reflected more patently by using such principles. These principles also provide relative flexibility to the judges.

However, Raz did mention that it is not easy to delineate rules from principles.[656] It is the author's view that in legal systems where correctness of a judgment is crucial and judges go to great lengths to analyse and apply the rules, certainty or uniformity is given less precedence in the scheme of things. In such situations, principles will have a slightly larger role in a subtle way in their application to the facts in a dispute. The author is of the school of thought that believes that in the application of principles, morality is in full force by the back door.[657] Raz is also of the same view, that morality prevails in such cases.[658]

Raz analysed the *principles* in detail in the context of the judges' power:

- Principles as grounds for *interpreting laws,* whereby any interpretation by the judges should conform to the general principles of a legal system that decides the coherence of purpose amongst various laws;

- Principles as grounds for *changing laws* where cases are modified using principles though the principles are used conservatively in this scenario;

[655]Ronald Dworkin, *Taking Rights Seriously*, 29–36. *See also*, Penner, "Law and Adjudication" 345, for further discussion on this aspect
[656]Raz, "Legal Principles" on discussion on the aspect that there is a thin line between rules and principles. *See also*, Penner, "Law and Adjudication" 354, for discussion on Raz's view.
[657]Refer to discussion on morality and natural Law in Chapter 3, §3.2.2.
[658]Raz, "Legal Principles," 838–47. *See also*, Penner, "Law and Adjudication" 354, for the discussion on this aspect and Raz's view.

- Principles as grounds for a *particular exception to laws* — more often used in non-common-law countries, but in common law countries also have principles that have been developed in the courts of equity,[659] for example — one must come with clean hands to the courts; or, no one can profit from their own wrong; or, the claimants cannot unreasonably delay in enforcing his rights through the courts, etc.;

- Principles as grounds for *creating new rules* when in particular situations, the judges are unable to find a particular law in any forum. However, any new rules that judges may apply are formulated on the basis of established principles;

- Principles as the sole grounds for action in particular cases such as in administrative law; the *implementation* through discretionary power by officials is governed by these principles.[660]

In order to understand the crucial differences between legal rules and principles, in the author's view, it is important to know how they have evolved. A *legal rule* can be created by a single judgment or a single legislation, but the *principle(s)* are gathered over a period through the analysis of many such judgments.

Raz said "...that legal principles do not exclude judicial discretion; they presuppose its existence and direct and guide it."[661] While the word 'discretion' leads many to believe it is arbitrary in nature, this is not the case in practice in common law systems. For example, even if there were no limits on discretionary power, the courts will still be "legally bound to act as they think is best according to their beliefs and values. If they do not, if they give arbitrary judgment by tossing a coin, for example, they violate a legal duty."[662] At a more concrete level, decisions/judgments made by the exercise of discretionary powers cannot be looked at in isolation, but has to be looked at through the prism of "some comprehensive theory or general principles and policies that is [sic] consistent with other decisions also thought right."[663]

---

[659]Refer, Chapter 2, §2.1.1.2
[660]Raz, "Legal Principles," 838–47. See also. Penner, "Law and Adjudication" 355–57.
[661] Raz, "Legal Principles," 838–47. This quote of Raz was even cited in Penner, "Law and Adjudication" 358.
[662]Ibid.
[663]Ibid.

6.2.1 Judges' Discretionary Power – in context of English law

In England & Wales, there are two schools of thought in relation to principles and rules. According to one jurisprudential school of thought, such principles are there as part of law, and therefore, the judges employ no judicial discretion. On the other hand, in another jurisprudential school of thought, there is an acknowledgment of judicial discretion and the fact that principles play a big role in judicial activities. It is the author's stance that no matter which school of thought we believe in, in legal practice or *law in action*, it is a fact, that judges do opt for principles, legal rules based on case laws, statutes, customs and policy reasons, and prioritise them.

According to Raz, few legal systems expressly provide that if the judges are unable to find a rule in a case, then they will not be able to render judgment. Raz has discussed the issue of employment of discretionary power by the judges in the following instances:[664]

- No sentences constructed in any language can be devoid of *vagueness*. Nonetheless, the courts have built rules of interpretation and there are principles as discussed above to guide the courts. However, it is important to note that these principles are vague and are quite broad.

- Judges are guided by the law as to what they need to consider when *applying the law*, but what weight the judges need to give in order to apply the rules (law of statute, customs or case law) or which rule will prevail or which rules need to be ignored is what judges have to consider. In other words, the judges have discretion to apply principles and to assess the relative importance of these principles.

- This special type of discretion is available to judges for them to apply *non- binding considerations*, but again this will be guided by principles.

---

[664]Raz, "Legal Principles," 838–47. *See also*, Penner, "Law and Adjudication" 357–58 for discussion on various scenarios highlighted by Raz.

The author has discussed in Chapter 4 the concept of overriding objective in *CPR 1998*, which allows the courts to exercise their discretionary power. Therefore, it can be argued that the principles supplementing and complementing the law are expressly included in *CPR 1998*.[665]

In many areas of both substantive and procedural law, common law sets its standards according to those of a 'reasonable person'. However, this community standard has been criticised, as they argue this is tantamount to the entry of judicial discretion by the back door. The criticism is due to the fact that there is a danger that judges can apply their own personal standards instead of the community standard in the 'reasonable person test'.[666]

In the current practice in England & Wales, in many areas of substantive law and procedural law, there is wide discretionary power that the judges in the English courts regularly employ in reaching their decisions. Numerous commentators who have analysed various judgments note that there were policy reasons behind these judgments, especially when there were no equivalent statutes and/or legislations to deal with those disputes.

6.3 Judges' Discretionary Power – in context of PRC law

In order to analyse the issue of judges' discretionary power in the PRC, the author will first discuss the pre-PRC era, and subsequently will discuss jurisprudential thinking in the current system. Finally, the author will discuss current practice of law/law in this context, in the PRC courts.

6.3.1 Historical Analysis of Judges' Discretionary Power in Pre-PRC Era

We have discussed in Chapter 3 the various invisible factors in relation to jurisprudential thought[667] which have influenced Chinese law over the centuries, and the legal thought of *conservatism*, which links ancient traditions with current schools of thought as prevailing in PRC, both of which still influence modern law.

---

[665] Anthony Clarke, "The Woolf Reforms: A Singular Event or an Ongoing Process," in *The Civil Procedure Ten Years On*, ed. Déirdre Dwyer (Oxford: Oxford University Press, 2009), 45. *See also,* the discussion of overriding objectives and secondary objectives in Chapter 4, §4.2.1.1.
[666] Negowetti, "Judicial Decisionmaking," 701.
[667] Refer, Chapter 3 §3.5 -3.6, Chinese Legal history and jurisprudence.

One jurisprudential thought in ancient China ensured that a ruler had all the legislative powers, and no officer could trespass upon this power. Legalism ensures that the officials' duties are thoroughly defined. Throughout legal history, Chinese judges had very limited discretionary powers, and in addition, they could even be held liable and could be punished for transgressing the limits of their power beyond the penal or administrative codes.[668] Therefore, in ancient Chinese legal practice, rulers insisted that officials have a thorough understanding of laws as compared to the general populace. Because of this, the codes were very detailed and well-defined.[669]

In ancient China, there were also the likes of Xunzi, as discussed in Chapter Three, who was of the view that when good, wise and capable men were selected for decision-making positions (such as judges of today), then it would not matter whether there were good laws. Xunzi was of the view that they would apply the external law in the textual form correctly by knowing the purpose of the law, and would thus do justice.[670] Was he, a few thousand years previously, alluding to the discretionary power of such wise men? It seems that such discretionary power could trump, if required, even the written law.

In the author's view, Xunzi was more likely alluding to the discretionary power of the judges, which was and is important in dealing with cases. However, the author feels that he was alluding to discretion in the weaker sense, rather than in the third sense as discussed above.[671] In the legal history of China, the discretionary powers of officials who sat as judges were curtailed by the drafting of Codes in detail, with strict directions not to 'invent' rules. One such direction was to only apply the rules of the Emperor. It was a rule for judges that previous cases were not to be cited as a precedent; they had to strictly state the Code and sub codes used in any judgments.[672]

The judges' capacity to even try using any residual discretionary power was curtailed by punishing them to ensure strict application of correct law. Any inadvertent, negligent or deliberate stepping out could result in punishment, thus discouraging judges from employing their residual discretionary power (even if there was any in the first place!). In addition, extensive supervisory rules also prevented the judges from stepping onto the path of equity by employing any discretionary power. This is

---

[668]MacCormack, *Spirit of Traditional Chinese Law*, 5.

[669]MacCormack, *Spirit of Traditional Chinese Law*, 5–6. Cf, the approach in Tang Codes discussed in §5.3.2.1.

[670]Wejen Chang, "Classical Chinese Jurisprudence and Development of Chinese Legal System" (2009–10), 240.

[671]Ronald Dworkin, *Taking Rights Seriously*, 36.

[672]MacCormack, *Spirit of Traditional Chinese Law*, 163.

in sharp contrast to developments in England & Wales, where many common law judges have assisted in development of laws in equity by developing new rules.[673]

The only clear cut discretionary power available to ancient Chinese judges was to resort to *analogy (pi fu)*, especially where it was difficult to find the exact rule to apply to the facts of a matter in front of them.[674] Analogy at times operated in situations where it was difficult for the judges to match the facts with the existing Code. In these scenarios, it was then possible for judges to decide based on the "spirit of the law, the meaning of the provisions, or the intention of the legislator [as] the basis of the analogy."[675] In the author's view, it does seem that ancient PRC judges were adopting a technique similar to the modern English concept of the statutory interpretation, where the intent of legislators needs to be investigated. However, many judges, unlike in the common law system, were not prepared to broaden the meaning of rules, and to a certain extent not even allowed to embark on this path. This seems to be the major difference between the historical common law and the historical Chinese legal system.[676]

As recently as the 18th and 19th centuries, *Qing Board of Punishments* in the context of criminal proceedings used to promote the 'value of consistency and certainty in the application of rules of penal code'.[677] This was another example of curtailing the discretionary power of the judges.

6.3.2   Principles and Philosophy in Current Legal System in PRC

We have seen in the previous Chapter[678] how principles govern the practice of law and rules in the courts. Most of the principles in relation to the PRC are relatively new and came to the forefront only after 1949. This is unlike the gradual development of such principles in the common law over centuries. In the PRC judicial organs are governed by following constitutional principles (that are further applicable to civil litigation):

---

[673]Refer, Chapter 2, §2.1.1.2.
[674]MacCormack, *Spirit of Traditional Chinese Law*, 166.
[675]MacCormack, *Spirit of Traditional Chinese Law*, 170 for discussion on Marinus Johan Meijer, "An Aspect of Traditional Chinese Law," *T'oung Pao* 66 (1980): 348.
[676]Supported in MacCormack, *Spirit of Traditional Chinese Law*, 173.
[677]MacCormack, *Spirit of Traditional Chinese Law*, 6.
[678]Refer, Chapter 5, §5.3 as to discussion of principles that are taken into account by the judges in the context of their employment of discretionary power in legal reasoning.

◆ All citizens are equal before the law.[679]

◆ In judicial proceedings, the laws are applied by judges equally to all citizens.[680]

◆ The People's Courts exercise their judicial power independently, in accordance with the provisions of law, and are not subject to interference by any administrative organs, public organisations or individuals.[681]

◆ Citizens of all nationalities (in the PRC) have the right to use their own written and spoken language.[682]

◆ Except in special circumstances, all hearings shall be public.[683]

The Supreme Peoples' Court ("SPC"), the highest court in the PRC, has been given the power to interpret applications of law.[684] This power is also available with People's Procuratorates which have the power to exercise supervision over the judicial activities of the People's Courts to ensure they conform to the law.[685] In the context of differences in opinion, if any, between the Supreme Court and People's Procuratorates in relation to legal interpretation, then the National People's Congress Standing Committee ("NPCSC") has the power to decide on the final interpretation.[686] The SPC regularly publishes such interpretations of important laws for the benefit of all.

A factor that has significantly influenced the official ambivalence about the need to contain discretionary power is that the courts are often not seen as law-making institutions.[687] At one end of the spectrum is the anti-corruption drive and on the other

---

[679]See Art. 33 of *Constitution of PRC 1982*.

[680]See Art. 5 of *Organic Law of People's Courts of People's Republic of China 1979*.

[681]See Art. 4 of *Organic Law of Peoples Courts of People's Republic of China 1979 (as amended in 1983)*. A similar article, Art. 126, can be found in *Constitution of PRC 1982*.

[682]See Art. 8 of *Organic Law of People's Courts of People's Republic of China 1979 (as amended in 1983)*.

[683]See *Organic Law of Peoples Courts of People's Republic of China 1979 (as amended in 1983)*, Art. 7.

[684]See *Organic Law of Peoples Courts of People's Republic of China 1979 (as amended in 1983)*.
[685]Ibid.

[686]See *Resolution on Strengthening the Work of Legal Interpretation*, para. 2, adopted on June 10, 1981 by the Standing Committee of the Fifth NPC at its 19th Session.

[687]Woo, "Discretion in Contemporary Chinese Courts," 581–2.

end are the codified procedures for supervision of judges based on the ideology of *jiandu.*[688]

There is also the fact that the PRC courts are more concerned with the application of substantive law rather than uniformity in procedures; put simply, the outcomes of different adjudications are more important than the procedure. At the same time, PRC courts are extremely vigilant about situations where any infringement of the rights of the PRC could become an issue.[689] The dichotomy between maintaining legitimacy by applying the formal rules and thus maintaining *rule of law (fazhi)*, and providing justice in specific circumstances using *rule by man* through judge*s (renzhi)*, is also a constant here, as in any other legal system.[690]

In relation to the debates discussed above, Yang has delineated *three schools* of thoughts:[691]

◆   The first school of thought does not reject *renzhi* but stresses the need to have qualified legal professionals. This school is realist and accepts the fact that any rule has to be applied by a man/woman. It seems this school of thought is receptive to the discretionary power of judges;

◆   The second school of thought rejects *renzhi* in relation to officials who are seen to be abusing power but accepts renzhi in relation to revolutionary leaders and masses. The author's view is that Yang is likely to include the abuse of discretionary power of the officials;

◆   The third school of thought rejects the whole concept of *renzhi* and stresses ideological guidance based on CPC principles. This school of thought seems to suggest that such principles are part of the law, akin to Dworkin's debate in jurisprudence pertaining to law in action.

---

[688]Ibid., 582.
[689]Ibid.
[690]Ibid., 585.
[691]Woo, "Discretion in Contemporary Chinese Courts," 585, where Woo discussed Yang's ideas as discussed in Ganqiao Yang, *New Thoughts of Chinese Jurisprudence (Zhongguo Faxue Xin Siwei)* (Shanxi: Shanxi People's Publisher, 1989), 29–31.

6.3.3 Current Thinking and Practice about Application of Discretionary Power in PRC Courts

Woo has discussed three types of discretion that are available in the PRC in the context of legal philosophy – fact-based discretion, self-interested discretion and ideological discretion.[692]

In *fact-based discretion*, judges will adjudicate according to the facts about the dispute before them. They will take into account the need for harmony in society, rather than seeking the solution in terms of winners and losers.[693] The judges will attempt to extract the truth from the facts and even try to investigate and correct the parties' versions.

In *fact-based discretion*, the focus of the judges on the facts of the disputes in the initial years of development of the legal system may be the result of lack of formal training of adjudication professionals. As per the Confucian model, the effects of morality and accordingly, the need to maintain social harmony, is always in the minds of the judges. This mindset has become part of the legal system. Marxist philosophy also had its effects on the legal system, stating that the law should remain answerable to the populace.[694] Woo suggested that the role of judges is more as social crisis managers rather than as resolvers of the disputes of the parties.[695]

In *self-interested discretion*, Woo has cited the use of discretion for the self-interest of the judges. Self-interest involves matters such as invitations to lavish parties for judges, or other forms of corruption, and takes the form of *renqing an* (where disputes are resolved using favours), or *guanxi an* (where disputes are resolved through personal relations or connections).[696] This problem is not only associated with a few judges, but is also is backed by many litigants in the PRC.[697]

Another form of *self-interested discretion* seen in the PRC courts takes the form of *difang baohu zhuyi* (a form of local protectionism), where the local courts in a province will not accept a case from other provinces, because the local government is responsible for the budget of local judicial services. Judges tend to protect local

---

[692]Woo, "Discretion in Contemporary Chinese Courts," 586.
[693]Ibid., 587.
[694]Woo, "Discretion in Contemporary Chinese Courts," 588.
[695]Ibid.
[696]Ibid., 590.
[697]Ibid., 591.

litigants and commerce in their own provinces.[698] There is an attempt to curtail this discretionary power of the PRC judges through Codes.[699]

The scope for *ideological discretion* has been added explicitly in *CPL 1991*.[700] Woo has researched another form of judicial discretion in the PRC courts, famously called *ideological discretion*. The *Preamble of Constitution PRC 1982* as last amended in 2018 explicitly provides for the leadership of the Communist Party of China, with guidance on the basis of *Marxism-Leninism, Mao Zedong's thoughts* and *Xi Jinping's thoughts*. This enables the judges faced with disputes in their courts to ensure that the results are compatible with ideological philosophy or any policy issued by CPC.[701]

In the early years of the PRC, there used to be a policy in relation to disputes in the courts that the cases were to be reviewed by the local CPC party secretary (*shuji pi'an*) through the local political affairs committee procedure (*zhengfa weiyuanhui*). Now, the Procuratorate System supervises judges and ensures compatibility with ideological philosophy in the outcome and judgments. In the author's view, this is a major issue when international commercial disputes are to be dealt with in PRC courts.

CPL 1991 provides for supervisory procedures, where cases in the courts can be *re-opened* to check the unjust application of judicial discretion. This has the effect of limiting discretion, but also in a way increases judicial discretion at the same time.[702] Supervision of the justice system and system of procuratorates is even enshrined in the PRC constitution,.[703] Protests against the judgment of the courts can be lodged according of *CPL 1991*.[704]

The system of Procuratorates has the power to interpret laws that are related to its own work, which is not considered to be within the realm of the judiciary. However, the system of procuratorates seems to intervene in civil cases only when the state's interests are affected.[705] There is a provision for supervision by the masses,[706] as part of the concept of democratic supervision (*mizhu jiandu*), and the NPC can seek a report on this aspect from the system of Procuratorates and courts. This system of

---

[698]Ibid.
[699]See Art. 44 of *CPL 1991 (as amended in 1991)*, where power is curtailed in the *Civil Procedure Code* by prohibiting judges from accepting gifts, and there is the possibility of criminal prosecution if they do.
[700]See Art. 14 of *CPL 1991 (as amended in 2012)*, where State Procuratorates have been provided to supervise the trials.
[701]Woo, "Discretion in Contemporary Chinese Courts," 418.
[702]Ibid., 601.
[703]See Art. 129 of *Constitution of PRC 1982*.
[704]See Art. 208 of *CPL 1991 (as amended in 2012)*.
[705]Woo, "Discretion in Contemporary Chinese Courts," 607.
[706]See Art. 7(7) of *Judges Law 1995*.

supervision from multiple areas has led to a situation where PRC judges are happy to be in the administrative role and leave decision making to the adjudication committee.[707]

Ideological discretion is thus affected by supervision, as it is a tool to accomplish precisely that.[708] The principle of *democratic centralism*[709] ensures that all judges submit to the adjudication committees. These Committees in turn submit to Procuratorates. Procuratorates in turn should submit to the National People's Congress.[710]

In current legal practice in the PRC, the general view about the discretionary power of the judges is that it is a power conferred on the judges by law, in order to enable them to arrive at flexible decisions based on facts, evidence, legal principles and justice, especially when there is a gap in law or where the law is ambiguous.[711] Guo has stated that many in the PRC confuse *discretionary power* of the judges with arbitrariness, when actually it means *independence and freedom to decide* without taking help or advice from outside.[712]

However, as the legal practice and system is still evolving in PRC, these practices are discouraged by the central CPC. At the same time, there are many examples from the news that concern judicial transfers or discharge of judges on socially sensitive cases. Such news is not uncommon in the PRC.[713]

In summary, in recent years, with the enactment of many procedural codes, *self-interest* discretion has been checked, to some extent, by good implementation of anti-corruption policies; however *ideological discretion* has, in fact, been codified.[714] *Fact-based discretion* has been adopted as part of the inquisitorial system, so it is

---

[707]Woo, "Discretion in Contemporary Chinese Courts," 609.

[708]Ibid.

[709]See Art. 3 of *Constitution of PRC 1982*.

[710]Refer to Figure 10 in Chapter 4.

[711]Zhenghua Li, "Theory of Discretionary Power," *Contemporary Law Review*, no. 4 (2000): 94, translated from quotation in Shandong Province People's Court Changle County, "The Application of Judges' Discretionary Power in China (Translated)." http://wfclfy.chinacourt.org/article/detail/2013/05/id/954542.shtml, accessed on July 16, 2016. Translated into English at the author's request.

[712]XiangGuo Hu and China Court Net Bozhou Qiaocheng Channel, "The Discretionary Power of Judge in Civil Proceedings and Its Improvements in China (Translated)." http://www.chinacourt.org/article/detail/2013/11/id/1122865.shtml, accessed on July 16, 2016. Translated into English at the author's request.

[713]Woo, "Discretion in Contemporary Chinese Courts," 593.

[714]Ibid., 594.

present in the system. However, *mizhu jiandu* and *principle of democratic centralism* have the potential to create issues in the adjudication of commercial disputes.

6.3.3.1   Judicial Discretion in Day to Day Practice of PRC Courts

The PRC courts are governed by the philosophy of *youti zhengti* in which the court is a single entity, and the judges are just part of the whole legal system. The judicial activities carried out by the judges are part of the legal system.[715] In the PRC today, looking at day to day work in the courts, discretionary power is exercised by the judge in lots of judicial activities in civil litigation.[716] For example:

- ♦ In ascertaining evidence from cases, in particular, the materiality and authenticity of evidence. This discretionary power is relevant in the function of evidence for ascertaining the facts. The judges have wide discretion in such judicial activities, in particular, in criminal litigation.[717]

- ♦ The judges are equipped with wide discretionary power in relation to their ability to investigate, to decide on issues of admissibility for adducing evidence in their courts, to decide on the requirements for Standards of Proof, and similar issues throughout the adjudication process.

- ♦ The judges are regarded as experts in finding the real facts, as sometimes even the parties to the dispute are unable to adduce the evidence, and judges are duty-bound to find the truth. In this context, the judges have discretionary power that has been provided by statutes.[718]

- ♦ In the context of statutes general standards are mentioned such as in PRC's criminal law, for example, including "serious

---

[715]Ibid., 604.

[716]Guodang Xu, *The Debate About the Trains of Thought for Drawing up a Chinese Civil Code,* (Beijing: Publishing House of CUPL, 2001) as cited in Hu and China Court Net Bozhou Qiaocheng Channel, "The Discretionary Power of Judge in Civil Proceedings and Its Improvements in China (Translated)," accessed on July16, 2016. Translated into English at the author's request.

[717] Shu-Shan Guo, "The Discussion about Judges' Discretionary Power in Our Country." www.66law.cn/domianblog/20248.aspx, accessed on July 24, 2016. Translated into English at the author's request.

[718]See Arts. 64 & 65 of *CPL 1991 (as amended in 2012).*

nature" or "bad social impact." Those general standards can only be applied using the discretionary power of the judges.[719]

In addition to the above scenarios, PRC scholars, like their counterparts in western jurisprudence, also consider that the discretionary power of judges is necessary for the following reasons in legal practice:[720]

♦ New types of relationships are developing in contemporary PRC, especially in the commercial sector of its fast-moving economy. The need for frequent amendments to law cannot be a reasonable expectation, and therefore, there is a need for judges to exercise their discretionary power. This employment of discretionary power will ensure the certainty that people expect from the PRC courts, and will also increase the legitimacy of the civil justice system.

♦ The judges' discretionary power is needed in any complex societies and relationships, to ensure all types of disputes can be resolved, in particular, in scenarios which the NPC could not anticipate in advance, or where judges could not wait for clarifications from the SPC, to resolve the disputes before them.

♦ There is an inherent conflict between accuracy of judgments and the cognitive ability of judges. The judges are trained in the PRC's inquisitorial system to find out the facts of disputes. However, the judges' role in finding such facts only arises after the dispute has evolved. It is impossible for the judges to find all facts and the ultimate truth. Under modern evidence law, the approach that the judges take is the 'free evaluation of evidence', which, when the facts are not very clear, entitles the judges to take decisions based on their legal knowledge and experience. This approach cannot exist without the judges having discretionary power.

---

[719] Guo, "The Discussion about Judges' Discretionary Power in Our Country."
[720] Jie Liu and China Court net Meishan City Dongpo channel, "Restriction and Guidance on Judges' Discretion (Translated)." http://www.chinacourt.org/article/detail/2013/05/id/959246.shtml, accessed on July 24, 2016. Translated into English at the author's request.

◆　　There is a tremendous case-load on the judges in the PRC, since it is the most populous country in the world. The exercise of discretionary power will enable the judges to consider the state of affairs, balance the interests of the stakeholders and render judgments in a timely manner, while ensuring that they have efficiently employed the judicial resources available in the PRC.

◆　　The judges are not machines or robots that can mechanically apply the law, and therefore, they "need to be positive and creative, rather than be in passive inaction, detached from the facts ...."[721]

However, scholars in the PRC have warned against the possible misuse of discretionary power by judges and have described it as a double-edged sword for the following reasons.[722]

◆　　The exercise of discretionary power may lead to arbitrary decisions and abuse of power without proper training and strict rules of professional conduct.

◆　　The judges who exercise discretionary power may hold different views about the same matter or persons, and these views are not even fixed. An individual judge's opinions about the same facts might differ at different times and places, or with their changed emotions. Therefore, there is an argument that the law conferring overly wide discretionary power on the judges may bring in an element of arbitrariness, affecting the legitimacy of the courts.

◆　　The misuse of discretionary power has the potential to greatly exacerbate issues of corruption within the judiciary.

---

[721] Hu and China Court Net Bozhou Qiaocheng Channel, "The Discretionary Power of Judge in Civil Proceedings and Its Improvements in China (Translated)," accessed on July 16, 2016. Translated into English at the author's request.

[722] Liu and China Court net Meishan City Dongpo channel, "Restriction and Guidance on Judges' Discretion (Translated)," accessed on July 24, 2016. Translated into English at the author's request.

The above observations in relation to exercise of discretion, a real need in a fast-developing economy, cannot be considered melodramatic. It must be appreciated that the PRC has in a very short span of time grown into a gigantic economy.

Scholars have cited two main problems with judges' discretionary power in the PRC— either *PRC judges exercise their discretionary power insufficiently, or the judges exercise their discretionary power excessively.*[723] The author will discuss these two problems as follows:

- ♦ The *first problem* is that the judges either do not know how to employ their discretionary power efficiently, or they do not know how to exercise this power. One of the reasons could be that PRC judges are habituated to hear cases totally in accordance with laws or rules, as *legalism* has strong roots in the PRC.[724] Therefore, when PRC judges encounter new circumstances or vague codes, they are not fully prepared or equipped to deal with those circumstances. The PRC is undergoing a social and economic transformation and such encounters with unique circumstances are becoming more common day by day.[725]

- ♦ The *second problem* that has been observed is that the judges sometimes use excessive discretionary power, especially under the law of evidence. The judges exercise their excessive discretionary power in relation to fact-finding and evidence.[726]

From the above, it seems, while there is a concept of discretionary power for judges in the PRC, at the moment it is not well-developed. It is also unbalanced in a few

---

[723]Hui Xing Liang, *Judging Methods* (Beijing: Beijing University Press, 2005), 76 as cited in Changle County, "The Application of Judges' Discretionary Power in China (Translated)," accessed on July 24, 2016. Translated into English at the author's request.

[724]Refer to Chapter 3, §3.4.1.3.

[725] Guohua Sun, *Chinese Law Dictionary*, Jurisprudence Volume (Chinese Procuratorial Press, 1997), 542. It was cited in Changle County, "The Application of Judges' Discretionary Power in China (Translated)," accessed on July 24, 2016. Translated into English at the author's request.

[726]Changle County, "The Application of Judges' Discretionary Power in China (Translated)," accessed on July 24, 2016. Translated into English at the author's request.

aspects, such as in the area of the application of law to facts and ascertaining the facts themselves.[727] This problem is compounded due to the following:

♦ The current state of legislation and guidance are very general and not specific in nature, as a result of which PRC law can be ambiguous, and at times too flexible and vague. It can therefore be argued, in these circumstances, that the discretionary power of the PRC judges is wider even compared to that of judges in the liberal and democratic western world.[728] This problem of excessive discretionary power is further compounded by a lack of proper procedural security and guidance.[729]

♦ Lack of training and guidance of the PRC judges in issues related to economic prosperity as the economy has developed too fast. Judges not only need laws, but also the ability to explain the law and its application.[730]

♦ PRC citizens and even external stakeholders in the PRC economy need more awareness about rights, in cases where discretionary power has been abused by judges.[731]

♦ There is a fear of punishment among PRC judges, especially if a wrong decision were to be made, or if for some reason, the rendered judgment did not comply with guidelines from supervisors and committees further up in the hierarchy. This possibility makes PRC judges wary of exercising their discretionary power.

---

[727]Changle County, "The Application of Judges' Discretionary Power in China (Translated)," accessed on July 24, 2016. Translated into English at the author's request.

[728]Hu and China Court Net Bozhou Qiaocheng Channel, "The Discretionary Power of Judge in Civil Proceedings and Its Improvements in China (Translated)," accessed on July 16, 2016. Translated into English at the author's request.

[729]Hu and China Court Net Bozhou Qiaocheng Channel, "The Discretionary Power of Judge in Civil Proceedings and Its Improvements in China (Translated)."

[730]Ibid.

[731]Ibid.

CHAPTER SEVEN — IMPORTANT JUDICIAL ACTIVITIES – COMMON LAW v. CHINESE LAW

7.1 Introduction to Judicial Activities

Having discussed the judges' power including discretionary power, the author will now discuss three important concepts within the area of judicial activities, where such power is used. These selected judicial activities are:

- Judicial Statutory Interpretation; and

- Judicial use of Case Precedent; and

● Issues of Burden and Standards of Proof considered by judges;

7.2 Judicial Statutory Interpretation

The issue of statutory interpretation arises in every legal system because of the following reasons, as discussed by Easterbrook:[732]

● Legislatures lack time to look into all issues;

● Legislative process is a process of compromises between legislators;

● Legislative process is a complicated process comprising lobbying groups and multiple opinions. No draft legislation can imagine all the potential problems for which laws need to be legislated, or how the effects of such legislation will be experienced in society;

● In the author's view, statutes have sometimes been given a particular meaning or concept through the process of interpretation, and due to the doctrine of precedents in common law, subsequent judges are bound to follow that meaning.

For a century, there has been a debate between *rule-based* statutory interpretation and *rule-free* interpretation.[733] These debates have spawned many theories in relation to statutory interpretation:[734]

● A few scholars give precedence to text in the statute (this is called *textualism*);

---

[732]Frank H. Easterbrook, "Legal Interpretation and Power of Judiciary," *Harv. J. L. & Pub. Pol'y* 7, no. 1 (1984): 88–90.
[733] Tina Hunter, "Interpretive Theories: Dworkin, Sunstein, and Ely," *Bond Law Review* 17, no. 2 (2005): 78.
[734]Ibid., 79–80.

- Some focus on the structural argument, looking at the position of words within the statute;

- A few scholars give precedence to the judicial purpose behind the statute as a whole;

- A few scholars look at external sources to learn the history of legislative intent.

The various philosophies pertaining to statutory interpretation can be distinguished by looking at different approaches. The approach that looks to the past in the form of tests, structure and legislative intent and is more akin to the *rule-based* approach and is referred to as '*originalism*' by scholars. This approach to judicial interpretation will result in reducing judicial discretion but will enhance judicial discipline. However, this approach fails to take into account the changing ethos of society and developments in law that can adapt to new circumstances, as it is too focused on wisdom from the past.[735]

On the other hand, the philosophy of statutory interpretation that is more forward looking, argues on values, and seeks to fill gaps in legislations and find reasons behind the particular statute, is called '*non-originalism*'.[736] This approach is becoming popular in many jurisdictions as it takes on current values but also at the same time looks to the future.

The author will do a comparative analysis by going deeper into the specific details of judicial statutory interpretation in the jurisdictions of England & Wales and the PRC.

7.2.1 Judicial Statutory Interpretation in England & Wales

Lawyers in the seventeenth century were inclined towards reasoned judgments rather than legislation(s), due to legal reasoning contained in those judgments. The main reason for such preference was that scholars were against the idea of superiority of legislations over other matters. To these scholars, legislations seem to be above the

---

[735]Ibid., 80–81.
[736]Ibid., 80–81.

will of the common man.[737] Hedley even was of the view that Parliament got its authority from common law and not the other way around.[738]

Coke stated that the judges at common law could invalidate even laws from Parliament if the legislated law was unreasonable. This view remained for a long time in England, though it was sometimes relegated to the background. In later years, scholars took the view that the process of integration of statutes and case law was similar in the common law. According to Hale, the process of integration involved regular use, interpretation (broad and narrow), exposition and extension.[739] A view also prevailed that it is quite possible that judges may not even consider a particular statute legislated by Parliament, thus not incorporating it into the practice.[740] However, the current status quo is as follows:

- The judges in England & Wales are currently bound by the fundamental principle of the English Legal System, that the legislations originated in Parliament are supreme. This means that the Parliament can draft laws concerning anything. No Parliament can bind a future Parliament. In addition, a valid Act of Parliament cannot be questioned by the courts. Parliament is the supreme lawmaker in England & Wales.

- The judges are also bound by the common law doctrine of *stare decisis*, more commonly called the doctrine of precedents. This doctrine will be discussed later in this Chapter.

- The third method through which the judges are bound is through various rules of judicial interpretation. There is also the *Interpretation Act 1978*,[741] which provides common

---

[737]Gerald J. Postema, "Classical Common Law Jurisprudence (Part II)," *Oxford U. of Commw. L.J.* 3, no. 1 (2003): 18. According to Postema, jurisprudents such as Hedley and Blackstone were not in favour of granting legislations priority over the case authorities. Postema quoted Hedley who said in 1610, "...the parliament hath his power and authority from the common law, and not the common law from the parliament." Hedley also said, "the common law is of more force and strength than the parliament ... The parliament may find some defects in the common law and amend them ... But that the parliament may abrogate the whole law, I deny, for that were includedly to take away the power of the parliament itself, which power it hath by the common law."
[738]Postema, "Classical Common Law Jurisprudence - II," 18.
[739]Ibid., 20.
[740]Ibid.
[741]c 30. Some changes to this Act are outstanding, that will be applied in the near future. See *SI 2016/157* Sch. para. 1(3).

definitions to assist the judges in their judicial activities. This is needed in practice because even though Parliamentary legislations are drafted with utmost care, no legislation can foresee all possible scenarios. Additionally, the words in the statutes themselves at times could be ambiguous and may need clarification, which can come from understanding the intent of the legislation.

The task of interpreting statutes is carried out by the judges. Historically, English statutes are *corrective* rather than *preventative*. They try to be as specific as possible. This is different from statutes in the civil jurisdiction, which are all-encompassing and very detailed.[742] Parliament through statutes can also override the case law, and this guidance is available to the judges in these statutes.

One noticeable feature of statutory interpretation in England and Wales is that all stakeholders understand that the statutes are bringing about incremental change to the pre-existing common law. The law before the advent of common law also remains, though in the background. [743] Practitioners of law need to appreciate that the continuity of law in England & Wales is completely different from other continental systems such as Germany, which make complete changes in Codes every other century, completely discarding the previous laws. However, there is continuity in the evolution of the common law over the years and centuries.

7.2.1.1 Presumptions

Before the judges interpret any statute before them, there are a few presumptions that they will always keep in mind. These presumptions will be taken to be true unless a good argument is provided to demonstrate that a particular presumption should not apply to the statutes. A few examples of these presumptions are as follows:

♦ It will be presumed by the judges that the existing law has not been changed, unless the Act containing statues shows a clear intention to change the existing law;

---

[742] Lundmark, *Divide between Common and Civil Law*, 304.
[743] Ibid., 339.

- ◆ Each area of law has its unique points; for example, in the field of criminal law, it will be presumed that *mens rea* (criminal intent) is required in criminal cases;

- ◆ Presumption against interference with vested rights;

- ◆ Strict construction of penal laws in favor of the citizens;

- ◆ Presumption against retrospective operation;

- ◆ Presumption that the statutes do not affect the Crown.

7.2.1.2 Rules of Statutory Interpretation

The author will start with the dicta of Donaldson J.:[744]

> The duty of the Courts is to ascertain and give effect to the will of Parliament as expressed in its enactments. In the performance of this duty the Judges do not act as computers into which are fed the statutes and the rules for the construction of statutes and from whom issue forth the mathematically correct answer. The interpretation of statutes is a craft as much as a science and the judges, as craftsmen, select and apply the appropriate rules as the tools of their trade [emphasis added]. They are not legislators, but finishers, refiners and polishers of legislation which comes to them in a state that require varying degrees of further processing.

The author will now consider the rules of statutory interpretation independently:

- ◆ The *first rule* is the *literal rule* that means that as a starting point, judges must give all the words in a statute their ordinary and natural meaning. The literal rule is strict, and it ensures that the judges have to follow the rule, even if the meaning that comes out after such statutory interpretation is absurd. It was the dominant rule in the late nineteenth century. Scholars

---

[744]See *Corocraft Ltd v Pan American Airways Inc* [1968] 3 WLR 714, 732. (Donaldson J).

have argued that orthodox judges, who are cagey about creating law, tend to put too much faith in draftsmanship.[745] In *R. v The Judge of the City of London Court*,[746] Lord Esher MR was willing to follow the law even if the wording of the statute was absurd.

Nevertheless, it will always be a starting point in most cases. However, senior judges have always shown resistance to departing from this rule, as can be seen in the dicta of Lord Simonds in *Magor and St Mellons Rural District Council v Newport Corporation*: in the context of statutory interpretation where a judge in the lower court attempted to openly espouse the cause of filling the gaps while embarking on an exercise of statutory interpretation, Simonds called the process "naked usurpation of legislative function under the thin disguise of interpretation". [747]

However, there have been cases where absurdity has been observed; for example, see this case taken from the criminal law (cited in the footnotes).[748]

♦   The *second rule* of statutory interpretation is commonly known as the '*golden rule*'. Under this rule, if the literal interpretation is going to result in an absurd result, which no Parliament would have intended at all, then the judges can substitute a reasonable meaning. The origins of this rule are in *Grey v Pearson* (1857) where Lord Wensleydale said:

> ... the grammatical and ordinary sense of the words is to be adhered to, <u>unless that would lead to some absurdity, or some</u>

---

[745]See *The Law Commission Report on Interpretation of Statutes* 1969, LC021, where it was said the literal rule assumes an unattainable perfection in draftsmanship.

[746][1892] 1 QB 273 (CA) (Lord Esher MR) said on p. 290 "the words of an Act are clear, you must follow them, even though they <u>lead to a manifest absurdity</u> [emphasis added]. The Court has nothing to do with the question whether the Legislature has committed an absurdity."

[747][1952] AC 189, 191 (Lords Simonds).

[748]See *R v Harris* (1836) 7 C & P 446. In this case, an Act existed that made it an offence to "stab, cut, or wound any person". Harris bit off his victim's nose. Did he commit the offence? The Court held that he would have required the use of an instrument/implement (e.g. a knife). Harris was found not guilty. If a word has a technical meaning, then according to the first rule of statutory interpretation, it should be given this technical meaning.

repugnance or inconsistency with the rest of the instrument [emphasis added], in which case the grammatical and ordinary sense of the words may be modified, so as to avoid that absurdity and inconsistency, but no further.[749]

There have been a few prominent cases in this field where golden rules were applied. In one particular case, for example, the judge clarified the meaning of a word in the statute (see footnote).[750] Such clarifications might *narrow* or *broaden* the meaning.

The *second* rule allows the judges some leeway, but it still raises many interesting questions; for example, what level of absurdity is acceptable? This issue has gradually been analysed in the courts, for example, Lord Blackburn in *River Wear Commissioners v Adamson* said:

> I believe that it is not disputed that what Lord Wensleydale used to call the golden rule is right, viz., that we are to take the whole statute together, and construe it all together, giving the words their ordinary signification, unless when so applied they produce an inconsistency, or an absurdity or inconvenience so great as to convince the Court [emphasis added] that the intention could not have been to use them in their ordinary signification, and to justify the Court in putting on them some other signification, which, though less proper, is one which the Court thinks the words will bear.[751]

Even though the golden rule was a great improvement over the literal rule as it addresses the issues of absurdity, inconsistency

---

[749]6 HL Cas 61,106 (Lord Wensleydale).
[750]See, *Adler v George* [1964] 2QB 7. According to s 3 of the *Official Secrets Act 1920*, c 75 "no persons shall in the vicinity of any prohibited place obstruct any member of Her Majesty's forces". Defendant was actually on the airfield. The courts had to determine whether "in [the] vicinity of" includes on/in the premises. The court said that in the vicinity did include 'on or in' as well, as it would be absurd to define "in the vicinity' as a prohibited place, but to stop considering it prohibited when someone is actually on or in it.
[751]See *River Wear Commissioners v Adamson* (1877) 2 App. Cas. 743,764-65. It was also quoted in The *Law Commission Report on Interpretation of Statutes* 1969, LC021.

or inconvenience for the first time, it still failed to provide a clear means to test the existence of absurdity or inconsistency, or how to measure it.[752]

♦ The *final rule* is called the '*mischief* approach'. This rule was developed during the time when fewer laws were legislated in Parliament and in fact, most laws were coming out of the common law courts. The starting point for this approach came from the Barons of the Court of Exchequer in *Heydon's Case* (1584),[753] where the judges met and considered all statutes of all kinds (may it be penal or beneficial, restrictive or enlarging the common law), and they decided that the following four points were to be considered by the judges under this rule:

  ➤ What was the common law before the making of the Act?

  ➤ What was the mischief and defect for which the common law did not provide?

  ➤ What remedy had Parliament resolved, and what was appointed to cure the disease of the Commonwealth?

  ➤ The true reason for the remedy was also stated: and then the office of all the judges were always to make such construction as shall suppress the mischief, and advance the remedy, and to suppress subtle inventions and evasions for continuance of the mischief, and *pro privato commodo*, and to add force and life to the cure and remedy, according to the true intent of the makers of the Act, *pro bono publico*.

---

[752]The Law Commission *Report on Interpretation of Statutes* 1969, LC021, 19.
[753]3 Co Rep 7a. *See also, Magistrates and Town Council of Glasgow v Commissioners of Police of Hillhead* (1885) 12 R. 864, which said that "it is a settled principle that the court should so construe an Act of Parliament as to apply the statutory remedy to the evil or mischief which it is the intention of the statute to meet."

However, the judges for many years were only willing to accept either the *literal rule* or the *golden rule*. In relation to this cautious approach, Lord Tenterden CJ in *Brandling v Barrington* said:

> ...that ... there is always danger in giving effect to what is called the equity of a statute, and <u>that it is much better and safer to rely on and abide by the plain words</u> [emphasis added], although the Legislature might possibly have provided for other cases had their attention been directed to them. [754]

In addition to the undercurrents seen in the 1950s and 1960s, the tide was slowly changing. Judges were more willing to be creative, with Lord Denning saying that "[the] judges are not the slaves of words but their masters."[755] It was clear that the first rule ignores the limitation of draftsmanship and even the judges in the highest courts can differ on the meaning of the same word. Therefore, this task of statutory interpretation is difficult. While the mischief rule seems to be satisfactory, however, the *Law Commission Report 1969* was of the view that:

> Heydon's Case is also somewhat outdated in its approach, <u>because it assumes that statute is subsidiary or supplemental to the common law</u> [emphasis added], whereas in modern conditions many statutes mark a fresh point of departure rather than a mere addition to, and qualification of, common law principles. [756]

Over the years, England & Wales has adopted the *purposive* approach. This purposive approach will always take into account the presumptions as discussed above. Lord Griffiths in a landmark case said:

> The days have long passed when the courts adopted a strict constructionist view of interpretation which required them to adopt the literal meaning of the language. <u>The courts now adopt a purposive approach</u> [emphasis added] which seeks to give effect

---

[754](1827) 6 B & C 467, 475 (Lord Tenterden CJ).
[755]See *Allen v Thorn Electrical Industries Ltd* (1968) 1 QB 481, 503 (CA) (Lord Denning MR).
[756]See *The Law Commission Report on Interpretation of Statutes* 1969, LC021, 20. *Refer also*, to views of Hedley and Coke as discussed earlier in Chapter 3, §3.2.1.

to the true purpose of legislation and are prepared to look at much extraneous material that bears upon the background against which the legislation was enacted.[757]

The purposive approach was spreading in England & Wales, as can be seen in the Ninth Wilfred Fullagar Memorial Lecture, delivered by Lord Scarman at Monash University on September 9, 1980:

> ... when I, as an English judge, read some of the decisions of the High Court of Australia, I think they are more English than the English. In London no-one would now dare to choose the literal rather than a purposive construction of a statute: and 'legalism' is currently a term of abuse [emphasis added].[758]

It is interesting to note that within a few months of this lecture, the Australian Parliament enacted section 15AA of the *Interpretation Act 1901*[759] that empowered Australian judges and provides as follows:

> In the interpretation of a provision of an Act, a construction that would promote the purpose or object underlying the Act (whether that purpose or object is expressly stated in the Act or not) shall be preferred to a construction that would not promote that purpose or object.

In 2001, a senior judge, Spigelman CJ of the Supreme Court of New South Wales in Australia commented:

---

[757]See *Pepper (Her Majesty's Inspector of Taxes) v Hart* [1993] AC 593, 617 (Lord Griffiths), [1992] UKHL 3.

[758]The Right Honourable Lord Scarman, (Ninth Wilfred Fullagar Memorial Lecture), "The Common Law Judge and the Twentieth Century - Happy Marriage or Irretrievable Breakdown?" *Monash L. Rev.* 7, no. 1 (1980): 6. Lord Scarman was also quoted in RR Geddes, "Purpose and Context in Statutory Interpretation," 129.www.judcom.nsw.gov.au/publications/education-monographs-1/monograph4/07_geddes.pdf.

[759]Inserted into the principal Act by the *Statute Law Revision Act 1981*, s 115.

> The law of statutory interpretation has become the most important
> single aspect of legal practice [emphasis added]. Significant areas
> of the law are determined entirely by statute. No area of the law
> has escaped statutory modification.[760]

In most common law jurisdictions, where the purposive approach is followed, judges will not embark upon literal statutory interpretation like robots, but in fact, will take into account the purpose of the statute, the historical view and even the policy considerations that led to the drafting of the statute. It is best to end this brief discussion on statutory interpretation with the words of Mason CJ:

> No one would suggest nowadays that statutory interpretation is
> merely an exercise in ascertaining the literal meaning of words.
> Statutory interpretation calls for reference not only to the context,
> scope and purpose of the statute but also to antecedent history and
> policy as well as community values [emphasis added].[761]

Presently, in order to follow the purposive approach, English judges may also use internal aids that are available with Parliamentary legislations, and external (outside the Act) aids.

7.2.1.3 Internal and External Aids to Statutory Interpretation, Purposive Approach

A few examples of the Internal aids to Statutory Interpretation that can be utilised by judges in England & Wales are as follows:

- ◆ The long and short title of the Act;

- ◆ The Preamble of the Act;

- ◆ Section headings may be used if they do not contradict the rest of the statute;

---

[760] J. J. Spigelman, "The Poet's Rich Resource: Issues in Statutory Interpretation," *Australian Bar Rev.* 21, no. 3 (2001): 224. Spigelman CJ was also quoted in Geddes, "Purpose and Context in Statutory Interpretation," 128.
[761] A. Mason, "Changing the Law in a Changing Society," *Commw. L. Bull.* 18, no. 3 (1992): 569.

♦ Schedules to the Act.

A few examples of External aids to Statutory Interpretation in England & Wales are as follows:

♦ Dictionary;

♦ Historical Setting;

♦ Evidence of past customary practice;

♦ Related statutes or similar Acts;

♦ Law Commission Reports;

♦ Treaties and International Conventions;

♦ Hansards and Parliamentary Reports;[762]

♦ EU Community Law.

Once Parliamentary reports were allowed, it opened the route for the judges to use the *'purposive approach'*. Even though this rule is similar to the mischief rule, the focus in this rule is on Parliament's intention in drafting the legislation, and not the common law.

7.2.1.4 Rules of Language for Statutory Interpretation

There are also a few rules of language that judges take into account when embarking on the task of statutory interpretation, for example:

---

[762]*Pepper v Hart [1993] AC 593*, the House of Lords significantly relaxed the general prohibition on using such materials for the purposes of statutory interpretation. This was after years of prohibition in referring to the Hansard and other Parliamentary Reports due to primacy of parliamentary privilege.

♦ *Ejusdem generis* — general words following particular ones normally apply only to such persons or things that are of the same genus or class.[763]

♦ *Noscitur a sociis* — the meaning of a word can be ascertained from the other words used. For example, see an old case from 1875, in the footnotes.[764]

♦ *Expressio unius est exclusio alterius* —this means that the express member of one member within the class excludes other members from the class by implication, as can be seen by the footnoted example.[765]

7.2.1.5 Judicial Interpretation in context of Civil Procedure

The concept of overriding objectives has been discussed previously:[766] overriding objectives are used in resolving conflicts between various rules of the *CPR 1998*. It is a very useful tool especially when the wording of the *CPR 1998* is silent or is not clear. For example, in one case (see footnotes), [767] the purposive approach to interpreting the civil procedural rules was used to lift a stay of procedure, because this stay was allowed only due to very technical application of rules. The overriding objective should have guided the conduct of the parties.

---

[763]A word will take its meaning from the *foregoing* words. For example, if in any act it is stated "no tradesmen, artisan, workmen, labourer or other person whatsoever shall work on a Sunday" then it may mean "other person whatsoever" does not include occupations such as estate agents, barbers or farmers.

[764]See *Muir v Keay* (1875) LR QBD 594 where the court at that time considered the *Refreshment Houses Act 1860,* c27, and thereafter considered the meaning of 'entertainment'. This Act dealt with public refreshment, resorts and entertainment. The courts had to decide how to determine the meaning of entertainment. They looked at the other words and found it could not refer to theatrical or musical entertainment. The word referred to refreshment rooms, reception and accommodation of the public.

[765]See the case of *Tempest v Kilner* (1846) 3 CB 249. A contract for the sale of goods, wares, and merchandise for £10 or more had to be evidenced in writing. Applying this rule of language, it could be argued then, that the contract for sales of stocks and shares did not have to be evidenced in writing because they were not goods, wares or merchandise.

[766]Refer, Chapter 4, §4.2.1.

[767]See *B v B [2005] EWCA Civ 237* In this case, the judgment clearly stated the duty imposed on the parties and their lawyers under *CPR 1998* r. 1.3 (to assist the courts to further the overriding objective). The Court was of the view that a lengthy and costly litigation could have been avoided if the lawyers had communicated with the defendant's solicitors shortly after the new proceedings commenced.

The *CPR 1998* has been drafted with 'purposive approach to interpretation'.[768] It is particularly useful in the following scenarios:

- ◆ Civil procedural rules are silent;

- ◆ Civil procedural rules are ambiguous;

- ◆ Civil procedural rules are in conflict with old rules that led to the previous body of cases.

The above discussions lead us to the role of the authority of case precedents in analysing the Code. It is unthinkable that in the common law system, old cases are not considered relevant. However, there are relevant cases from the time of pre-*CPR 1998* rules. Cases before the new *CPR 1998* came into existence are not relevant, as can be seen from the case of *Biguzzi v Rank Leisure*.[769] The case of *Biguzzi* was tried before the court immediately after the new *CPR 1998* came into existence. However, in the later case of *Garratt v Saxby*,[770] it was said that previous cases could have some persuasive force. In particular, Dyson LJ said:

> Although it has been said on a number of occasions that decisions on pre-CPR procedural rules are not binding for the purpose of interpreting the CPR, *there are circumstances in which they may be of considerable persuasive force* [emphasis added]. In my view, this is a good example.[771]

However, the circumstances where old cases could be binding are very limited and judges have shown caution in utilising pre-*CPR 1998* authorities. It is relevant at this point to bring in the dicta of Brooke LJ in a particular case:

---

[768]Déirdre Dwyer, "What is the Meaning of CPR r 1.1(1)," in *The Civil Procedure Rules Ten Years On*, Déirdre Dwyer (Oxford: Oxford University Press, 2009), 73.

[769]See [1999] 1 WLR 1926 (CA). See also the discussion of the case in *Biguzzi v Rank Leisure [1999] 1 WLR 1926 (CA), [1999] 4 ALL ER 934, Biguzzi v Rank Leisure [1999] 1 WLR 1926 (CA), [1999] 4 ALL ER 934, Biguzzi v Rank Leisure [1999] 1 WLR 1926 (CA), [1999] 4 ALL ER 934.* See also, *Dwyer, "Overriding Objective,"* 67.

[770][2004] EWCA Civ 341. *Garratt v Saxby [2004] EWCA Civ 341.*

[771]Ibid., [18]. *Garratt v Saxby [2004] EWCA Civ 341, [18].*

It is clear, in my view, that what Lord Woolf was saying was that reference to authorities under the former rules is generally no longer relevant. Rather it is necessary to concentrate on the intrinsic justice of a particular case in the light of the overriding objective.[772]

In the years following the advent of *CPR 1998*, there have been scholarly articles which submit that old cases can only be used in situations where difficulties arise.[773] However, it is clear that judges are adopting a cautious approach. Lord Woolf later released *Practice Direction on the Citation of Authorities, 2001*,[774] where he made an attempt to reduce reliance on case precedents in matters of civil procedural law. This *Practice Direction* advises users of *CPR 1998* that minor cases should not be cited, unless the judgment has established a new principle or extended the law.

In summary, case precedents will only need to highlight the consistency of approach of the civil courts. However, most civil procedural lawyers will disagree with the above views, including the author, as the relevant *White Book*[775] itself highlights many case precedents, and new cases are added every year to make the book even thicker.[776]

7.2.1.6   Human Rights Act 1998

After World War II, the *European Convention of Human Rights* ("*ECHR*") entered into force on September,3, 1953. *The Human Rights Act 1998* ("*HRA 1998*") is an Act of Parliament of the United Kingdom that came into force on October,2, 2000. It incorporated *EHCR* into the UK law and ensured that the remedies for breach of human rights pursuant to *ECHR* are available in local courts in the UK. There are different types of rights available in *HRA 1998*:

---

[772]*Walsh v Misseldine [2000] CP Rep 74*, [79], where Brooke LJ cited May LJ from the case of *Purdy v Cambran* [2000] CP Rep 67.

[773]A. Zuckerman, *Zuckerman on Civil Procedure: Principles of Practice*, 2nd ed. (London: Sweet and Maxwell, 2006), [1.51]. Zuckerman's views were also discussed in Dwyer, "Overriding Objective," 67.

[774]See *Practice Direction (Citation of Authorities) [2001] 1 WLR 2001*.

[775]*White Book* is a famous textbook for English civil law practitioners, guiding them on civil procedural rules.

[776] Dwyer, "Overriding Objective," 68, where the issue of *White Book* becoming thicker every year is discussed to highlight the issue of complexity that could be avoided.

- ◆ A few of them ensure that all primary and subordinate legislations must be read and given effect according to *HRA 1998*;

- ◆ High Court or superior courts can declare the law invalid and incompatible with *HRA 1998,* and the courts can give notice to the relevant Ministry within the Executive;

- ◆ Jurisprudence of *ECHR* is taken into account by the English courts according to section 2 of *HRA 1998*.[777]

- ◆ All public bodies (including courts and tribunals)[778] are under the obligation to act in accordance with *HRA 1998* pursuant to sections 6-8 of *HRA 1998*.

7.2.1.6.1 HRA's Effects on CPR 1998

The foregoing discussion on the concept of overriding objective states that cases should be dealt with justly in the context of civil procedural rules. The philosophy of *overriding objective* also fits well with *HRA 1998*.[779] It was even reported in the case of *Goode v Martin* (Times, January, 24, 2002): it was stated that *HRA 1998* functions as an extra tool in the interpretation of procedural rules.[780]

Section 6(1) of *HRA 1998* brings into effect Article 6 of *ECHR* that provides:

---

[777]s 2 of *HRA 1998* Interpretation of Convention rights provides:

(1) A court or tribunal determining a question which has arisen in connection with a Convention right must take into account any — (a) judgment, decision, declaration or advisory opinion of the European Court of Human Rights, (b) opinion of the Commission given in a report adopted under Article 31 of the Convention, (c) decision of the Commission in connection with Article 26 or 27(2) of the Convention, or (d) decision of the Committee of Ministers taken under Article 46 of the Convention.

[778]s 6 (3) of *HRA 1998* provides:

... "public authority" includes —

(a) a court or tribunal, and (b) any person certain of whose functions are functions of a public nature.

[779]However, the recent referendum, popularly called BREXIT, which came up while the author was writing this book, and whose effect will not be known for a few more years, has not yet been taken into account.

[780]See Blake, *Practical Approach to Effective Litigation*, 57 for further discussion on *HRA 1998* and *CPR 1998*.

221

In the determination of his civil rights and obligations or of any criminal charge against him, everyone is entitled to a fair and public hearing within a reasonable time by an independent and impartial tribunal established by law. Judgment shall be pronounced publicly [emphasis added] but the press and public may be excluded from all or part of the trial in the interest of morals, public order or national security in a democratic society, where the interests of juveniles or the protection of the private life of the parties so require, or the extent strictly necessary in the opinion of the court in special circumstances where publicity would prejudice the interests of justice.

Briefly, *HRA 1998* is applicable to the right to public hearing, the right to have access to the courts in litigation, the right to having unbiased judges with no conflict of interest, the right to adversarial procedure, equality of time and facilities, the right to hearing within a reasonable time, the right to receive reasons for a judgment and the right to fair proceedings.

In a case in the Court of Appeal, it was noted:

> … that a judgment should contain reasons that are sufficient to demonstrate that the essential issues that have been raised by the parties have been addressed by the domestic court and how those issues have been resolved. It does not seem … that the Strasbourg jurisprudence goes further and requires a judgment to explain why one contention, or piece of evidence, has been preferred to another [emphasis added].[781]

7.2.2   Judicial Statutory Interpretation in PRC

Historically, the theory of statutory interpretation in PRC law is usually found in the PRC's civil law. Lately, there has been a trend within PRC legal studies to develop the study of statutory interpretation as an independent subject.

The right of interpretation of the statutes/codes is treated as an independent right. This right has been monopolized by the legislative authority and to a limited extent by the judicial authorities at the highest level within the hierarchy. The judges' right to interpret the law is not available in the PRC legal system. Because the PRC is in the

---

[781]See *English v Emery Reimbold and Strick Ltd* [2002] EWCA Civ 605.

midst of colossal economic and social change due to accelerated economic changes, there is a need to adapt the codes to these powerful changes within society.

7.2.2.1 Historical Judicial Interpretation

For centuries, it was the Emperor of ancient China that was vested with most of the legislative authority, and the power associated with the application of those laws.[782] Therefore, ancient Chinese sovereign emperors were a major source of law. Moreover, all the judicial branches existed at the central level only and were relatively not very advanced.[783]

In relatively modern times, the Qing Dynasty in 1905 introduced fairly modern judicial reforms.[784] However, there is some evidence from Xunzi's writings that the *purposive interpretation* that is currently followed in the common law systems was in some form already thought of in ancient China. He appears to have suggested that the 'spirit of law' (*yi*) was more important than the law in texts (*shu*). Xunzi was of the view that if one did not know the *yi* but was only aware of *shu*, no matter how broad the judges' knowledge was of the relevant law (*shu*), according to him, there would still be some gaps when handling actual cases.[785] However, it is likely that Xunzi was alluding to the concept at the philosophical level.

For the sake of completeness, and as discussed earlier,[786] there was a concept of benevolence and humanity (*jen*) that was applied in many ways in practice in ancient China. This concept was framed on the Confucian, especially Neo-Confucian, school of thought.

---

[782] Zhenbao Jin, "From a Supplementary Legislator to a Legitimate Judicial Lawmaker - on the Role of the Supreme People's Court in Developing the Law in Mainland China," in *Towards a Chinese Civil Code: Comparative and Historical Perspectives*, Lei Chen and C H van Rhee (Dordrecht: Martinus Nijhoff Publishers, 2012), 30, where Zhang's views were discussed from Jinfan Zhang, *Tradition of Chinese Law and Its Transformation in Late Qing (Zhonggua Falu de Chuantong Yu Jindai Zhuanxing)* (Beijing: Beijing Law Press, 1997), 21–34.

[783] Zhenbao Jin, "Role of SPC," 29, where Zhang's views were discussed further from Jinfan Zhang, *Tradition of Chinese Law and Its Transformation in Late Qing (Zhonggua Falu de Chuantong Yu Jindai Zhuanxing)* (Beijing: Beijing Law Press, 1997), p. 92–103.

[784] Zhenbao Jin, "Role of SPC," 30, where there was discussion on Zhang from Sheng Zhang, "Institutions and Practice of Independent Adjudication of Dali Yuan in the Early History of the Republic of China (*Minchu Daliyuan Shenpan Duli de Zhidu Yu Shijian*)," *Journal of China University of Political Science and Law (Zhengfa Luntan) 20* (2002): 146.

[785] Wejen Chang, "Classical Chinese Jurisprudence and Development of Chinese Legal System" (2009–10), 235.

[786] Refer, Chapter 3, § 3.4.1.1 for discussion on Confucians and Neo-Confucians and their philosophy.

However, this took time and it was only in 1912, when the Republic of China came into existence, that *Dali Yuan* was established with independent power for carrying out statutory interpretation. *Dali Yuan* had exclusive jurisdiction over what appears to be points of law from Provincial High Courts that were tasked to bridge the gaps between the old and new China of the time.[787] However, the reign of *Dali Yuan* did not last very long after the arrival of the new government of the PRC in 1949.

The principle of checks and balances between the various organs of government under the concept of separation of powers, soon gave way to the principles of *democratic centralism*.[788] The concept of democratic centralism was borrowed from *Marxism* and *Leninism*, where there was absolute freedom for the party members to argue issues, but once the decision had been made by the central leadership using the majority decision, it was then expected to be followed by everyone.[789]

At the time of the formation of the PRC, the Communist Party of China instructed that all existing laws were to be abolished; this was in relation to the *Abolition of the Six Laws of the Kuomintang Regime and the Establishment of the Judicial Principle in the Liberated Areas (Feichu Guomindang de Liufa Quanshu yu Queli Jiefangqu de Sifa Yuanze de Zhishi).*[790] The adjudicative works carried out by the existing courts had to follow and rely on the policies of the CPC in addition to following the guidelines, laws, regulations and resolutions promulgated by the People's government and the People's Liberation Army, before a complete legal system came into existence.

The above instructions led to the Supreme People's Court ("SPC") taking greater responsibility and gradually clarifying various policies. However, it was not until 1977, when economic development in the PRC accelerated, that the SPC began issuing more Opinions on many new economic and civil laws, coming into prominence as a result.

---

[787]Yuansheng Huang, "Sources of Law in Civil Adjudication of the Dali Yuan in the Early Republic of China (Minch Dali Yuan Minshi Shenpan Fayuan)," in *100 Selected Precedents of the Dali Yuan (Dali Yuan Minshi Panli Baixuan),* ed. Yuansheng Huang (Taibei: Wunan Book Co. Ltd., 2009), 60. It was further discussed in Sun Jin, "On the Practical Level of Judicial Interpretation of the Law - Reasoning Made by Judges in Judgments," 30. http://www.court.gmw.cn/html/article/201212/28/115659.shtml, accessed on July, 9, 2016. Translations done at the author's request.

[788]Dingjina Cai, *History and Reforms: The Legal History of the New China (Lishiyu Biange: Xin Zhongguo Fazhi Jianshe de Licheng)* (Beijing: Press of China's University of Political Science and Law, 1999), 2, as discussed in Sun Jin, "On the Practical Level of Judicial Interpretation of the Law - Reasoning Made by Judges in Judgments," 30.

[789]The concept of *democratic centralism* is enshrined in Art. 3 of *Constitution of PRC 1982*.

[790]It was promulgated by the Central Committee of the CCP in February1949.

Under the *PRC Constitution of 1954*, the power of judicial interpretation was vested in the Standing Committee of National People's Congress ("NPCSC").[791] Even when the Constitution was altered in 1982, the power of judicial interpretation remained vested in NPCSC.[792] Pursuant to the Resolution of the NPCSC on *Statutory Interpretation of 1955*,[793] the SPC was conferred with the *delegated power* of statutory interpretation. This delegated power was later confirmed through another *Resolution of 1981*.[794] SPC has utilized this delegated power actively, and many scholars have commented that this was a significant contribution towards building a complete legal system in the modern PRC.[795] It is important to discuss the key points from this *Resolution of 1981,* which are as follows:

- ◆ All articles in laws requiring further definition or supplementary stipulations shall be interpreted or stipulated by NPC Standing Committee pursuant to the law;

- ◆ All questions arising from courts' civil trials concerning the specific application of laws and decrees shall be interpreted by SPC.

However, the SPC's power of statutory interpretation under their delegated power is not to be confused with power in relation to case precedent as seen in common law jurisdictions such as England & Wales.

According to the author, the SPC is now very similar to a legislative body, albeit supplementary. It is interesting to note the comments of Jin, who states:

> Strictly speaking, this practice is indeed *de facto* law-making process and the SPC is playing the role of a supplementary legislative body, not subject to any substantive and procedural

---

[791]See Art. 31 of *Constitution of PRC 1954.*

[792]See Art. 67 of *Constitution of PRC 1982.*

[793]See *Resolution of the NPCSC on Statutory Interpretations, 1955.*

[794]See *Resolution of the NPCSC on Strengthening the Work of Statutory Interpretations, 1981*, adopted on June, 10, 1981.

[795]Zhenbao Jin, "Role of SPC," 31n14, where it was discussed that in the National People's Congress, *Work Report of the 10th Standing Committee of the National People's Congress of 8 March 2008* (Beijing), Mr. Banggu Wu while addressing the 2nd Plenary Session of the 1st Conference of the 11th NPC stressed the need for a complete *socialist legal system with Chinese characteristics* composed of the Constitution of the PRC, national laws, administrative regulations and local regulations.

restriction stipulated in Law of Legislation of the People's Republic of China of 2000.[796]

The delegated power of the SPC as a supplementary legislative body is, in practice, not even restricted by any substantive and procedural restrictions as prescribed in the *Law of Legislation 2000*,[797] in particular, section 4, Articles 39-42. This issue has been discussed by Jin.[798]

Apart from the two resolutions of 1955 and 1981, the delegated power of SPC is enhanced through another law that was promulgated in 1979, and then amended in 2006.[799] The SPC has also promulgated *Several Provisions on Judicial Interpretation Work (Guangyu Sifa Jieshi Gongzuo de Ruogan Guiding) in 1997 (as amended by '2007* Provisions'),[800] which itself enhanced the power of the SPC to carry out judicial statutory interpretation on various issues such as specific application of law for the People's Courts in their adjudicative work, the legal effect of the judicial interpretations promulgated by the SPC, and the procedure for enacting judicial interpretations.[801]

The *2007 provisions* introduced a few democratic norms in the judicial interpretations. According to these *Provisions, both 1997 and as amended in 2007*, the judicial interpretations of the SPC are expressly declared to have the force of law and shall take effect when they are promulgated. Thus this date is different from the date when the law was promulgated. Furthermore, if the statutory interpretation is not correct, the process by which the SPC can modify the incorrect version is very cumbersome. The author finds it chaotic and is supported in this opinion by Jin, who also feels that process needs improvement.[802]

The SPC, according to the *Provisions 2007*, may promulgate four types of judicial interpretations, namely, *jieshi* (Interpretation), *guiding* (Provisions), *pifu* (Reply) and *jueding* (Decision), all of which have the effect of law and shall be published in the

---

[796]Zhenbao Jin, "Role of SPC," 31.
[797]See *Law of Legislation of PRC 2000* (as revised in 2015).
[798]Zhenbao Jin, "Role of SPC," 31.
[799]See, Art. 33 of *Organic Law of People's Courts of People's Republic of China 1979 (as amended in 1983). Organic Law of Peoples Courts of People's Republic of China 1979 (as amended in 1983).*
[800]*Several Provisions on Judicial Interpretation Work (Guanyu Sifa Jieshi Gongzuo de Ruogan Guiding) 2007 Fa Fa [2007] No. 12.* This Provision repealed Rules of the *Supreme People's Court on the Work of Judicial Interpretation [1997], Fa Fa [1997] No. 15.*
[801]Jinfan Zhang, *Tradition of Chinese Law and Its Transformation in Late Qing (Zhonggua Falu de Chuantong Yu Jindai Zhuanxing)* (Beijing: Beijing Law Press, 1997), 39.
[802]Zhenbao Jin, "Role of SPC," 43.

Gazette of the SPC. Briefly, each of the four types of judicial interpretations will be discussed below:[803]

- ♦ *Jieshi* is the most important type of statutory interpretation. It refers to judicial interpretations of the specific statute, or interpretations that guide the application of law in special types of cases or issues. For example — *Opinions on Several Issues concerning the Implementation of General Principles of Civil Law of 1988,* the *Interpretation of Several Issues concerning the Implementation of Contract Law of 1999* and the *Interpretation of the Securities Law of 2001.*[804]

- ♦ *Guiding* rules are enacted to regulate issues concerned mostly with non-substantive issues such as Procedural rules for the relevant substantive law, such as *2007 provisions.* However, the distinction between *guiding* and *jieshi* is not very clear.

- ♦ *Pifu* refers to judicial interpretations made in response to inquiries from the Higher People's Courts and Military courts of the People's Liberation Army concerning legal issues in pending cases.

- ♦ *Jueding* is made for the purpose of modifying or nullifying the existing SPC's judicial interpretations.

The lower courts do not have any power of statutory interpretation; all the delegated power is limited completely to the SPC. The reason cited by PRC scholars for this lack of power in the lower courts is that it is "to secure uniform statutory interpretations among all the courts at different levels."[805]

In this Chapter, it is important to consider the jurisprudential aspect of statutory interpretation in the PRC. The judiciary in the PRC is not a separate branch and there is no concept of separation of powers. However, the way the SPC carries out statutory interpretation, it is more like an extension of the NPC. PRC scholars have described the jurisprudence of judicial interpretation as being based on the Chinese socialist

---

[803]Ibid., 41.
[804]Ibid., 40.
[805]Ibid., 39.

political system, where the "principle of '*democratic centralism*', or the principle of the unity of deliberation and execution" [806] prevails. This means that the SPC implements the decisions of the NPC, which are then supervised by the NPC.

7.2.2.2 Current Practice of Judicial Statutory Interpretation in PRC

From the above discussion, [807] it is clear that the SPC has been delegated the responsibility for carrying out statutory interpretation for a great many legislations, resolutions, and customary practices. SPC \ actively utilizes this power to guide the lower courts. However, as discussed above, there is no power available to the lower courts with regards to statutory interpretation.

In order to resolve substantive disputes, PRC legal philosophers have divided the practice of statutory interpretation to two levels. First is the *narrow* level, limited to interpreting the legal terminology and sentences of the PRC code. On the other hand, at the *broader* level, statutory interpretation is done in the broader context of people, society, concepts, and so on.

The above is an example of dual centers of statutory interpretation, both with the NPC and SPC. While the SPC has been active in issuing guidelines, the same cannot be said of the NPC in relation to their task of issuing statutory interpretations. Therefore, the guidance given by SPC is very general in nature, while the judges in the lower courts in practice have to deal with the issue of statutory interpretation in a particular case with very specific facts. Therefore, whatever judicial interpretations are available from NPC or SPC provide only general guidance. In addition, these interpretations, in practice, ignore the judicial interpretations that may be required in specific cases in the lower courts.

The judge's role in dealing with cases in any jurisdiction is usually a three-step process, which is first to understand the facts of the commercial disputes, then apply the relevant law with proper interpretation applicable to material facts, and finally reach a conclusion in law.

When judges deal with a legal case, they could either be looking for relevant facts from the points of law, or they could be looking at points of law to find material facts. A question arises: in a case before the lower courts in the PRC, is the application of law to the facts any different from the process of judicial interpretation?

---

[806]Ibid., 45.
[807]Refer Chapter 7, § 7.2.2.1.

As discussed above, the judges in the lower courts are not recognized in law as persons having any power to carry out statutory interpretation in the current PRC legal system. However, as also discussed above, statutory interpretation is inseparable from the application of law in the judges' work in the courts. At the same time, to assist the lower courts, there is a constitutional structure and the institution of '*replies*', which enables the lower courts to seek clarifications from the SPC.

In addition, as the limits of lower court judges in relation to statutory implementation is clear, there is also a provision of '*appeal on points of law*'. In the process of appeal on points of law, either party may have a chance to get a legal opinion from the Court of Appeal, or to have them checked by the Supreme Court.

Due to this conflict in day-to-day work, there is a big difference in practice and theory of statutory interpretation. Is this a reason why many of the judgments in the PRC legal system are short on reasons, as compared to the English Legal system or even other civil jurisdictions? The paucity of reasons in the judgment can leave the litigants unsatisfied, and in the author's view can even affect the legitimacy of the courts.

Another problem that has been on the rise in the PRC courts in recent years due to the above problem is something called *tong'an bu tong'pan* (similar cases, different rulings).[808] It is very important to note what Jin has said about the current practice:

> It can be safely said that PRC courts, including the SPC, have not developed a consistent and predictable pattern or theory of legal interpretation. The most important reason might be that the judiciary in PRC is not an independent branch of state power.[809]

Furthermore, the PRC courts are obliged to apply not only the laws and regulations, but also philosophies applicable at that particular time, or policies that have been adopted by NPC and/or CPC.[810] In a famous case in Shandong High Court,[811] a claimant was deprived of his constitutional right to education because a defendant went as an imposter in the Claimant's name. The judges, before they could receive clarification from the SPC, were of the view that civil law cannot be used to protect

---

[808]Zhenbao Jin, "Role of SPC," 31.
[809]Ibid., 34.
[810]Ibid.
[811]See a famous case of *Qi Yuling* of 2001 and its discussion in Zhenbao Jin, "Role of SPC," 34.

the claimant's constitutional rights. Scholars were of the view that there was an Article available in *General Principles of Civil law* 1986,[812] which could have been used by the judges to find a remedy in this case. The lack of discretionary power came to the forefront.

In fact, none of the judges at any level mentioned that provision in their judgment.[813] Was it the judges' unwillingness to take the initiative? Was it the fear of punishment or the risk of appeal, or was it that the local committee had advised them to ignore the relevant article? In England & Wales, the active lawyers would have ensured that the judges take into consideration any relevant statutes or any principles that could be argued in the legal framework.

On the other end of the spectrum is the accusation of judicial activism: by enacting *in abstracto* judicial interpretations, the SPC has been actually playing the role of legislator.[814] However, over the years, before issuing *Opinions*, the SPC has been seeking the views of the public. In the author's view, it is difficult to comprehend and reconcile with the judges' role, where the judges themselves take public opinion as a benchmark to give their Opinion. In the author's view, the SPC's role is rapidly moving into the area of legislature, and it is clearly an example of judicial activism. However, it seems this is not condemned by the NPC or other stakeholders, or even the public.

7.3 Doctrine of Precedents

The role of case precedents is instrumental in the practice of law in most jurisdictions. The doctrine of *stare decisis* has been instrumental in the development of common law,[815] and in a way it also limits judicial discretion. The judges in later cases must follow the law developed in the previous cases. Judicial precedent promotes certainty,

---

[812]See Art. 106(2) of the *General Principles of Civil Law 1986*, Order No. 37 of the President of the People's Republic of China (and as revised by *Decision of the Standing Committee of the National People's Congress on Revising Certain Laws 2009*), which specifies: "Any citizen or legal person who, with fault attributable to them, infringes upon the property of the state or any collective, or upon the property, personal or family interest of other persons, shall bear civil liability."

[813]See Zhenbao Jin, "Role of SPC," 35 for the discussion on the case.

[814]Zhenbao Jin, "Role of SPC," 41.

[815]Henry de Bracton in the thirteenth century published the rulings in over two thousand cases, which greatly assisted in rationalising the law of that time in England. The publication of a yearly book started from then. Slowly, more case reports were published with greater accuracy. With the advent of positivism, the idea that if there is no law by legislature, then the judgment must be taken as the law, also contributed to its development. For further discussion on this topic, see Lundmark, *Divide between Common and Civil Law*, 347–9.

consistency; expectations of the litigants are managed, and, in a way, this assists in developing a rule of law.[816] Precedents are "prima facie commitments that future cases will be decided accordingly".[817]

Case precedent ensures that the discretionary power of judges is curtailed, and at the same time it assists in the evolution of the law. Scholars have argued for a long time as to what comes first – legal reasoning or the application of case precedents. One school of thought argued that the common law developed as the judges in medieval England could not remember their reasons and had to cite cases, but another school of thought argued that it was the common law that demanded that reasons in the judgments that led to its development.[818]

In simple words, it means that the judges in other courts, when deciding later cases, must enforce the rules established by the courts in earlier cases. This rule will be applied based upon the hierarchy of the courts in jurisdictions. The doctrine of precedents has been criticised because the judges seem to be making law through their judgments, which are then followed by the lower courts, when in fact, the judges should always be subordinate to the legislators. The legislators are the right people to balance different political-interest groups; only then can they formulate the policy reasons behind much legislation. In addition, it has been argued that if a policy reason is introduced into a case by the judges, then it is arguable that a new policy reason cited in a case is actually a new law. Furthermore, it should be retroactively applicable to the facts that had happened before. [819]

It is also very common that when the cases go to appeal, the judgments are written by many judges. Not infrequently, the judges differ and argue vehemently whether the principle at stake is actually a principle in law, and whether such a principle should even be considered by them. At stake might be the principle obtained from a previous case. These are all the challenges and criticisms that the doctrine of precedents must overcome. Nonetheless, even in the continental system, such criticisms are a part of the daily life of the courts at the level of adjudication.

---

[816]Cohen, "Judges' Reasons," 508.

[817]Cohen, "Judges' Reasons," 509. On this page, Cohen discussed the view of Frederick Schauer about the importance of giving reasons.

[818]Cohen, "Judges' Reasons," 509.

[819]Penner, "Law and Adjudication," 364–8, where Dworkin's 'Right Thesis' was discussed and quoted. The quote is originally taken from R. Dworkin, "Hard Cases," *Harv. L. Rev.* 88, no. 6 (1975): 1057–1109.

7.3.1 Doctrine of Stare Decisis in England & Wales

For centuries in England, the binding value of a case was supposed to be limited to the parties only, and any case was at best the evidence of the law. Mansfield, a famous English jurist in the eighteenth century had said, "Precedent though it be evidence of law, is not the law itself, much less the whole of the law."[820] Postema defined the concept of common law as follows:

> The authority and force of any component of the common law depends on its integration into the framework of the whole and its satisfaction of a shared sense of reasonableness rooted in this framework [emphasis added]. If a judicial ruling is entrenched and regarded to be peremptory, thereby blocking all subsequent assessment of its reasonableness and coherence with the whole …, Hedley argued, then the common law in general could no longer claim authority.[821]

Many jurisprudents have argued that the *principle of fairness* ensures that all cases should be treated in the same manner. This is the most important reason for the evolution of the doctrine of *stare decisis*. On the practical side, the publication from 1865 onwards of *Law Reports* supervised by the judges in the cases, a few private case reports such as All England Reports from 1936, and weekly law reports from 1953, also contributed in development of the common law. Since 2001, the judgments in the higher courts have been issued with neutral citations. However, there are many unreported cases. In the words of Park, CJ in *Mirehouse v Rennell* (1833) 1 Cl. & Fin. 527, "Precedent must be adhered to for the sake of developing the law as a science." This demonstrates the importance of case precedents in England & Wales.

There is no statutory code/rule stating that the lower courts must follow the case law from the higher appellate court. However, there is only one statutory rule,[822] which is that the rulings from the Court of Justice of the European Union on the issue of Human rights will be binding on the courts in England & Wales. In addition, the highest court of England & Wales was the only court that was bound by its own courts'

---

[820]See Postema, "Classical Common Law Jurisprudence - II," 14, where Mansfield was quoted.
[821]Postema, "Classical Common Law Jurisprudence - II," 14.
[822]See sec. 3(1) *European Communities Act 1972*.

previous decisions unless the previous decision had been made *per incuriam*.[823] However, from 1966 onwards,[824] the House of Lords decided through this *Practice Statement* that they can overrule their previous decisions, if there was a mistake in previous decisions or if there are changes in the society, subject to their exercising caution by not disturbing retrospectively the basis of contracts, settlements of property, and fiscal arrangements.

Therefore, in 1966, the House of Lords decided on their own to develop their own rule without waiting for the legislature to legislate on this aspect of judicial activities. The Court of Appeal, an appellate court lower than the House of Lords (currently Supreme Court), is bound to follow its own judgment with a few exceptions.

It is important to note that only the *ratio decidendi*, the legal reasoning aspect of the decision, is *binding* on the courts within this system of judicial precedents. Any observations made by the judges on any legal question or issue, but not arising in such a manner as requiring a decision, is known as *obiter dictum* (meaning 'by the way', an incidental remark). These observations are *persuasive in nature but are not binding* on the lower courts.

In practice, in order to apply a case precedent, similar facts in a decided case are first analysed with reference to the facts in the case before the judges, or it may involve distinguishing the facts between these two or more cases. There is no set methodology but will depend on the judges' understanding of law. The methodology to find an applicable relevant statute(s) for the particular circumstances of a case is not that different from this methodology of finding relevant cases.

It is important to appreciate that there has been a debate that by using this doctrine, the judges have been making law by back door and, as discussed in Chapter 3 §3.2.4, are in fact bringing their own world view into the reasoning. This is a critical issue in cases where the judges are not selected from every section of society or when some section of society is prevented, due to various reasons, from becoming judges. This is important as the judges are not elected by the populace. The judgments and legal reasoning in the cases are described in great detail and are accordingly a good source for the lawyers/academics to learn the legal reasons, including the facts of the case. The cases are also important for training of judges within the judicial system.

---

[823] See *London Street Tramways v London County Council* [1898] AC 375. The meaning of *per incuriam* is due to lack of care that if the previous important case made in the same court or statute was not brought to the notice of the House of Lords.

[824] See *Practice Statement (Judicial Precedent)* (*HL*) 1966, [1966] 3 All ER 77, [1966] 1 WLR 1234.

7.3.2 Guiding Case System in China

In this section, the author will first analyse the history and tradition of a case guidance system in ancient China to decide the disputes. The author will then proceed to analyse the current guiding case system in the PRC.

7.3.2.1 History of Case Guidance (pre-PRC)

In ancient China, even though the feudal system and legislative activities were not fully established, there were still cases reported from every dynasty since the West Zhou dynasty.[825] These cases continue to have a general effect on other cases. One group of cases is from the era before the Qin Dynasty,[826] at which time not only were the Codes not fully shaped in the context of law, but the societal rules were also not fully fashioned.

On the other hand, there were cases that used to have a general effect only, and originated between the Qin to Qing Dynasties, when all the power was concentrated in the hands of the emperors. During that time, there were no clear concepts such as fairness, especially procedural fairness, and in fact the statutory system was just evolving with comprehensible and precise codes. However, the economy of ancient China was thriving. Legal philosophies and jurisprudential debates thrived, as discussed in Chapter 3, §3.4, §3.5, §3.6 & §3.7 affecting the ongoing codification and even affecting the issue of procedural fairness. For example, during the *Qing* dynasty, previous case references were required in specific cases due to nascent legal jurisprudence that was still developing at that time. In practice this resulted in increased complexity during application of statutes.[827]

The compilation of cases developed as a result of demands from Chinese society in between the Qin to Qing dynasties.[828] There was little compilation of cases before the Qin dynasty. In the Ming and Qing Dynasties, *lvli heyi* was applied to the cases.

---

[825]Ducai Liu, "A Study of Judicial Precedent in Traditional China. (Zhongguo Gudai Panli Kaolun)," *Social Sciences in China (Zhonguo Shehui Kexue)*, no. 4 (2007): 150. Liu's comments on legal history was discussed in Jinting Deng, "The Guiding Case System in Mainland China," *Frontiers of Law in China* 10, no. 3 (2015): 4.

[826]The Qin dynasty was from 221-206 BCE. Refer to Table of Dynasties of ancient China in Table VIII.

[827] Shirong Wang, "The Functions of Cases in Traditional Chinese Law. (Panli Zai Zhongguo Chuantongfa Zhong de Gongneng)," *Chinese Journal of Law (Faxue Yanjiu)*, no. 1 (2006): 125–34. Wang was discussed in Deng, "The Guiding Case System in PRC," 4.

[828]Xingliang Chen, "The Jurisprudence of the Case Guidance System (Anli Zhidao Zhidu de Fali Kaocha)," *Law and Social Development (Fazhi Yu Shehui Fazhan)* 18, no. 3 (2012): 74–76. Chen's findings were discussed in Deng, "The Guiding Case System in PRC," 4.

According to this principle, statutes and cases were compiled together.[829] In some ways, there was a similarity between the application of previous cases and statutory interpretation by analogy as practised during the Qing Dynasty. The only difference was that it was compulsory for judges in ancient China to apply the correct statutes. However, unlike with the statutes, there was no punishment for not using a previous case or even using the previous case incorrectly.[830]

In ancient China, guiding cases represented the will of the emperor and were also issued under the name of the emperor. The guiding cases were intended to be seen as if originating from the emperor (*fazi junchu*).[831] Most guiding cases were from the family and criminal branch of law as compared to commercial and civil litigation.[832] Most of the these deciding cases in ancient China were in fact used to supplement the existing statutes.[833] Scholarly articles note that these guiding cases did not restrict judicial discretion, which was already restricted to a considerable extent by the relevant statutes. In fact, these guiding cases were required due to the demands of society.[834] These guiding cases were very useful in meeting the needs of society, and they provided flexibility in relation to several issues during adjudication of disputes during those times.

In the Song, Yuan, Ming and Qing Dynasties, the guiding cases even created exceptions that were to be given priority over the then-existing written codes.[835] These guiding ancient cases also served other purposes such as having educational and declaratory functions for target audiences. However, unfortunately, the legal reasoning was not clearly postulated in those guiding cases.[836]

In ancient China, there was another institution, called *BiFu*, that was mostly utilised in criminal law. This institution would guide the lower courts to use the details

---

[829]Sibin Yang, "On Basic Characteristics and Exchanges of Ancient China's Case System. (Zhongguo Gudai Panli Zhidu de Yanbian Yu Jiben Tezheng)," *Law Science Magazine (Faxue Zazhi)*, no. 2 (2008): 121n5. *See also*, Deng, "The Guiding Case System in PRC," 4, where Yang was cited.

[830]MacCormack, *Spirit of Traditional Chinese Law*, 186.

[831]Xingliang Chen, "The Jurisprudence of Case Guidance System," n.20 at 74, *See also*, Deng, "The Guiding Case System in PRC," 11, where Chen was cited and analysed.

[832]Deng, "The Guiding Case System in PRC," 5.

[833] Shirong Wang, "The Functions of Cases in Traditional Chinese Law. (Panli Zai Zhongguo Chuantongfa Zhong de Gongneng)," n.18 at 130. *See also*, Sibin Yang, "Basic China's Case System," 123n5. *See also*, Deng, "The Guiding Case System in PRC," 8, where both Wang and Yang were cited and analysed in detail.

[834]Deng, "The Guiding Case System in PRC," 8.

[835] Shirong Wang, "The Functions of Cases in Traditional Chinese Law. (Panli Zai Zhongguo Chuantongfa Zhong de Gongneng)," 134n18. *See also*, Deng, "The Guiding Case System in PRC," 8, where Wang's views were discussed in detail.

[836]Liu, "A Study of Judicial Precedent in Traditional China. (Zhongguo Gudai Panli Kaolun)," 148–15n16. *See also*, Deng, "The Guiding Case System in PRC," 8, where Liu was cited.

provided in the guiding cases, to classify crimes which were based on a set of facts. From this, a punishment appropriate to the facts could be delivered. This process was akin to matching of the crimes (*qingzui xiangfu*) of the guiding case(s) with the crime before the judges.[837]

Another reason for seeking the appropriate criminal code for the award of punishment was that all crimes had statutory penalties that could be found in the codes and were absolute in nature (*juedui queding fadingxing*).[838] Even if the cases had been decided by *BiFu*, those cases could also be re-issued as guiding cases.[839]

Deng analysed thirty cases that were adjudicated in the lower courts, which were able to use *BiFu* to find similar cases with an "analogy of relationship, legal elements, or certain equitable feelings." This analogy was executed through the principle of *juzhong mingqin; juqing mingzhong* principle.[840]

In ancient China, if the crime in front of the officials of the lower courts was less severe than the available guiding case, that crime would be punished less severely. Similarly, if the crime were more severe than the available guiding case, then the crime would be punished more severely. *BiFu* is not allowed in the current PRC legal system, as *BiFu* goes against the Latin principle '*nulla poena sine lege*', which means that there cannot be any penalty without a law.[841]

The case guiding system in ancient China needed a very detailed approval process, as it was necessary for the system to be seen as originating from the emperor. For example, in the Han Dynasty, *Tingwei*, the supreme judiciary of the time, was authorized to make guiding cases, called '*jueshibi*', from reported cases that had been approved by the emperor.[842]

---

[837]Xinyu Chen, "Bifu and Leitui - Starts from Biyin Lvtiao. (Bifu Yu Leitui Zhibian - Cong 'Biyin Lvtiao' Chufa)," *Tribune of Political Science and Law (Zhengfa Luntan)* 29, no. 2 (2011): 118n2. *See also*, Deng, "The Guiding Case System in PRC," 11, where Chen's analysis was discussed in detail.
[838]Deng, "The Guiding Case System in PRC," 11.
[839]Xinyu Chen, "Bifu and Leitui - Starts from Biyin Lvtiao. (Bifu Yu Leitui Zhibian - Cong 'Biyin Lvtiao' Chufa)," 114. It was discussed in Deng, "The Guiding Case System in PRC," 11. Deng cited Chen's views on cases that were decided according to *BiFu,* but were later reissued as guiding cases, such as the 30 cases compiled in Volume 47 of *Criminal Laws of Qing Dynasty.*
[840]The analysis of the 30 cases was carried out by Xinyu Chen, "Bifu and Leitui - Starts from Biyin Lvtiao. (Bifu Yu Leitui Zhibian - Cong 'Biyin Lvtiao' Chufa)," 115n5, 116 –18. *See also*, Deng, "The Guiding Case System in PRC," 11, where Chen's analysis was discussed in detail.
[841]Deng, "The Guiding Case System in PRC," 12.
[842]Sibin Yang, "Basic China's Case System," 122n5, as cited in Deng, "The Guiding Case System in PRC," 19.

Lastly, the author would like the readers to ponder that thousands of years ago, Lord Lu, a high judicial officer of the Zhou dynasty, gave instructions to jurists, as recorded by Shang-shu:

> In a case of an offence less serious than one for which a heavy punishment is prescribed, a lighter punishment should be imposed; in a case of an offence more serious than one for which a light punishment is prescribed, a heavier punishment should be imposed.[843]

7.3.2.2 Case Guidance System (post-1985)

Lower courts in the PRC have been using the *Gazette* of published cases since 1985. The Gazette is published by the Supreme People's Court. In recent years, the SPC has compiled *Cases of People's Courts* and *Guide Books of Judicial Cases in China*.[844] Over the years, many departments as well as the lower courts in various provinces have started publishing guide books of cases resulting in books, academic articles, and so forth.[845]

This formed the foundation upon which the guiding case system was formally established on November, 26, 2010, when the SPCC issued the *Provisions on Case Guidance Work*,[846] announcing the establishment of the Guiding Case System in mainland China.[847] Later in the same year, the Supreme People's Procuratorate and the Public Security Ministry issued provisions on the case guidance system to guide work in their institutions, though this is more akin to 'administrative instructions' than judicial power, which is only vested in the SPC.[848]

---

[843]Wejen Chang, "Classical Chinese Jurisprudence and Development of Chinese Legal System" (2009–10), 235. Chang took the discussions and quote from Qu Wanli, shi jing quan shi [ANNOTATION ON THE BOOK OF SONGS] 326, 347, 362, 372, 376, 395, 506, 527, 546 (1983) (Taiwan)(ROC), 259.

[844]*Guide Books of Judicial Cases* in China was compiled by the SPCC, the National Judges College and the Renmin University Law School together as discussed in Deng, "The Guiding Case System in PRC," 2n1.

[845]Deng, "The Guiding Case System in PRC," 2.

[846]*Fa Fa [2010]* No. 51 November 26, 2010.

[847]For example, pursuant to *Provisions on Guiding case system* of SPC, the SPC has issued *The Notice of the First Set of Guiding Cases* and published four guiding cases, then the second on April, 14, 2012, the third on September 18, 2012, the fourth on February 7, 2013, the fifth on November 15, 2013, the sixth on January 29, 2014, and the seventh on July 8, 2014.

[848]Deng, "The Guiding Case System in PRC," 2.

In March 2011, during the fourth session of the eleventh NPC, the ex-chairman of the Standing Committee of the NPC, Mr. Wu Bangguo, declared that the statutory framework with Chinese characteristics has been fully established in the PRC as part of the socialist legal system. On May, 13, 2015, the SPC issued the *Detailed Rules of Implementation of the Provisions of the Supreme People's Court on Case Guidance Work* ("Detailed Rules").[849] Given that (based on the date of promulgation) the PRC legal system is so recent in origin, the level of expectation that anyone can have from the PRC legal system cannot be high.

Scholars of PRC law assert that the next wave of reforms will be based on case guiding systems rather than on legislations and the SPC's opinions.[850] This view is also based on the fact that many of these scholars are dissatisfied with the vague codes and equally vague statutory interpretations provided by the SPC.[851]

It is important to highlight Deng's analysis of the guiding case management system:

> However, in both ancient and current China, <u>statutes are primarily relied on to centralize power</u> [emphasis added], and guiding cases are supplementary; while in early common law, cases are dominant and statutes are supplementary.[852]

It is important to note that even in the common law systems, and in particular the *CPR 1998*, there is a growing reliance on the written laws/statutes/codes. Some scholars are of the view that statutes are growing more important even in prominent common law countries, such as England & Wales, the US and India.[853]

It is believed that guiding cases can fill the gaps between the law as determined by the relevant codes in the area of substantive law, their interpretation by the judges, and the application of these laws to the specific set of facts.[854] This focus on interpretation and application is important, as the PRC is a vast land mass comprising many provinces, and the quality of the judges who interpret codes and apply laws in the lower courts has been questioned by many scholars. On the other hand, the

---

[849]*Fa Fa [2015] No. 130.*
[850]Deng, "The Guiding Case System in PRC," 3.
[851]Refer above §7.2.2.
[852]Deng, "The Guiding Case System in PRC," 5.
[853]Melvin Aron Eisenberg, *The Nature of Common Law* (Cambridge: Harvard University Press, 1988), 1. *See also*, Deng, "The Guiding Case System in PRC," 6, for discussion on Eisenberg's views.
[854]Deng, "The Guiding Case System in PRC," 6.

increasing prosperity levels amongst the populace, achieved in just two decades, are also raising expectations in relation to judicial efficiency pertaining to PRC courts.

Another aim, it appears, of the guiding case system is to regulate the exercise of judicial discretion, and last but not least to resolve the longstanding issue of similar cases receiving different rulings in the PRC courts.[855] These guiding cases also have a political and declaratory function. Since these cases within the case guidance system are backed by reasons and methodologies, it can also be an important arena for training judges in the lower courts. Another objective of the case guidance system is to ensure that the lower courts rely less on the Reply system,[856] and to increase judicial efficiency in the PRC courts.[857]

The SPC has been standardizing the format in which the cases selected for case guidance are written. The lower courts are motivated 'to cooperate in reporting, compiling and applying guiding cases, constructing relevant working and incentive mechanisms, and building case database.'[858] The SPC and High Court has recently organised meetings to fulfil this function. These meetings also clarified that the interpretations of the guiding cases lead the system towards uniformity in all the courts.

The *Guiding cases* are published in SPC's *Gazette,* its web site, and People's Court Daily in both paper and electronic versions. Many PRC scholars have praised the new system, but others have criticised the lack of facts in the guided cases. These scholars have even questioned the criteria by which the cases are selected in the Case Guiding System.

In selecting cases for the Guiding Cases system, the SPC requires the selected cases should meet the following five conditions: [859]

◆   The facts of the cases have aroused wide public concern;

---

[855]Zelin Su, "Fully Exploit the Function of the Guiding Case System with Chinese Characteristics; Courts, Positively Enforce Historical Missions of People's Application. (Chongfen Fahui Zhongguo Tese Anli Zhidao Zhidu Zuoyong Jiji Lvxing Renmin Fayuan Lishi Shiming)," *Journal of Law Application (Falv Shiyong)* 7 (2011): n. 12 at 5.
[856]Refer §7.2.2.2.
[857]Mingguo Chen and Weiming Zuo, "Practical Obstacles and Countermeasures of Guiding Cases. (Zhidaoxing Anli de Yingyong Zhangai Jiqi Kefu - Sichuan Fayuan Anli Yingyong Shidian Gongzuo de Chubu Fenxi)," *Journal of Law Application (Falv Shiyong)* 5 (2012): 69–70.
[858]Ibid., 10.
[859]See Art. 2 of *Provisions of the Supreme People's Court Concerning Work on Guiding Cases, Fa Fa [2010]* No. 51 November 26, 2010.

- The cases involve circumstances, where relevant laws only stipulate principled provisions and the legal provisions are of relatively general nature;

- Cases are of a typical nature;

- Cases are difficult, complicated or are cases of new types within the PRC legal system;

- Other cases that can serve as guide.

Furthermore, Hu said, "A guiding case must be a just decision, a decision with its social effect and legal effect organically unified, and a model followed by judges."[860]

Mr. Hu, Director of Research Office of SPC, has clarified that the lower courts must follow the guided cases.[861] Mr. Hu also stated that the guided cases were not a new type of statutory interpretation, and clarified their binding nature.[862]

It is not clear that "erroneous application of law" as grounds for appeal in Article 170 of *Civil Procedure Law 1991 (as amended in 2012)* includes 'erroneous application of guiding cases'.[863] Guiding cases are not grounds for such appeal, but it seems they are related to the correct position of law. However, the lower courts can depart from the guiding cases provided reasons are given.[864] In any event, the legislated Codes will prevail in the PRC; here, it diverges from common law's case precedent system, where the *ratio decidendi* even involving a statute will prevail. Therefore, it seems the SPC intentionally uses the word "guiding (*zhidaoxing*) *anli*" instead of "*panli*" to

---

[860]Comment by Mr. Hu Yunteng, Director of the Research Department of the Supreme People's Court, available at http://cgc.law.stanford.edu/why-guiding-cases-matter/#hyunteng (last viewed Jan. 29, 2014). *See also*, the same comment cited in Jocelyn E. H. Limmer, "China's New 'Common Law' Using China's Guiding Cases to Understand How to Do Business in People's Republic of China," *Willamette J. Int'l L. & Dis. Resol.* 21, no. 2 (2013): 35. The author has used the revised version of Limmer's paper that is available on ssrn.com.
[861]Yunteng Hu, "The Constructing Cases Guidance System with Chinese Characteristics Exclusive Interview of Dr. Hu, Yunteng, Member of Judicial Committee and the Director of the Research Office in Supreme People's Court," *China L.*, no. 1 (2011): 4–6,58–60. *See also*, Deng, "The Guiding Case System in PRC," 20, where Hu was cited.
[862]Hu's statement was discussed in Deng, "The Guiding Case System in PRC," 21. Deng has disagreed with Hu. However, Hu's views will likely prevail over Deng's views, because Hu is from the SPC.
[863]Deng, "The Guiding Case System in PRC," 22.
[864]Deng, "The Guiding Case System in PRC," 22, where Hu's statement was discussed in this context.

cautiously differentiate the guiding cases from normal cases and common law cases.[865]

It appears from reading the translation of various scholars that even though guiding cases are not laws, and therefore should not be cited in the 'Judgment's Key Points' section of a statement of claim submitted to a Chinese court, they can nonetheless be cited in the reasoning section.[866] Further guidance on this issue has been given by Deng, but is beyond the scope of this book.[867]

In the author's view, even though Deng has clarified the PRC law in relation to case guidance in a very succinct way. However, when comparing the system to the common law system, he has failed to fully grasp what the common law is in terms of the judges' power to make law or whether they can indeed make law in the common law system. The kind of training and autonomy the judges have in common law is unimaginable in the PRC system. The whole jurisprudence of the current common law revolves around this issue.

It is time to delineate the detailed rules as published by the SPC in *Detailed Rules of Implementation of the Provisions of the Supreme People's Court on Case Guidance Work* ("Detailed Rules"),[868] and analyse them. These rules have in fact been issued to prevent inconsistency in application. The key elements of these *Detailed Rules* are as follows:

◆ Article 7 – Where the Case Guidance Office deems it necessary to further study a potential case to be included as a guiding case, it may consult relevant State organs, departments and social organizations, members of the case guidance work expert committee, as well as experts and scholars. This is to ensure that the People's courts at all levels shall take them as a reference in future, when they try similar cases.

---

[865]Deng, "The Guiding Case System in PRC," 24.
[866]Limmer, "China's New 'Common Law' Using China's Guiding Cases to Understand How to Do Business in People's Republic of China," 36.
[867]Deng, "The Guiding Case System in PRC," 22, 27–28.
[868]Fa Fa [2015] No. 130.

- ◆ Article 9 –Where a case under adjudication by a People's court at any level is similar to a guiding case published by the Supreme People's Court in terms of basic facts and the application of law, then it is incumbent on the People's court to render a judgment/ruling by referencing the headnotes of the judgment/ruling on the guiding case. This means that the binding effect of a guiding case is limited by the law to a reference, rather than being a binding precedent that must be followed.

- ◆ Article 10 –When a People's Court at any level refers to a guiding case in the adjudication of a similar case, it shall quote the guiding case as part of the reasons for judgments/rulings; however, it shall not quote the same as a basis for judgment/ruling. Therefore, PRC judges are not allowed to use guiding cases as the legal basis for judgment. Instead, PRC judges can refer to a guiding case in the reasoning part of the judgments. If it were to be compared to the common law, then it would be as if common-law judges were to look for the reasons cited from another published decision as guidance only, to develop their legal reasoning in their case. On proper analysis, it is the author's view that the detailed rules, therefore, are an attempting to limit the judges' discretion in their ability to reference previous decisions.

- ◆ Article 11 –During the process of case handling, case handling officers must search relevant guiding cases. Having analyzed Article 11 the author feels that now there is an obligation on the judges to actively participate in finding decisions from the case guiding system. However, the training aspect in relation to this article would be a big challenge throughout the PRC.

7.4 Burden and Standards of Proof

In civil litigation, any party making allegations in a statement of case/claims must prove those allegations in order to win their case. The proof will be dependent on *weight and reliability* of the evidence. A party who has to prove the allegations, has the Burden of Proof in the civil litigation and that party has to provide enough evidence to satisfy the courts. An opponent, a Defendant, has to similarly prove his defence. This process is followed in most jurisdictions for trying civil litigation cases. However, the jurisprudential school of thoughts can influence the thinking of the judges and the legal system.

A good advocate or lawyer constantly reminds the courts as to which side has the requisite Burden of Proof, as sometimes it is not clear from the allegations in parties' statements of case. The most common example of such instances in England & Wales is where the judges are also in doubt in cases involving interpretation of contracts.[869] At times, the courts can decide based on the fact that a particular party is in the better position to adduce evidence in the dispute.[870]

However, the next question is how much evidence each party must submit to the courts to discharge the Burden of Proof. The answer can be found in the concept called *Standards of Proof*. Most civil cases are decided based on the *balance of probabilities,* except the Standards of Proof will be higher in cases that have elements of a criminal nature such as contempt or fraud or deceit. Any lawyer in practice must analyse evidence objectively. For the sake of completeness, the test for Standard of Proof is 'beyond reasonable doubt' in criminal cases, and any jury should be left with no doubt before convicting anyone.

7.4.1 Standards of Proof in context of England & Wales v. Standards of Proof in Civil Law Jurisdictions

As discussed above, the balance of probabilities has been understood from various cases to mean that something is '*more probable than not*'.[871] In simple terms, this means that in order to win, any party must prove that at least fifty-one percent of the allegations in his civil case are true, or the defendant must prove that the allegations are fifty-one percent untrue. If either party can provide this level of proof, then that party will win the case. However, there is no mathematical formula for deciding the percentages, and that figure of fifty-one percent is used to provide a simple explanation. Every lawyer will try their best to ensure that they provide as much *relevant and admissible* evidence as necessary to prove his case, for example, at seventy percent or even more on the test of probability.

---

[869]See *The Glandarroch* [1894] P 226, and *Hurst v Evans* [1917] 1 KB 352.

[870]See *Joseph Constantine Steamship Line Ltd v Imperial Smelting Corp Ltd* [1942] AC 154.

[871]See Lord Denning's view in *Miller v Minister of Pensions* [1947] 2 All ER 372, 374. In another common law jurisdiction, Canada also has a similar test for Standards of Proof, which states that if there is a higher probability for this to happen than not, then in that case the Burden of Proof of such party shall thereby be released. In English Law, in the courts it would mean that either the burden has been discharged or it is not discharged at the end of the trial.

In a recent case, Lord Nicholls of Birkenhead succinctly explained the concept of Standards of Proof in the case *In Re H (Minors) (Sexual Abuse: Standard of Proof)*:[872]

> The balance of probability standard means that a court is satisfied an event occurred if the court considers that, on the evidence, the occurrence of the event was more likely than not. When assessing the probabilities, the court will have in mind as a factor, to whatever extent is appropriate in the particular case, that <u>the more serious the allegation the less likely it is that the event occurred and, hence, the stronger should be the evidence before the court concludes that the allegation is established on the balance of probability</u> [emphasis added]. Fraud is usually less likely than negligence. Deliberate physical injury is usually less likely than accidental physical injury. ...built into the preponderance of probability standard is a generous degree of flexibility in respect of the seriousness of the allegation.

The Standards of Proof is also called '*preponderance of evidence*'[873] in the United States. The test for Standards of Proof in civil litigation is lower than in the criminal law, where the requirement for Standards of Proof is 'beyond reasonable doubt'. In addition, it is an appropriate time to appreciate that the test for Standards of Proof in the common law system are lower than in the continental civil tradition. In civil law jurisdictions, the test for Standard of Proof is defined in terms of "*moral certainty* or as *intime conviction.*"[874]

---

[872]See H and others (Minors) (A.P.) (Respondents) [1995] UKHL 16, [73] (Lord Nicholls). *See also*, in the same case at [76] (Lord Nicholls) for further discussion of test of Standards of Proof that was to be applied in *Children Act 1989* cases. Accordingly, there is the test of balance of probabilities, which is same test as applied in civil litigation. According to the judges, there are only two tests of Standards of Proof, one for criminal law and one for the civil law. The test of balance of probabilities as applicable to the civil law cases has in-built flexibility.

[873]Chao-yang (Xiamen Municipal Intermediate People's Court Chen, Xiamen), "Standards of Proof in Civil Proceedings: From the Perspective of Judicial Impartiality and Efficiency," *J. of Southwest U. P. Sc. & L.*, no. 1 (2002): 9–19, where an American scholar was quoted and discussed: "the general standard of proof in civil action is Preponderance of Probability. That means the facts alleged will be deemed to be true when jury is convinced that the probability for its existence based on the evidence available, is higher."

[874]Dominique Demougin and Claude Fluet, "Deterrence Vs Judicial Error: A Comparative View of Standards of Proof," *J. of Inst. and Theoretical Econ.* 161, no. 2 (2004): 161. https://ssrn/abstract=585770. See also, *French Code de Procédure Pénale* (as on 5 June 2016), Art. 353; *German Zivilprozessordnung 2005 (as amended in 2013)*, § 286 (1); *German Strafprozessordnung 1987* (as amended in 2014), § 261.

While the definition of Standards of Proof is easy, how the judges in the English courts go about deciding on the matter is quite complex. They will consider the following points very carefully:[875]

- Quality of relevant evidence and not just quantity of evidence;

- The judges will repeat this exercise again and again against each cause of action stated in the Statements of Case of the parties.

Standards of Proof in the common law system such as in England & Wales is an *objective concept* but in the continental tradition, it is a *subjective concept*. In spite of the difference, the goal of judiciary is the same in both systems. Both the common law and civil law jurisdictions operate within conditions of uncertainty.[876]

Facts or allegations that are highly improbable will require stronger evidence. However, the probability of a fact happening does not alter the balance of probability test.[877]

The subjective aspect of the continental law tradition can be appreciated by analysing an example taken from the *German Code*, § 286 (1) of *Code of Civil Procedure* which provides:

> Paying due regard to the entirety of the proceedings, including the evidence presented, if any, it is for the court to decide, based on its **personal** conviction [emphasis added], whether a factual claim is indeed true or not.

---

[875]Susan Blake, *A Practical Approach to Effective Litigation*, 8th ed. (Oxford: Oxford University Press, 2015), 554.

[876]James Brook, "Inevitable Errors: The Preponderance of Evidence Standard in Civil Litigation," *Tulsa L.J.* 18, no. 1 (1982): 79–109. *See also*, Christoph Engel, "Preponderance of the Evidence Versus Intime Conviction: A Behavioural Perspective on Conflict between American and Continental European Law," *MPI Collective Goods Preprint No.2008/33* (2008): 2, where Brook was discussed in the context of uncertainty of evidence in any civil litigation.

[877]See *Re H & others (A.P.) (Respondents)* [1995] UKHL 16, [76] (Lord Nicholls).

It is clear from the above reading of § 286 (1) that in the German Code, *'personal convictions''* of the judges are very important.[878] The continental system relies upon the experience and convictions of the judges in deciding cases.[879] Kaplan, Mehren & Schaefer have discussed this in greater depth:

> What is the degree of conviction to which the civil court must be brought in ordinary situations before it is justified in holding that the burden of establishing a proposition has been met? [A German treatise says]: "The judge may and must always content himself with a degree of certainty that is appropriate for practical life, one which silences doubts without entirely excluding them." Evidently a rather high degree of probability is called for, and there is a tendency toward at least verbal equation of the civil with the criminal standard [emphasis added].[880]

However, scholars have argued that in jurisdictions where the concept of *objective* Standards of Proof is dominant, such as in the common law jurisdictions of the US and England & Wales, the evidence and arguments will still be processed by the judges' human minds. The human mind is always susceptible to bias, prejudices, and external influence, and the subjectivity of the judges cannot be avoided.[881] Thus common law decisions are still error prone due to the subjective element involved in processing the evidence.

The philosophy behind the concept of *balance of probabilities* in common law is that it minimises the frequency of errors by the judges, so that generally they are able to

---

[878]Engel, "Preponderance of the Evidence versus Intime Conviction: A Behavioural Perspective on Conflict Between American and Continental European Law," 5.

[879]Engel, "Preponderance of the Evidence versus Intime Conviction: A Behavioural Perspective on Conflict Between American and Continental European Law," 5. Engel brings in the views of other scholars, to discuss the issue in continental jurisdiction such as Germany regarding as to how a German judge will decide various aspects of a case in his/her mind. For example, he discusses Schulz's view that the test is empirical, built on *"ethos, experience and intuition"*, and *"the psychic state of taking a fact for true."*

[880]Benjamin Kaplan, Arthur T. von Mehren, and Rudolf Schaefer, "Phrases of German Civil Procedure (Pt.1)," *Harv. L. Rev.* 71, no. 7 (1958): 1242. *See also*, where the same quote was analysed in E. Sherwin and K. M. Clermont, "A Comparative View of Standards of Proof," *Am. J. Comp. L.* 50, no. 2 (2002): 243. *See also*, Sherwin and Clermont, "Comparative Standard of Proof," 256, where it was discussed as to how the French legal system seems to put lots of faith in judges' intuitive conviction. In the author's view, if judges are selected from a particular elite end of the society, then it could be dangerous for the society.

[881]Refer, Chapter 5, §5.5.

find the truth in the cases before them.[882] However, the question that could be asked is: why are the common law jurisdictions satisfied with finding the truth on a scale of averages, rather than adopting the more stringent concept of Standards of Proof as in the Civil law jurisdiction? Does it really minimise the errors, as common law jurisdictions seek to find truth on the basis of the possibility of success in an average number of cases it handles? Sherwin and Clermont answered these questions within the context of civil law jurisdictions by explaining that there are many reasons why these civil jurisdictions have higher Standards of Proof — such as settlement of disputes without having to worry over the quality of settlement, discouraging litigation to reduce costs, etc., but above all the reason is to enhance the legitimacy of judicial decisions.[883]

Based on the above analysis, the author is going to discuss a few logical questions. Does it then mean that the decisions in civil-law countries are perfect? It could also mean that the burden is so high in civil law traditions, that the party which has the Burden of Proof might not be able to meet the Standards of Proof required in the civil law courts, even though that party could have won the same case within a common law jurisdiction. As a result of these stringent requirements, the party might end up losing the case in the civil law jurisdiction. Does it then really help the civil law legal system to increase the legitimacy of the courts in civil law countries, if many Claimants will end up dejected because of the high Burden of Proof? Would this not affect the legitimacy of the courts?

Additionally, in many civil law jurisdictions as compared to common law jurisdictions, the exact details of these stringent requirements as to Standards of Proof is not clear.[884] How much evidence will be sufficient for it to be classed as certain in the eyes of the judges, for the Standards of Proof to be met in any civil law jurisdictions? Does it involve any exercise of discretion by the judges? It is said that civil law judges usually apply variable standards in this context.[885] Interventions from the civil law judges are very common, while, on the other hand, the judges in common law jurisdictions will let the parties' lawyers present the case to them.[886]

---

[882]Demougin and Fluet, "Comparative Standards of Proof," 193.
[883]Sherwin and Clermont, "Comparative Standard of Proof," 252–54. *See also*, Demougin and Fluet, "Comparative Standards of Proof," 193, where Sherwin & Clermont's views were discussed in detail.
[884]Sherwin and Clermont, "Comparative Standard of Proof," 45.
[885]Ibid., 47.
[886]Refer, Chapter 5, §5.2.

Additionally, in the common law, there are lots of 'exclusionary principles'[887] that have the potential to exclude relevant evidence from being submitted to the judges. It is difficult to measure and thus confirm that errors are, in fact, minimized in the common law system as compared to the civil law system, based on the test of 'balance of probablities'. In any event, the focus in the civil law system is on finding the ultimate truth. In addition, in the civil law jurisdiction there is a possibility of changing even the Burden of Proof midway due to judicial interventions. In contrast, in the civil law jurisdictions, there are fewer exclusionary principles in relation to what the courts may be willing to accept as evidence.

In the end, no system is perfect, and many scholars have written on the debates between different types of legal systems. Many mathematical studies have also been carried out to find the answers to the above questions. For the sake of completeness, mathematical studies have shown that the common law test for Standards of Proof is better at providing incentives to members of society to act correctly rather than minimising errors, but the civil law test of Standards of Proof is more likely concerned with finding the truth.[888] Such questions are essential to be kept in mind while pursuing comparative study.

In the author's view, since there are so many variables such as exclusionary rules within the context of law of evidence in the common law, the unpredictability of judges' interventions in the civil jurisdictions (which could shift the Burden of Proof, or even make the causes of actions to be looked at differently) then it is likely that no firm conclusions from mathematical models can be drawn as to which of the two systems is better in minimising errors in courts.

---

[887]*Exclusionary principles* were developed in the area of criminal legal systems in most common law jurisdictions. These principles were developed in the context of law of evidence, whereby particular evidence can be excluded because its *prejudicial value exceeds the probative value*. As a result of which evidence such as confessions, improperly obtained evidence etc. can be excluded at the judge's discretion, some of which were codified later through legislations.

In the civil cases as well, the judges have discretion as provided in *CPR 1998* r. 31.1 (2) that provides that the court can give directions on — (a) the issues on which it requires evidence; (b) the nature of the evidence which it requires to decide those issues; (c) the way in which the evidence is to be placed before the court. However, there is more flexibility in civil litigation on parties to present the cases, but common law has developed some exclusion principles such as in the case of *ITC Film Distributors v Video Exchange* [1982] 2 All ER 246, where the claimant was granted an injunction to prevent the use of evidence by the defendant. The said evidence was picked up by the defendant due to the claimant's error. However, there are rules that has been developed in common law on admissibility of evidence such as in the case of *First Subsea Ltd v Balltec Ltd* [2013] EWHC 1033. In this case, it was decided that the focus of the judges will be on relevance, weight and probative effect of evidence. Judges will likely exhibit a cautious approach where the evidence is second-hand and will exclude evidence that can be tampered with and will likely allow indirect evidence where direct evidence is not available. For further knowledge on this topic, the readers should refer to Blake, *A Practical Approach to Effective Civil Litigation*, 547–49.

[888]Demougin and Fluet, "Comparative Standards of Proof," 205.

Lastly, due to the subjectivity of judges towards evidence being mandated in civil law jurisdictions, in the author's view, the selection of judges is a crucial issue. It is important that the judges are selected from all sections of society.

7.4.1.1 Standards of Proof in Interim Hearings under CPR 1998 in England & Wales

The above discussion was about Standards of Proof in general. However, when there are interim applications in courts, common-law judges in England & Wales have devised many tests pertaining to Standards of Proof. In a normal trial, as discussed earlier, if one of the parties proves the case as more probable than not, then that party will win the case in the courts.[889] The importance of Burden of Proof is that once the Burden of Proof is discharged by the appropriate test of Standards of Proof, then the courts will consider the facts as having happened in a dispute. [890] However, interlocutory hearings are different.

In any interlocutory hearings, the purpose is not to resolve the disputes; rather the parties are trying to regulate their position until the trials are over, or to obtain case management directions, or other similar issues. It needs to be appreciated that fact-finding processes involving witnesses' credibility, demeanour and cross-examination are not usually available to English judges in such interim hearings.

In addition, reliance circumstantial or contemporaneous evidence is not an option for the judges. From the case of *Prince of Wales v Associated Newspapers Ltd*,[891] it is clear that judges will decide any interim application on the basis of written applications containing facts and any fact that is disputed by the Respondents' version of the story. Judges will not usually go into the merits of the cases unless there are applications, for example applications for summary judgements or security for costs.

---

[889]See *Miller v Minister of Pensions* [1947] 2 All ER 372.

[890]Stuart Sime, "Disputes of Fact in Interim Applications," in *The Civil Procedure Rules Ten Years On*, ed. Déirdre Dwyer (Oxford; New York: Oxford University Press, 2009), 274. *See also, Re B (children) (care proceedings: standard of proof)* [2008] UKHL 35, Judge Baroness Hale said at [32] that:
"In our legal system, if a judge finds it more likely than not that something did take place, then it is treated as having taken place. If he finds it more likely than not that it did not take place, then it is treated as not having taken place. He is not allowed to sit on the fence. He has to find for one side or the other. [emphasis added] Sometimes the burden of proof will come to his rescue: the party with the burden of showing that something took place will not have satisfied him that it did. But generally speaking a judge is able to make up his mind where the truth lies without needing to rely upon the burden of proof."
[891][2006] EWCA Civ 1776; [2008] Ch 57.

In all such interim applications, the English judges have a duty to balance the aim of the interim applications along with the overriding objective.[892] The courts will try to avoid the interim hearings turning into mini-trials. In order to balance the interests of all parties in these applications, the courts have formulated various tests for Standards of Proof.

In order to understand these tests, it is important to understand what needs to be proved in England & Wales:[893]

- ◆ Law through statutes or case precedent may require that some facts need to be proved to establish legal right. These are called *facts in issue* that need to be proved on balance of probabilities by a party having the Burden of Proof;

- ◆ In any case, there are a few facts that are required to be proved in order to predict the occurrence of material facts. These facts also need to be proved on balance of probabilities by a party having the Burden of Proof;

- ◆ Facts that are to become part of the foundation from which the fact of issue needs to be inferred, do not need to be proved to have happened.

The different types of tests for Standards of Proof are applicable in the interlocutory or the interim hearings. In such interim hearings, the judges are not concerned with resolving the disputes or deciding the conflicting evidence presented to the courts. The default test for Standards of Proof in such interim hearings is that the applicants have a '*good arguable case*'. However, different Standards of Proof have developed over the years for interim hearings, to ensure that the tests for Standards of Proof are fit for the purpose.[894]

The flexibility shown by tests is an example of common-law judges' discretionary power. More importantly, it also showcases the ability of the common law to adapt to different circumstances, or to the nature of applications, and to balance the interests of even other stakeholders not party to the disputes.

---

[892]Sime, "Interim Application – Dispute of Facts," 271–74.
[893]See *Re B (children) (care proceedings: standard of proof)* [2008] UKHL 35, [3]. (Lord Hoffmann)
[894]Sime, "Interim Application - Dispute of Facts," 276–9.

A few of the tests for Standards of Proof that have been developed over the years by the English courts for various types of interim applications in courts are as follows:

♦ Test of 'Good arguable case' — In this test, a party needs to prove that the merits of the case have a few serious arguments. Sime is of the view this test is very similar to the usual *prima facie* test that the applicants have to satisfy in many different applications.[895] Cases have highlighted that this test can vary depending on the cases.[896]

♦ Test of 'better argument on the material available' — In this test, the applicants must prove their case a bit more on evidence as compared to the test of 'good arguable case'.

♦ Test of 'Serious cases on merits' — In the interim injunction applications, the applicants need to satisfy the courts that there is a *serious question that needs to be tried* in the dispute and accordingly, the applicants need to prove a prima facie case on merits on evidence. [897]

♦ Test of 'Real Prospect of success' — In these applications, the applicants have to prove that there is a '*realistic*' in contrast to a '*fanciful*' prospect of success in the main dispute.[898] From the recent case *ED & F Man Liquid Products Ltd v Patel*,[899] the test from dicta of Potter LJ must be as follows: "*case is better than merely arguable*" and "*must carry some degree of conviction.*"

♦ Test of 'Equal prospect of success' — In applications for interim injunctions, in exceptional cases, the court had awarded a mandatory injunction on the basis of test of equal

---

[895]Sime, "Interim Application - Dispute of Facts," 277.
[896]Sime, "Interim Application - Dispute of Facts," 277. See also, *WPP Holdings Italy SRL v Benatti* [2007] EWCA Civ 263; [2007] 1 WLR 2316.
[897]See *American Cyanamid Co v Ethicon Ltd* (No 1) [1975] AC 396 (HL).
[898]See *Swain v Hillman* [2001] 1 All ER 9.
[899][2003] CPLR 384, [8] (Potter LJ); [2003] EWCA Civ 472.

prospect of success with the opponent and accordingly the requirement of evidence will reflect that.[900]

♦ Test of 'High degree of assurance' — As discussed earlier, the courts expect to be convinced that the merits of the case are *quite high*,[901] before they will grant the mandatory injunction. This means court would like to be satisfied a bit more on evidence.

♦ Test of 'obvious case' — This test has been used by the courts before granting a prohibitory injunction.

♦ Test of 'No reasonable grounds' — This test is very similar to the test of Standards of Proof, and it requires the party to show that there is no reasonable ground for the opponent to argue a particular cause of action.

♦ Test of 'Reasonable possibility' — It is granted to the applicants where there is a *reasonable possibility* that the applications for freezing injunction might be made in future.[902]

♦ Test of 'real possibility' — In the applications for obtaining the search orders to preserve evidence, the applicants have to satisfy the courts with evidence that there is a *real possibility* that the material evidence will be destroyed.[903]

♦ Test of 'extremely strong prima facie case' —In this test, the applicants' burden in relation to Standards of Proof is *higher* as compared to just showing to the courts that they have a good arguable case. This test is used in obtaining search orders.

♦ Test of 'strong prima facie case' — This test is used by showing there is a *strong prima facie* case against respondents

---

[900]See *Leisure Data v Bell* [1988] FSR 367 (CA). In this case, it appears that the mandatory injunction was granted as an exception because the applicant/claimant gave a wide-ranging undertaking to protect the defendant's position and on the facts of the case, only the claimant would have been able to commercially use the computer program.
[901]See *Chambers v British Olympic Association* (2008) LTL 18 July 2008; [2008] EWHC 2028 (QB).
[902]See *Lichter v Rubin* [2008] EWHC 450 (Ch); The Times, 18 April 2008.
[903]See *Anton Piller KG v Manufacturing Processes Ltd* [1976] Ch 55. See also *CPR 1998* r. 25.1(1)(h).

who included false information in the witness statement that was verified by a Statement of Truth.[904]

♦ Test of 'Solid Evidence' — In this test, the applicants must show clear evidence that the respondents have incriminating evidence against which an order of the court is requested.

♦ Test of 'Overwhelming case' —The test is more stringent than that for a case that is merely a serious issue to be tried.[905] Accordingly, the judge needs to be satisfied a bit more on evidence.

♦ Test of 'Reason to believe' — These tests are applied when the courts have to decide whether the claimants should provide security for costs to the defendants, in case the claimants were to lose the case in future trials.[906]

7.4.2 Standards of Proof in context of PRC Procedural Law

We have seen from the above discussion,[907] how the civil law tradition differs from the common law traditions, and even the philosophy behind approaches pertaining to Standards of Proof. The discussion on Standards of Proof in PRC law will be no different. Chen wrote as far back as in 2002, while working in Xiamen Intermediate People's Court, that the discussion on Standards of Proof is a matter of practice of law.[908]

In the civil law tradition or in the PRC, unlike with common law, the starting point for any discussion would be the relevant codes from *CPL 1991*. The relevant codes from *CPL 1991 (as amended in 2012)* are as follows:

■ Article 63 of *CPL 1991 (as amended in 2012)* provides:

---

[904]Sime, "Interim Application - Dispute of Facts," 277–8.
[905]See *Lansing Linde Ltd v Kerr* [1991] 1 WLR 251; [1991] 1 All ER 418. See also, *Phoenix Partners Group LLP v Asoya*g [2010] IRLR 594. *See also, Cayne v Global Natural Resources plc* [1984] 1 All ER 225.
[906]See *CPR 1998* r. 25.13(2) (c).
[907]Refer Chapter 7, §7.4.1.
[908]Chao-yang (Xiamen Municipal Intermediate People's Court Chen, Xiamen), "Standards of Proof," 1.

Evidence shall include as follows: (1) Statements of parties concerned; (2) documentary evidence; (3) material evidence; (4) audio-visual material; (5) testimony of witnesses; (6) statements of the parties; (7) expert conclusions; and (8) records of inspection.

The above-mentioned evidence must be verified before it can be taken as a basis for ascertaining a fact [emphasis added].

■ Article 64 of *CPL 1991 (as amended in 2012)* provides:

If, for objective reasons, a party and his agent are unable to collect the evidence by themselves or if the people's court considers the evidence necessary for the trial of the case, the People's court shall investigate and collect it [emphasis added]. The People's court shall, in accordance with the procedure prescribed by the law, examine and verify evidence **comprehensively and objectively** [emphasis added].

■ Article 93 of *CPL 1991 (as amended in 2012)* provides:

In the trial of civil cases, the People's Court shall distinguish between right and wrong on the basis of the facts being clear [emphasis added] ....

■ Article 170 of *CPL 1991 (as amended in 2012)* in the context of appeal in the second instance court provides:

... (3) if in the original judgment the facts were incorrectly or not clearly ascertained [emphasis added] and the evidence was insufficient, the People's Court of second instance shall make a written order to set aside the judgment and remand the case to the original people's court for retrial, or the people's court of second instance may amend the judgment after investigating and clarifying the facts.

Article 64 of *CPL 1991 (as amended in 2012)* clearly provides that the judges will examine the evidence '*comprehensively and objectively*'. In the author's view, this test for Standard of Proof is a combination of the common law test and the civil law test. First, the Standards of Proof test in PRC are very comprehensive. They are similar to the continental European standards but again any *subjectivity of the judges* is ruled out by using the word '*objectively*'.

This objective test is similar to the common law test and can be differentiated from the civil law test for Standards of Proof, for example as seen earlier from German Codes. The same article also allows the judges to investigate and collate the evidence. It seems to be the case that the focus in PRC courts is on finding the truth. It also means that the burden on the parties to prove their case in terms of Standards of Proof is very high. In the author's view, the claimants can win a case in the English jurisdiction but may end up losing the same case in the PRC courts because Standards of proof are set too high. It is also quite possible that case itself might not be accepted by the courts to be litigated as discussed earlier.[909]

From the various articles, the Standards of Proof in criminal proceedings, administrative law proceedings or civil proceedings are nearly the same in the PRC legal system; namely that the evidence must be found 'objectively' by the judges. Nonetheless, as discussed in the context of the common law, even if the test is objective in terms of finding facts, the subjectivity of the judges' cognition is still involved in assessing this evidence. Cheng has also discussed this point in his book on evidence.[910] But then again, how high the test of Standards of Proof should be in the PRC courts is still debated even among academics and practising lawyers.

This debate swings between two poles. Chen and Wei suggest that it should be '*objectively true*' and it should mean that the judges must find as to what actually happened in the case.[911] However, other scholars have suggested the test for Standards of Proof to be *'facts are clear and evidence is sufficient'* and are part of

---

[909]Refer §7.4.1

[910]Yiyun Cheng, *Science of Evidence* (Beijing: People's Public Security University of China Press, 1991), 114. *See also*, Chao-yang (Xiamen Municipal Intermediate People's Court Chen, Xiamen), "Standards of Proof," where Cheng's views on the issue of judges' role in PRC in relation to objective evidence was discussed.

[911]Chao-yang (Xiamen Municipal Intermediate People's Court Chen, Xiamen), "Standards of Proof." Chan and Wei's views were discussed in Chao-Yang's article. *See also*, Guangzhong Chen, Haiguang Chen, and Xiaona Wei, "The System of Criminal Evidence and Epistemology - Discussion between Legal Truth and Relative Truth," *China Legal Science*, no. 1 (2001): 37-52.

three-stage tests *'objectivity, legality and certainty'*.[912] A few PRC scholars have suggested the test for Standards of Proof is to be *'legally true'* or *'relatively true'*.[913]

In the author's view, this excessive focus bordering on obsession to find the 'objective truth' in the PRC legal system can cause delay and has the potential to waste judicial resources. PRC scholar Li's views on the risks of adopting high Standards of Proof are as follows: [914]

- it can create inefficiency;

- it can scare the claimants due to the sheer burden of the high Standards of Proof;

- it can create possibilities for a retrial pursuant to Art 170(3) of *CPL 1991 (as amended in 2012)* to fulfil the requirement of *'objective truth'*. This could affect finality of judgment; and

- it can necessitate the need to carry out further investigations

In the author' view, excessive judicial intervention in order to seek the comprehensive and objective truth is not beneficial to enhance the legitimacy of the legal system because these interventions have the potential to create a perception of bias against one of the parties. For the sake of completeness, Article 3 of *Some Provisions of the Supreme People's Court on Evidence in Civil Procedures (No. 33 of [2001])* provides that the PRC courts can participate in collecting evidence and will direct the parties in relation to it.[915]

---

[912]Chao-yang (Xiamen Municipal Intermediate People's Court Chen, Xiamen), "Standards of Proof." Xiong's article was discussed in Chao-Yang. *See also*, Zhihai Xiong, "Objective and Subjective Norms of Procedural Testimony," *Modern Law Science* 22, no. 5 (2000): 75-80.

[913]Chao-yang (Xiamen Municipal Intermediate People's Court Chen, Xiamen), "Standards of Proof." Fan's article was discussed in this comprehensive article. *See also*, Chongyi Fan, "Opinions on Objective Truth," *China Legal Science*, no. 1 (2000): 114-120.

[914]Chao-yang (Xiamen Municipal Intermediate People's Court Chen, Xiamen), "Standards of Proof." *See also*, Guoguang Li, *Guidance and Reference on Economic Trail* (Beijing: Legal Press, 2001).

[915]See Art. 3 *Some Provisions of the Supreme People's Court on Evidence in Civil Procedures (No. 33 of [2001])* provides: "The People's court shall inform the parties concerned of the requirements for producing evidences and the the of the corresponding legal liabilities so that the parties concerned may produce evidence actively, completely, correctly and honestly within the reasonable time period. Any party who cannot independently collect evidences <u>due to objective reasons may request the People's court to collect after investigations</u> [emphasis added]."

However, with the introduction of these latest Rules of Evidence, the litigants taking advantage of the philosophy of the PRC courts about seeking the '*objective truth*' cannot now force a retrial easily, as time limits are also set for the presentation of evidence by the litigants.[916]

In the author's view, there are so many uncertainties in any story having facts, human emotions, perceptions, prejudices, and biases; therefore, it is nearly impossible to find 'absolute truth', not just in the PRC but in any jurisdiction. Another factor, in the author's view, is that focus on such high Standards of Proof will definitely affect procedural justice. However, the author has earlier discussed the issue of substantive and procedural justice in the PRC jurisdiction.[917]

It is a fact that in commercial and civil cases, the parties are not on equal footing. This focus on high Standards of Proof needs to take this into account. The financially weaker parties are not fighting their case on an even footing as a financially stronger business entity. PRC scholars have recognised this dilemma and have therefore suggested a different version of Standard of Proof that is '*legal truth*'.[918]

As a comparativist, it appears to the author that the PRC legal system, because it has such high Standard of Proof requirements, is more concerned with substantive justice as compared to procedural justice.

Standards of Proof at the time of filing a case are also high and therefore, many cases do not even pass this initial high barrier pertaining to Standard of Proof. This issue can even affect the litigation rights of parties, which are enshrined in the *PRC Constitution* and *CPL 1991*.[919] Standards of Proof at trial, as discussed above, seem to prefer substantive justice over procedural justice. However, the author agrees that a few causes of actions may demand higher Standards of Proof such as cause of actions pertaining to commercial fraud, misrepresentation in contracts and so forth. However, the requirements for high Standards of Proof cannot be taken as a requirement for all types of cases in civil and commercial litigations.

---

[916]See *Rules on Civil Evidence, Interpretation of Laws issued by the Supreme People's Court, No. [2001] 33, December 21, 2001.*
[917]Refer, Chapter 4, §4.2.2 & §4.3.4.2.
[918]Chao-yang (Xiamen Municipal Intermediate People's Court Chen, Xiamen), "Standards of Proof."
[919]See Art. 2 of *CPL 1991 (as amended in 2012)*.

CHAPTER EIGHT — CAN WE UNDERSTAND CHINA? CONCLUSIONS & RECOMMENDATIONS

8.1 Conclusions

In this book, the author has carried out a comparative analysis from various viewpoints and perspectives, for example, the effects of *invisible factors & contexts* in the civil justice system and how the two jurisdictions' legal systems have advanced on the recognised principles of civil and commercial litigations. The comparative analysis of individual invisible factors was carried out at the end of each chapter. In this section, the author focuses on *an overview* of these analyses based on various practical aspects of economic development, augmented number of international projects originating in the PRC and further concluding remarks on the key findings.

The strengths and weaknesses of the law in both jurisdictions have been analysed through a comparative analysis of the invisible factors and contexts. Hopefully, the analysis carried out in the book will assist various stakeholders *to understand PRC a bit better.* The understanding of invisible factors and contexts is also required to understand one's own jurisdiction. This is in fact important for lawyers and judges, who usually originate from elite sections of society, particularly in many common law jurisdictions, and who may therefore assume, due to their elite background and education, that they know everything about the world or are aware of the aspirations and challenges of all segments of their own societies.

The *reason the author selected* the jurisdictions of England & Wales and the PRC for the comparative study is that there are similarities between the two jurisdictions as both of these countries are leading trading and economic powers. On one hand, London (following the *common law system*) has been an international financial centre for over two centuries, while on the other hand, the PRC, following its own version of law ("PRC law") and influenced by many different schools of thought, has emerged as an economic superpower of the twenty-first century and is increasingly getting involved in international projects in many countries, for example through the Belt and Road Initiative.[920]

England & Wales, both being part of the United Kingdom, have a common substantive and procedural law within the unified and common civil justice system. As discussed in Chapter 1, the increase in international projects has meant that many PRC citizens involved in commerce now must engage with foreign jurisdictions. The key findings in this book can help by acquainting them with invisible factors and contexts associated with other legal systems, helping them to protect their commercial interests.

Many of the International projects that originate in the PRC involve issues of Contract and Tort law, Investment law, Private International Law, Public International law, Banking Law, Environment Law, Maritime Law, Civil Procedural Law, and Alternative Dispute Resolution including Arbitration law and so forth. There is always an interaction of PRC law with the local law of the country where these international projects are carried out.

The PRC is also involved in setting up Dispute resolution centers in many parts of world, for example in Hong Kong ("PRC") and Singapore. These dispute resolution centres are based on Chinese/PRC law characteristics and aim to resolve disputes arising in International projects. Additionally, many stakeholders can knock on the doors of PRC courts. Therefore, it is important for these stakeholders to understand the *invisible factors and contexts* that influence PRC law and also how the issues of *law in action* will pan out,[921] where PRC law or any law with Chinese characteristics is applicable or even where it has an indirect influence through a back door channel.

In order to understand the markedly unique PRC law, stakeholders from common law jurisdictions need a **benchmark** to comprehend the PRC legal system's strengths, weaknesses, opportunities and threats. In the author's view, those benchmarks can be provided through a comparative analysis of invisible factors and contexts such as legal system, jurisprudence & philosophy, legal history, judges' powers including discretionary power and how the judicial activities are carried out pursuant to the PRC law as compared to the common law system. This book has attempted to fill this gap and be that initial benchmark study for such stakeholders, be they from the PRC or from countries outside the PRC.

---

[920]Refer, Chapter 1, §1.5.
[921]Refer to Chapter 5.

In addition, economic growth in any nation, particularly with respect to trading powers, not only leads to increase of Gross Domestic Product in any country, but also steers the country towards am upsurge in export, import, buying & selling of goods and services, conceptualising & implementation of global projects and other market activities. The PRC's economy and its international projects are the perfect example of this phenomenon. The upswing in commerce & trade has piloted the country towards further investments (domestic & foreign direct investment), increased international and domestic trade, growth in both internal and external migration of people. Because of this, augmented transactions, both domestically and internationally, are carried out by that nation's own citizens and business organisations.

The likelihood of *commercial disputes* arising during the upsurge of commercial activities, and possibly progressing to commercial litigation in the civil justice system or to arbitration, is a sizeable impediment to enhancing trade and enlarging the GDP of the country by increased trade and commerce. These potential commercial disputes could become even bigger stumbling blocks, if there were issues of trust in the civil justice system of the nation from which the business and projects originate. The benchmark study carried out in this book will assist stakeholders to avoid these potential disputes turning into conflicts, including political & military conflicts, in particular where there are big-ticket international projects between PRC organisations and organisations from other countries.

An important feature of this book has been the focus on the use of Maxeiner's distinction between *culturalism* and *functionalism*. This has allowed a comparison between the problems in a legal system or body of law from the *interior point of view* so that the readers can see how lawyers,[922] judges, arbitrators and other juridical stakeholders think of the legal process while using the *law in action* in both the PRC legal system and the common law of England & Wales. The author has discussed in various chapters of this book how the thought process of the judges,[923] in particular, during the exercise of their discretionary power,[924] is affected by *contexts and invisible factors*.

In addition, civil process in any jurisdiction is the mirror image of society and is affected by *contexts and invisible factors*. An understanding of the proper contexts and invisible factors through a comparative analysis will assist the readers to understand even the *external law* of both the common law system and the PRC system

---

[922]Refer, Chapter 4, §4.3.3.
[923]Refer to Chapter 5.
[924]Refer to Chapter 6.

in the proper context.[925] To put it clearly, even the substantive law of codes, statutes, case precedents and so forth needs to be read and understood against the backdrop of contexts and invisible factors.

The author's advice to other researchers and stakeholders is to immerse themselves in the various aspects of PRC law and culture as part of the first step of comparative methodology, if they wish to take this benchmark study further. The contexts and invisible factors within a stakeholder's own jurisdictions are usually taken for granted, but in any comparative studies, it is crucial to understand the invisible factors and contexts within the PRC. It is hoped that the analysis in the book will assist PRC businessmen and corporations who have stakes outside the PRC, or who are arbitrating or litigating disputes in the common law system or even in other civil law based systems.

This book hopefully will assist the stakeholders and readers to avoid *assumptions* based on their own invisible factors and contexts, and/or the PRC's legal system. As a word of warning, the author is not immune from the influence of invisible factors and biases; however, a great effort has been made to ensure that any discussion and analysis remain objective without any bias against either common law or PRC Law. Diversity of thought is what makes this world a beautiful place but there is also a need to avoid potential conflicts and disputes for the sake of the next generation.

It is believed that the findings in this book can also be useful in analysing the opportunities and threats that lie ahead for both jurisdictions, in particular, the effects of such threats and opportunities on sustaining and enhancing economic prosperity and commercial transactions, on enhancing the trust of stakeholders with commercial interests in both the legal systems, on reducing transaction costs by an effective civil justice system in the market economy, on initiating reforms in the respective jurisdictions, and so forth.

It is noteworthy that in recent years there has been a surge in reforms carried out in Civil Procedure law in many countries such as England & Wales, Norway, Japan and so forth. As discussed above, the main reason for such a surge is globalization, which has led to increased business and commercial activities as a result of interaction between countries, their corporate businesses and between citizens of these countries. Most reforms that were carried out in any jurisdiction were compelled to take into account the needs of stakeholders from outside that jurisdiction.

---

[925]Refer Chapter 4, §4.3.3.

As an example, reforms were carried out in Norway and have been in force from January 1, 2008 due to the effects of globalisation. According to those reforms:

> It is important that procedure be in principle familiar and understandable also for parties coming from abroad. <u>The courts are increasingly dealing with cases originating in transnational activities which involve non Norwegian parties</u> [emphasis added].[926]

The above example from Norway is also relevant for the PRC.[927] The next logical step is for the author to recommend the possible reforms that can be undertaken in both the jurisdictions based upon the key findings and discussion carried out in this book. One such area is effectiveness of the judges in both the systems, in particular in the PRC. In the author's view, *judicial effectiveness* will be a significant factor in the PRC maintaining its status as an economic superpower, while it will also be important for London with its common law system to retain its position as the leading financial centre of the world.

Lastly, even the perception among those involved in commerce of issues in the PRC – such as 'similar cases, different rulings' in different courts within PRC (*tong'an bu tong' pan*),[928] or local protection by the courts (*defang bao hu zhu yi*),[929] or misunderstandings in relation to discretionary power of judges in any civil law system, such as confusing it with arbitrariness – can be fatal to trade and commerce in the PRC in the long-term. In particular, it will deter stakeholders from resolving any disputes arising out of the PRC's big-ticket international projects such as the Belt and Road Initiative, in dispute resolution centres based on PRC law or in PRC courts.

Lastly, the understanding that judicial effectiveness during *law in action* is part of the *service* industry needs to gain traction within the PRC political and legal set-up,

---

[926] I. L. Backer, "The Norwegian Reform of Civil Procedure," *Scandinavian Studies in Law* 51 (2007): 41–76. See also, Oscar G. Chase and Vincenzo Varano, "Comparative Civil Justice," in *The Cambridge Companion to Comparative Law*, ed. M. Bussani and U. Mattei (Cambridge; New York: Cambridge University Press, 2012), 221, where Backer was quoted and analysed.

[927] The PRC, an economic superpower, is actively involved in many international projects. This means that interests in PRC's legal system is bound to increase from external stakeholders. Most of the foreign stakeholders will not really be interested in the PRC's Constitutional Law or Family law, but one area they will encounter regularly due to commercial interests is the Civil Procedural law and the invisible factors and contexts affecting the PRC's *law in action*.

[928] Refer to, Chapter 7, §7.2.2.

[929] Refer, Chapter 6, §6.3.3.

particularly for resolving commercial disputes on international projects. However, this change in mind-set will require a fundamental change in selection, training, retention, and on-the-job training of the judges/arbitrators in the civil justice systems. This is relevant as these judges/arbitrators will ultimately decide on commercial disputes.

The selection and training of judges and other employees in the legal system will be the key issue for administrators in the PRC. In addition, to maintain consistency in applying the law at all levels in all provinces of the PRC will not be easy because of its vast landmass. This issue is compounded by the fact that various judicial activities are still developing in the PRC,[930] and there is still a dearth of understanding of newly developed substantive laws and the issues surrounding them. For example, in English Courts, the judges have devised many interim remedies by taking into account the commercial needs of businesses. Any such exercise of judicial discretion is unthinkable in the PRC where judges are also supervised by the Procuratorate system.[931]

Therefore, as discussed above, the need to look at the civil justice system in the PRC in economic terms will definitely bring into focus the *software part of the legal system*; that is, the transforming role of judges in relation to commercial disputes, training of judges, independence of judges, supervision of judges and so forth. In order for judges to exercise discretionary power or be significantly more willing to exercise their discretionary power to grant appropriate remedies in commercial disputes, is where the greatest challenge lies in the PRC.

The effects of invisible factors such as historical jurisprudence, current legal system, origins of legal and civil procedure system are crucial in the software part of the legal system in the PRC. Stakeholders from the common law system will find this software aspect of the PRC legal system somewhat challenging, but the comparative analysis provided in this book, will help them to appreciate the reasons behind the differences that exist between the systems. However, to bring about reforms in this area in the PRC is an uphill task. Given the global undercurrents at play, it is uncertain, if it is conceivable, to bring about major reforms in the software part of the legal system.[932] The answer to the question is again beyond the scope of this book.

---

[930]Refer, Chapter 2, §2.2, Chapter 7, §7.2.2 & §7.3.2.
[931]Refer, Chapter 2, §2.2.1 and §2.4.
[932] Some of these global undercurrents include trade disputes originating within the World Trade Organisation ("WTO"), and doubts raised by a few countries as to the relevance of WTO given the huge trade deficit large economies like the US, EU, and India have with the PRC. In addition, the world order is currently in a state of flux with the emergence of the PRC as an economic superpower along with

In the author's view, the *hardware of the legal system* in the form of laws, codes, procedures, and guidance is easily understood,[933] but the software part of the legal system, that is, issues pertaining to the judges, needs to be developed and nurtured constantly. The PRC has done well in the hardware part of the legal system, drafting a lot of substantive and even procedural law in the last decade. According to Gillespie, judicial effectiveness is actually enhanced by judicial power more than by judicial independence, as in the early stages of development, the judiciary itself needs protection.[934]

The PRC's legal system is relatively new, in relation to its position as an economic superpower. It goes without saying that its legal system has only been evolving for the last three decades, as compared to a thousand years of development of the common law. These are a few of the substantial challenges that cannot be ignored by the PRC or stakeholders in the PRC's legal system.

8.2 Recommendation for Reforms in PRC

As discussed in section §8.1, there are opportunities for both the jurisdictions to carry out meaningful reforms based on their experiences with one another. The comparative analysis carried out in the book can be utilised to carry out specific reforms in both jurisdictions.

A Chinese proverb says "stones from other mountains may help to polish a piece of local jade." This is true as a general statement in life; however, even for the author as a comparativist to suggest recommendations for reforms in a country of size of PRC is a daunting task. As a first step, before the author even attempts to recommend reforms arising out of this research, it is important to quote Sherwin and Clermont in relation to mistakes that a comparativist can make while giving recommendations:

> A comparativist should be sufficiently immersed in the different
> legal cultures to understand the context in which legal rules operate
> and the attitudes an insider might take toward the rules. To the

other BRICS economies such as India, Russia, Brazil and South Africa. For the PRC, to manage these uncertainities may be a priority in the immediate future.

[933]Refer, Chapter 1, §1.2, where Mr. Wu Bangguo, a senior PRC official, confirmed that the socialist legal system with Chinese characteristics was established in China in 2011 after promulgating many new substantive and procedural laws within a short span of two decades.

[934]Refer, Chapter 5, §5.4.

extent the comparativist is not an insider, he or she should also approach the rules of a different system with modesty and respect. Then, in drawing lessons for home system, the comparativist should remain cautious. <u>He should be suspicious of drawing easy generalities or making confident calls for legal transplants</u> [emphasis added].[935]

To introduce legal reforms in the PRC is an uphill task. In the author's view, any scholar should ask two fundamental questions about the PRC that were also looked into by Chang, when introducing reforms through ideas that are borrowed from foreign jurisdictions: [936]

- ■ What are the PRC's long-term goals in respect of its civil justice system or in respect of any one aspect of its civil justice system?

- ■ What will be the immediate tasks that need to be assigned to its new legal system after bringing in the requisite reforms?

From the comparative analysis, the author recommends the following *specific* reforms in the PRC legal system:

- ■ First, as discussed earlier, the software part of the PRC's legal system needs to be improved considerably. The focus on selection of judges, their training, and consistency within all courts should be the focus. The discretionary power of judges and their willingness to use it will also be for the evolution of any legal system. The administrative part of the courts also needs strengthening.

- ■ Second, judicial efficiency can be enhanced and more clarity can be introduced by adopting tests of Standards of Proof from

---

[935]E. Sherwin and K. M. Clermont, "A Comparative View of Standards of Proof," *Am. J. Comp. L.* 50, no. 2 (2002): 244.
[936]Wejen Chang, "Classical Chinese Jurisprudence and Development of Chinese Legal System" (2009–10), 272.

common law in commercial disputes, rather than the judges aiming for perfect substantive justice in PRC courts. [937] In addition, there could be different Standards of Proof at different stages of litigation, for example, at the time of submission of the claims, at the time of interim hearings, during the trials and so forth. The PRC courts expecting a very high Standard of Proof at the time of submission of claims is not practical. This reform will also enhance judicial legitimacy in the eyes of stakeholders with commercial interests.

- Third, the next recommendation would be that the ideological supervision of judges should be removed in cases of commercial disputes, in contrast to the ordinary civil disputes litigated in the PRC courts. This step will ensure the enhanced trust of foreign stakeholders in the PRC legal system.

- Fourth, at this stage of legal development of the civil justice system, the laws, rules, Guidance from SPC and so on are all scattered in multiple locations, and the local courts in various provinces also have their own local guidance. All this adds greatly to the number of rules and bye-rules that litigants need to look into in order to litigate commercial or civil disputes. Therefore, it may be worthwhile to carry out a major housekeeping exercise to collate all of these in one place and create a massive online guide, which can be updated regularly (even online).

The availability of an online guide in English can be useful for stakeholders who are not from the PRC, but who have a genuine interest in the PRC's legal system. It is the author's view that for a large country like the PRC, this kind of house-keeping exercise is like a drop in the ocean. In the practice of law, an important concept is cross-referencing and, in particular, the availability of a means of cross-referencing information and rules. However, with the increase of laws in PRC, there is a requirement to maintain consistency in civil

---

[937]See Chao-yang (Xiamen Municipal Intermediate People's Court Chen, Xiamen), "Standards of Proof in Civil Proceedings: From the Perspective of Judicial Impartiality and Efficiency," *J. of Southwest U. P. Sc. & L.*, no. 1 (2002): 9–19, for discussion on *judicial efficiency* in context of test of Standards of Proof.

litigation. A very similar example of means of cross-reference (but at a different level) was available in the past, such as with the Tang Codes, which were divided into two sections – general principles and specific offences (though in the context of criminal law).[938]

- Fifth, in order to increase consistency in practice before the PRC courts, there should be Practice Directions. Practice Directions are available for practice in English civil courts and they are read together with the *Civil Procedure Rules 1999*. The recommendation for Practice Directions for the PRC can be added to the author's recommendations to collate *CPL 1991 (as amended in 2012)*, other relevant laws, other civil procedure rules and directions from the SPC in one book. In the same book or as an annex to the book, there can be local court rules for the reference of the litigants.

  These Practice Directions can even have draft standard orders, local court guides, details about the rules of practice of courts, relevant telephone numbers, guidance as to requirements of evidence in courts and so forth. This will be of immense assistance to foreign stakeholders in the PRC legal system. However, this adjective law needs to be flexible, so that it in itself does not become the means for procedural injustice at the level of local court officials.

  The above recommended undertaking appears to be daunting, but with the extraordinary resources that are available in the PRC, it is the author's view that it can be completed in a few months. All the above can even be updated regularly every day for the benefit of the stakeholders.

- Sixth, with many of the SPC's provisions/interpretations, there are very few days between the date of promulgation of any new Code and date at which they are applicable and effective in practice. The author recommends a gap of at least

---

[938]Geoffrey MacCormack, *The Spirit of Traditional Chinese Law*, The Spirit of the Laws (Athens; London: University of Georgia Press, 1996), 14–15. *See also*, Table VIII for Tang Dynasty.

3-4 months between these two dates. It will assist the commercial stakeholders to plan their businesses accordingly.

- Seventh, with the massive economic growth in the PRC, the number of stakeholders from abroad who have an interest in PRC laws will certainly grow. The procedures for commercial dispute resolution should become more friendly for foreign stakeholders, and there could even be a provision for separate commercial courts in the PRC for such cases. As discussed in the analysis, such practical measures are not just good from the point of view of procedural justice but can also ensure even stronger economic growth for the PRC by raising the trust of stakeholders in its civil justice system.

- Eighth, the requirements as to the pleadings in PRC courts should become more liberal: the prerequisite for any evidence to pass the hurdle of a very high Standard of Proof at the time of filing of claims should not be mandatory. The fear in the PRC legal system in relation to frivolous claims passing the net can be managed by imposing penalty in form of legal costs on claimants bringing these types of claims.

However, the above recommendations will avoid the scenario of genuine claimants being denied access to the PRC's civil justice system at this early stage of civil procedure. These recommendations will provide better access to justice for most claimants. In commercial litigation, it is essential that many of the stakeholders in the civil justice system are made aware of high Standards of Proof in relation to the evidence that is required of them even at the docking stage (the first stage in civil litigation, where claimants submit their claim forms in the courts).

If foreign claimants' applications are rejected due to a lack of evidence based on the test of Standards of Proof, it can create a bad impression of the PRC's legal system. The PRC civil justice system can easily take steps to avoid this.

In fact, foreign stakeholders who have not analysed the invisible factors and relevant contexts as discussed in this book will just end up assuming that these are akin to non-tarriff barriers for investment and trade in PRC. The strict requirements for accepting pleadings pursuant to Articles 119-123 of *CPL 1991 (as amended in 2012)* could be modified for law in action.

The issue of turning away cases at the docking stage due to legal technicalities, or due to lack of training of the judges who would rather reject and disallow any case instead of dealing with novel issues, is a major stumbling block in the PRC. In the author's view, this serious gap should be remedied to maintain the universal principles of access to justice. The reason for the rejection of cases could also be due to the increasing workload of judges and increase in civil cases in the PRC courts.[939] The discretionary power of judges to reject cases is definitely not an asset to the PRC legal system.

Any requirement of filing of defence only arises pursuant to *CPL 1991 (as amended in 2012)* after the case has been accepted at the docking stage. Even though after 1998, the case filing division was separated from the division responsible for adjudication within the court systems, the discretionary power exhibited by the rotational judges in the case filing division has been extraordinary, especially for rejecting cases rather than allowing them to be adjudicated in the courts on merits and evidence.

This aspect of the legal system needs an overhaul, in particular, in relation to commercial disputes. To be fair there has been an attempt to increase efficiency in this area. As a result, a full-fledged case registration system has been fully available from 2015.[940] There will be no use for any rules or laws or codes or procedures or any comparative analysis, if the cases of the claimants cannot even pass this initial docking stage.

---

[939]Margaret Y. K. Woo, "Manning the Courthouse Gates: Pleadings, Jurisdictions, and the Nation-State," *Nev. L.J.* 15, no. 3 (2015): 1285. This article highlights that the number of civil cases that were filed at the first instance between 1991 – 2010 increased annually by more than 10%. According to the author, it is a heavy workload on legal administration and deserves immediate attention in terms of capacity building for the future.

[940]See *Opinion on the Implementation of the People's Courts Reform of the Case-filing Registration System*, promulgated by Supreme People's Court on April 1, 2015, effective May 1, 2015.

- Lastly, in the PRC, for a long time, the laws were seen as a means to sustain market economy, but the author recommends that with massive economic growth, there is a scope for role reversals. As a result, the requirements of the PRC's socialist market economy can instead act as a catalyst to bring in changes in the laws and or codes as required by stakeholders with commercial interests. These stakeholders could even be foreign. The need for legitimacy in the PRC's civil justice system is as strong today as it was in 1978, as stated by the then-President of the SPC, Mr. Jiang Hua.[941]

- The 2012 amendments to *CPL 1991* have given more case management power to the PRC's judges in respect of the litigants, and the author recommends that in commercial litigation, a move towards a really adversarial process can assist foreign stakeholders to appreciate the PRC's legal system, and therefore, can even lead to the making of an effective civil litigation system in the PRC. In this respect, experiences from the common law system can be borrowed for the PRC legal system.

- Any remedy, interim or permanent, invariably requires an exercise of discretion by the judges. In the author's view, while legal reforms are a work in progress, a lot of work still needs to be done in the PRC to ensure good software in the legal system. Ensuring this will involve capacity building, training of judges, and continuous professional development for the judges to ensure they are independent and fearless. The exercise of discretion in courts or an effective *law in action* is in fact dependent on judges, as well as on well-trained lawyers to argue cases in the courts.

- It is important for reformers to note that laws can be amended or new legislations introduced, but the customary practices and ethos of any group of people are difficult to change.

---

[941] See Minshi Shenpan Gongzuo Tongdeng Zhongyao (Civil Trial Is Equally Important), available at http://www.geilibook.com/book/2441/157831.html and http://www.geilibook.com/book/2441/157832.html. Quoted in Woo, "Manning the Courthouse Gates," 1274.

Bearing this in mind, any reforms, including the author's recommendations, should be introduced with caution. In the author's experience, and in the opinion of many PRC scholars, any attempt at reform will need to balance two opposing views: on the one hand, one group of policy makers seem to highlight and even boast about the old civilisational virtues of the past while incorporating new ideas across-the-board regularly, and on the other hand, there is the group of policy makers who completely reject new ideas and border on being paranoid about safeguarding the ancient Chinese ethos or Chinese characteristics. It must be understood that a bridge between the old and new traditions is essential for many of PRC scholars and reformers.[942]

The author does not recommend letting go of the PRC's greatest asset, which is its *civilisational values*. However, modern ideas can be useful to improve the existing system in the PRC. The author also fully recommends that many ancient jurisprudential aspects can be extracted from the current PRC's practice of conservatism, and can be incorporated into the local laws, rules and procedures. A few examples of relevant ancient concepts are – preservation of ancient moral traditions and humanity, great respect for the wisdom of ancestors, and concern for order and maintenance of social stability and the rejection of anarchy.[943]

A word of caution: given the advent of globalisation, combined with unprecedented urbanisation, it is essential that policy makers appreciate that though it is good to have an element of conservatism, overdoing it in relation to the practice of law can have damaging effects on the aims of the PRC's system. Take, for example, the Confucian concept of managing the present using the past or respecting old institutions, as recommended by Ming Tai-Tsu, the founder of

---

[942]Refer, Chapter 3, §3.7.

[943]See MacCormack, *Spirit of Traditional Chinese Law*, 32 for discussion on the key elements of *conservatism*, in particular, the effect of *conservatism* in the context of the symbolic spirit of Law in China.

the Ming Dynasty;[944] he gave guidance in this respect to his successors. In the author's view, this kind of practice may be troublesome in the current era, where the only constant is not just change, but rapid change. This phenomenon is experienced not only in the PRC, but across the entire digitally-connected, interdependent world.

There is a popular trend in the context of reforms in many countries which hold to different legal systems,[945] for example, the US, Australia, England, Germany, Austria, France, Spain, and Russia, in relation to civil procedural systems, to improve case management powers of judges. Another trend has been to provide flexibility in the procedural steps that need to be taken in the civil justice system according to the complexity of the cases, to reduce delays and legal costs.

There is another trend in civil justice systems, where preliminary matters related to evidence and plenary proceedings are arranged systematically to avoid delay and to ensure that the actual trial is more effective. Similarly, a popular trend in common law systems is the move towards summary procedures which rely less on oral evidence in proceedings. In addition, there have been reforms, for example in England & Wales, where each party to litigation must provide any evidence that goes against them, or the litigants can seek assistance from the courts to obtain such evidence.

Lastly, the PRC's current legal system can avoid the pitfalls of the more mature common law system. In spite of the reforms that have been carried out in England & Wales, there is still an urgent need for additional reforms to correct systemic issues. These are additional warning signs to the fast-evolving PRC legal system, in particular, the civil justice system.

A few of the reforms that are needed in the common law jurisdiction of England & Wales are as follows:

---

[944]MacCormack, *Spirit of Traditional Chinese Law*, 41 highlighted in the context of *conservatism* that Confucius used to stress "on conserving and reestablishing the good customs of past." Another example he discussed was that Ming Tsai-Tsu, founder of Ming Dynasty ordered his descendants not to change the old institutions.
[945]Refer, Chapter 1, §1.4.3.

- Costs to litigants to obtain remedies in the civil justice system are increasing by the day. The excessive cost of delivery of justice within the civil justice system has to be avoided, as it bars litigants from access to justice. During litigation the focus and discussion shifts at times to increasing legal costs rather than to obtaining justice or arguing substantive points. This recommendation from the author is not new and was even provided by Anthony Clarke, Justice of the Supreme Court of the UK, when he referred to the 'holy trinity of complexity, costs and delay' as things to be avoided during reforms.[946]It is a fact that due to the multitude of variables in disputes, no civil procedure can be ever be perfect and there will always be complaints.[947]

- The process of bringing reforms to the civil justice system is very delicate, and as a recommendation, any suggested reforms should not be implemented in haste. The elements of efficiency and right to justice are very important. However, Lord Justice Clarke has mentioned that there are no short-cuts to eliminating delay and excessive expense in civil litigation.[948] The failure of civil justice reforms in earlier decades was because the rules had become too technical, and in addition, the culture of litigation as practised by the judges and the lawyers was not changed.[949]

- The author recommends that that any further reforms even in England & Wales will require a change in culture as invisible factors influence every aspect of law, in particular law in

---

[946]Anthony Clarke, "The Woolf Reforms: A Singular Event or an Ongoing Process," in *The Civil Procedure Ten Years On*, ed. Déirdre Dwyer (Oxford: Oxford University Press, 2009), 33. Justice Clarke was referring to the words of scholar Neil Andrews. Justice Clarke again in the same article on page 42 has advised that "... there are no short cuts where procedural reforms is concerned; there is no doing in haste and repenting at leisure."

[947]Clarke, "Woolf Reforms- Singular Event?" 34, where Justice Clarke cited Pound. Pound said '[D]issatisfaction with the administration of justice is as old as law.' *See also*, Pound, "Dissatisfaction with Administration of Justice," 729. The dissatisfaction with the civil justice system was highlighted as far back as the 13th century, in the *Magna Carta* in 1215 CE, which said in its Art. 40: 'To no one will we sell, to no one will we refuse or delay, right or justice.'

[948]Clarke, "Woolf Reforms- Singular Event?" 35. *Refer also*, Chapter 2 §2.1.2 for discussion on failure of civil justice reforms in the 18th & 19th centuries. This failure resulted in major reforms, particularly the Lord Woolf Reforms 1999. *See also*, Lord Woolf, *Access to Justice: Final Report to the Lord Chancellor on the Civil Justice System in England and Wales* (London: HMSO, 1996).

[949]Clarke, "Woolf Reforms- Singular Event?" 43.

action at the courts. This is relevant even for an established and mature legal system such as in England & Wales. Therefore, any reform in the civil justice system must bring in a change of culture along with the procedural and structural reforms.

- According to the author and many jurisprudents, lawyers and judges are the worst people to suggest and implement judicial reforms as they have deep vested financial interests in maintaining the status quo in terms of complexities and notions of law. The author recommends that law, rules, adjective law and so forth should be made simple for laymen and commercial people. By reducing litigation costs, commerce will further improve in any jurisdiction.

- The author wishes to highlight that in the context of reforms of the civil justice system in England & Wales, Lord Justice Anthony Clarke's was of the view that the following needs to be taken into an account:[950]

- Satellite litigation within the main litigation, where parties fight over smaller issues such as extension of time, should be avoided as much as possible as it uses a lot of court's resources;

- The carrot and stick approach, where the courts ensure parties reach consensual settlements through mediation, or via Part 36 offers from the parties to resolve the dispute (the carrots), while the stick of the court functions as a threat of punishment for any conduct of parties that is not in accordance with the overriding objectives of civil litigation;[951]

- Litigation costs should be within reasonable limits. The Woolf reforms had shortcomings in the area.

---

[950]Clarke, "Woolf Reforms- Singular Event?" 41–49.
[951]Refer, Chapter 4, §4.2.1 & §4.2.1.1.

- Reforms in relation to the rules should be there to change the litigation culture, and it should be a continuous process.

- Reforms should set the agenda for today as well as for tomorrow.

- Lastly, Comparative law is popular in continental traditions such as in France & Germany; however common law systems such as England & Wales has been slow in the uptake of foreign ideas, and therefore a bit more needs to be done in this regard in practice. However, to be fair, the higher courts and above have been observed lately to be more willing to accept and incorporate foreign ideas. [952]

8.3 Concluding Remarks

The lawyer's role in providing relevant advice for commercial disputes with PRC connections, whether the lawyer is from the common law system or from the PRC jurisdiction, is dependent on their understanding the invisible factors and contexts surrounding the disputes. Disregarding the invisible factors and contexts or excessively focusing on the black letter law in the form of codes or statutes or case law and so on can prove to be quite costly for litigants involved in cross-border litigation, in particular when disputes have a PRC connection.

The exercise of discretionary power of judges is needed in granting interim remedies, managing case-management power in courts and even to some extent in granting of the final remedies. Similarly, the role of judges' discretionary power in litigation is fundamentally decisive in most cases. In any jurisdiction, the discretionary power of judges,[953] their willingness to exercise this power during judicial activities,[954] and the limits of such power must be analysed in a cultural context; this cannot be disregarded by any litigants or their legal representatives. In any dispute having a PRC connection, the legal representatives of litigants ignore this advice from the author at their own peril.

---

[952]*See Fairchild v Glenhaven Funeral Services Ltd* & others [2002] UKHL 22, [32] (Lord Bingham).
[953]Refer, Chapter 6 with regard to the discussion on discretionary power of judges.
[954]Refer, Chapter 7 for a few examples of judges' role in judicial activities in courts.

In section §8.2 of this book, the author has been audacious enough to suggest a few reforms. Over the years, a lot of reforms have been carried out in many jurisdictions using *legal transplants*, that is, borrowing law from another jurisdiction. Legal transplant is one of the many approaches available to administrators, and it remains a popular method.[955] Legal transplants are useful in areas where there are no laws or there are gaps, or even in order to arrive at a proved uniform outcome.[956] Even Lord Bingham said in relation to the utility of legal transplant in the context of England & Wales, the mother of the common law system:

> Development of the law in this country cannot of course depend on a head-count of decisions and codes adopted in other countries around the world, often against a background of different rules and traditions. The law must be developed coherently, in accordance with principle, so as to serve, even-handedly, the ends of justice. If, however, a decision is given in this country which offends one's basic sense of justice, and if consideration of international sources suggests that a different and more acceptable decision would be given in most other jurisdictions, whatever their legal tradition, this must prompt anxious review of the decision in question. In a shrinking world... there must be some virtue in uniformity of outcome whatever the diversity of approach in reaching that outcome [emphasis added].[957]

Even though there could be benefits in legal transplant to bring in legal reforms, it is important to appreciate the warnings of Chase in relation to the issue of legal transplants. Chase was of the view that even the most elegant foreign law will not have the desired effects in a completely different jurisdiction with a different culture; he was alluding to invisible factors and contexts, which have been discussed in this book.

In addition, any resultant conflict arising out of the borrowed ideas from a very different legal system or jurisdiction will affect the legitimacy of the legal system that has borrowed the ideas. Furthermore, it needs to be appreciated that any borrowed

---

[955]Chen Lei, "Contextualizing Legal Transplant: China and Hong Kong," in *Methods of Comparative Law*, ed. Pier G. Monateri (Cheltenham, U.K.; Northampton, MA: Edward Elgar Pub., 2012), 193.
[956]Ibid.
[957]See *Fairchild v Glenhaven Funeral Services Ltd* & others [2002] UKHL 22, [32] (Lord Bingham). *See also*, Lei, "Contexualizing Legal Transplant in PRC," 193., where Lord Bingham was quoted & analysed.

and incorporated procedural code or concepts from other jurisdictions can affect the society in which the code/idea was introduced.[958]

Any law reformers, before borrowing ideas or codes from another jurisdiction, should not ignore the fact that scholars drafting that code from that other jurisdiction could have analysed the issues from a completely different perspective. This is illustrated by an example from Ramseyer's study on Japan. Ramseyer initially concluded that the Japanese prefer mediation over litigation; however, further analysis showed that this preference for mediation only came about because in Japan, there were institutional barriers to pursuing litigation.[959] Haley traced this phenomenon to Japanese elites that had created those institutional barriers in order to maintain the status quo.[960] Therefore, it is important for reformers to understand the context behind the ideas or codes before robotically adopting foreign codes/ideas in their own jurisdiction.

In order for any civil justice system to command the respect and confidence of its stakeholders, there is a need for the *concept of proportionality* in the justice system. The issue of proportionality is important to the adjective law, which means "Procedural requirements should be proportionate to the subject matter of the litigation."[961] An understanding of how the justice system adapts to particular circumstances of commercial activities within the context of commercial litigation is vital for any civil justice system irrespective of the kind of legal system.

The concept of *proportionality* is also relevant in terms of limits of the law to "intrude upon the private rights. The proportionality principle is one way of expressing those limits."[962] For example, to achieve the objectives of the pre-judgment remedies in a commercial dispute, the exercise of discretionary power of the judges should not exceed the required minimum to achieve those objectives. The judges' use of sanctions or adverse costs orders against the litigants are exceptions to the concept of proportionality.

The concept of proportionality requires the *optimum* exercise of discretionary power by the judges and more importantly, the willingness of the judges to exercise their discretionary power. In the end, in the words of Lord Woolf, the civil justice system

---

[958]Oscar G. Chase, "Some Observations on the Cultural Dimension in Civil Procedure Reform," *Am. J. Comp. Law* 45, no. 4 (1997): 866.

[959]See Oscar G. Chase, "Some Observations on the Cultural Dimension in Civil Procedure Reform," 869 for discussion on Ramseyer and Haley.

[960] Ibid.

[961]Jackson, *The Reform of Civil Litigation*, 20.

[962]Ibid., 18.

needs to be just, fair, offer appropriate procedures at reasonable cost, deal with the issues at a reasonable speed, be understandable to those who need to use it (including foreign citizens), be responsive and provide certainty, be effective, and be adequately resourced and organised.[963] This is where the PRC legal system faces its biggest challenge as compared to other legal jurisdictions and legal systems, particularly for *law in action*.

The software part of the legal system of the PRC, or indeed any system, is where the real challenge lies; it does not matter whether the hardware of the legal system in the form of numerous drafted codes or rules or substantive law is perfect or not. In the end, what will matter the most is whether the software part of the legal system, that is the judges, have the capacity to fulfil the following:

    i.   whether the judges can appreciate the changing business and commercial environment; and

    ii.   whether the judges can appreciate the need for an efficient relationship between the civil justice system and the local economy and, to some extent, the global economy; and

    iii.   the level of confidence and trust the stakeholders will have in the civil justice system to protect their commercial interests; and

    iv.   whether the judges are given discretionary power and, last but not least, whether the judges are willing to exercise this discretionary power without any fear or external influence.

The above issues are extremely relevant to the economic superpower of the day, the PRC. The PRC has been one of the success stories for creating wealth for its citizens and for being actively involved in international trade and commerce with its footprints expanding in all parts of the world through these trading activities and international projects like the Belt and Road Initiative ("BRI"). An efficient legal system is key to sustaining and enhancing the growth momentum of the PRC.

---

[963]Lord Woolf, *Access to Justice: Final Report to the Lord Chancellor on the Civil Justice System in England and Wales* (London: HMSO, 1996), section 1.

A key test for ensuring that any legal system is efficient is the recognition by stakeholders of this fact, in particular the stakeholders from outside the jurisdiction. External stakeholders identifying the English legal system as an example of an efficient legal system with ethical, autonomous, empowered and well-trained judges is quintessential to the ability of London to remain a financial center of world. The PRC legal system would do well to emulate this, to enhance its own success. Needless to say, any shortcoming in attaining this objective can also have long term effects on the success of the PRC's international projects and its economy in the long run.

The intention of the PRC to move into the dispute resolution sector, at least for their international projects, will require the readers, legal students and practitioners to appreciate the subtle comparative analysis accomplished in this book. A few of the issues will also remain relevant to the common law system, such as England & Wales, where one of the world's leading financial center is located, and which many commercial interests from around the world still use as the preferred choice of law in their contracts.

BIBLIOGRAPHY

Adam, "Ethonologische Rechtsforschung," in *Lehrbuch der Volkerkunde*, ed. Adam and Trimborn (1958), 189-n.a.

Maurice Adams and Dirk Heirbaut, eds., *The Method and Culture of Comparative Law: Essays in Honour of Mark Van Hoecke* (Oxford: Hart Publishing, 2015).

Janet E. Ainsworth, "Categories and Culture: On the 'Rectification of Names' in Comparative Law," *Cornell L. Rev.* 82, no. 1 (1996): 19-42. http://scholarship.law.cornell.edu/clr/vol82/iss1/3.

Ruggero J. Aldisert, *The Judicial Process, Readings, Materials, and Cases*, American Casebook Series (St. Paul, Minn.: West Publishing Comp
any, 1989).

ALI/UNIDROIT, *Principles of Transnational Civil Procedure*, rev. ed., Cambridge Books Online (Cambridge: Cambridge University Press, 2007).

Neil Andrews, *English Civil Procedure: Fundamentals of New Civil Justice System* (Oxford; New York: Oxford University Press, 2003).

Neil Andrews, "Fundamental Principles of Civil Procedure: Order Out of Chaos," in *Civil Litigation in a Globalising World*, ed. X.E. Kramer and Rhee, H (The Hague: T.M.C. Asser Press, 2012), 19-38.

Aristotle and J. A. K. Thomson, trans., *The Ethics of Aristotle: The Nicomachean Ethics*, Reprinted ed. (London: Penguin, 1961).

I. L. Backer, "The Norwegian Reform of Civil Procedure," *Scandinavian Studies in Law* 51 (2007): 41-76.

Benjamin J. Bai and Guoping Da, "Strategies for Trade Secrets Protection in China," *Northwestern J. Of Technology and Intellectual Property* 9, no. 7 (2011): 351-75. http://scholarlycommons.law.northwestern.edu/njtip/vol9/iss7/1.

Anne Barron, et al., *Introduction to Jurisprudence and Legal Theory: Commentary and Materials* (London: Butterworths, 2002).

Jeremy Bentham, *An Introduction to the Principles of Morals and Legislation* (New York: Dover Publications, 1996).

Harold J. Berman, ed., *Talks on American Law: A Series of Broadcasts to Foreign Audiences by Members of the Harvard Law School Faculty*, ed. Harold J. Berman (New York: Vintage Books, 1961).

Paul Schiff Berman, *Global Legal Pluralism: A Jurisprudence of Law beyond Borders* (Cambridge; New York: Cambridge University Press, 2012).

Kathryn Bernhardt and Philip Huang, *Civil Law in Qing and Republican China*, Law, Society, and Culture in China. (Stanford, Calif.: Stanford University Press, 1999).

William Blackstone, *Commentaries on the Laws of England* (Chicago: Chicago University Press, 1979).

Susan Blake, *A Practical Approach to Effective Litigation*, 7th ed. (Oxford: Oxford University Press, 2009).

Susan Blake, *A Practical Approach to Effective Litigation*, 8th ed. (Oxford: Oxford University Press, 2015).

Susan Blake, Julie Browne, and Stuart Sime, *A Practical Approach to Alternative Dispute Resolution*, 3rd ed., Practical Approach Series (Oxford: Oxford University Press, 2014).

Patricia Blazey and Kay-Wah Chan, *The Chinese Commercial Legal System* (Pyrmont, NSW, Australia: Lawbook Co., 2008).

M.K. Block, et al., "An Experimental Comparison of Adversarial Versus Inquisitorial Procedural Regimes," *Am. L. & Economics Rev.* 2, no. 1 (2000): 170-94.

M. H. Bond, *The Oxford Handbook of Chinese Psychology* (Hong Kong: Oxford University Press, 2010).

Samuel L. Bray, "The System of Equitable Remedies," *UCLA L. Rev.* 63, no. 3 (2016): 530-93.

James Brook, "Inevitable Errors: The Preponderance of Evidence Standard in Civil Litigation," *Tulsa L.J.* 18, no. 1 (1982): 79-109.

Nicolas Browne-Wilkinson, "Territorial Jurisdiction and The New Technologies," *Israel L. Rev.* 25, no. 2 (1991): 145-55.

Yuanshi Bu, ed., *Chinese Business Law* (Oxford: Hart Publishing, 2010).

Yuanshi Bu, ed., *Chinese Civil Law* (Oxford: Hart Publishing, 2013).

Paul Burrows and Cento G. Veljanovski, eds., *The Economic Approaches to Law* (London; Boston; Sydney; Wellington; Durban; Toronto: Butterworths, 1981).

Paul Burrows and Cento G. Veljanovski, "Introduction to: Economic Approaches to Law," in *The Economic Approaches to Law*, ed. Paul Burrows and Cento G. Veljanovski (London; Boston; Sydney; Wellington; Durban; Toronto: Butterworths, 1981).

Mauro Bussani and Ugo Mattei, eds., *The Cambridge Companion to Comparative Law*, Cambridge Companions to Law (Cambridge: Cambridge University Press, 2012).

Dingjing Cai, *History and Reforms: The Legal History of the New China (Lishiyu Biange: Xin Zhongguo Fazhi Jianshe de Licheng)* (Beijing: Press of China's University of Political Science and Law, 1999).

Ernest Caldwell, "Social, Change and Written Law in Early Chinese Legal Thought," *L. and History Rev.* 32, no. 1 (2014): 1-30.

David Campbell and Philip Thomas, *Fundamental Legal Conceptions as Applied in Judicial Reasoning; and Other Legal Essays*, Reprinted ed. (Oxford: Routledge, 2016).

Fabang Chai, *New Civil Procedure* (Beijing: Law Press, 1992).

Lord Chancellor, *Civil Procedure Rules: Practice Directions, Pre-Action Protocols and Forms* (London: HMSO, 2000).

Dennis Chang, "Towards a Jurisprudence of a Third Kind --One Country, Two Systems," *Case W. Res. J. Int'l L.* 20, no. 1 (1988): 99-125.

Wejen Chang, "Classical Chinese Jurisprudence and Development of Chinese Legal System," *Tsinghua China L. Rev.* 2, no. 2 (2010): 207-72.

Yi Chang, Chief Editor, *The Civil Procedure Law* (Beijing: China University of Law and Political Science and Law Press, 1996).

Chao-yang (Xiamen Municipal Intermediate People's Court Chen, Xiamen), "Standards of Proof in Civil Proceedings: From the Perspective of Judicial Impartiality and Efficiency," *J. of Southwest U. P. Sc. & L.*, no. 1 (2002): 9-19.

O. G. Chase, "American 'Exceptionalism' and Comparative Procedure," *Am. J. Comp. L.* 50, no. 2 (2002): 277-301.

Oscar G. Chase and Vincenzo Varano, "Comparative Civil Justice," in *The Cambridge Companion to Comparative Law*, ed. M. Bussani and U. Mattei (Cambridge; New York: Cambridge University Press, 2012), 210-40.

Oscar G. Chase, "Some Observations on the Cultural Dimension in Civil Procedure Reform," *Am. J. Comp. Law* 45, no. 4 (1997): 861-70.

Albert H. Y. Chen, "The Developing Chinese Law and the Civil Law Tradition," *China Rev.* (1996): 29-59. http://www.jstor.org/stable/23453139.

Guangzhong Chen, Haiguang Chen, and Xiaona Wei, "The System of Criminal Evidence and Epistemology - Discussion between Legal Truth and Relative Truth," *China Legal Science*, no. 1 (2001): 37-52.

Jianfu Chen, *Chinese Law: Context and Transformation*, Numen Book (Leiden; Boston: Martinus Nijhoff Publishers, 2008).

Jianfu Chen, "Civil Codification and Foreign Influence in China - Towards China's Own Civil Code," *Culture, Law and Order: Chinese and Western Traditions, Macao Ricci Institute* (2004).

Lei Chen and C. H. (Remco) van Rhee, eds., *Towards a Chinese Civil Code: Comparative and Historical Perspectives* (Dordrecht: Martinus Nijhoff Publishers, 2012).

Mingguo Chen and Weiming Zuo, "Practical Obstacles and Countermeasures of Guiding Cases. (Zhidaoxing Anli de Yingyong Zhangai Jiqi Kefu - Sichuan Fayuan Anli Yingyong Shidian Gongzuo de Chubu Fenxi)," *Journal of Law Application (Falv Shiyong)* 5 (2012): 67-71.

Xingliang Chen, "The Jurisprudence of the Case Guidance System (Anli Zhidao Zhidu de Fali Kaocha)," *Law and Social Development (Fazhi Yu Shehui Fazhan)* 18, no. 3 (2012): 73-80.

Xinyu Chen, "Bifu and Leitui - Starts from Biyin Lvtiao. (Bifu Yu Leitui Zhibian - Cong 'Biyin Lvtiao' Chufa)," *Tribune of Political Science and Law (Zhengfa Luntan)* 29, no. 2 (2011): 113-21.

Zexian Chen, Chief Editor, *Contemporary Chinese Law* (Beijing: China Procuratorial Press, 2009).

Yiyun Cheng, *Science of Evidence* (Beijing: People's Public Security University of China Press, 1991).

H. Chodosh, "Comparing Comparisons: In Search of Methodology," *Iowa L. Rev.* 84, no. 5 (1999): 1025-1132.

Hiram E. Chodosh, *Global Justice Reform: A Comparative Methodology* (New York: New York University Press, 2005).

T'ung-Tsu Ch'u, *Law and Society in Traditional China*, Selected Works of Modern Chinese Learning: English Version (Beijing: The Commercial Press, 2011).

J. Church and A. B. Edwards, "Comparative Law/Comparative Method," in *Introduction to South African Law and Legal Theory*, W. J. Hosten, et al. (Durban: Butterworths, 1995), 1261-70.

Civil Justice Reform (Hong Kong), *Final Report of the Working Party on Civil Justice Reform* (Hong Kong, 2004). http://www.civiljustice.gov.hk/eng/archives_fr.html>.

Anthony Clarke, "The Woolf Reforms: A Singular Event or an Ongoing Process," in *The Civil Procedure Ten Years On*, ed. Déirdre Dwyer (Oxford: Oxford University Press, 2009), 33-49.

J. Clore, *Civil Litigation*, 2nd ed., Legal Practice Course Companion (London: Routledge-Cavendish, 1998).

Hugh Collins, "Law as Politics: Progressive American Perspectives," in *Introduction to Jurisprudence and Legal Theory: Commentary and Materials*, Anne Barron, et al. (London: Butterworths, 2002), 279-333.

Jerome A. Cohen, "China's Troubled Path to WTO," *Int'l Financial L. Rev.*, 1st September 2001, 71.

Jerome A. Cohen, ed., Chen, Fu-Mei Chang, *Essays on China's Legal Tradition*, Studies in East Asian Law (Princeton: Princeton University Press, 1981).

Mark Cohen. "Case Filing" in China's Courts and their Impact on IP cases." Posted on March 24, 2012. Accessed on September 30, 2016. https://chinaipr.com/2012/03/24/case-filing-in-chinas-courts-and-their-impact-on-ip-cases/.

Mathilde Cohen, "When Judges Have Reasons not to Give Reasons: A Comparative Law Approach," *Wash. & Lee L. Rev.* 72, no. 2 (2015): 483-572.

Standing Committee, *Parliamentary Debates: House of Commons Official Report: Civil Procedure Bill* (London: HMSO, 1997).

First Standing Committee on Delegated Legislation. [Civil Procedure (Amendment no 2) Rules 2005.], *Parliamentary Debates: House of Commons Official Report: Civil Procedure (Amendment No 2) Rules 2005* (London: HMSO, 2005).

Third Standing Committee on Delegated Legislation, *Parliamentary Debates: House of Commons Official Report: Draft Civil Procedure (Modification of Enactments) Order 1998* (HMSO, 1998).

Fourth Standing Committee on Delegated Legislation, *Parliamentary Debates: House of Commons Official Report: Draft Civil Procedure (Modification of Crown Proceedings Act 1947) Order 2005* (London: HMSO, 2005).

Lord Evershed, *Committee on Supreme Court Practice and Procedure, Final Report*, Cmd 8878 (1953).

E. J. Couture, "The Nature of Judicial Process," *Tul. L. Rev.* 25, no. 1 (1950-51): 1-28.

Vivian Grosswald Curran, "Cultural Immersion, Difference and Categories in U.S. Comparative Law," *Am. J. Comp. L.* 46, no. 1 (1998): 43-92. http://www.jstor.org/stable/841076.

Danny Danziger and John Gillingham, *1215: The Year of Magna Carta* (New York: Simon & Schuster, 2004).

Rene David and John E.C. Brierley, *Major Legal Systems in the World Today*, 3rd ed. (London: Sweet & Maxwell, 1985).

Dominique Demougin and Claude Fluet, "Deterrence Vs Judicial Error: A Comparative View of Standards of Proof," *J. of Inst. and Theoretical Econ.* 161, no. 2 (2004): 193-206. https://ssrn/abstract=585770.

Jinting Deng, "The Guiding Case System in Mainland China," *Frontiers of Law in China* 10, no. 3 (2015): 449-74.

A. V. Dicey, *Introduction to the Study of the Law of Constitution* (London; New York: Macmillan, 1902).

C. Dickens, *Bleak House* (Hammondsworth: Penguin, 1996).

Yong Ding, "Research for Abusing Litigation of Blemish in Resolutions of Companies in Germany and Enlightenment," *Journal of Comparative Law*, no. 4 (2013): 35-48.

Scott Dodson, "The Challenge of Comparative Civil Procedure," *Ala. L. Rev.* 60, no. 1 (2008): 133-50.

Hao Dong, *On Judicial Interpretation* (Beijing: Press of China's University of Political Science and Law, 2007).

Antony Duff, et al., *The Trial on Trial: Volume I: Truth and Due Process* (Oxford: Hart Publishing, 2004).

R. Dworkin, "Hard Cases," *Harv. L. Rev.* 88, no. 6 (1975): 1057-1109.

Ronald Dworkin, *Law's Empire (Legal Theory)*, New ed. (Oxford: Hart Publishing, 1998).

Ronald Dworkin, *Taking Rights Seriously* (London: Duckworth, 1977).

Déirdre Dwyer, ed., *The Civil Procedure Rules Ten Years On* (Oxford; New York: Oxford University Press, 2009).

Déirdre Dwyer, *The Judicial Assessment of Expert Evidence* (Cambridge: Cambridge University Press, 2008).

Déirdre Dwyer, "What is the Meaning of CPR r 1.1(1)," in *The Civil Procedure Rules Ten Years On*, Déirdre Dwyer (Oxford: Oxford University Press, 2009), 65-73.

Frank H. Easterbrook, "Legal Interpretation and Power of Judiciary," *Harv. J. L. & Pub. Pol'y* 7, no. 1 (1984): 87-100.

Edward J. Eberle, "The Method and Role of Comparative Law," *Wash. U. Global Stud. L. Rev.* 8, no. 3 (2009): 451-86.

Melvin Aron Eisenberg, *The Nature of Common Law* (Cambridge: Harvard University Press, 1988).

Christoph Engel, "Preponderance of the Evidence versus Intime Conviction: A Behavioural Perspective on Conflict between American and Continental European Law," *MPI Collective Goods Preprint No.2008/33* (2008): 1-28.

William Ewald, "The Jurisprudential Approach in Comparative Law: A Field Guide to 'Rats'," *Am. J. Comp. L.* 46, no. 4: 701-7.

Elizabeth Fahey and Zhirong Tao, "The Pretrial Discovery Process in Civil Cases: A Comparison of Evidence Discovery between China and the United States," *B.C. Int'l & Comp. L. Rev.* 37, no. 2 (2014): 281-333.

Chongyi Fan, "Opinions on Objective Truth," *China Legal Science*, no. 1 (2000): 114-20.

Keith A Findley, "Innocents at Risk: Adversary Imbalance, Forensic Science, and the Search for Truth," *Seton Hall L. Rev.* 38, no. 3 (2008): 893-973.http://scholarship.shu.edu/shir/vol38/iss3/7.

R. Finkelstein, "The Adversarial System and the Search for the Truth," *Monash U. L. Rev.* 37, no. 1 (2011): 135-44.

Owen M. Fiss, "'Against Settlement'," *Yale L.J.* 93, no. 6 (1984): 1073-92.

Nicholas H. D. Foster, "Company Law Theory in Comparative Perspective: England and France," *Am. J. Comp. L.* 48, no. 4 (2000): 573-622.

Joel Friedman and Michael Collins, *The Law of Civil Procedure: Cases and Materials*, 4th ed., American Case Book Series (St. Paul, Minn.: West Academic Publishing, 2013).

Xin Fu. "Try to Describe the Relation and Difference of Commercial Law, Economy Law and Civil Law." Posted on August 8, 2004. Accessed on June 15, 2016. http://www.law-lib.com/lw/lw_view.asp?no=3507.

Lon L. Fuller, "The Adversary System," in *Talks on American law: A Series of Broadcasts to Foreign Audiences by Members of the Harvard Law School Faculty*, ed. Berman and Harold J. (New York: Vintage Books, 1961), 35-36.

Lon Fuller, "The Forms and Limits of Adjudication," *Harv. L. Rev.* 92, no. 2 (1978): 353-409.

Lon L. Fuller, *The Law in Quest of Itself* (Boston, Mass.: Beacon Press, 1940).

Yu-Lan Fung and Derk Bodde, trans., *A History of Chinese Philosophy. Vol. 2, The Period of Classical Learning (from the Second Century B.C. to the Twentieth Century A.D.)*, 7th ed. (Princeton: Princeton (N.J.) Princeton University Press, 1983).

Yu-Lan Fung and Derk Bodde, trans., *A History of Chinese Philosophy. Vol. 1, The Period of the Philosophers (from the Beginnings to Circa 100 B.C.)* (Princeton: Princeton University Press, 1983).

RR Geddes. "Purpose and Context in Statutory Interpretation." Accessed on 28 May, 2015. www.judcom.nsw.gov.au/publications/education-monographs-1/monograph4/07_geddes.pdf.

Fabien Gélinas, et al., *Foundations of Civil Justice: Toward a Value-Based Framework for Reform* (Heidelberg; New York; Dordrecht; London: Springer, 2015).

E. Genzmer, "Zum Verhaltnis von Rechtsgeschichte und Rechtvergleichung ('In German')," *ARSP* 41 (1954/55): 326-47.

David J. Gerber, "Comparing Procedural Systems: Towards an Analytical Framework," in *Law and Justice in Multistate World: Essays in Honor of Arther T. von. Mehren*, James A. R. Nafziger and Symeon C. Symeonides (2002), 665-74, http://ssrn.com/abstract=12342579.

John Gillespie, "Rethinking the Role of Judicial Independence in Socialist-Transforming East Asia," *I.C.L.Q.* 56, no. 4 (2007): 837-70.

C. Glasser, "Solving the Litigation Crisis," *The Litigator* (1994): 14.

David M. Gooden and Douglas Walton, "Defeasibility in Judicial Opinion – Logical or Procedural," *Informal Logic* 28, no. 1 (2008): 6-19.

James Gordley, "Comparative Legal Research: Its Function in the Development of Harmonized Law," *Am. J. Comp. L.* 43, no. 4 (1995): 555-68.

James Gordley, "The Functional Method," in *Methods of Comparative Law*, in *Methods of Comparative Law*, ed. Monateri. Pier G., Research Handbooks in Comparative Law. (Cheltenham, U.K.; Northampton, MA: Edward Elgar Pub., 2012), 107-19.

Peter Gottwald, "Comparative Civil Procedure," *Ritsumeikan L. Rev.* 22 (2005): 23-35.

J. Gould and W. L. Kolb, *A Dictionary of the Social Sciences*, 1st ed. (London: Tavistock, 1964).

S. J. Gray, "Towards a Theory of Cultural Influence on the Development of Accounting Systems Internationally," *ABACUS* 24 (1998): 1-16.

J. A. G. Griffith, *The Politics of the Judiciary*, 5th ed. (London: Harper Collins, 1997).

Hyman Gross and R. Harrison, eds., *Jurisprudence: Cambridge Essays*, ed. Hyman Gross and Ross Harrison (Oxford: Clarendon Press, 1992).

Bernard Grossfeld, "Global Accounting: Where Internet Meets Geography," *Am. J. Comp. L.* 48, no. 2 (2000): 261-306.

Bernhard Grossfeld and Edward J. Eberle, "Patterns of Order in Comparative Law: Discovering and Decoding Invisible Powers," *Tex. Int'l. L.J.* 38, no. 2 (2003): 291-316.

Gongyun Gu, *Tutorial of Commercial Law* (Shanghai: Shanghai People's House, 2001).

Wang Guiguo and John Mo, eds., *Chinese Law* (The Hague; London; Boston: Kluwer Law International, 1999).

Wang Guiguo, "The Legal System of China," in *Chinese Law*, ed. Wang Guiguo and John Mo (The Hague; London; Boston: Kluwer Law International, 1999), 1-21.

Rongxing Guo, *An Introduction to the Chinese Economy: The Driving Forces Behind Modern Day China* (Singapore: John Wiley & Sons (Asia) Pte. Ltd., 2010).

Shu-Shan Guo. "The Discussion About Judges' Discretionary Power in Our Country." Posted on June 30, 2010. Accessed on July 24, 2016. www.66law.cn/domianblog/20248.aspx_Dan Harris. "Where to Locate in China? or Why Weifang Isn't Suzhou." Posted on January 1, 2014. Accessed on September 30, 2016. http://chinalawblog.com/2014/01/where-to-locate-in-china-or-why-weifang-isnt-suzhou.html

Harold Cooke Gutteridge, *Comparative Law: An Introduction to the Comparative Method of Legal Study and Research* (Cambridge: Cambridge University Press, 2015).

W. J. Habscheid, "The Fundamental Principles of the Law of Civil Procedure," *Comp. & Int'l L.J. S. Afr.* 17, no. 1 (1984): 1-31. www.jstor.org/stable/23246919.

J. Hage, "Comparative Law as Method and the Method of Comparative Law," *Maastricht European Private Law Institute Working Paper No. 2014/11* (2014), www.ssrn.com. www.ssrn.com.

Dan Harris. "China Litigation and Case Acceptance." Posted in March 24, 2013. Accessed on September 30, 2016. http://www.chinalawblog.com/2012/03/china-litigation-and-case-acceptance.html.

H. L. A. Hart, *The Concept of Law*, 2nd ed. (Oxford: Oxford University Press, 1994).

H. L. A. Hart, "Definition and Theory in Jurisprudence," *L. Quarterly Rev.* 70 (1983): 37-60.

H. L. A. Hart, *Essays on Bentham: Jurisprudence and Political Theory* (Oxford: Oxford University Press, 1982).

H. L. A Hart, "Positivism and Separation of Law and Morals," *Harvard L. Rev.* 71, no. 4 (1958): 593-629.

Keith Hawkins, ed., *The Uses of Discretion*, Rev. ed. (Oxford: Clarendon Press, 1995).

G. Jr. Hazard, "Civil Litigation without Frontiers- Harmonization and Unification of Civil Code," *World Congress on Procedural Law: Procedural Law on the Threshold of a New Milllenium* (2002), Walter Hans Rechberger and Thomas KlickaWien: Manzsche, 2002.

Qinhua He, "The Birth and Growth of Modern Jurisprudence in China," *Frontiers of Law in China* 1, no. 4 (2006): 486-513.

John W. Head, *Great Legal Traditions: Civil Law, Common Law, and Chinese Law in Historical and Operational Perspective* (Durham, N.C.: Carolina Academic Press, 2011).

Jacqueline Hodgson, "Conceptions of the Trial in Inquisitorial and Adversarial Procedure," in *The Trial on Trial: Volume 2: Judgment and Calling to Account*, ed. A. Duff, Farmer, S Marshall, and V. Tadros (Oxford; Portland; Or: Hart, 2004), 223-42.

Mark Van Hoecke, "Deep Level Comparative Law," *EUI Working Paper Law No. 2002/13* (2002). www.cadmus.eui.eu/bitstream/handle/1814/191/law02-13pdf?sequence=1.

W. J. Hosten, trans., Scott, "Romeinse Reg, Regsgeskiedenis en Regsvergelyking," *THRHR* 25 (1961): 16 (Pretoria: N.A., 1961).

D. Howarth, "Making Sense Out of Nonsense," in *Jurisprudence: Cambridge Essays*, ed. Hyman Gross and Ross Harrison (Oxford: Clarendon Press, 1992), 29-53.

C. Stephen Hsu, ed., *Understanding China's Legal System: Essays in Honor of Jerome A. Cohen* (New York: NYU Press, 2003).

Minjie Hu, "The Practical Obstacles and Road Selection of Administrative Guiding Case. (Xingzheng Zhidaoxing Anli de Shijian Kunjing Yu Lujing Xuanze)," *Law Science (Faxue)*, no. 1 (2012): 149-54.

XiangGuo Hu. "The Discretionary Power of Judge in Civil Proceedings and Its Improvements in China (Translated)." China Court Net Bozhou Qiaocheng Channel. Posted on November 6, 2013. Accessed on July 16, 2015, http://www.chinacourt.org/article/detail/2013/11/id/1122865.shtml.

Xin Hu, "Bifu in Criminal Law of Ancient China (Zhongguo Gudai Xingfa Zhong de Bifu)," *Law Review (Faxue Pinglun)*, no. 2 (1994): 84-87.

Yunteng Hu and Tongzhi Yu, "Research on Several Important Difficult Questions of the Guiding Case System. (Anli Zhidao Xhidu Ruogan Zhongda Yinan Zhengyi Wenti Yanjiu)," *Chinese Journal of Law (Faxue Yanjiu)*, no. 6 (2008): 3-24.

Yunteng Hu, "The Constructing Cases Guidance System with Chinese Characteristics Exclusive Interview of Dr. Hu Yunteng, Member of Judicial Committee and the Director of the Research Office in Supreme People's Court," *China L.*, no. 1 (2011): 4-6,58-60.

Philip C. C. Huang, *Chinese Civil Justice, Past and Present* (Lanham: Rowman & Littlefield, 2012).

Philip C. C. Huang and Kathryn Bernhardt, eds., *The History and Theory of Legal Practice in China: Toward a Historical-Social Jurisprudence*, The Social Sciences of Practice (Book 3) (Leiden: Brill Academic Publishing, 2014).

Yuansheng Huang, "Sources of Law in Civil Adjudication of the Dali Yuan in the Early Republic of China (Minch Dali Yuan Minshi Shenpan Fayuan)," in *100 Selected Precedents of the Dali Yuan (Dali Yuan Minshi Panli Baixuan), Ed. Yuansheng Huang*, ed. Yuansheng Huang (Taibei: Wunan Book Co. Ltd., 2009).

Tina Hunter, "Interpretive Theories: Dworkin, Sunstein, and Ely," *Bond Law Review* 17, no. 2 (2005): 78-101.

Haihong Huo, "Chinese Expression or Theory of Civil Procedure Law," *Legal System and Social Development*, no. 4 (2013): 3-9.

Lord Justice Jackson (Editor-in-chief), *Civil Procedure: Volume I & II*, general editors B. Fontaine and I. R. Scott. [Civil procedure 2015], The White Book Service 2015 (London: Sweet & Maxwell, 2015).

Lord Justice Jackson (Editor-in-chief), *Civil Procedure: Volume I & II*, general editors B. Fontaine and I. R. Scott. [Civil procedure 2016], The White Book Service 2016 (London: Sweet Maxwell, 2016).

The Rt. Hon. Lord Justice Jackson, *The Reform of Civil Litigation* (London: Sweet & Maxwell, 2016).

Jack I. H. Jacob, *The Fabric of English Justice*, Hamlyn Lecture Series (London: Sweet & Maxwell, 1987).

Michael James, *Litigation with a Foreign Aspect: A Practical Guide* (Oxford; New York: Oxford University Press, 2009), http://ssrn.com/abstract=1113916.

P. Jessup, *Transnational Law* (New Haven: Yale University Press, 1956).

Ping Jiang and Jian Mi, "The Civil Law Tradition and Contemporary Chinese Law [Part II]. (Lun Minfa Chuantong Yu Dangdai Zhangguo Falii (Xia))," *The Tribune of Political Science and Law (Zhengfa Luntan)*, no. 3 (1993): 1-8.

Sun Jin. "On the Practical Level of Judicial Interpretation of the Law - Reasoning Made by Judges in Judgments." Accessed on 22 December 2015. http://www.court.gmw.cn/html/article/201212/28/115659.shtml.

Zhenbao Jin, "From a Supplementary Legislator to a Legitimate Judicial Lawmaker- on the Role of the Supreme People's Court in Developing the Law in Mainland China," in *Towards a Chinese Civil Code: Comparative and Historical Perspectives*, Lei Chen and C H van Rhee (Dordrecht: Martinus Nijhoff Publishers, 2012), 29-60.

Zhenbao Jin, "On the Power of the Supreme People's Court to Issue Judicial Interpretations in Abstracto (Lun Zuigao Renmin Fayuan de Chouxiang Sifa Jieshi Quan)," *Journal of Comparative Law (Bijiao Fa Yanjiu)*, no. 2 (2010): 55-66.

Junjian Jing, "Legislation Related to the Civil Economy in the Qing Dynasty," in *Civil Law in Qing and Republican China*, Kathryn Bernhardt, Philip C. Huang, and Mark A. Allee, Law, Society, and Culture in China. (Stanford, Calif.: Stanford University Press, 1994), 42-84.

J. A. Jolowicz, "Adversarial and Inquisitorial Models of Civil Procedure," *I.C.L.Q.* 52, no. 2 (2003): 281-95.

J. A. Jolowicz, "Civil Litigation: What's it For?" in *The Civil Procedure Ten Years On*, ed. Déirdre Dwyer (Oxford: Oxford University Press, 2009), 51-63.

J. A. Jolowicz, "Civil Litigation: What's it For?" *Camb. L.J.* 67, no. 3 (2008): 508-20.

J. A. Jolowicz, *On Civil Procedure*, Cambridge Studies in International and Comparative Law (Book 13) (Cambridge; New York: Cambridge University Press, 2000).

J. A. Jolowicz, "On the Comparison of Procedures," in *Law and Justice in Multistate World: Essays in Honour of Arther T. Von Mehren*, ed. James Nafziger and Symeon Symeonides (New York: Transnational Publishers, 2002), 721-40.

Ann D. Jordan, "Lost in Translation: Two Legal Cultures, Common Law Judiciary and the Basic Law of Hong Kong Special Administrative Region," *Cornell Int'l L. J.* 30, no. 2 (1997): 335-80.

Benjamin Kaplan, Arther T. von Mehren, and Rudolf Schaefer, "Phrases of German Civil Procedure (Pt.1)," *Harv. L. Rev.* 71, no. 7 (1958): 1193-1268.

Neal Kumar Katyal, "Judge as Advicegivers," *Stan. L. Rev.* 50, no. 6 (1998): 1709-1824.

Kevin C. Kennedy, "Equitable Remedies and Principled Discretion: The Michigan Experience," *U. Det. Mercy L. Rev.* 74, no. 4 (1997): 609-56.

Perry Keller, ed., *Chinese Law and Legal Theory*, The International Library of Essays in Law and Legal Theory (Second Series) (London: Routledge, 2001).

A. D. Kessler, "Our Inquisitorial Tradition: Equity Procedure, Due Process, and the Search for an Alternative to the Adversarial," *Cornell L. Rev.* 90, no. 5 (2005): 1181-1275.

Zentaro Kitagawa, "The Development of Comparative Law in East Asia," in *The Oxford Handbook of Comparative Law*, ed. Mathias Reimann and Reinhard Zimmermann (Oxford: Oxford University Press, 2008), 237-60.

T. Kojima, "Legal Families in Procedural Law Revisited - Report to World Congress of Procedural Law," *World Conference on Procedural Law (10th) in Transnational Aspects of Procedural Law*, Italo Andolina (Taormina, Italy, 1998).

Hein Kotz, "Comparative Law in Germany Today," *Revue Internationale de Droit Compare* 51, no. 4 (1999): 753-58.

X. E. Kramer and C. H. van Rhee, eds., *Civil Litigation in a Globalising World* (Hague: T.M.C. Asser Press, 2012).

Nicola Lacey, "Modern Positivism: H. L. A. Hart and Analytical Jurisprudence," in *Introduction to Jurisprudence and Legal Theory: Commentary and Materials*, by Anne Barron, et al. (London: Butterworths, 2002), 143-89.

Edouard M. Lambert, "Conception Generale et Definition de la Science due Droit Compare," *Procesverbaux Des Seances et Documents, Congres International de Droit Compare I* (1905): 26.

F. H. Lawson, *Selected Essays*, European Studies in Law (Amsterdam; New York: North-Holland Pub. Co., 1977).

Tahirih V. Lee, ed., *Basic Concepts of Chinese Law*, Chinese Law: Social, Political, Historical, and Economic Perspectives (London: Routledge, 1997).

James Legge, trans., *The Ch'un Ts'ew with the Tso Cheun in 5 the Chinese, Taiwan (ROC) (1883)*, Taiwan (ROC) (1883) (Oxford: Clarendon Press, 1971).

Chen Lei, "Contextualizing Legal Transplant: China and Hong Kong," in *Methods of Comparative Law*, ed. Pier G. Monateri (Cheltenham, U.K.; Northampton, MA: Edward Elgar Pub., 2012), 192-209.

Buyun Li, *Constitutionalism and China* (Beijing: Law Press, 2006).

Guoguang Li, *Guidance and Reference on Economic Trail* (Beijing: Legal Press, 2001).

Xiliang Li, "The Demarcation of 'Stakeholder' in Civil Procedure Law," *Science of Law (Journal of Northwest University of Political Science and Law)*, no. 1 (2012): 139-47.

Yuwen Li, "Professional Ethics of Chinese Judges," *China Perspectives [Online Journal]* (2003), Http://chinaperspectives.revues.org/274, accessed on 25 June 2016.

Zhenghua Li, "Theory of Discretionary Power," *Contemporary Law Review*, no. 4 (2000): 18-19, 66.

Hui Xing, Liang, *Judging Methods* (Beijing: Law Press, 2005).

Qi Chao Liang, *The Collection of Yin Bing Shi, Vol. 5* (Shanghai: Shanghai Guangzhi Publishing House, 1936).

Linxia Liang, *Delievering Justice in Qing China: Civil Trials in Magistrate's Courts*, British Academy Post-Doctoral Fellowships Monograph (London: British Academy, 2008).

Shuwen Liang, ed., *Research for Problems in Implementation of Civil Procedure Law* (Beijing: People's Court Press, 2000).

Zhiping Liang, "Explicating Law: A Comparative Perspective of Chinese and Western Legal Culture," *J. Chinese L.* 3, no. 1 (1989): 55-92.

Huang Lie, "Rule of Law in China: Ideal and Reality," in *Constitutionalism and China*, in *Constitutionalism and China*, Buuyun Li (Beijing: Law Press, 2006), 175-90.

Jocelyn E.H. Limmer, "China's New 'Common Law' Using China's Guiding Cases to Understand How to Do Business in People's Republic of China," *Willamette J. Int'l L. & Dis. Resol.* 21, no. 2 (2013): 96-133.

Ducai Liu, "A Study of Judicial Precedent in Traditional China. (Zhongguo Gudai Panli Kaolun)," *Social Sciences in China (Zhonguo Shehui Kexue)*, no. 4 (2007): 145-55, 207-8.

Jie Liu. "Restriction and Guidance on Judges' Discretion (Translated)." China Court net Meishan City Dongpo channel. Posted on May 16, 2013. Accessed on July 24, 2016, http://www.chinacourt.org/article/detail/2013/05/id/959246.shtml.

Kaixiang Liu, "About the Nature, Accordance and Features of Commercial Law," *Modern Law Science*, no. 5 (1997): 26-34.

Li Liu, "Discussion on Case Guiding System (Lun Woguo de Anli Zhidao Zhidu)," *Journal of Hubei University of Police (Hubei Jingguan Xueyuan Xuebao)*, no. 1 (2013): 132-34.

Nanping Liu and Michelle Liu, "Justice without Judges: The Filing Division in People's Republic of China," *U.C. Davis J. Int'l L. & Pol'y* 17, no. 2 (2011): 283-344.

Weimin Liu, "The Difference Between Thought of Civil Law and Thought of Commercial Law in Juridical Application," *Speed Reading (Published by Xihua University, Chengdu)*, no. 9 (2014): 256-57.

Karl Llewellyn, "Some Realism About Realism- Responding to Dean Pound," *Harv. L. Rev.* 44, no. 8 (1931): 1222-64.

K. N. Llewellyn, *The Common Law Tradition: Deciding Appeals* (New York: Aspen Law and Business, 1960).

Thomas Lundmark, *Charting the Divide Between Common and Civil Law* (New York; Oxford: Oxford University Press, 2012).

Wei Luo, *Chinese Law and Legal Research*, Chinese Law Series (Book 8) (Littleton, Colorado: Fred B. Rothman & Co, 2005).

Wei Luo, *The Civil Procedure Law a/nd Court Rules of the People's Republic of China*, Chinese Law Series (Book 10) (Littleton, Colo.: Fred B Rothman and Co, 2006).

Arabella Lyon, "Rhetorical Authority in Athenian Democracy and the Chinese Legalism of Han Fei," *Philosophy & Rhetoric* 41, no. 1 (2008): 51-71.

Lord Mackay, *Halsbury's Laws of England, Volume 12: Civil Procedure* (London: LexisNexis, 2009).

M. Martinek, "Rechtsverglechung Als Akademische Disziplin in Deutschland," *Ritsumeikan Law Review (International Edition)* 17 (2000): 79-117.

A. Mason, "Changing the Law in a Changing Society," *Commw. L. Bull.* 18, no. 3 (1992): 1166-72.

Ugo Mattei, "An Opportunity not to be Missed – A Future of Comparative Law In the United States," *Am. J. Comp. L.* 46, no. 4 (1998): 709-18.

Geoffrey MacCormack, "Scandinavian Realism," *The Juridical Rev.* (1970): 33-55.

Geoffrey MacCormack, *The Spirit of Traditional Chinese Law*, The Spirit of the Laws (Athens; London: University of Georgia Press, 1996).

Geoffrey MacCormack, *Traditional Chinese Penal Law*, rev. ed., Law in East Asia Series. (London: Simmonds & Hill Publishing, 2013).

Neil MacCormick, *Legal Reasoning and Legal Theory*, Clarendon Law Series (Oxford: Clarendon Press, 1978).

Thomas O. Main, "The Procedural Foundation of Substantive Law," *Wash. U. L. Rev.* 87, no. 4 (2009): 801-42. http://ssrn/abstract=1113916.

Thomas O. Main, "Traditional Equity and Contemporary Procedure," *Wash. L. Rev.* 78, no. 2 (2003): 429-514.

Henry S. Maine, *Dissertations on Early Law and Custom* (Delhi: B. R. Pub Corporation, 1985).

F.W. Matiland, *Equity: A Course of Lectures*, Reissue ed. (Cambridge: Cambridge University Press, 2011).

James R. Maxeiner, "Legal Methods as a Point of Reference for Comparative Studies of Procedural Law," *XIIIth World Congress on Procedural Law,* Salvador -Bahia, 16 to 22 September 2007 (Bahia, Brazil, 2007): 1-13, Http://ssrn.com/abstract=1232579.

Stephen McCaffrey and Thomas Main, *Transnational Litigation in Comparative Perspective: Theory and Application*, 1st ed. (New York; Oxford: Oxford University Press, 2009).

Sebastian McEvoy, "Descriptive and Purposive Categories of Comparative Law," in *Methods of Comparative Law*, ed. Pier G. Monateri (Cheltenham, U.K.; Northampton, MA: Edward Elgar Publishing, 2012), 144-61.

Peggy McInerney. "Modern Legal in China is Only 35 Years Old." UCLA Int'l Institute. Posted on January 28, 2014. Accessed on April 12, 2016. http://web.international.ucla.edu/Institute/article/136768.

Marinus Johan Meijer, "An Aspect of Traditional Chinese Law," *T'Oung Pao* 66 (1980): 199-216.

Chuncai Meng, "Civil Procedure Law," in *Chinese Law*, ed. Guiguo Wang and John Mo (The Hague, London, Boston: Kluwer Law International, 1999), 179-216.

Sen Meng, *New Introduction to Jurisprudence* (Shanghai: Shanghai Commercial Press, 1911).

John Henry Merryman, trans, Peidong & Lu Gu, Zhengping, *The Civil Law Tradition*, 2nd ed. (Beijing: Beijing Law Press, 2004).

Ralf Michaels, "The Functional Method of Comparative Law," in *The Oxford Handbook of Comparative Law*, ed. Mathias Reimann and Reinhard Zimmermann (Oxford: Oxford University Press, 2008), 339-82.

Peter Middleton, *Review of Civil Justice and Legal Aid*, Report to the Lord Chancellor (London: Lord Chancellor's Department, 1997).

Catherine Mitchell, *Interpretation of Contracts (Current Controversies in Law)*, 1st ed., Current Controversies in Law (Book 2) (London: Routledge-Cavendish, 2007).

John Shijian Mo, "The General Principles of Civil Law," in *Chinese Law*, ed. Guiguo Wang and John Mo (The Hague, London, Boston: Kluwer Law International, 1999), 95-176.

John Shijian Mo, "Non-Judicial Means of Dispute Settlement," in *Chinese Law*, ed. Guiguo Wang and John Mo (The Hague, London, Boston: Kluwer Law International, 1999), 757-807.

Pier Giuseppe Monateri, "Methods in Comparative Law: An Intellectual Overview," in *Methods of Comparative Law* (Cheltenham, U.K.; Northampton, MA, USA: Edward Elgar Pub., 2012), 7-24.

Charles A. Moore, ed., *The Chinese Mind: Essentials of Chinese Philosophy and Culture* (Honolulu: University of Hawaii Press, 1978).

Peter L. Murray, "A Morning at the Amtsgericht: German Civil Justice in Practice," in *Law and Justice in Multistate World: Essays in Honor of Arther T. von Mehren*, James Nafziger and Symeon Symeonides (New York: Transnational Publishers, 2002), 779-92.

P. L. Murray and Rolf H. Sturner, *German Civil Justice* (Durham, N.C.: Carolina Academic Press, 2004).

Chen, Nanjun, "The Schism of the Legislation of Civil- Commercial Law: The Rational Choice of Legislation of Commercial Law in China," Ph.D. Thesis, Huaqiao University, Quanzhou, 2007.

Nicole E. Negowetti, "Judicial Decisionmaking, Empathy, and the Limits of Perception," *Akron L. Rev.* 47, no. 3 (2015): 693-751.

Richards Nobles and David Schiff, "The Evolution of Natural Law," in *Introduction to Jurisprudence and Legal Theory: Commentary and Materials*, by Anne Barron, et al. (London: Butterworths, 2002), 35-90.

Richard Nobles and David Schiff, "Debating with Natural Law; the Emergence of the Legal Positivism," in *Introduction to Jurisprudence and Legal Theory: Commentary and Materials*, Anne Barron, et al. (London: Butterworths, 2002), 91-142.

J. Normand and K. Kerameus, "Provisional Remedies in Transnational Litigation," World Congress on Procedural Law (10th) in *Transnational Aspects of Procedural Law*, ed. Italo Andolina (Taormina, Italy, 1998).

F. S. C. Northrop, *The Complexity of Legal and Ethical Experience: Studies in the Method of Normative Subjects*, 1st ed. (Boston: Little, Brown, 1959).

Roderick O'Brien, "The Survival of Traditional Chinese Law in the People's Republic of China," *Hong Kong L. J.* 40, no. 1 (2010): 165-74.

W. B. Odgers, "Changes in Procedure and in the Law of Evidence," in *A Century of Law Reform: Twelve Lectures on the Changes in the Law of England During the Nineteenth Century* (London: The Macmillan Company, 1901).

W. Blake Odgers and W. Blake Odgers, *The Common Law of England (V1)*, reproduction of 1920 book (Ithaca, New York: Cornell University Library, 2009).

William Blake Odgers and Simon Goulding, eds., *Odgers on Civil Court Actions*, 24th ed. (London: Sweet & Maxwell, 1996).

OECD, *What Makes Civil Justice Effective*, OECD Economic Department Policy Notes, No. 18 June 2013 (2013). www.oecd.org/eco/growth/civil%20Justice%20Policy%20note.pdf.

John O'Hare and Kevin D. Browne, *Civil Litigation*, 13th ed. (London: Sweet & Maxwell, 2007).

Esin Örücü, *The Enigma of Comparative Law: Variations on a Theme for the Twenty-First Century* (Leiden; Boston: Martinus Nijhoff Publishers, 2004).

V.V. Palmer, "From Lerotholi to Lando: Some Examples of Comparative Law Methodology," *Global Jurist Frontiers* 4, no. 2 (2004): 1-29.

Jianfeng Pan, "Scientific Reforms of Civil Trial Procedure System in China - Reflection on the Civil Procedure and its Relationship," *Tribune of Political Science and Law*, no. 5 (2012): 99-113.

Tim Parkes, "The Civil Procedure Rules Ten Years on: The Practitioners' Perspectives," in *The Civil Procedure Rules Ten Years On*, Déirdre Dwyer (Oxford: Oxford University Press, 2009), 435-51.

Randall Peerenboom, "Judicial Accountability and Judicial Independence: An Empirical Study of Individual Case Supervision in the People's Republic of China," *The China Journal* 55 (2006): 67-92.

James Penner, "Law and Adjudication: Dworkin's Critique of Positivism," in *Introduction to Jurisprudence and Legal Theory: Commentary and Materials*, by Anne Barron, et al. (London: Butterworths, 2002), 334-426.

James Penner, David Schiff, and Richard Nobles, "Approaches to Jurisprudence, Legal Theory, and the Philosophy of Law," in *Introduction to Jurisprudence and Legal Theory: Commentary and Materials*, Anne Barron, et al. (London: Butterworths, 2002), 3-34.

Anne Peters and Heiner Schewenke, "Comparative Law Beyond Post-Modernism," *I.C.L.Q.* 49, no. 4 (2000): 800-834. htttp://justor.org/stable/761761.

A. E. Plastas, "The Functional and the Dysfunctional in the Comparative Method of Law: Some Critical Remarks," *Electronic J. Comp. L.* 12, no. 3 (2008). www.ejcl.org.http://www.ejcl.org/123/.

F. Pollock and F. Maitland, *The History of English Law Before the Time of Edward I, Volume 1 & 2* (Cambridge: Cambridge University Press, 1988).

Gerald J. Postema, "Classical Common Law Jurisprudence (Part I)," *Oxford U. of Commw. L.J.* 2, no. 2 (2002): 155-80.

Gerald J. Postema, "Classical Common Law Jurisprudence (Part II)," *Oxford U. of Commw. L.J.* 3, no. 1 (2003): 1-28.

R. Pound, "The Causes of Popular Dissatisfaction with the Administration of Justice," *Reports of the American Bar Association* 29 (1906): 395-417.

Ernest Rabel, *Aufgabe und Notwendigkeit der Rechtsvergleichung*, in *Gesammelte Aufsatze III*, ed. Leser, 1967, Rabel (1925), 1.

Ernst Rabel, *The Conflict of Laws; a Comparative Study*, foreword by William Draper Lewis and Hessel E. Yntema, Michigan Legal Studies (Ann Arbor: University of Michigan Law School, 1958).

Gustav Radbruch, *Einführung in die Rechtswissenschaft* (Stuttgart: K. F. Koehler, 1969).

John Rawls, *The Law of Peoples* (Cambridge, Mass.: Harvard University Press, 1999).

John Rawls, *A Theory of Justice*, 2nd ed. (Cambridge, Mass: Belknap Press of Harvard University Press, 1999).

J. Raz, "Legal Principles and the Limits of Law," *Yale L.J.* 81, no. 5 (1972): 823-54.

Mathias Reimann and Reinhard Zimmermann, eds., *The Oxford Handbook of Comparative Law*, 1st ed. (Oxford: Oxford University Press, 2008).

Mathias Reimann, "Comparative Law and Neighbouring Disciplines," in *The Cambridge Companion to Comparative Law*, ed. Mauro Bussani and Ugo Mattei, Cambridge Companions to Law (Cambridge; New York: Cambridge University Press, 2012), 13-34.

Mathias Reimann, "The Progress and Failure of Comparative Law in the Second Half of the Twentieth Century," *Am. J. Comp. J.* 50, no. 4 (2002): 671-700. http://www.jstor.org/stable/41616734.

Robert Reiner, "Classical Social Theory and Law," in *Introduction to Jurisprudence and Legal Theory: Commentary and Materials*, in *Jurisprudence and Legal Theory: Commentary and Materials*, Anne Barron, et al. (London: Butterworths, 2002), 230-78.

John C. Reitz, "How to Do Comparative Law," *Am. J. Comp. L.* 46, no. 4 (1998): 617-36.

J. Resnik, "Managerial Judges," *Harv. L. Rev.* 96, no. 2 (1982): 374-448.

Michael D. Risinger, "'Substance' and 'Procedure' Revisited: With Some Afterthoughts on the Constitutional Problems of 'Irrebuttable Presumptions'," *UCLA L. Rev.* 30, no. 2 (1982): 189-216.

C. H. van Rhee and R. Verkerk, "Civil Procedure," in *Elgar Encyclopaedia of Comparative Law*, ed. J.M. Smits (Cheltenham: Edward Elgar Publishing, 2006), 120-34.

C. H. van Rhee, ed., *European Traditions in Civil Procedure*, Ius Commune Europaeum (Book 54) (Antwerp: Intersentia, 2005).

C. H. van Rhee and A. Uzelac, eds., *Truth and Efficiency in Civil Litigation: Fundamental Aspects of Fact-Finding and Evidence-Taking in a Comparative Context*, Ius Commune Europaeum (Book 111) (Cambridge: Intersentia, 2012).

C. H. van Rhee and A. Uzelac, eds, *Evidence in Contemporary Civil Procedure: Fundamental Issues in a Comparative Perspective*, Ius Commune Europaeum (Cambridge: Intersentia, 2015).

Max Rhenstein, "Comparative Law and Legal Systems," reprinted in 1 Max Rhenstein International Encyclopaedia of the Social Sciences, 1 Gesammelte Schiriften (N.a.: MacMillan Publishers, 1968), 204-10.

Norbert Rouland, *Legal Anthropology*, trans. Philippe G. Planel (California: Stanford University Press, 1994).

Teemu Ruskola, "The East Asian Legal Tradition," in *The Cambridge Companion to Comparative Law*, in *The Cambridge Companion to Comparative Law*, ed. M. Bussani and U. Mattei (Cambridge; New York: Cambridge University Press, 2012), 257-77.

The Right Honourable Lord Scarman, (Ninth Wilfred Fullagar Memorial Lecture), "The Common Law Judge and the Twentieth Century - Happy Marriage or Irretrievable Breakdown?" *Monash L. Rev.* 7, no. 1 (1980): 1-15.

David Schiff, "Modern Positivism: Kelsen's Pure Theory of Law," in *Introduction to Jurisprudence and Legal Theory: Commentary and Materials*, Anne Barron, et al. (London: Butterworths, 2002), 190-229.

Carl E. Schneider, "Discretion and Rules: A Lawyers' View," in *The Uses of Discretion*, ed. Keith Hawkins (Oxford: Clarendon Press, 1992), 47-88.

R. B. Schlesinger, "The Past and Future of Comparative Law," *Am. J. Comp. L.* 43, no. 3 (1995): 477-82.

Peter F. Schlosser, "Coordinated Transnational Interaction in Civil Litigation and Arbitration," *Mich. J. Int'l L.* 12, no. 1 (1990): 150-72.

Paul J. Schmidt, "A Review of China's New Civil Evidence Law," *Pacific Rim L. & Pol. J.* 12, no. 2 (2003): 291-313.

T. J. Scott. "The Comparative Method of Legal Research." Accessed on April 21, 2015. http://italeem.iium.edu.my/2014.

Shandong People's Court. "The Application of Judges' Discretionary Power in China (Translated)." Changle County, Shandong Province People's Court. Posted on May 5, 2013. Accessed on July 16, 2015, http://wfclfy.chinacourt.org/article/detail/2013/05/id/954542.shtml.

Ming Shao, "Abuse of Civil Litigation Law and Regulation," *Tribune of Political Science and Law*, no. 6 (2011): 175-80.

Ying Shao and Run Shao, "Commercial Law in Practice: Discuss Problems of Law Application in Our Commercial Trial," *Market Modernization*, no. 19 (2014): 40-41.

Zongling Shen, ed., *Jurisprudence (Fa Li Xue)*, 3rd ed. (Taipei: Beijing University Press, 2009).

E. Sherwin and K. M. Clermont, "A Comparative View of Standards of Proof," *Am. J. Comp. L.* 50, no. 2 (2002): 243-76.

H. S. Shin, "Adversarial and Inquisitorial Procedure in Arbitration," *Rand J. Economics* 29, no. 2 (1998): 378-405.

Stuart Sime, "Disputes of Fact in Interim Applications," in *The Civil Procedure Rules Ten Years On*, ed. Déirdre Dwyer (Oxford; New York: Oxford University Press, 2009), 271-81.

Stuart Sime, *A Practical Approach to Civil Procedure*, 5th ed. (Oxford: Oxford University Press, 2002).

Stuart Sime, *A Practical Approach to Civil Procedure*, 17th ed. (Oxford: Oxford University Press, 2014).

Stuart Sime, *A Practical Approach to Civil Procedure*, 9th ed. (Oxford: Oxford University Press, 2016).

Stuart Sime, *A Practical Approach to Civil Procedure*, 14th ed., Practical Approach Series (Oxford: Oxford University Press, 2011).

Laura Slater, *Civil Litigation Practice: An Expert Guide* (London: Ark Group, 2015).

Lawrence B. Solum, "Procedural Justice," *S. Cal. L. Rev.* 78, no. 1 (2004): 181-322.

John Sorabji, Andenas Mads, et al., "The Road to New Street Station: Fact, Fiction and Overriding Objective," in *Legal Studies Research Paper Series: Paper No. 21/2011* (Cambridge, 2011), 1-18.

Benjamin A. Spencer, "The Restrictive Ethos in Civil Procedure," *Geo. Wash. L. Rev.* 78, no. 2 (2010): 353-73.

J. J. Spigelman, "Judicial Accountability and Performance Indicators," *Civil Justice Quarterly* 21 (2002): 1-28.www. http://ssrn.com/abstract=1802176.

J. J. Spigelman, "The Poet's Rich Resource: Issues in Statutory Interpretation," *Australian Bar Rev.* 21, no. 3 (2001): 224-34.

Zelin Su, "Fully Exploit the Function of the Guiding Case System with Chinese Characteristics; Courts, Positively Enforce Historical Missions of People's Application. (Chongfen Fahui Zhongguo Tese Anli Zhidao Zhidu Zuoyong Jiji Lvxing Renmin Fayuan Lishi Shiming)," *Journal of Law Application (Falv Shiyong)* 7 (2011): 3-6.

Stephen N. Subrin, "On Thinking about a Description of a Country's Civil Procedure," *Tul. J. Int'l & Comp. L.* 7 (1999): 139-52.

Stephen N. Subrin, "How Equity Conquered Common Law: The Federal Rules of Civil Procedure in Historical Perspective," *U. Pa. L. Rev.* 135, no. 4 (1987): 909-1002. www.jstor.org/stable/3312053.

Guohua Sun, *Chinese Law Dictionary*, Jurisprudence Volume (Chinese Procuratorial Press, 1997).

G. Swanson, "Framework for Comparative Research: Anthropology and the Theory of Action," in *Comparative Methods in Sociology: Essays on Trends and Applications*, ed. Vallier Ivan and Aptter. David E. (Berkeley: University of California Press, 1971), 141-202.

Lewis Talbot, Nadine H. Shelton, and Chief editor Mauro Cappelletti, eds., *International Encyclopaedia of Comparative Law. Volume XVI: Civil Procedure.* (Tubingen: Mohr Sieback, 2014).

Weijian Tang, "The Evolution of Civil Procedure System of China," *Frontiers L. China* 7, no. 2 (2012): 190-210.

Kristie Thomas, "Dynamism in China's Civil Procedure Law: Civil Justice with Chinese Characteristics," in *The Dynamism of Civil Procedure - Global Trends and Developments*, ed. C. Picker and G. Seidman (London: Springer, 2015), 119-39.

Ching-I Tu, "Conservatism and Constructive Forum: The Case of Wang Kuowei (1877-1927)," *Monumenta Serica (Journal of Oriental Studies)* 28 (1969): 188-214.

Karen G. Turner, James V. Feinerman, and R. Kent Guy, eds., *The Limits of the Rule of Law in China*, Asian Law Series (Seattle: University of Washington Press, 2015).

UNDROIT. "Principles of Transnational Civil Procedure." UNIDROIT (as adopted and promulgated by). Updated September 27, 2016, accessed on March 20, 2016 and October 30, 2016. http://www.unidroit.org/instruments/transnational-civil-procedure, accessed many times between April-November 2016.

F. Venter, ed., et al, "Regsnavorsing - Metode en Publikasie, ('Legal Research - Method and Publication')," 1st ed. (Kaapstad: Juta, 1990).

E. Vescovi, "Improvement of Civil Litigation: Lessons from Administrative Procedures," in *Justice and Efficiency: General Reports and Discussions (Eight World Conference on Procedural Law, Utrecht, 1987)*, ed. W. Wedekind (Kluwer, 1989).

Liming Wang, "The Achievements and Prospects of Court Reforms in China," *Frontiers L. China* 1, no. 1 (2006): 1-13.

Rui Wang, Feimin Wang, and Danning Li, "Comparative Research of Basic Principles between Civil Law and Commercial Law," *Journal of North China University of Technology* 20, no. 4 (2008): 26-32.

Shizhou Wang, *Civil Procedure in China*, International Encyclopaedia of Laws (Alphen aan den Rijn: Wolters Kluwer Law & Business, 2014).

Shirong Wang, "The Functions of Cases in Traditional Chinese Law. (Panli Zai Zhongguo Chuantongfa Zhong de Gongneng)," *Chinese Journal of Law (Faxue Yanjiu)*, no. 1 (2006): 125-34.

Yanchuan Wang, "The Dual Development of Commercial Law and the Growing Logic of Modern Commercial Law," *Journal of Northwest University (Philosophy and Social Science Edition)* 45, no. 1 (2015): 58-65.

Zhixiang Wang and Zengrun Wang, trans., *Soviet Civil Procedure* (Beijing: Law Press, 1957).

Chen Weizuo, *Chinese Civil Procedure and the Conflict of Laws*, Tsinghua Chinese Law Series. (Beijing: Tsinghua University Press, 2011).

Richard W. Wigley and Xu Jing. "Evidence Collection and Alternatives to Discovery in PRC Litigation." Posted on April 15, 2011. Accessed on December 22, 2015, www.chinalawinsight.com/2011/04/articles/dispute-resolution/evidence-collection-and-alternatives-to-discovery-in-prc-litigation.

John Henry Wigmore, *A Treatise on the Anglo-American System of Evidence in Trials at Common Law -V3* (Whitefish: Literary Licensing, 2012).

Margaret Y. K. Woo and Mary E. Gallagher, eds., *Chinese Justice: Civil Dispute Resolution in Contemporary China* (Cambridge: Cambridge University Press, 2011).

Margaret Woo, "Law and Discretion in Contemporary Chinese Courts," *Pacific Rim L. & Pol'y J.* 8, no. 3 (1999): 581-616.

Margaret Y. K. Woo, "Manning the Courthouse Gates: Pleadings, Jurisdictions, and the Nation-State," *Nev. L.J.* 15, no. 3 (2015): 1261-92.

Lord Woolf, *Access to Justice: Interim Report to the Lord Chancellor on the Civil Justice System in England and Wales* (London: HMSO, 1995).

Lord Woolf, *Access to Justice: Final Report to the Lord Chancellor on the Civil Justice System in England and Wales* (London: HMSO, 1996).

Jialin Wu, *Xian Fa Xue ('Constitutional Law')* (Beijing: The Press of Central Radio and TV University, 1985).

Jing-Xiong Wu, *A Study of Legal Philosophy* (Shanghai: Shanghai Law Translation & Edition Press, 1933).

Zhihai Xiong, "Objective and Subjective Norms of Procedural Testimony," *Modern Law Science* 22, no. 5 (2000): 75-80.

Guodang Xu, *The Debates about the Trains of Thought for Drawing up a Chinese Civil Code*, (Beijing: Publishing House of CUPL, 2001).

Xuelu Xu and Peng Liang, "Research for the Principle of Honesty and Credibility in Commercial Law," *Law Review (Published by Wuhan University)*, no. 3 (2002): 32-41.

Ganqiao Yang, *New Thoughts of Chinese Jurisprudence (Zhonggguo Faxue Xin Siwei)* (Shanxi: Shanxi People's Publisher, 1989).

Sibin Yang, "On Basic Characteristics and Exchanges of Ancient China's Case System (Zhongguo Gudai Panli Zhidu de Yanbian Yu Jiben Tezheng)," *Law Science Magazine (Faxue Zazhi)*, no. 2 (2008): 121-24.

Liang Yue and Wei Han, "On the Thought of Commercial Law - Analysis with Comparison to Civil Law Thought," *Legal System and Society (Published by Yunan Provincial People's Association)*, no. 19 (2009): 6-7.

Joachim Zekoll, "Comparative Civil Procedure," in *The Oxford Handbook of Comparative Law*, ed. Mathias Reimann and Reinhard Zimmermann (Oxford: Oxford University Press, 2008), 1327-62.

Xianyi Zeng and Xiaohong Ma, "A Dialectic Study of the Structure and Basic Concept of Traditional Chinese Law and an Analysis of the Relationship Between Li (Ceremony) and Fa (Law)," *Frontiers of Law in China* 1, no. 1 (2006): 34-52.

Jinfan Zhang, *Tradition of Chinese Law and Its Transformation in Late Qing (Zhonggua Falu de Chuantong Yu Jindai Zhuanxing)* (Beijing: Beijing Law Press, 1997).

Mingkai Zhang, *Criminal Law*, 4th ed. (Beijing: Law Press, 2011).

Mo Zhang, "International Civil Litigation in China: A Practical Analysis of the Chinese Judicial System," *B.C. Int'l & Comp. L. Rev.* 25, no. 1 (2002): 59-96, http://lawdigitalcommons.bc.edu/iclr/vol25/iss1/3.

Sheng Zhang, "Institutions and Practice of Independent Adjudication of Dali Yuan in the Early History of the Republic of China (Minchu Daliyuan Shenpan Duli de Zhidu Yu Shijian)," *Tribune of Political Science & Law (Zhengfa Luntan)* 20, no. 4 (2002): 146-52.

Shiming Zhang, "Re-Examination of Abolishing Consular Jurisdiction," *Frontiers L. China* 10, no. 2 (2015): 343-64.

Weiping Zhang, "Restatement of China's Principle of Debate in Civil Litigation," *Legal Research (Cass J.L.)* 18, no. 6 (1996): 46-56.

Bo Zhao, *Legal Principles and Chinese Law: A Philosophical Investigation*, CRBS-Dissertatiereeks (Hague: Boom Eleven International Publishing, 2009).

Cui Zhou, "Research for Behaviour Preservation: Interpretation of Articles 100-105 in Civil Procedure Law," *Science of Law (Journal of Northwest University of Political Science and Law)* 33, no. 4 (2015): 92-106.

Guobin Zhu, "Constitution Law and State Structure," in *Chinese Law*, ed. Wang Guiguo and John Mo (The Hague; London; Boston: Kluwer Law International, 1999), 23-61.

Yikun Zhu, *Concise Chinese Law* (Beijing: Law Press, 2007).

Yikun Zhu, *China's Procedural Law* (Beijing: Law Press China, 2003).

Reinhard Zimmermann, "An Introduction to German Legal Culture," in *Introduction to German Law*, ed. Werner F. Ebke and Matthew W. Finkin (Hague, Boston: Kluwer Law International, 1996), 1-n.a.

A. Zuckerman, *Civil Procedure: Principles of Practice*, 2nd Revised ed. (London: Sweet & Maxwell, 2006).

A. A. S. Zuckerman, *Civil Justice in Crisis: Comparative Perspectives of Civil Procedure* (Oxford: Oxford University Press, 2000).

A. A. S. Zuckerman, "Quality and Economy in Civil Procedure – The Case for Commuting Correct Judgements for Timely Judgments," *Oxford J. of Legal Stud.* 14, no. 3 (1994): 353-88.

Konrad Zweigert, Hein Kotz, and Tony Weir, trans., *An Introduction to Comparative Law: Volume I: The Framework*, 2nd Revised ed. (Oxford: Clarendon Press, 1987).

Konrad Zweigert and K. Kotz, trans., Tony Weir, *An Introduction to Comparative Law*, 3rd Revised ed. (Oxford: Clarendon Press, 1998).

INDEX

+

CPSIA information can be obtained
at www.ICGtesting.com
Printed in the USA
LVHW101521130919
631006LV00011B/191/P